Gophers Illustrated

Welcome Home...

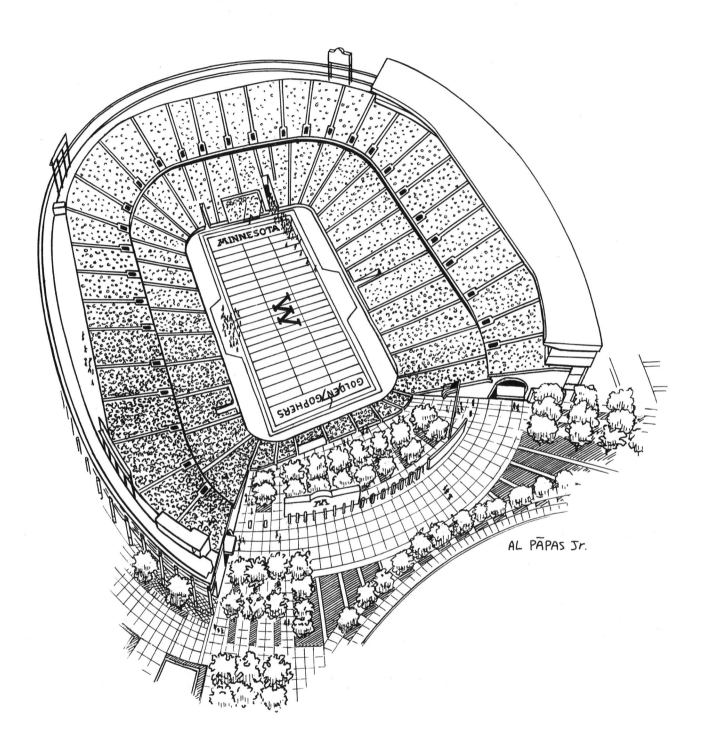

AL PĀPAS Jr.

GOPHERS

Illustrated

The Incredible Complete History
of Minnesota Football

METICULOUSLY RESEARCHED AND DRAWN BY *Al Papas Jr.*

University of Minnesota Press
Minneapolis
London

Earlier versions of some of the content of this book were published as
Gopher Sketchbook by Nodin Press in 1990.

Published by the University of Minnesota Press
111 Third Avenue South, Suite 290
Minneapolis, MN 55401-2520
http://www.upress.umn.edu

Library of Congress Cataloging-in-Publication Data
Papas, Al.
Gophers illustrated : the incredible complete history of Minnesota football / Meticulously
Researched and Drawn by Al Papas, Jr.
      p. cm.
Earlier versions of some of the content of this book were published as *Gopher Sketchbook* by
Nodin Press in 1990.
ISBN 978-0-8166-6756-7 (hc : alk. paper)
1. University of Minnesota—Football—History. 2. Football players—United States—Portraits. I.
Papas, Al. Gopher Sketchbook. II. Title.
GV958.U529P38 2009
796.332'6309776579—dc22   2009029172

Printed in the United States of America on acid-free paper

16 15 14 13 12 11 10 09   10 9 8 7 6 5 4 3 2 1

To my parents, Al and Bea Papas

How I Came to Write This Book

MY FIRST MEMORY OF SPORTS WAS GOPHER FOOTBALL. I was playing on the floor at my father's feet while he listened to a game on the radio. He, himself, had served under Fritz Crisler and Bernie Bierman until a leg injury ended his varsity season. Under the rules of those days, his play time wasn't enough to qualify for an "M." The rules changed the following year, when he would have had more than enough, but he was not able to return to campus for his letter. He loved the game but loved my mom more: he left the team to earn a living. Not getting the "M" was a sore disappointment just the same.

He took me to my first game, and the goose bumps would swell on his arms as they played the "Minnesota Rouser." The song soon did the same for me.

Once, while I was sick in bed, he sat with me as I wondered about his football days. When I asked if he had ever scored a touchdown for the Gophers, he looked hurt as he answered, "No." I silently made an oath I would someday cross the goal line in his name, but I had neither the size nor ability to follow through and went to art school instead.

At a young age my father was stricken with cancer. His doctor, Bill Proffitt, was one of his football buddies. Proffitt wrote a petition to get Dad that elusive "M," which was presented to him shortly before his death (he was never told it was only honorary). He was thrilled to receive it, and from time to time he would ask my mother to place it on his chest. In his weakened condition he would close his eyes, smile, and glide his fingers over it.

I reflected on this many years later and felt driven to check out the archives at the university to see if there was anything about my dad there. To my surprise I saw his name at the top of Bernie Bierman's first game starting lineup: he was the first Gopher of the "Golden Era." He would have been surprised to know that.

While doing this archival exploring I happened on the most illuminating material about Gopher football history. The grabber was holding the program of the 1903 Michigan game in my hands—it was like cradling the Gutenberg Bible. I returned to the archives repeatedly to record the most interesting stuff. I had wanted to draw some of the All-Americans to make a small booklet. Dad, an artist, had created a "1933 Gopher Sketchbook" in his college days. He had wanted to continue it, so this seemed a good idea for me to expand.

I called on some of his old football friends. I enjoyed meeting them and appreciated their friendliness. The grandson of an All-American taught me the secret on how to drop-kick (it can still be done with the modern ball).

There were always research surprises from unexpected places. I wasn't so interested in the fields the Gophers had played on until I saw an odd 1895 reference to the Minnesota Driving Club. A casual question to a librarian about what a driving club was (a sulky racetrack) led him to find this place on a map. It turned out that the former track circled my house. I then mentioned to a friend that she also lived near a racetrack where the Gophers played in 1882, and she directed me to a place where I could find an obscure map to give me a more exact location. I was able to pin down the spot where the Gophers played their first intercollegiate game. Today it is a one-block street, a site whose significance was lost to memory among all living people.

And then there was K. C. Poehler, whose grandfather played with the earliest Gophers team. He loaned me a priceless book that became a backbone for my research. I met K.C. through an accident report when he witnessed my parked car smashed to bits by a hit-and-run, and he took off after the culprit. What good fortune for me, eh? Dave Samuelson, a lifetime collector of football publications, had written a letter to someone else, who then passed it along to me; his memorabilia, including record books dating back to 1913, kept me busy. Bob Patrin, a historian, gave me a book I otherwise didn't have access to.

Of course, most information came from reading old books, yearbooks, programs, newspapers, and even directories that preceded telephones. Records were sometimes wrong from mistaken rewriting over time. Old reporters' memories, too, proved flawed when compared to play-by-plays: this led me to make a series of game charts, which were common in the old days and fascinating to look at. One thing led to another . . . some nights I didn't sleep but instead thought of ideas for new kinds of revealing charts. I didn't want to lose any precious information.

Karen Zwach from the Athletic Communications department of the University of Minnesota helped me find pictures and directed me to additional help. She was a key person for whom I give many thanks. This project would have bogged down without her, but that can also be said for many others.

I never would have started this book if it were planned to be what it is now. But, like eating popcorn, I craved more and then more little bits of information, and *Gophers Illustrated* grew one tasty nibble at a time.

Al Papas Jr.
June 2009

Roster of Contents

Game Preparation

FOOTBALL CAN BE TRACED BACK TO THE 11TH CENTURY WHEN SOME ENGLISHMEN WERE EXCAVATING A FORMER BATTLEFIELD. THEY UNEARTHED THE SKULL OF A DANISH SOLDIER. IN CONTEMPT FOR THEIR PRIOR RULER, THEY BEGAN KICKING THE HAPLESS HEAD AROUND. IT ATTRACTED ATTENTION TO WHERE ALL THE DIGGERS LEFT THEIR WORK TO JOIN IN. THIS SPONTANEOUS NEW "GAME" WAS DUBBED "KICKING THE DANE'S HEAD."

OF COURSE, THIS WAS ALL TAKEN IN BY SOME KIDS WHO FOUND THEIR OWN HEAD. IT WAS A BIT HARD ON THE FEET SO THEY SUBSTITUTED THE HEAD WITH A COW'S BLADDER. IT THEN BECAME KNOWN AS "KICKING THE BLADDER." SOMETIME AFTER THIS EXOTIC BEGINNING, THE GAME BECAME KNOWN AS "FUTEBALLE" BECAUSE THE BLADDER, THAT IS BALL, WAS DIRECTED BY FOOT.

THERE WASN'T MUCH FOR RULES. IT WAS MOSTLY MAYHEM. THEY STARTED BY DROPPING A BALL BETWEEN TWO VILLAGES. PLAYERS, WHICH MIGHT NUMBER IN THE HUNDREDS, WOULD KICK IT TO THE CENTER OF THE OPPOSING TEAM'S TOWN. SHOPKEEPERS CLOSED DOWN WHEN THEY HEARD THE RIOTOUS TEAMS COMING.

TO END THIS BEHAVIOR, RULES CAME INTO BEING. A FIELD AND GOAL LINE WAS CREATED.

SO POPULAR THIS GAME BECAME THAT PEOPLE NEGLECTED ARCHERY PRACTICE OVER IT. BOW AND ARROW WAS VITAL TO NATIONAL DEFENSE SO KING HENRY II BANNED FUTEBALLE. EXCEPT FOR OCCASIONAL GAMES THAT WERE STILL ALLOWED, IT REMAINED BANNED FOR 400 YEARS.

WITH THE INTRODUCTION OF THE GUN, GAMES WERE ALLOWED BACK BY KING JAMES I IN THE 17TH CENTURY. MORE STANDARDIZED RULES CAME ABOUT AS THE GAME ADVANCED TO WHAT WE CALL SOCCER.

ONE DAY IN 1838, AT RUGBY, A FRUSTRATED PLAYER, WHO COULDN'T GET IN A KICK, PICKED UP THE BALL AND RAN WITH IT. IT WAS A FOUL DEED, BUT AN INTERESTING ONE. THE IDEA CAUGHT ON AND SOCCER TOOK A SECOND DIRECTION. THE GAME OF RUGBY WAS BORN.

FOOTBALL, OR SOME FORM OF IT, CAME TO AMERICA IN THE 1820'S.

PRINCETON AND RUTGERS PLAYED THE FIRST INTERCOLLEGIATE GAME IN 1869 UNDER SOCCER RULES.

MORE TEAMS BEGAN TO PLAY. HARVARD WAS STILL SHORT AN OPPONENT IN 1875 WHEN THEY LOOKED TO CANADA FOR A CHALLENGE. McGILL ACCEPTED. AS THE CANADIANS PRACTICED, THE HARVARD CAPTAIN WATCHED IN AMAZEMENT AS THEY PICKED UP THE BALL AND RAN WITH IT. TO BE POLITE, HE OFFERED TO PLAY THE GAME WITH HALF SOCCER AND HALF RUGBY RULES. IT ENDED IN A SCORELESS TIE.

THESE NEW BALL CARRYING RULES WERE MORE FUN TO PLAY. THE SOCCER STYLE WAS DISCARDED. HARVARD CHALLENGED YALE IN 1876. AMERICAN FOOTBALL WAS BORN.

A WHOLE VOLUME COULD BE WRITTEN ON THE EVOLUTION OF AMERICAN RULES. FOR A WHILE KICKING WAS STILL MOST IMPORTANT. A FIELD GOAL SCORED MORE POINTS THAN A TOUCHDOWN. THE SHAPE OF THE BALL CHANGED FROM SPHERICAL TO PROLATE SPHEROID.

IN 1905 A SWARTHMORE PLAYER WAS SO DELIBERATELY BEATEN UP THAT PRESIDENT TEDDY ROOSEVELT THREATENED TO BAN THE GAME IF SOMETHING WASN'T DONE ABOUT IT. FOOTBALL WAS MOSTLY A BRAWL.

PASSING WAS INTRODUCED TO HELP CHANGE THE EMPHASIS AWAY FROM THIS BRUTE FORCE. IT DID THE TRICK TO LET SMALLER TEAMS COMPETE WITH BIGGER ONES MORE EVENLY.

FOOTBALL BECAME MORE REFINED. IT TOOK DEEP ROOT INTO MINNESOTA SOIL. AS YOU READ, YOU WILL NOTE MINNESOTA'S PART IN INTRODUCING MANY ELEMENTS THAT HAVE ADVANCED THE GAME AND ARE INTEGRAL TO IT TODAY.

MOST IMPORTANTLY, THIS BOOK DEALS WITH MINNESOTA'S GREATEST INDIVIDUALS AND SEEKS TO BE AS COMPLETE AS POSSIBLE IN PORTRAYING ALL THEIR LIKENESSES UNDER ONE COVER.

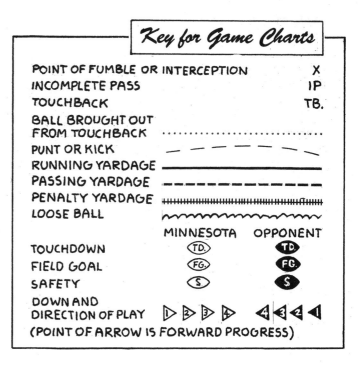

THERE ARE THOSE WHO CAME TO FULL BLOOM AND THERE ARE THOSE WHO WERE SEEDLINGS THAT WENT ON TO GREATNESS ELSEWHERE. SOME HAVE BEEN FORGOTTEN OVER TIME AND ARE HERE RECALLED TO THE PLACE OF HONOR THEY DESERVE.

STILL THEY ARE BUT A BRANCH OF THE MIGHTY TREE OF THOUSANDS OF PLAYERS WHO ADORNED THE COLORFUL MAROON AND GOLD LEAVES OF AUTUMN.

ALL-AMERICAN SELECTIONS WERE STARTED BY YALE GRAD WALTER CAMP IN 1889. SELECTIONS BY OTHERS CAME, TOO, BUT WERE NOT ACCEPTED WITH AS MUCH AUTHORITY. EASTERN TEAMS WERE AT THE CENTER OF THE GAME, THEN, SO CAMP DIDN'T ALWAYS NOTICE DESERVING PLAYERS FROM THE WEST. MANY GOPHERS BECAME ALL-AMERICANS AND EVEN CONSENSUS ALL-AMERICANS. A LESSER NUMBER BECAME FAMOUS FOR MAKING THE CAMP TEAM. ALL ARE RECOGNIZED WITHIN THIS BOOK.

CUSTOMS, RULES AND PEOPLE FROM OTHER FACETS OF THE GAME ARE ALSO REMEMBERED. DIAGRAMS OF SOME OF THE MOST HISTORIC GAMES ARE SHOWN. THE KEY TO THEM IS FOUND AT RIGHT.

THESE PAGES SERVE AS A BRIEF DOCUMENT TO THE CONTRIBUTIONS AND GREATNESS OF UNIVERSITY OF MINNESOTA INDIVIDUALS TO THE SPORT OF FOOTBALL AND TO THE U OF M.

Key for Game Charts

POINT OF FUMBLE OR INTERCEPTION	X
INCOMPLETE PASS	IP
TOUCHBACK	TB.
BALL BROUGHT OUT FROM TOUCHBACK	· · · · · · · ·
PUNT OR KICK	– – – –
RUNNING YARDAGE	————
PASSING YARDAGE	- - - - -
PENALTY YARDAGE	++++++++
LOOSE BALL	∼∼∼∼∼

	MINNESOTA	OPPONENT
TOUCHDOWN	TD.	TD.
FIELD GOAL	FG.	FG.
SAFETY	S	S
DOWN AND DIRECTION OF PLAY	▷ ▷ ▷ ▷	◁ ◁ ◁ ◁
(POINT OF ARROW IS FORWARD PROGRESS)		

1887 TEAM
BACK: ARTHUR MANN, WILLIAM WILLARD, FRED MANN, EDMUND ALLEN, WALTER HEFFELFINGER, HAL WATSON, HENRY MORRIS
FRONT: ALONZO MEADS, WILLIAM HOYT, PAUL GOODE, ALFRED PILLSBURY, JOHN CORLISS, JOHN HAYDEN

The Starting Lineup

PLAYERS, IN THE BEGINING, COULD BE RECRUITED FROM OUTSIDE OF THE CAMPUS. WALTER "PUDGE" HEFFELFINGER WAS ONE OF THEM. HE WAS A HIGH SCHOOL STUDENT FROM MINNEAPOLIS CENTRAL WHEN HE JOINED SOME FANS TO SEE THE GOPHERS OFF FOR AN AWAY GAME. THE TEAM WAS IN NEED OF ANOTHER PLAYER WHEN CAPTAIN PILLSBURY NOTICED THE STRAPPING LAD. "PUDGE" WAS INVITED TO COME ALONG AND SO HE JOINED THE TEAM.

HEFFELFINGER EVENTUALLY WENT TO COLLEGE AT YALE. WHILE THERE HE WAS SELECTED TO BE ON THE FIRST EVER ALL-AMERICAN TEAM. HE REPEATED THE DISTINCTION THE FOLLOWING TWO YEARS AND HAS MADE MOST OF THE ALL-TIME TEAMS SINCE.

AS AN EARLY INNOVATOR OF THE GAME, HE WAS THE FIRST GUARD TO LEAVE HIS POSITION AND RUN INTERFERENCE FOR THE BALL CARRIER. HE ALSO INVENTED THE SHIN GUARDS AND WAS THE FIRST FOOTBALL PLAYER TO EVER SIGN A PRO CONTRACT. HE DID THIS IN 1892 AT $500 TO PLAY FOR ONE GAME.

UPON RETURNING HOME HE AGAIN TOOK UP THE MAROON AND GOLD COLORS. IN 1895 HE SERVED AS MINNESOTA'S PAID COACH. AFTER THAT HE HELPED PART TIME WITHOUT PAY FOR 15 YEARS. YOU COULD ALSO FIND HIM PLAYING AGAINST MINNESOTA ON AN EX-COLLEGIAN TEAM TO TEST THE GOPHERS' METTLE.

HEFFELFINGER'S LAST GAME WAS IN A 1933 CHARITY CONTEST IN MINNEAPOLIS. AT AGE 65 HE FINALLY TOOK HIMSELF OUT OF THE ACTION FOR NOT BEING TOUGH ENOUGH. HIS PLAYING DAYS SPANNED 50 YEARS AND HE WAS, OF COURSE, ENSHRINED IN THE FOOTBALL HALL OF FAME.

3

Kickoff!

THE FIRST FOOTBALL PLAYED AT THE U OF M WAS ON THE WOODED HILL OVER-LOOKING THE CORNER OF UNIVERSITY AND PLEASANT. IT WAS AN INTRAMURAL GAME HELD ON OCTOBER 12, 1879. THE FRESHMEN BEAT THE SOPHOMORES BY FIVE GOALS. THEY HAD THE ADVANTAGE BY HAVING THE MOST PLAYERS. A SECOND GAME WAS PLAYED WITH EVEN SIDES. THIS TIME THE SOPHOMORES CAME OUT ON TOP 6-5. FINALLY THE SOPHOMORES AND SENIORS CHALLENGED THE OTHER CLASSES. THE CHALLENGE WAS ACCEPTED BUT NO GAME WAS PLAYED "OWING TO THE NON-ARRIVAL OF THE BALL."

DURING THE SAME YEAR C.C. CAMP FROM YALE, INTRODUCED FOOTBALL AT SHATTUCK MILITARY ACADEMY IN FARIBAULT. HE LAID OUT THE FIRST REGULA TION FIELD IN THE NORTHWEST. USING THE RUGBY STYLE OF PLAY THE HIGH SCHOOL ORGANIZED A TEAM OF STUDENTS AND FACULTY. THEY WON THEIR FIRST GAME AGAINST SEABURY DIVINITY. THEY CHALLENGED MANY COLLEGES ALONG THE WAY INCLUDING MINNESOTA. BETWEEN THE YEARS 1886-1890 SHATTUCK HELD THE WINNING EDGE OVER THE GOPHERS 4-3.

MINNESOTA TRIED TO BEGIN ITS INTERCOLLEGIATE COMPETITION IN 1880 BUT CARLETON DECLINED TO PLAY.

TWO YEARS LATER THE GOPHERS CHALLENGED HAMLINE. THE SCHOOLS WERE ABOUT EQUAL IN SIZE AND MET AT THE STATE FAIR GROUNDS IN SOUTH MINNEA-POLIS AS SHOWN HERE. THE GROUNDS WAS ONE OF TWO COMPETING STATE FAIRS OF ITS DAY.

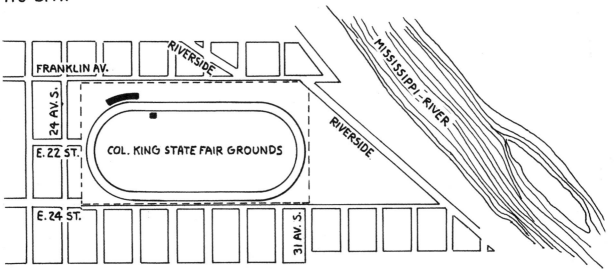

HAMLINE COMPLAINED ABOUT PLAYING ON A RACE TRACK. THEY ALSO SAID THEIR FACULTY MADE THEM PROMISE TO BE HOME BY 6:30 P.M. OR THEY WOULDN'T BE ALLOWED TO COME AGAIN. MINNESOTA THREATENED A "REAL CHARIVARI" TO THE HAMLINE FACULTY IF THEY DIDN'T FOLLOW THROUGH.

THE FIRST POINTS WERE MADE BY CAPTAIN A.J. BALDWIN. IT WAS IN THE SOCCER STYLE OF PLAY AND A SCORE WAS WORTH TWO POINTS. THE GOPHERS WENT ON TO WIN THE GAME 4-0. LADIES FROM BOTH SCHOOLS GAVE "ELEGANT FLORAL OFFERINGS TO THE VICTORS." THE DATE WAS SEPTEMBER 30, 1882.

TWO WEEKS LATER THE TEAMS MET AGAIN AT A NOW LONG-FORGOTTEN LOCATION. THIS TIME HAMLINE WON 2-0 AND THE GOPHERS ENDED THEIR FIRST SEASON WITH A 1-1-0 RECORD.

John William Adams

JOHN ADAMS PLAYED CENTER FOR THE GOPHERS FROM 1881 TO 1886.

IN 1882 HE COMPETED IN MINNESOTA'S FIRST INTERCOLLEGIATE GAME AND WAS AMONG THE FIRST "M" LETTERMEN. THE FOLLOWING YEAR HE SERVED AS TEAM CAPTAIN.

HE WAS THE INVENTOR OF THE EXPRESSION "SKI-U-MAH."

HIS FOOTBALL DAYS WEREN'T OVER AFTER HE LEFT MINNESOTA. AS SHOWN IN THIS DRAWING HE WENT ON TO PLAY IN THE EAST FOR THE UNIVERSITY OF PENNSYLVANIA.

IN 1891 THIS GOPHER BECAME PENNSYLVANIA'S FIRST ALL-AMERICAN.

Foot Notes (EARLY DAYS)

 BECAUSE OF GOOD SEASONS, MINNESOTA PROCLAIMED ITSELF AS "CHAMPIONS OF THE NORTHWEST" IN 1890 AND 1891.

 EARLY PLAYERS OF THE 1880'S PAID FOR THEIR OWN UNIFORMS AND TRAVEL EXPENSES AS WELL AS CONDITIONED THE FIELD THEMSELVES.

 T.U. "TULE" LYMAN VOWED HE WOULD NEVER LEAVE COLLEGE UNTIL HE PLAYED ON A TEAM THAT BEAT MINNESOTA. HE FINALLY DID SO IN 1894 ON HIS SIXTH TRY IN FIVE YEARS. HE PLAYED FOR GRINNELL AND WISCONSIN.

MRS. AGUSTA NORWOOD SMITH, WHO TAUGHT ENGLISH FROM 1876-1880, SELECTED THE SCHOOL COLORS TO BE MAROON AND GOLD.

STARTING IN 1898, "THE GIVING OF SOME TOKEN OF HONOR TO OUR ATHLETES, A CUSTOM VERY COMMON IN OTHER COLLEGES, WAS DECIDED UPON. IT IS TO BE A LETTER 'M' TO BE WORN UPON THE SWEATER OF THE FOOTBALL PLAYER... ANY ONE PLAYING IN THREE CHAMPIONSHIP GAMES OF FOOTBALL... MAY WEAR THE INSIGNIA. BY CHAMPIONSHIP GAMES ARE MEANT GAMES WITH LARGE COLLEGES." THOSE WHO DIDN'T FULLY QUALIFY FOR THE FULL "M" CAME TO RECEIVE THE LESSER "ENGLISH M" (SHOWN ON THE LEFT). THE "ENGLISH M" WAS DROPPED IN 1933. ALL PLAYERS SEEING ANY ACTION COULD RECEIVE THE FULL "M" FROM THEN ON.

WITHOUT A COACH IN 1892 MINNESOTA WENT UNDEFEATED AND WON THE CHAMPIONSHIP OF THE NORTHWESTERN LEAGUE. THE GREAT CHICAGO COACH, AMOS ALONZO STAGG, CLAIMED THAT "IF I HAD THE UNIVERSITY OF MINNESOTA TEAM I COULD MAKE (THEM) ONE OF THE BEST IN THE UNITED STATES..."

UNDER THE DIRECTION OF WALLIE WINTER, THE FOLLOWING YEAR, THEY REPEATED AS UNDEFEATED CHAMPIONS. FOR A LAST GAME THEY HOPED TO TAKE ON CORNELL TO CLAIM VICTORY OVER AN EASTERN TEAM. CORNELL BACKED OUT AT THE LAST MOMENT SO MINNESOTA TRIED TO REPLACE THEM WITH LEHIGH. IT ALSO DIDN'T MATERIALIZE. HOPES HAD BEEN GREAT AS THE SCHOOL PAPER STATED, "THE DEFEAT OF LEHIGH WOULD GIVE US THE FIFTH RANK AMONG AMERICAN COLLEGES ON THE FOOTBALL FIELD. ONLY THE 'BIG FOUR,' YALE, HARVARD, PRINCETON AND 'U' OF PENNSYLVANIA, WOULD THEN BE AHEAD OF US."

SOMETIMES, IN EARLY DAY AWAY GAMES, NOT ALL THE GOPHERS ARRIVED FOR THE KICKOFF. BECAUSE THEY GOT THERE ANY WAY THEY COULD THEY MIGHT BE LATE OR LOST. TO HAVE THE PRESCRIBED ELEVEN PLAYERS THEIR OPPONENTS WOULD "LOAN" THEM SOME OF THEIR OWN. IT WAS SAID THEY WEREN'T MUCH HELP.

"BABE" LOOMIS, IN A PLAYER SWAP, TOOK THE SIDE OF THE EX-COLLEGIATES AGAINST THE GOPHERS IN 1895. ON A CERTAIN PLAY HE WAS SUPPOSED TO KICK. IN THE CONFUSION HE FORGOT AND LATERALED TO HIS BROTHER. HIS BROTHER, PLAYING FOR THE GOPHERS, RAN IT BACK FOR A SCORE.

Alf Pillsbury

HIS NAME MAY SOUND FAMILIAR BECAUSE
HE WAS OF THE PILLSBURY MILLS
FAMILY. HIS FATHER WAS JOHN S.
PILLSBURY, THE "FATHER OF THE
UNIVERSITY" AND FORMER GOVERNOR
OF THE STATE.

"PILLY" WAS THE EARLIEST GOPHER
STANDOUT. HE PLAYED QUARTER
(QUARTERBACK) AND ON THE RUSH LINE.
HIS CAREER LASTED EIGHT YEARS WHILE
SERVING AS CAPTAIN DURING
1887 AND 1889.

PILLSBURY'S GREATEST
CONTRIBUTION MAY HAVE BEEN
IN CHANGING MINNESOTA FROM
THE SOCCER TO RUGBY STYLE
OF GAME. THIS HE DID IN 1886
DUE TO HIS INFLUENCE OF
OWNING THE ONLY BALL IN
TOWN!

Thomas Peebles

BECAUSE HE HAD JUST ARRIVED FROM PRINCETON, WHERE HE LEARNED KNOWLEDGE OF HOW THE GAME WAS PLAYED, THOMAS PEEBLES WAS ASKED BY THE UNIVERSITY PLAYERS TO HELP THEM OUT. THE PROFESSOR OF MENTAL AND MORAL PHILOSOPHY THUS BECAME MINNESOTA'S FIRST FOOTBALL COACH IN 1883.

DURING THE FIRST GAME HE ALSO SERVED AS REFEREE. THIS CAME ABOUT AS A COMPROMISE WHEN CARLETON WAS CHALLENGED OVER THEIR ROSTER AND THEIR WANTING TO PLAY RUGBY STYLE.

PEEBLES LIKED THE SOCCER STYLE OF PLAY BUT THE RUGBY STYLE GAINED FAVOR UNDER SECOND "COACHER" FRED JONES.

Fredrick S. Jones

PEEBLES AND JONES CREATED INTEREST BY DIVIDING THE MINNESOTA TEAM UP AND PLAYING ONE ANOTHER. IF PEEBLES' SIDE SCORED HE WOULD HOLLER OUT FOR PRINCETON. IF JONES' TEAM SCORED HE WOULD CHEER FOR HIS ALMA MATER, YALE.

JONES TOOK A KEEN INTEREST IN THE GAME. HIS GUIDING HAND EARNED HIM THE TITLE "FATHER OF MINNESOTA FOOTBALL."

AFTER HIS TIME AS COACH HE SERVED AS FACULTY REPRESENTATIVE ON THE ATHLETIC BOARD. HE WAS INSTRUMENTAL IN OBTAINING THE LAND FOR NORTHROP FIELD AND SIGNING DR. HENRY L. WILLIAMS AS COACH.

The Yale Connection

AFTER FRED JONES STEPPED DOWN, MINNESOTA HAD GAME COACHES FOR ONE SEASON. FOLLOWING THAT, TOM ECK NOTCHED THE FIRST CHAMPIONSHIP FOR THE GOPHERS IN 1890.

MINNESOTA'S FIRST NATIVE-BORN COACH WAS EDWARD "DAD" MOULTON FROM MINNEAPOLIS. AT 14 HE ENLISTED IN THE FIRST MINNESOTA HEAVY ARTILLERY DURING THE CIVIL WAR. AFTER THAT, IN THE MID-1870'S, HE WAS KNOWN AS THE CHAMPION SPRINTER OF AMERICA. HE DID THIS PROFESSIONALLY AND IT LED HIM INTO BECOMING AN ATHLETIC TRAINER. HE MOSTLY KEPT THE GOPHERS IN GOOD PHYSICAL SHAPE RATHER THAN COACH THEM IN THE GAME.

THE TEAM CAPTAIN, IN THOSE DAYS, WOULD OFTEN DOUBLE UP AND BE MORE OF A COACH THAN THE COACH. THE SEASON AFTER MOULTON LEFT, MINNESOTA HAD NO COACH AT ALL AND WENT UNDEFEATED.

EDWARD W. MOULTON

IF IT WASN'T THE CAPTAIN RUNNING THE SHOW, IT MIGHT BE A RECENTLY "RETIRED" PLAYER WHO WAS WELL-RESPECTED. SINCE THE "GREAT" ONES WERE FROM THE EAST, THE GOPHERS HEAVILY RELIED ON YALE GRADS AND ADOPTED THEIR STYLE OF PLAY.

"WALLIE" WINTER CAME ALONG AFTER HAVING BEEN AN ALL-AMERICAN TACKLE AT YALE. HE WAS CONSIDERED MINNESOTA'S FIRST "REAL" COACH. HE WORKED HIS PLAYERS HARD AND WOULD, FOR A FEW DAYS BEFORE GAMES, PUT HIS TEAM THROUGH RUGGED SCRIMMAGES. THE PLAYERS CONSIDERED THE ACTUAL GAMES AS BREATHERS COMPARED TO THE SCRIMMAGES IN 1893.

THOMAS COCHRANE, JR., AGAIN FROM YALE, CAME NEXT. THE PROGRAM WAS SUFFERING FINANCIALLY, SO HE GAVE A LECTURE TO RAISE FUNDS. IT WAS CALLED "FOOTBALL AS PLAYED IN THE EAST." HE STAYED FOR ONLY ONE YEAR.

ALEXANDER N. JERREMS

"PUDGE" HEFFELFINGER RETURNED HOME FROM YALE TO SERVE FOR THE NEXT SEASON. "DAD" MOULTON ALSO RETURNED AS TRAINER AFTER A STINT AT MICHIGAN.

NEXT TO TAKE HIS TURN WAS ALEX JERREMS. HE WAS BORN IN SYDNEY, AUSTRALIA, BUT GREW UP IN CHICAGO. HE MOSTLY LEARNED THE GAME AT YALE WHILE PLAYING BACKFIELD POSITIONS.

THE YALE CONNECTION ENDED TEMPORARILY WITH THE ARRIVAL OF JACK MINDS. HE HAD BEEN AN ALL-AMERICAN FULLBACK AT PENNSYLVANIA, WITH A REPUTATION AS A KICKER.

IN 1899 A COUPLE OF MINNESOTA ALUMNI DECIDED TO GIVE CO-COACHING A TRY AND THEIR TEAM ENDED UP LAST IN THE CONFERENCE.

THE TIME FINALLY CAME WHEN MINNESOTA LANDED DR. HENRY WILLIAMS AS ITS FIRST FULL-TIME SALARIED COACH. HE GOT A THREE-YEAR CONTRACT FOR $2,500, STARTING IN 1900.

WILLIAMS PREVIOUSLY HAD PLAYED BALL WITH HEFFELFINGER AT YALE. AFTER THAT HE ASSISTED ARMY IN THEIR FIRST VICTORY OVER NAVY. HE COMMUNICATED WITH THE CADETS BY MAIL. THEY LEARNED HIS NEW THEORY OF PLAY THIS WAY AND WENT OUT AND WON. HE WOULD BECOME MINNESOTA'S WINNINGEST COACH.

JACK MINDS

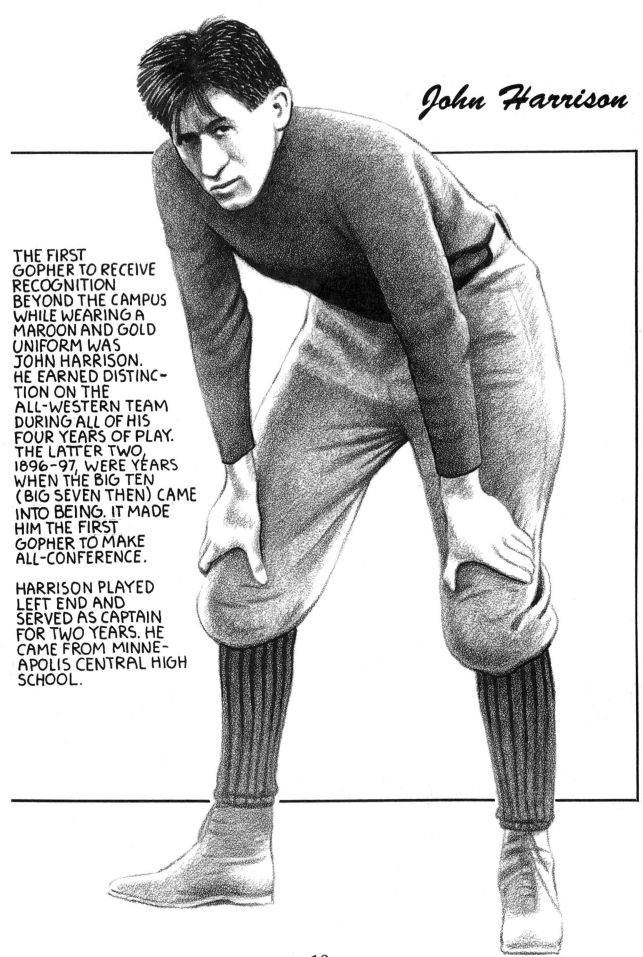

John Harrison

THE FIRST GOPHER TO RECEIVE RECOGNITION BEYOND THE CAMPUS WHILE WEARING A MAROON AND GOLD UNIFORM WAS JOHN HARRISON. HE EARNED DISTINC- TION ON THE ALL-WESTERN TEAM DURING ALL OF HIS FOUR YEARS OF PLAY. THE LATTER TWO, 1896-97, WERE YEARS WHEN THE BIG TEN (BIG SEVEN THEN) CAME INTO BEING. IT MADE HIM THE FIRST GOPHER TO MAKE ALL-CONFERENCE.

HARRISON PLAYED LEFT END AND SERVED AS CAPTAIN FOR TWO YEARS. HE CAME FROM MINNE- APOLIS CENTRAL HIGH SCHOOL.

'Johnny' Campbell   Lt. Edwin Glenn

A TACTIC BY PRINCETON PLAYERS IN THE FIRST COLLEGIATE GAME WAS TO USE THE BLOOD-
CHILLING REBEL YELL LEFT OVER FROM THE CIVIL WAR. THEY WOULD USE IT AT STRATEGIC
MOMENTS TO GAIN A PSYCHOLOGICAL EDGE. THIS GOT THEM UNNECESSARILY WINDED,
HOWEVER, SO THEY GOT SCHOOLMATES ON THE SIDELINES TO DO THE YELLING FOR THEM.
IT RESULTED IN CHEERING AT GAMES, WHICH EVENTUALLY EVOLVED INTO FANCY YELLS
AND ROUSING SONGS. THE FIRST SPECIFIC CROWD CHANT WAS THE "LOCOMOTIVE"
CHEER AT PRINCETON. THESE CHEERS WOULD BE STARTED BY ANYONE IN THE CROWD.

IN 1892 LT. EDWIN GLENN DEVELOPED THE ORGANIZED "ROOTERS" WHICH WAS UNIQUE TO MINNE-
SOTA. THE PROFESSOR OF MILITARY SCIENCE AND TACTICS STARTED WITH ABOUT 20 FAITHFUL,
WHO WOULD FOLLOW THE GOPHERS WHEREVER THEY PLAYED, TO LEND A VOCAL HAND.

ANOTHER MINNESOTA INVENTION, CHEERLEADING, WAS CREATED BY "JOHNNY" CAMPBELL ON
NOVEMBER 12, 1898. THIS POPULAR IDEA SPREAD THROUGHOUT FOOTBALLDOM AS WELL AS INTO
OTHER SPORTS. IN LATER YEARS CAMPBELL LED A CONTINGENT KNOWN AS THE SOUTH ST. PAUL
"HOOK 'EM COWS." THEIR VOCAL AND COWBELL RINGING VOLUME WERE WELL-REPRESENTED AT
GOPHER GAMES. HE DIDN'T MISS A HOME GAME FOR 42 YEARS.

11

Dr. Henry
L. Williams

THIS HALL OF FAMER WAS ONE OF HIS ERA'S GREAT-
EST OFFENSIVE COACHES. HIS PLAYS WERE CLEVER
AND ILLUSIVE, CENTERING ON POWER AND
SPEED. HE INVENTED THE MINNESOTA SHIFT,
WHICH HAD DRAMATIC EFFECT ON THE GAME.

AS A MEMBER OF THE N.C.A.A. RULES COMMITTEE
HE WAS THE FIRST TO PROPOSE LEGALIZATION
OF THE FORWARD PASS.

12

GIL DOBIE PLAYED QUARTERBACK IN 1900-01. HE WAS AT HIS BEST ON DEFENSE AND RETURNING PUNTS.

AT THE END OF HIS PLAYING DAYS HE STUCK AROUND TO ASSIST UNDER HENRY WILLIAMS. HE HAD FOUND HIS NICHE IN COACHING, WHERE HE WOULD CONTINUE ON TO THE HALL OF FAME.

SOME OF THE STOPS ALONG THE WAY FOR "GLOOMY GIL" WERE NORTH DAKOTA, WASHINGTON, NAVY, CORNELL AND BOSTON COLLEGE.

HE COACHED HIS WHOLE WASHINGTON CAREER (1908-16) WITHOUT SUFFERING A DEFEAT. WASHINGTON STILL HOLDS THE ALL-TIME COLLEGIATE UNDEFEATED STRING OF 63 GAMES. THE RECORD 59-0-4 WAS MADE FROM 1907-17. SANDWICHED BETWEEN TIES WERE 39 VICTORIES IN A ROW... THE SECOND-LONGEST WIN STRING IN COLLEGE HISTORY.

AT CORNELL HE WENT THREE YEARS WITH A PERFECT WINNING RECORD. TWO OF THOSE YEARS WERE BACK-TO-BACK NATIONAL CHAMPIONSHIPS IN 1921 AND 22.

Gilmore Dobie

IN HIS 33 YEARS OF COACHING, DOBIE COMPILED A 180-45-15 MARK WITH A .781 WINNING PERCENTAGE.

Champions of the West

IT WAS HALLOWEEN, 1903. THE POINT-A-MINUTE MEN FROM MICHIGAN HAD COME TO GOPHERLAND WITH THEIR TRICKS AND TREATS. THEY WERE DEFENDING THEIR TITLE AS "CHAMPIONS OF THE WEST." INDEED, THEY WERE CHAMPIONS OF THE ENTIRE NATION! THEY HADN'T LOST A GAME IN THREE SEASONS. THE YEAR BEFORE THEY HAD THROTTLED STANFORD IN THE FIRST-EVER ROSE BOWL GAME 49-0. SO FAR, THIS SEASON, THEY HAD OUTSCORED OPPONENTS 447-0. THEIR BIG GUN WAS WILLIE HESTON WHO WOULD EVENTUALLY HAVE A LIFETIME 93 TOUCHDOWNS.

MICHIGAN COACH, FIELDING YOST, HAD VISITED TWO WEEKS BEFORE TO PERSONALLY SCOUT THE GOPHERS. WHEN HE RETURNED TO MICHIGAN HE PROMPTLY TOLD FOUR PLAYERS TO PRACTICE THEIR PUNTING. UP UNTIL THEN, MICHIGAN HAD NOT PUNTED ALL YEAR. TEAM SESSIONS WERE TOUGH BECAUSE OF THEIR RESPECT FOR THE MINNESOTANS. MICHIGAN'S STRENGTH WAS IN THEIR PHYSICAL CONDITIONING. THEY WERE INJURY-FREE AND THEIR TEAMWORK WAS CONSIDERED PERFECTION.

MINNESOTA HAD ALSO PREPARED FOR THE GREAT BATTLE. HIGH-SCORING GAMES WERE COMMON IN THIS ERA. ONCE A BALL CARRIER FOUGHT PAST THE LINE OF SCRIMMAGE HE WAS, MORE OR LESS, FREE TO THE GOAL LINE. TO STOP THIS, COACH WILLIAMS (WITH THE HELP OF PUDGE HEFFELFINGER) INVENTED THE SEVEN MAN DEFENSIVE LINE. FOUR MEN WOULD PLAY AS DEFENSIVE BACKS TO BOX IN HESTON. MINNESOTA'S GREATNESS WAS ITS SPEED AND PHYSICAL STRENGTH. THEY WERE, HOW- EVER, NOT IN AS GOOD PHYSICAL CONDITION AS WAS MICHIGAN. THERE WAS DOUBT AS TO WHETHER SOME PLAYERS WOULD START. THE ODDS WERE 10-8 FOR MICHIGAN.

FANS GOT READY FOR THE GAME, TOO. SOME BOYS WERE ARRESTED AND FINED TWO DOLLARS BY A ST. PAUL MAGISTRATE. THEY HAD BEEN APPREHENDED FOR "PRACTICING" THE "SKI-U-MAH" YELL AT A NIGHTLY HOUR. THERE WAS A GREAT RALLY PUT ON BY THE MEDIC ROOTING CLUB. 2000 STUDENTS ALSO ATTENDED A "MONSTER" BONFIRE WHICH WAS LIT ON THE DRILL GROUNDS. FANS CAME FROM ALL OVER THE REGION AND FROM AS FAR AWAY AS NEW YORK. CONFIDENCE WAS INTENSE ON BOTH SIDES.

GAME DAY CAME WITH PERFECT INDIAN SUMMER WEATHER. EXCITED FANS WERE FILLING NORTHROP FIELD SIX HOURS BEFORE KICKOFF TIME. THOSE WHO COULDN'T GET IN CLUNG TO TELEGRAPH AND TELEPHONE POLES TO SEE. THE LIMBS OF TREES WERE SPROUTING PEOPLE. ALL AVAILABLE HOUSE TOPS WERE CROWDED. KIDS STOOD ON BARRELS IN WAGONS, WITH HOPES OF GETTING A VIEW.

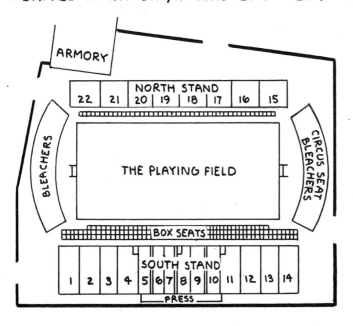

THE CROWD WAS WELL-DECORATED IN MAROON AND GOLD. THE MEDICAL STUDENTS PARADED ONTO THE FIELD GUIDING A DONKEY AND PIG DRESSED IN MINNESOTA COLORS. MICHIGAN COLORS WERE TIED TO THEIR TAILS. THE "ORGANIZED" AND "UNORGANIZED" ROOTERS VIED FOR THE MOST NOISE. THE GIRLS' MEGAPHONE BRIGADE WAS SAID TO HAVE MADE AS MUCH, IF NOT MORE, NOISE AS ANY. THE WHOLE NATION LOOKED UPON THE BANKS OF THE MISSISSIPPI FOR AN EPIC CONTEST FEATURING MINNESOTA'S GREATEST TEAM TO DATE.

◀ THE "NEW" NORTHROP FIELD

THE FIRST HALF WENT TO MINNESOTA ALTHOUGH THERE WAS NO SCORING. IT WAS PLAYED MOSTLY IN MICHIGAN TERRITORY. MICHIGAN WOULD STIFFEN WHEN MINNESOTA WAS WITHIN RANGE TO SCORE. THE GOPHERS OUT-FIRST-DOWNED THE WOLVERINES 17-3.

IN THE SECOND HALF MICHIGAN'S CONDITIONING PAID OFF WITH A LONG MARCH OVER THE GOAL LINE. TIME WAS BECOMING A FACTOR IN THE SCHEDULED 70 MINUTE GAME. THE GAME, HOWEVER, WASN'T OVER YET...

Early Rules

SOME OF THE RULES OF THE GAME IN 1903 WERE AS FOLLOWS:

THE FIELD WAS 110 YARDS LONG AND THE KICKOFF WAS FROM THE 55 YARD LINE; A TEAM HAD TO ADVANCE THE BALL FIVE YARDS IN THREE TRIES TO MAKE A FIRST DOWN; THE SCORED-UPON TEAM HAD THE OPTION OF KICKING OR RECEIVING. BEFORE 1903 THE SCORED-UPON TEAM ALWAYS KICKED OFF.

STARTING IN 1903 THE QUARTERBACK, WHO WAS FIRST TO RECEIVE THE BALL, COULD ADVANCE THE BALL BEYOND THE SCRIMMAGE LINE ONLY IF HE FIRST RAN FIVE YARDS TO THE LEFT OR RIGHT OF THE "SNAPPER-BACK." THIS TYPE ADVANCE WAS ONLY ALLOWED BETWEEN THE 25 YARD LINES. THE FIELD WAS DESIGNED IN A CHECKERBOARD

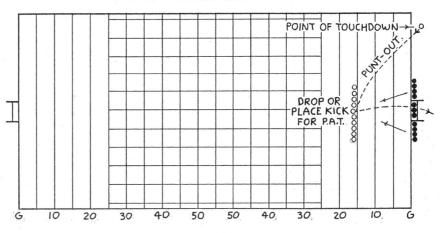

PATTERN FOR THE SAKE OF THE REFEREE TO KEEP TRACK OF THIS LATERAL MOVEMENT.

ANOTHER NEW RULE ENDED ROUGHING OF THE PUNTER. PREVIOUSLY THE PUNTER COULD KICK AND SCAMPER DOWN FIELD TO PICK UP THE BALL AND ADVANCE IT AS IF THE PLAY HAD BEEN A RUN. TO PREVENT THIS, THE RECEIVING TEAM WOULD FLATTEN THE KICKER BEFORE HE COULD GET STARTED. NOW THE KICKER COULD NOT BE TOUCHED NOR COULD HE RECEIVE HIS OWN KICK.

A TOUCHDOWN WAS WORTH FIVE POINTS. THE SCORE COUNTED WHEN THE BALL WAS TOUCHED DOWN ON THE GROUND OR WHEN THE CARRIER WAS TACKLED PAST THE GOAL LINE. HE WOULD TRY TO PUT THE BALL AS CLOSE TO THE GOAL POSTS AS POSSIBLE BECAUSE THE POINT AFTER WAS ATTEMPTED 15 YARDS OUT FROM WHERE THE TOUCH-DOWN WAS MADE. SINCE THE POSTS WERE RIGHT ON THE GOAL LINE, TO SCORE NEAR THE SIDE OF THE FIELD OFFERED A HARD ANGLE FROM WHICH TO KICK THE POINT AFTER. GREAT STRUGGLES MIGHT OCCUR IN THE END ZONE FOR POSITION.

TO OVERCOME THESE BAD KICKING ANGLES A PUNT-OUT WAS ALLOWED. AN OFFENSIVE PLAYER WOULD TAKE THE BALL FROM THE POINT OF TOUCHDOWN AND PUNT IT TO A TEAMMATE BEYOND THE 15 YARD LINE IN FRONT OF THE GOAL-POSTS. THE RECEIVER WOULD PLACE OR DROP-KICK IT FOR THE SCORE. THE DEFENDERS WOULD LINE UP ON THE GOAL LINE AND TAKE OFF AT THE PUNT-OUT.

Sig Harris

AT ONE POINT QUARTERBACK SIG HARRIS, FROM MINNEAPOLIS CENTRAL, WAS TACKLED AND CARRIED BACKWARD. HIS CRIES OF "DOWN!" ENDED THE PLAY IN TIME TO PREVENT A SAFETY. HARRIS WAS VALUED FOR HIS PUNTING AND PUNT RETURNS. HE WAS ALSO THE FINAL DEFENSIVE STOPPER ON WILLIE HESTON. DURING A HESTON END RUN THE TWO COLLIDED AND WERE BOTH KNOCKED OUT. THEY WERE REVIVED AND CONTINUED PLAY. AFTER MICHIGAN'S SCORE HARRIS RETURNED THE KICKOFF 43 YARDS. IT WAS THE DAY'S MOST SPECTACULAR PLAY AND GAVE MINNESOTA IMPORTANT FIELD POSITION.

HE EVENTUALLY BECAME COACH OF THE FRESHMEN SQUAD. BEFORE MICHIGAN GAMES, HE WOULD GIVE THE VARSITY ROUSING SPEECHES TO SPUR THEM ON TO VICTORY.

16

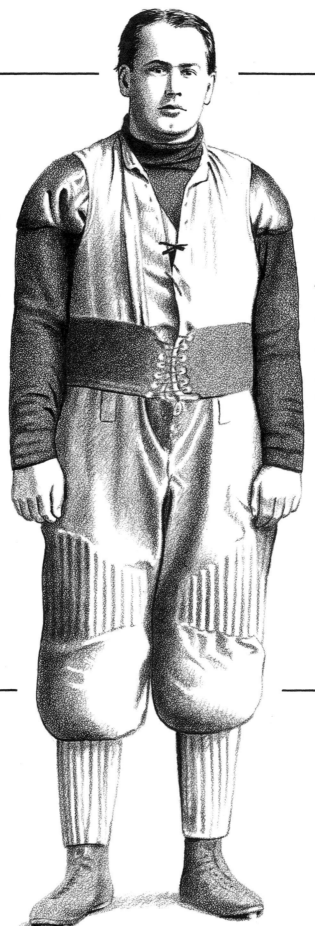

WITH MINUTES TO PLAY THE GOPHERS ROSE ABOVE THEIR FATIGUE TO FIGHT DOWN THE FIELD. A GREAT SPEARHEAD IN THE STRUGGLE WAS FRED SCHACHT.

SCHACHT WAS THE HEAVIEST LINEMAN FOR MINNESOTA AT 5'11" TALL AND 210 POUNDS. HE WORE A CORSET, MUCH TO THE DISGUST OF THE MICHIGAN COACH... BUT HE JUST WANTED TO LOOK GOOD.

LINEMEN WERE ALLOWED TO RUN WITH THE BALL, AND SO, FROM TACKLE, HE WAS THE TEAM'S BEST GROUND-GAINER. WITH HIS SPEED AND WEIGHT HE WOULD HIT THE LINE AND POUND OUT MANY OF THE MOST CRITICAL YARDS IN THE GOPHER'S TOUCHDOWN DRIVE.

Fred 'Germany' Schacht

THE FERGUS FALLS GIANT BECAME MINNESOTA'S FIRST CONSENSUS ALL-AMERICAN. HE FAILED TO MAKE WALTER CAMP'S TEAM, THOUGH.

HE DIED OF BRIGHTS DISEASE JUST THREE YEARS AFTER THE MICHIGAN GAME.

FINALLY, EGIL BOECKMANN CRACKED THE GOAL LINE. THE PUNT-OUT TRY WENT TO ED ROGERS. TWO WEEKS BEFORE, AGAINST IOWA, HE HAD KICKED 10 CONVERSIONS. THIS ONE WAS TO BE HIS BIGGEST. HE COOLLY DROP-KICKED IT THROUGH TO TIE THE GAME.

THERE WAS NOTHING TO HOLD THE JOYOUS FANS AS THEY FLOODED ONTO THE FIELD. A POLICEMAN GOT HIS RIBS BROKEN WHILE TRYING TO HOLD BACK THE BURSTING TIDE. THE BAND PLAYED "HOT TIME."

ROGERS AND THE MICHIGAN CAPTAIN AGREED TO END THE GAME RATHER THAN CLEAR THE HUMANITY OFF THE FIELD. THERE WERE ONLY A FEW MINUTES LEFT AND DARKNESS WAS SETTING IN, ANYWAY.

Ed Rogers

BEFORE BECOMING THE MINNESOTA CAPTAIN, ROGERS PLAYED SIX YEARS AT CARLISLE. HE WAS CAPTAIN THERE, TOO.

AFTER HIS PLAYING DAYS, THE CHIPPEWA LEFT END FROM WALKER, MINNESOTA COACHED ST. THOMAS AND CARLISLE.

HE BECAME A MEMBER OF THE FOOTBALL HALL OF FAME.

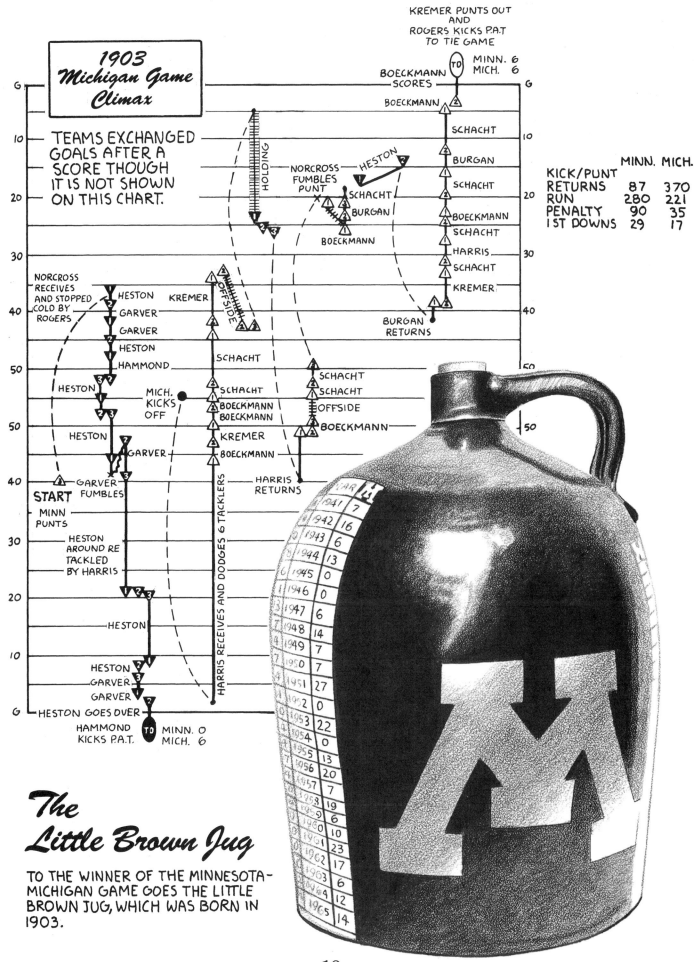

1903
Michigan Game
Climax

TEAMS EXCHANGED
GOALS AFTER A
SCORE THOUGH
IT IS NOT SHOWN
ON THIS CHART.

KREMER PUNTS OUT
AND
ROGERS KICKS P.A.T
TO TIE GAME

MINN. 6
MICH. 6

BOECKMANN
SCORES

BOECKMANN

SCHACHT

BURGAN

SCHACHT

BOECKMANN

SCHACHT

HARRIS

SCHACHT

KREMER

BURGAN
RETURNS

HOLDING

NORCROSS
FUMBLES
PUNT

HESTON

SCHACHT

BURGAN

BOECKMANN

KICK/PUNT	MINN.	MICH.
RETURNS	87	370
RUN	280	221
PENALTY	90	35
1ST DOWNS	29	17

NORCROSS
RECEIVES
AND STOPPED
COLD BY
ROGERS

HESTON

GARVER

GARVER

HESTON

HAMMOND

HESTON

HESTON

GARVER

GARVER
FUMBLES

KREMER

OFFSIDE

SCHACHT

SCHACHT
BOECKMANN
BOECKMANN

KREMER

BOECKMANN

SCHACHT
SCHACHT

OFFSIDE

BOECKMANN

HARRIS
RETURNS

HARRIS RECEIVES AND DODGES 6 TACKLERS

START

MINN.
PUNTS

HESTON
AROUND RE
TACKLED
BY HARRIS

HESTON

HESTON
GARVER
GARVER

HESTON GOES OVER

HAMMOND
KICKS P.A.T.

MINN. 0
MICH. 6

MICH.
KICKS
OFF

GARVER

The
Little Brown Jug

TO THE WINNER OF THE MINNESOTA-
MICHIGAN GAME GOES THE LITTLE
BROWN JUG, WHICH WAS BORN IN
1903.

YEAR	M
1941	7
1942	16
1943	6
1944	13
1945	0
1946	0
1947	6
1948	14
1949	7
1950	7
1951	27
1952	0
1953	22
1954	0
1955	13
1956	20
1957	7
1958	19
1959	6
1960	10
1961	23
1962	17
1963	6
1964	12
1965	14

19

THE GREAT MINNESOTA-MICHIGAN GAME OF 1903 WAS OVER, BUT NOT THE EXCITE-MENT. YOU WOULD THINK THE LATE MINNEAPOLIS AMERICAN LEAGUE BASEBALL TEAM OF 1901 HAD RETURNED AND WON A WORLD SERIES OR SOMETHING. CONSIDERING THE OPPOSITION, A TIE WAS AS GOOD AS A WIN THIS DAY. THE GOPHERS WERE BEING PROCLAIMED THE NEW "CHAMPIONS OF THE WEST."

ALTHOUGH STREET CARS WERE LINED UP FOR BLOCKS TO CARRY THE LIVELY THRONG FROM THE GAME, MOST ENDED UP WALKING. IT WAS TWO MILES TO DOWNTOWN AND ITS CELEBRATIONS. COULD SUCH EXCITEMENT EVER HAPPEN AGAIN?

THE FRIENDLY MOB SNAKED DOWN THE STREETS BY ZIG-ZAGGING FROM ONE SIDE TO THE OTHER. RIDES WERE GIVEN IN WHEEL BARROWS WHETHER PEOPLE WANTED TO BE PASSENGERS OR NOT. THEATERS WERE PUNCTUATED BETWEEN ACTS WITH CRIES OF "SKI-U-MAH!" A POLICEMAN CONFISCATED A RICKETY OLD WAGON THAT FANS WERE PULLING ALL OVER DOWNTOWN. AN AUTO DRIVER WAS LASSOED AND ALMOST PULLED FROM HIS VEHICLE BEFORE HE COULD STOP IT.

MOST OF THE ACTION WAS ON NICOLLET, BETWEEN WASHINGTON AND 7TH STREET. ANYTHING TO MAKE NOISE WAS USED. THE STREETS AND SIDEWALKS WERE JAMMED. HALLOWEEN TRICKS WERE PULLED ON MICHIGAN FANS WHO WERE UNWISE ENOUGH TO RIDICULE THE GOPHERS. THERE WERE STILL THOUSANDS IN THE STREETS AT 2 A.M.

A GOOD TIME WAS HAD BY ALL.

IN SPITE OF THE JOY, SOME BAD FEELINGS ALSO CAME OUT. MICHIGAN HAD THOUGHT MINNESOTA PLAYED OVERLY-ROUGH. MINNESOTA ACCUSED THE MICHIGAN COACH OF GIVING SIGNALS TO HIS QUARTERBACK FROM THE SIDELINES. IT TOOK A WEEK FOR BOTH SIDES TO CALM DOWN.

NOT GIVING UP COMPLETELY, MICHIGAN MADE A CHALLENGE TO HAVE A POST-SEASON GAME TO CONCLUSIVELY DECIDE THE CHAMPIONSHIP. MINNESOTA REFUSED BECAUSE THERE WAS NO PRECEDENT FOR SUCH A THING.

We'll cheer for Minnesota,
for the old Maroon and Gold.

We'll cheer for Minnesota
in our coffins when we're cold.

And when we're up in heaven
we'll yell to Ski-u-mah!

But if we go the other way
we'll give 'em Sis-boom-ah!

(ADAPTED FROM 1904 SONG)

IT WAS THE CUSTOM OF TRAVELING TEAMS TO BRING THEIR OWN WATER TO GAMES. THIS IS WHAT MICHIGAN DID IN 1903.

COACH YOST HAD HIS STUDENT MANAGER, TOMMY ROBERTS, GO TO A DOWNTOWN MINNEAPOLIS VARIETY STORE TO PURCHASE A WATER CONTAINER. HE BOUGHT A GRAY FIVE GALLON JUG FOR 35 CENTS.

THE JUG SAT BY THE MICHIGAN BENCH DURING THE GREAT STRUGGLE, BUT WAS LATER FORGOTTEN IN THE TEAM

Oscar Munson

DRESSING ROOM. TWO DAYS AFTER THE GAME, CUSTODIAN OSCAR MUNSON FOUND AND BROUGHT IT TO THE DIRECTOR OF PHYSICAL EDUCATION, DR. LOUIS COOKE.

IN HIS SCANDINAVIAN ACCENT MUNSON SAID, "LOOK DOC, JOST LEFT HIS YUG." COOKE REPLIED, "IF YOST WANTS IT, LET HIM COME AND GET IT."

COOKE PAINTED "MICHIGAN JUG, CAPTURED BY OSCAR," ON IT AS SHOWN ABOVE. HE THEN HUNG IT ON A HOOK ABOVE HIS OWN DESK WHERE IT STAYED FOR SIX YEARS.

IN 1909 THE TWO TEAMS MET AGAIN. CAPTAIN JOHN McGOVERN SUGGESTED TO THE MICHIGAN CAPTAIN THAT THE JUG BE A GAME TROPHY. MICHIGAN AGREED AND PROMPTLY WON IT OVER.

IT WASN'T UNTIL 1919, AT ANN ARBOR, THAT MINNESOTA WON IT BACK. AFTER THE VICTORY, THE JUG WAS FOUND CHAINED TO THE FLOOR OF THE SCHOOL GYMNASIUM TROPHY ROOM.

YOST SUGGESTED THE TEAMS PAINT THEIR SCHOOL COLORS ON IT. EVENTUALLY IT ENDED UP AS IT IS TODAY, WITH GAME SCORES AND THE MINNESOTA M ON ONE SIDE, AND THE MICHIGAN M ON THE OTHER.

Dr. Louis Cooke

"MOSE" STRATHERN, FROM HASTINGS, WAS TEAM CAPTAIN AND ALL-AMERICAN CENTER IN 1904. HIS SQUAD WENT 13-0-0 WHILE PILING UP 725 POINTS. THIS STANDS SECOND ONLY TO HARVARD'S ALL-TIME RECORD OF 765 POINTS IN 1886.

Moses Strathern

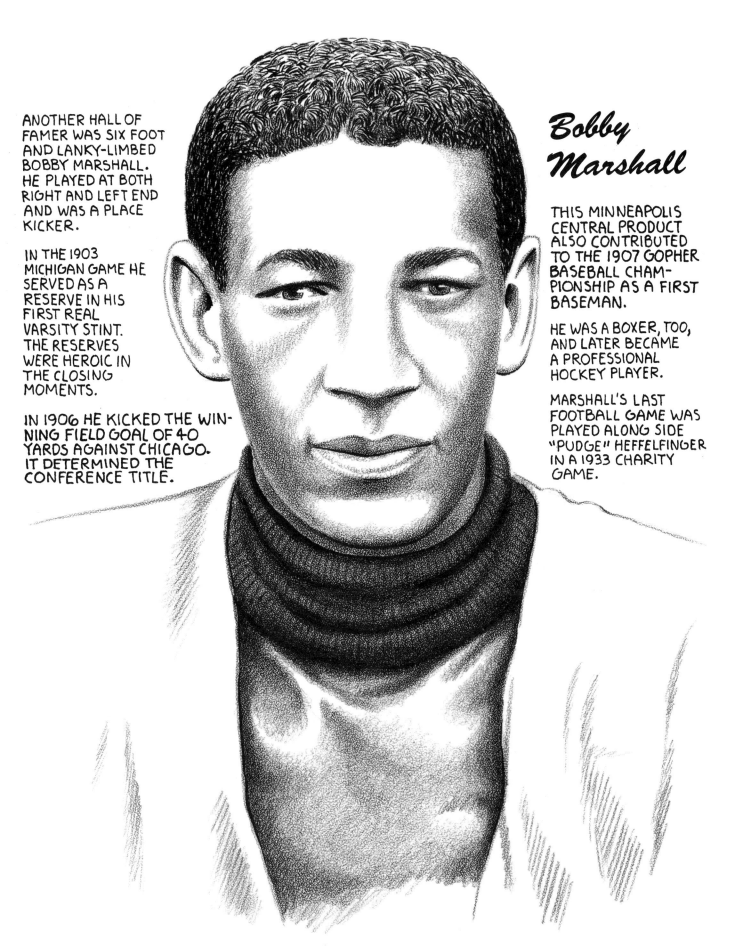

ANOTHER HALL OF FAMER WAS SIX FOOT AND LANKY-LIMBED BOBBY MARSHALL. HE PLAYED AT BOTH RIGHT AND LEFT END AND WAS A PLACE KICKER.

IN THE 1903 MICHIGAN GAME HE SERVED AS A RESERVE IN HIS FIRST REAL VARSITY STINT. THE RESERVES WERE HEROIC IN THE CLOSING MOMENTS.

IN 1906 HE KICKED THE WINNING FIELD GOAL OF 40 YARDS AGAINST CHICAGO. IT DETERMINED THE CONFERENCE TITLE.

Bobby Marshall

THIS MINNEAPOLIS CENTRAL PRODUCT ALSO CONTRIBUTED TO THE 1907 GOPHER BASEBALL CHAMPIONSHIP AS A FIRST BASEMAN.

HE WAS A BOXER, TOO, AND LATER BECAME A PROFESSIONAL HOCKEY PLAYER.

MARSHALL'S LAST FOOTBALL GAME WAS PLAYED ALONG SIDE "PUDGE" HEFFELFINGER IN A 1933 CHARITY GAME.

23

1904 Grinnell Game

THE SMELL IN THE AIR WAS THAT OF CARNAGE. WITH 20 GAMES LISTED ON THE SPORTS PAGE, 18 TEAMS WENT SCORELESS. THE VICTORS HAD RUN UP 712 POINTS TO 12 FOR THE LESS FORTUNATE. MICHIGAN ALONE HAD SCRUBBED WEST VIRGINIA 130-0. IT BETTERED THEIR OWN NATIONAL SCORING RECORD BY TWO. IT WOULDN'T BE ENOUGH TO SET A NEW RECORD, THOUGH, AS MINNESOTA TOOK IT OVER BY BURYING GRINNELL 146-0! LOCALS ACCLAIMED IT A "WORLD RECORD."

NEXT TO GRINNELL'S TEAM, THE MOST SHELL-SHOCKED PEOPLE MUST HAVE BEEN THE STATISTICIANS. THE PAPER HAD PLAY-BY-PLAY DESCRIPTIONS VERSUS A CHART OF THE ACTION THAT DIDN'T ALWAYS BALANCE. THE PLAY-BY-PLAY MIGHT LIST A FEW PLAYS IN A DRIVE WHERE THE CHART WOULD SHOW A FEW MORE. BECAUSE OF THIS SOME PLAYERS WOULD NOT GET FULL ACCOUNTINGS OF THEIR INDIVIDUAL EXPLOITS. THEY MIGHT SIMPLY GET A MENTION THAT THEY HAD A COUPLE GOOD GAINS. THE OVERALL YARDAGE SHOWED 485 MORE YARDS RUSHING THAN CAN BE CREDITED FOR INDIVIDUALLY. TOUCHDOWN PLAYS WERE RELATIVELY ACCURATE, THOUGH. CHARTS ON THESE PAGES SHOULD NOT BE TOO FAR OFF.

ANOTHER THING TO KEEP IN MIND WAS THE EMPHASIS ON KICKING BEING EQUAL TO RUNNING IN TABULATIONS. THEY WERE COUNTED TOGETHER IN AN OVERALL TOTAL "YARDS ADVANCED." EVEN A KICKOFF WAS CONSIDERED AN ADVANCE FOR THE KICKER.

THIS GAME WAS PLAYED IN TWO 25 MINUTE HALVES. THE GOPHERS MANAGED TO SCORE A TOUCHDOWN IN LESS THAN EVERY TWO MINUTES. THE HALFTIME SCORE WAS 73-0.

THE GRINNELL COACH SAID, "MINNESOTA'S OFFENSE WAS FASTER THAN WE EXPECTED." THE MAROON AND GOLD SHOWED CRUSHING INTERFERENCE AFTER HAVING STARTED PLAYS IN SUCH A HURRY THAT GRINNELL PLAYERS WERE NOT READY FOR THE SNAP. THEY WERE OFTEN OFFSIDE. THE MINNESOTA GAINS WERE SO GREAT THAT THE LITTLE FIVE YARD PENALTIES WERE NEVER TAKEN ADVANTAGE OF.

GRINNELL'S FUTILITY SAW THEM GET BUT THREE RUNS BEYOND THE LINE OF SCRIMMAGE ALL DAY. THEY WENT FOR ONE, THREE AND TWO YARDS. EVERYTHING ELSE WENT FOR A LOSS OR WAS STOPPED COLD AT THE LINE. THEY WOULD HIT THE LINE AND PILE UP IN A HEAP AND BE TOPPLED BACK.

WITH HOPE FOR ACHIEVING FIELD POSITION GRINNELL WOULD USUALLY ELECT TO KICK AFTER A GOPHER SCORE. DURING ONE STRETCH MINNESOTA REELED OFF FIVE TOUCHDOWNS WITHOUT GRINNELL HAVING A SINGLE POSSESSION FROM SCRIMMAGE.

MINNESOTA WAS ONLY OCCASIONALLY SLOWED DOWN BY FUMBLING. GRINNELL WOULD FUMBLE

STATISTICS	M	G
POSSESSIONS	30	15
PLAYS	132	37
FIRST DOWNS	54	0
KICKOFFS	11	17
PUNTS	2	6
FUMBLES	4	7
FUMBLES LOST	3	7
PENALTIES ASSESSED	7	0
YARDS PENALIZED	75	0
TOUCHDOWNS	26	0
P.A.T - GOOD	16	0
P.A.T. - NO GOOD	10	0

YARDS ADVANCED	M	G
RUSHING	1431	-4
KICKOFF RETURNS	303	41
PUNT RETURNS	52	32
RETURNS OFF TURNOVERS	70	0
KICKOFFS	544	646
PUNTS	97	205
TOTAL YARDS ADVANCED	2497	920

MINNESOTA SCORING DRIVES

TD.	SCORER	RUN	DESCRIPTION	DRIVE	PLAYS	FIRST DOWNS	CONVERSION		SCORE
1	THORPE	3		77	8	4	LARKIN	(NO GOOD)	5
2	OECH	3		30	3	1	LARKIN	(NO GOOD)	10
3	VITA	2		95	11	6	MARSHALL	(GOOD)	16
4	BRUSH	65		80	2	1	MARSHALL	(NO GOOD)	21
5	DAVIES	46	AROUND LE	46	1	0	MARSHALL	(GOOD)	27
6	BURDICK	3		51	7	3	MARSHALL	(GOOD)	33
7	BRUSH	3		83	8	4	MARSHALL	(GOOD)	39
8	MARSHALL	55	FROM PUNT MUFF	–	–	–	MARSHALL	(GOOD)	45
9	VITA	4		73	9	4	MARSHALL	(NO GOOD)	50
10	VITA	8		74	5	2	DAVIES	(GOOD)	56
11	DAVIES	55	AROUND RE	55	1	0	DAVIES	(GOOD)	62
12	BRUSH	10		70	6	4	DAVIES	(NO GOOD)	67
13	DAVIES	50	AROUND RE	65	2	1	DAVIES	(GOOD)	73
14	KREMER	4		4	1	0	MARSHALL	(GOOD)	79
15	VITA	8		70	11	4	MARSHALL	(GOOD)	85
16	ITTNER	4		71	10	5	MARSHALL	(GOOD)	91
17	GLEASON	15	OFF BLOCKED PUNT	–	–	–	MARSHALL	(GOOD)	97
18	ITTNER	72	THROUGH THE LINE	72	1	0	MARSHALL	(GOOD)	103
19	ITTNER	2		37	5	3	MARSHALL	(NO GOOD)	108
20	MARSHALL	45	AROUND RE	63	4	2	MARSHALL	(NO GOOD)	113
21	THORPE	16		20	2	0	MARSHALL	(GOOD)	119
22	KREMER	3		64	8	3	MARSHALL	(NO GOOD)	124
23	LUCE	16	OVER LT	16	1	0	MARSHALL	(GOOD)	130
24	GLEASON	12		61	7	3	LARKIN	(NO GOOD)	135
25	MARSHALL	10		10	1	0	MARSHALL	(NO GOOD)	140
26	MARSHALL	45	CIRCLED END	45	1	0	MARSHALL	(GOOD)	146

IT RIGHT BACK ON THE NEXT PLAY AND THE GOPHERS WOULD CONTINUE THEIR MARCH. JAMES KREMER, AT ONE POINT, RETURNED A KICKOFF FOR 40 YARDS. HE WAS INTERRUPTED BY A FUMBLE ONLY TO HAVE TEAMMATE EARL LUCE PICK IT UP AND CONTINUE FOR 15 MORE YARDS.

THE ONLY TIMES THE GOPHERS PUNTED WAS BECAUSE THEY PLACED THEMSELVES IN A HOLE DUE TO HOLDING PENALTIES.

AT LEAST THREE GOPHERS RUSHED OVER 100 YARDS. TWO OTHERS WERE CLOSE. PERCY BRUSH HAD 229+. SIGNAL CALLER, ARTHUR LARKIN, LED IN TOTAL YARDS ADVANCED WITH 362. BOBBY MARSHALL ADVANCED 330+ YARDS. THE TOTAL TEAM ADVANCED THE BALL A LITTLE UNDER ONE AND A QUARTER MILE.

GRINNELL DIDN'T LACK FOR YARDS ADVANCED STATISTICS. A FELLOW NAMED NOBLE LED FOR THE RED AND BLACK. HE, NATURALLY, WAS THE KICKER. HE BOOTED AWAY FOR 851 YARDS AND FIGURED IN A COUPLE RUNBACKS. HE HELD ALL HIS TEAM ADVANCE STATISTICS EXCEPT FOR 42 YARDS.

SCORING

	TD.	P.A.T.	PTS.
BRUSH	3		15
BURDICK	1		5
DAVIES	3	3	18
GLEASON	2		10
ITTNER	3		15
KREMER	2		10
LUCE	1		5
MARSHALL	4	13	33
OCECH	1		5
THORPE	2		10
VITA	4		20

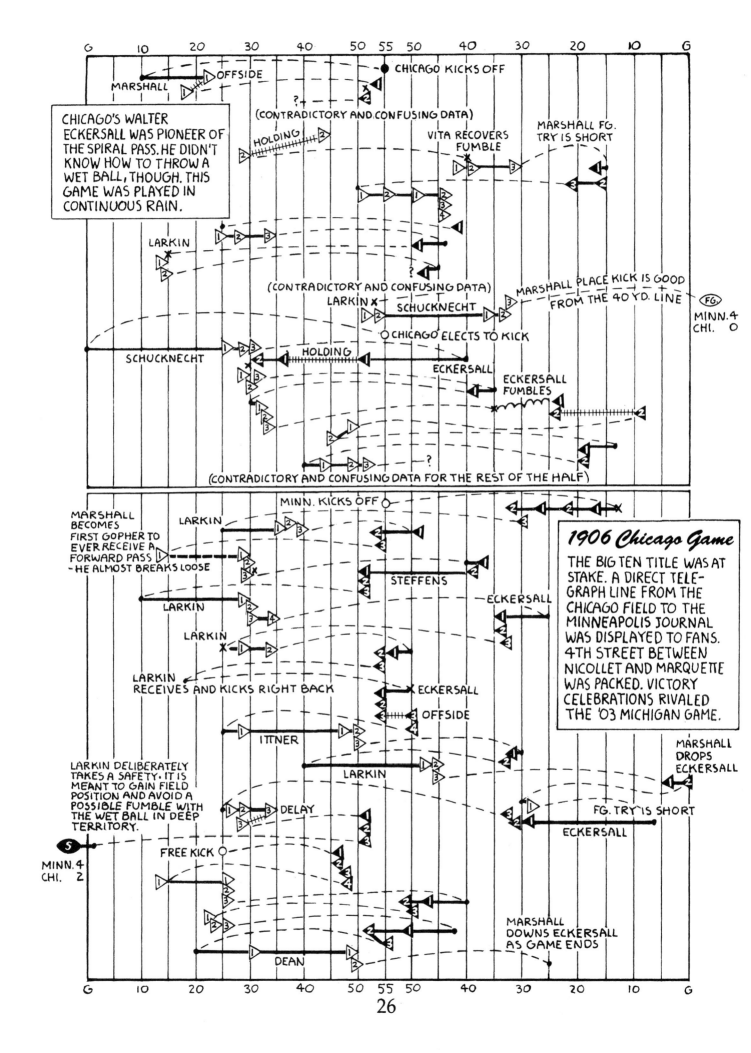

CHICAGO'S WALTER ECKERSALL WAS PIONEER OF THE SPIRAL PASS. HE DIDN'T KNOW HOW TO THROW A WET BALL, THOUGH. THIS GAME WAS PLAYED IN CONTINUOUS RAIN.

1906 Chicago Game

THE BIG TEN TITLE WAS AT STAKE. A DIRECT TELEGRAPH LINE FROM THE CHICAGO FIELD TO THE MINNEAPOLIS JOURNAL WAS DISPLAYED TO FANS. 4TH STREET BETWEEN NICOLLET AND MARQUETTE WAS PACKED. VICTORY CELEBRATIONS RIVALED THE '03 MICHIGAN GAME.

CHICAGO KICKS OFF

MARSHALL

OFFSIDE

? (CONTRADICTORY AND CONFUSING DATA)

HOLDING

VITA RECOVERS FUMBLE

MARSHALL FG. TRY IS SHORT

LARKIN

(CONTRADICTORY AND CONFUSING DATA)

LARKIN

SCHUCKNECHT

MARSHALL PLACE KICK IS GOOD FROM THE 40 YD. LINE

FG. MINN. 4 CHI. 0

CHICAGO ELECTS TO KICK

SCHUCKNECHT

HOLDING

ECKERSALL

ECKERSALL FUMBLES

? (CONTRADICTORY AND CONFUSING DATA FOR THE REST OF THE HALF)

MINN. KICKS OFF

MARSHALL BECOMES FIRST GOPHER TO EVER RECEIVE A FORWARD PASS - HE ALMOST BREAKS LOOSE

LARKIN

STEFFENS

ECKERSALL

LARKIN

LARKIN

LARKIN RECEIVES AND KICKS RIGHT BACK

ECKERSALL

OFFSIDE

ITTNER

LARKIN

MARSHALL DROPS ECKERSALL

LARKIN DELIBERATELY TAKES A SAFETY. IT IS MEANT TO GAIN FIELD POSITION AND AVOID A POSSIBLE FUMBLE WITH THE WET BALL IN DEEP TERRITORY.

DELAY

FG. TRY IS SHORT

ECKERSALL

S MINN. 4 CHI. 2

FREE KICK

MARSHALL DOWNS ECKERSALL AS GAME ENDS

DEAN

26

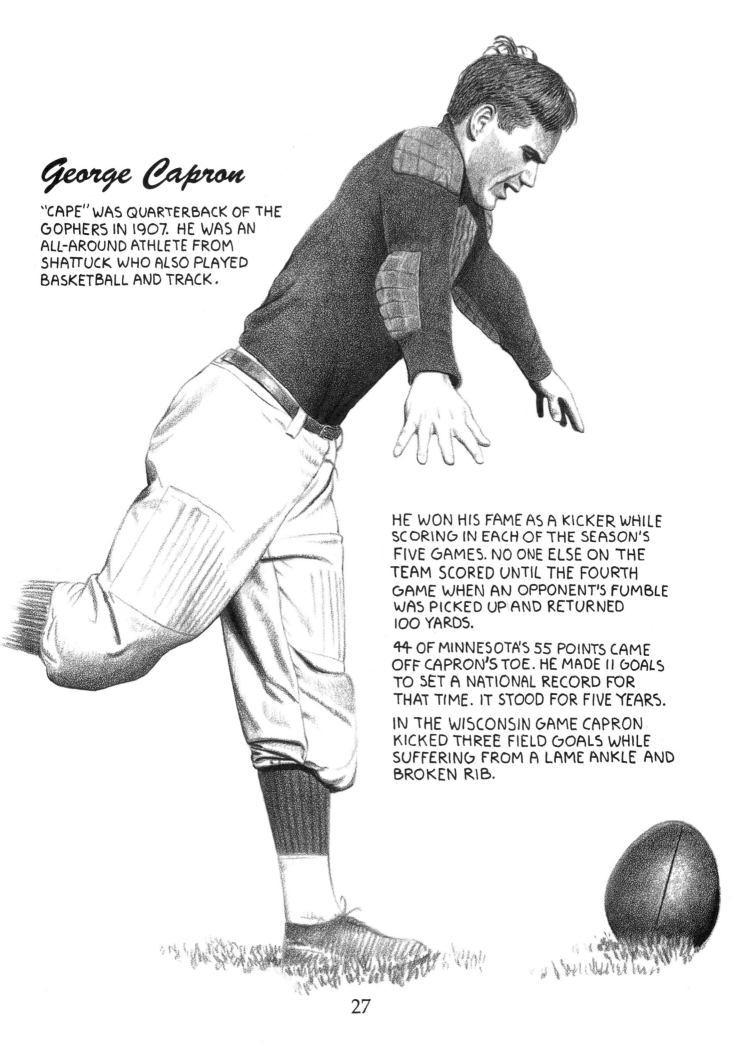

George Capron

"CAPE" WAS QUARTERBACK OF THE GOPHERS IN 1907. HE WAS AN ALL-AROUND ATHLETE FROM SHATTUCK WHO ALSO PLAYED BASKETBALL AND TRACK.

HE WON HIS FAME AS A KICKER WHILE SCORING IN EACH OF THE SEASON'S FIVE GAMES. NO ONE ELSE ON THE TEAM SCORED UNTIL THE FOURTH GAME WHEN AN OPPONENT'S FUMBLE WAS PICKED UP AND RETURNED 100 YARDS.

44 OF MINNESOTA'S 55 POINTS CAME OFF CAPRON'S TOE. HE MADE 11 GOALS TO SET A NATIONAL RECORD FOR THAT TIME. IT STOOD FOR FIVE YEARS.

IN THE WISCONSIN GAME CAPRON KICKED THREE FIELD GOALS WHILE SUFFERING FROM A LAME ANKLE AND BROKEN RIB.

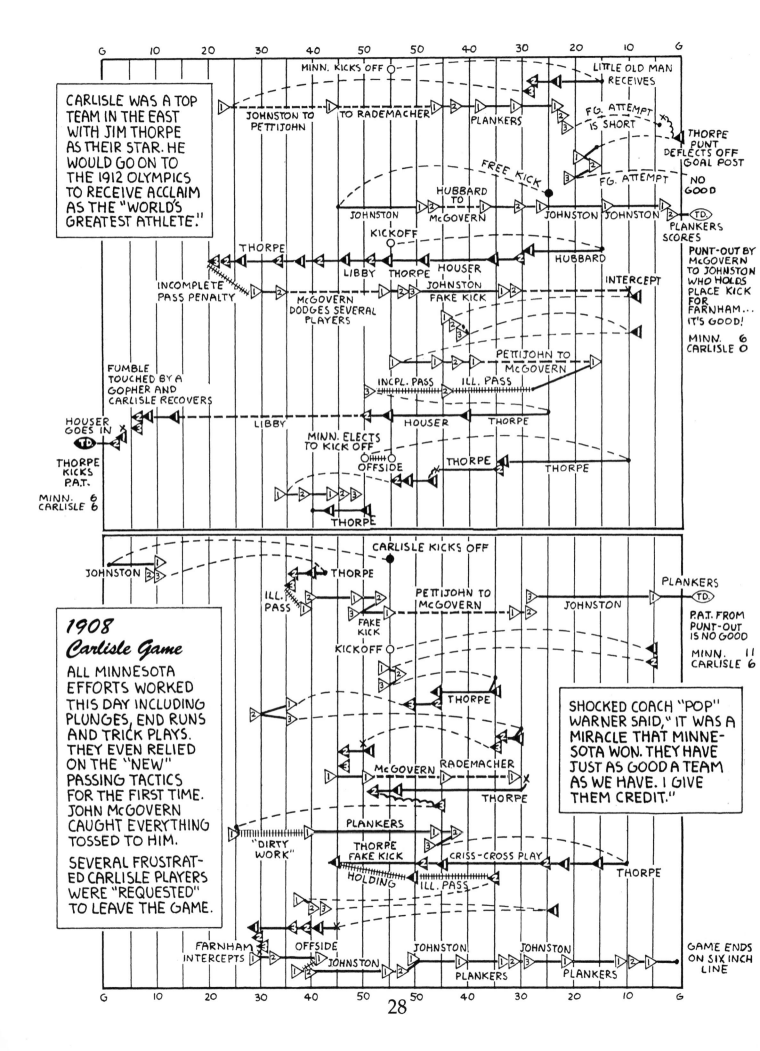

CARLISLE WAS A TOP TEAM IN THE EAST WITH JIM THORPE AS THEIR STAR. HE WOULD GO ON TO THE 1912 OLYMPICS TO RECEIVE ACCLAIM AS THE "WORLD'S GREATEST ATHLETE."

MINN. KICKS OFF
LITTLE OLD MAN RECEIVES
JOHNSTON TO PETTIJOHN
TO RADEMACHER
PLANKERS
FG. ATTEMPT IS SHORT
THORPE PUNT DEFLECTS OFF GOAL POST
FREE KICK
HUBBARD TO McGOVERN
JOHNSTON
FG. ATTEMPT
JOHNSTON JOHNSTON
NO GOOD
PLANKERS SCORES
THORPE
KICKOFF
LIBBY THORPE HOUSER
HUBBARD
PUNT-OUT BY McGOVERN TO JOHNSTON WHO HOLDS PLACE KICK FOR FARNHAM... IT'S GOOD!
INCOMPLETE PASS PENALTY
McGOVERN DODGES SEVERAL PLAYERS
JOHNSTON FAKE KICK
INTERCEPT
MINN. 6
CARLISLE 0
FUMBLE TOUCHED BY A GOPHER AND CARLISLE RECOVERS
PETTIJOHN TO McGOVERN
INCPL. PASS
ILL. PASS
HOUSER GOES IN
LIBBY
HOUSER
THORPE
THORPE KICKS P.A.T.
MINN. ELECTS TO KICK OFF
OFFSIDE
THORPE
THORPE
MINN. 6
CARLISLE 6
THORPE

JOHNSTON
CARLISLE KICKS OFF
THORPE
PLANKERS
JOHNSTON
ILL. PASS
PETTIJOHN TO McGOVERN
TD.
FAKE KICK
KICKOFF
P.A.T. FROM PUNT-OUT IS NO GOOD
MINN. 11
CARLISLE 6

1908 Carlisle Game

ALL MINNESOTA EFFORTS WORKED THIS DAY INCLUDING PLUNGES, END RUNS AND TRICK PLAYS. THEY EVEN RELIED ON THE "NEW" PASSING TACTICS FOR THE FIRST TIME. JOHN McGOVERN CAUGHT EVERYTHING TOSSED TO HIM.

SEVERAL FRUSTRATED CARLISLE PLAYERS WERE "REQUESTED" TO LEAVE THE GAME.

THORPE
McGOVERN
RADEMACHER
THORPE
PLANKERS
"DIRTY WORK"
THORPE FAKE KICK
CRISS-CROSS PLAY
THORPE
HOLDING
ILL. PASS

SHOCKED COACH "POP" WARNER SAID," IT WAS A MIRACLE THAT MINNESOTA WON. THEY HAVE JUST AS GOOD A TEAM AS WE HAVE. I GIVE THEM CREDIT."

FARNHAM INTERCEPTS
OFFSIDE
JOHNSTON
JOHNSTON
PLANKERS
JOHNSTON
PLANKERS
GAME ENDS ON SIX INCH LINE

28

John McGovern

NOT ONLY DID JOHN McGOVERN BECOME A CONSENSUS ALL-AMERICAN IN 1909, HE WAS THE FIRST GOPHER TO MAKE WALTER CAMP'S ELEVEN.

AS QUARTERBACK, HAILING FROM ARLINGTON, MINNESOTA, HE WAS AN INSPIRING CAPTAIN WITH GREAT GENERAL-SHIP ABILITIES.

ON OFFENSE HE WAS SLICK IN THE OPEN FIELD. HE WAS SMALL, SQUATTY, PIANO-LEGGED BUT POWERFUL TO THE POINT OF NOT GOING DOWN UNTIL BURIED. TACKLERS MIGHT RIP OFF HIS LOWER JERSEY AS HE WOULD DUCK THROUGH THE LINE. ON ONE 55 YARD TOUCHDOWN RUN HE WAS TACKLED TWICE AND SHOOK LOOSE. WITH LEGALIZATION OF THE PASS HE BECAME THE TEAM'S BEST RECEIVER.

HE WAS ALSO A SUPERB DROP-KICKER IN THE YEAR SUCH A SCORE WAS LOWERED TO THREE POINTS. IT WAS PREVIOUSLY WORTH MORE TO PACIFY SOCCER-STYLE FANS OF THE GAME. McGOVERN FIGURED IN MANY VICTORIES BECAUSE OF HIS KICKING.

DEFENSIVELY HE TACKLED WITH DEADLY PRECISION AND WAS KNOWN TO SNATCH AN INTERCEPTION NOW AND THEN.

EXCEPT FOR ONE GAME, HE PLAYED EVERY MINUTE OF EVERY GAME FOR THREE YEARS. HE EVEN PLAYED WITH A BROKEN COLLAR BONE SUFFERED TOWARD THE END OF 1909.

HIS SHOULDER INJURY HAMPERED HIS ABILITY TO REPEAT AS ALL-AMERICAN IN 1910. IT DIDN'T STOP HIM AT ALL FROM ENTERING THE HALL OF FAME.

James Walker

1910 WAS THE FIRST YEAR THE GAME WAS DIVIDED INTO QUARTERS INSTEAD OF HALVES AND MINNESOTA HAD ITS SECOND WALTER CAMP ALL-AMERICAN. THE MINNEAPOLITAN WAS FAST FOR HIS SIZE AND A TERROR ON DEFENSE, SMEARING THE OPPOSITION BEFORE THEY COULD GET SET UP.

IN THE FIRST GAME FOR WHICH THE LITTLE BROWN JUG WAS FOUGHT, IN 1909, HE SCORED ON A TACKLE ELIGIBLE PLAY. HE SERVED EVERY MINUTE ON THE FIELD OF ALL BUT ONE GAME FOR TWO YEARS.

IN HIS OLD AGE WALKER WAS STILL ANNOYED OVER A RULING NULLIFYING HIS BLOCKED KICK THAT TOUCHED A REFEREE. THE BALL WAS INCORRECTLY GIVEN TO MICHIGAN WHO USED THE ADVANTAGE TO WIN IN 1910.

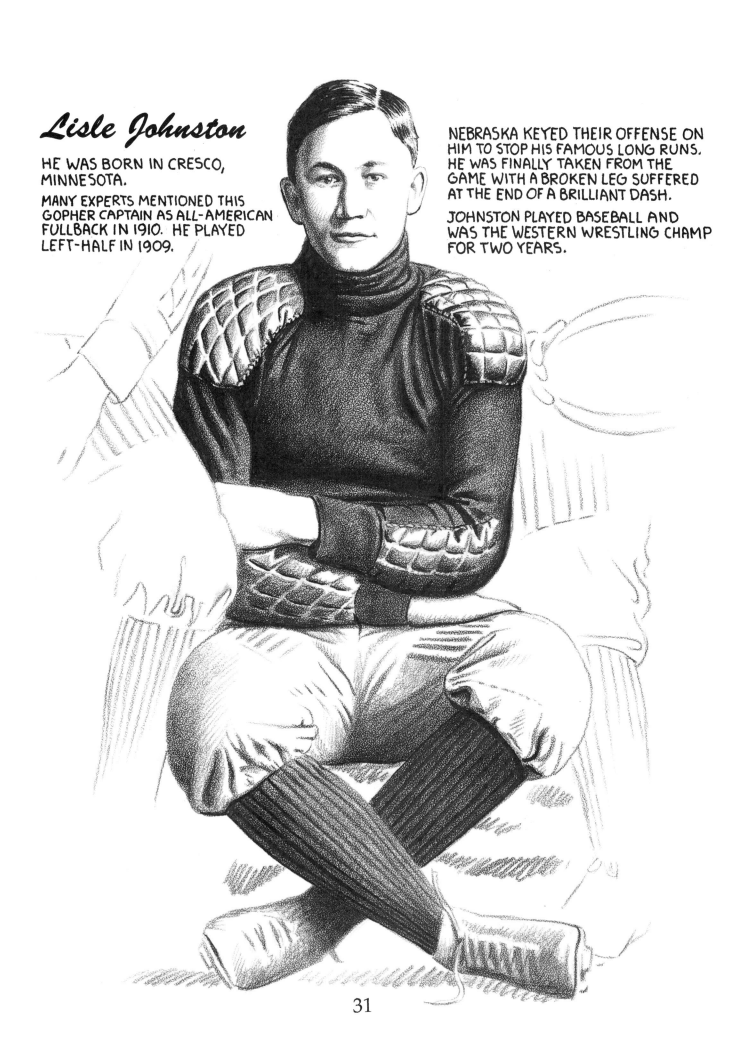

Lisle Johnston

HE WAS BORN IN CRESCO, MINNESOTA.

MANY EXPERTS MENTIONED THIS GOPHER CAPTAIN AS ALL-AMERICAN FULLBACK IN 1910. HE PLAYED LEFT-HALF IN 1909.

NEBRASKA KEYED THEIR OFFENSE ON HIM TO STOP HIS FAMOUS LONG RUNS. HE WAS FINALLY TAKEN FROM THE GAME WITH A BROKEN LEG SUFFERED AT THE END OF A BRILLIANT DASH.

JOHNSTON PLAYED BASEBALL AND WAS THE WESTERN WRESTLING CHAMP FOR TWO YEARS.

HE WAS ORIGINALLY FROM ST. CLOUD,
BUT WENT TO HIGH SCHOOL
AT NORTH ST. PAUL. WHILE
IN HIGH SCHOOL HE PLAYED
NO SPORTS.

Clark Shaughnessy

AT MINNESOTA HE PLAYED
TACKLE AND FULLBACK.
AS AN ALL-AMERICAN
IN 1913 HE EXCELLED
AS A KICKER WHILE
ALSO BEING A PASS
RECEIVER AND RUNNER.

IN THE 1912 IOWA
GAME HE GRABBED
THREE HAWKEYE
FUMBLES. ONE OF
THEM RESULTED IN
A TOUCHDOWN.

HIS GREATEST
ACHIEVEMENTS
CAME AS A COACH
FOR WHICH HE WAS
NAMED TO THE HALL
OF FAME.

HE COACHED TULANE,
LOYOLA, CHICAGO,
STANFORD, MARYLAND,
PITTSBURGH AND THE
L.A. RAMS.

WHILE AT CHICAGO
ONE OF HIS PLAYERS
WAS JAY BERWANGER,
THE FIRST-EVER
HEISMAN TROPHY
WINNER.

SHAUGHNESSY
STUDIED MILITARY
TACTICS FOR
FOOTBALL IDEAS.
FROM THE GER-
MAN GENERAL
HEINZ GUDERIAN,
HE TOOK THE
BLITZKRIEG TO
INVENT THE MAN-
IN-MOTION
FOR THE
T-FORMATION.

HE PERFECTED
THE USE OF
BRUSH BLOCKS TO
ENHANCE HIS INVEN-
TION'S SPEED AND
DECEPTION. A 1700
WORD VOCABULARY
WAS DEVISED THAT
ONLY HIS PLAYERS
COULD UNDERSTAND
FOR FAST PLAY CALLING.

THE FIRST YEAR HE
UNLEASHED HIS MAN-IN-
MOTION HE WON THE
NATIONAL TITLE.
BETWEEN THE FINAL
SEASON GAME AND VICTORY
IN THE ROSE BOWL, HE
TAUGHT HIS INVENTION
TO THE CHICAGO BEARS
WHO USED IT TO MOP UP
THE WASHINGTON
REDSKINS IN THE
N.F.L. TITLE GAME.

CLARK SHAUGHNESSY
REVOLUTIONIZED
FOOTBALL WITH HIS
MAN-IN-MOTION
TO MAKE IT THE
EXPLOSIVE AND
EXCITING GAME
IT IS TODAY.

Merton Dunnigan

THOUGH ORIGINALLY FROM MICHIGAN, HE MOVED TO MINNEAPOLIS WHERE HE ATTENDED WEST HIGH.

WALTER ECKERSALL NAMED "HAP" TO HIS ALL-AMERICAN TEAM IN 1915. WITH THE HELP OF DUNNIGAN'S EFFORTS THE GOPHERS WON THE BIG TEN TITLE THAT YEAR.

HE LATER RETURNED TO THE "U" AS AN ASSISTANT FOR COACH CLARENCE SPEARS.

Lorin Solon

HE THREW, RECEIVED AND RAN INTERFER-
ENCE EXCEPTIONALLY WELL. IN 1913 HE
RECEIVED ALL-AMERICAN RECOGNITION AT
END. THE FOLLOWING YEAR HE BECAME A
FULLBACK.

IN 1915, AGAINST IOWA STATE, HE CAUGHT
SIX PASSES, RAN BACK KICKOFFS OF 60 AND
35 YARDS AND SCORED FOUR TOUCHDOWNS.

IN THE MIDDLE OF THE 1915 SEASON IT WAS
LEARNED HE HAD PLAYED PRO BASEBALL
FOR A TEAM IN MONTANA THE PREVIOUS
SUMMER. NO OPPONENTS OBJECTED TO
HIS CONTINUED PLAY BUT MINNESOTA AUTHOR-
ITIES DISQUALIFIED HIM. BERNIE BIERMAN
TOOK OVER HIS POSITION AS TEAM
CAPTAIN.

Bernie Bierman

SUCH A GREAT COACH WAS BERNIE BIERMAN THAT HIS ATHLETIC ABILITY IS SOMETIMES FORGOTTEN.

AS A CHILD HE GOT A BONE INFECTION IN HIS LEG. TO IMPROVE HIS CONDITION HE TOOK UP SPORTS. IN HIGH SCHOOL HE BECAME A STAR FOR A CHAMPION LITCHFIELD TEAM.

AT MINNESOTA HE PLAYED LEFT HALFBACK WHILE SOMETIMES SUBSTITUTING FOR CLARK SHAUGHNESSY AT FULLBACK. HE PLAYED LEFT END, AS WELL.

HIS MOST OUTSTANDING SEASON WAS 1915, WHEN HE MADE ALL-AMERICAN DISTINCTION. HE ALSO WON THE CONFERENCE MEDAL FOR SCHOLASTIC AND ATHLETIC ACHIEVEMENT.

IN A GAME AGAINST WISCONSIN HE MANAGED TO INTERCEPT FOUR PASSES AND SCORE TWO TOUCHDOWNS.

BIERMAN LETTERED IN BASKETBALL AND TRACK, TOO. HE DID THE 100 YARDS IN TEN SECONDS AND THE 220 IN 22.5 SECONDS.

HE DIDN'T INTEND TO GO INTO COACHING AFTER LEAVING SCHOOL. IT WASN'T A PROMISING CAREER TO MAKE A LIVING. HE DID TRY ONE SEASON AT THE BUTTE, MONTANA HIGH SCHOOL, THOUGH. THEY WON THE STATE TITLE.

AFTER SERVING IN WORLD WAR I, HIS FRIEND, CLARK SHAUGHNESSY, ASKED HIM TO BE HIS ASSISTANT AT TULANE. EVENTUALLY BIERMAN TOOK OVER THE HEAD TULANE COACHING JOB HIMSELF.

HIS RECORD FOR THE GREEN WAVE BECAME 36-10-2, WHILE PRODUCING FOUR ALL-AMERICANS.

IN HIS FINAL SEASON, HIS TEAM ENDED UP BEING RATED SECOND IN THE NATION. HIS ONLY LOSS WAS TO NUMBER ONE RATED U.S.C. IN THE 1932 ROSE BOWL. THAT GAME ENDED AN 18 GAME WIN STRING.

MINNESOTA CALLED HIM HOME AND SOON HE WAS GREETED LIKE KING MIDAS, WHO TOUCHED THE CAMPUS TO BRING ON THE "GOLDEN ERA" OF MINNESOTA FOOTBALL.

Bert Baston

FROM ST. LOUIS PARK CAME MINNESOTA'S FIRST TWO-TIME WALTER CAMP ALL-AMERICAN. IT WAS BERT BASTON IN 1915-16. THE LATTER YEAR HE WAS CONSENSUS.

HE WAS THE RECEIVER IN THE GAME'S FIRST GREAT PASSING COMBINATION, WITH "PUDGE" WYMAN ON THE TOSSING SIDE.

IT WAS SAID BASTON HAD LEGS LIKE STEEL SPRINGS AND WOULD SNATCH PASSES JUST OVER THE FINGERTIPS OF HIS OPPONENTS. THIS LEFT WING DID IT TWICE IN A FLOCK OF HAWKEYES IN 1916. SOMETIMES HE WOULD JUGGLE THE BALL WITH ONE HAND WHEN TWO WEREN'T CONVENIENT. HE HAD AN INSTINCT FOR GETTING IN THE OPEN WHEN HE TIRED OF CROWDS.

HE COULD CLEAR THE WAY FOR HIS BACKS AND ON DEFENSE WAS HARD TO TAKE OUT OF A PLAY.

ON A WISCONSIN KICKOFF HE ONCE RETURNED 85 YARDS FOR A SCORE WHILE MAKING THE LAST 30 IN RECORD TIME. HE MISTOOK A TEAMMATE'S SHADOW FOR A PURSUER.

HE COULD ALSO BE USED TO KICK CONVERSIONS.

IN 1954 HE WAS INDUCTED INTO THE HALL OF FAME.

OTHER HONORS CAME TO HIM ON OTHER FIELDS. SIX MONTHS AFTER LEAVING THE PLAYING GRIDIRON HE WAS TWICE WOUNDED ON THE BATTLEFIELDS OF WORLD WAR I. HE RECEIVED THE DISTINGUISHED SERVICE CROSS.

AT FRITZ CRISLER'S REQUEST HE RETURNED TO THE "U" IN 1930. HE CONTINUED TO HELP AS AN ASSISTANT UNDER HIS FORMER TEAMMATES BERNIE BIERMAN AND GEORGE HAUSER. FOR 20 YEARS HE SHAPED SOME OF MINNESOTA'S FINEST WINGS.

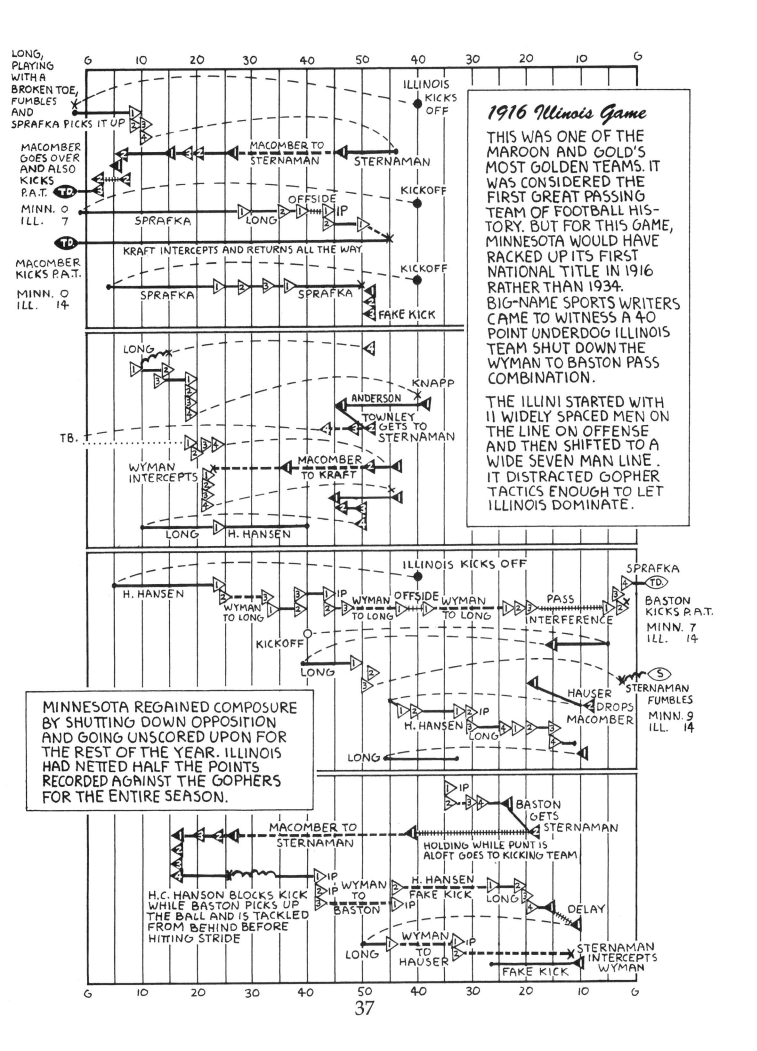

1916 Illinois Game

THIS WAS ONE OF THE MAROON AND GOLD'S MOST GOLDEN TEAMS. IT WAS CONSIDERED THE FIRST GREAT PASSING TEAM OF FOOTBALL HISTORY. BUT FOR THIS GAME, MINNESOTA WOULD HAVE RACKED UP ITS FIRST NATIONAL TITLE IN 1916 RATHER THAN 1934. BIG-NAME SPORTS WRITERS CAME TO WITNESS A 40 POINT UNDERDOG ILLINOIS TEAM SHUT DOWN THE WYMAN TO BASTON PASS COMBINATION.

THE ILLINI STARTED WITH 11 WIDELY SPACED MEN ON THE LINE ON OFFENSE AND THEN SHIFTED TO A WIDE SEVEN MAN LINE. IT DISTRACTED GOPHER TACTICS ENOUGH TO LET ILLINOIS DOMINATE.

MINNESOTA REGAINED COMPOSURE BY SHUTTING DOWN OPPOSITION AND GOING UNSCORED UPON FOR THE REST OF THE YEAR. ILLINOIS HAD NETTED HALF THE POINTS RECORDED AGAINST THE GOPHERS FOR THE ENTIRE SEASON.

WISCONSIN SEEMED TO BE HIS FAVORITE VICTIM. IN 1915 HE WAS THE GOPHERS ONLY CONSISTENT GROUND GAINER AGAINST THEM. THE FOLLOWING YEAR HE RETURNED A WISCONSIN PUNT 45 YARDS FOR A TOUCHDOWN AND FREQUENTLY MADE 15-20 YARD GAINS.

Claire 'Shorty' Long

"SHORTY" LONG WAS AN OPEN FIELD RUNNER WHO CAME FROM MINNEAPOLIS. HE WAS AN ALL-AMERICAN QUARTERBACK ON THE GREAT 1916 TEAM.

HAUSER CAME FROM CEDAR FALLS, IOWA TO BECOME A GOPHER ALL-AMERICAN IN 1917.

HE PLAYED RIGHT TACKLE AND WAS KNOWN TO BREAK UP MORE PLAYS IN THE TRENCHES THAN ANYONE ELSE. IN HIS SPARE MOMENTS HE MADE SACKS ON END RUNS, TOO.

HIS 1917 LINE ALLOWED ONLY ONE FIRST DOWN BY THE RUN ALL SEASON.

George Hauser

LINE COACHING TOOK HIM TO MINNESOTA, IOWA STATE, OHIO STATE AND BACK TO MINNESOTA. HE WAS CONSIDERED ONE OF THE BEST IN THE NATION. HE ALSO PUT IN A COUPLE OF YEARS AS HEAD COACH AT COLGATE, IN THE 1920'S, AND A FEW MORE AT MINNESOTA DURING WORLD WAR II.

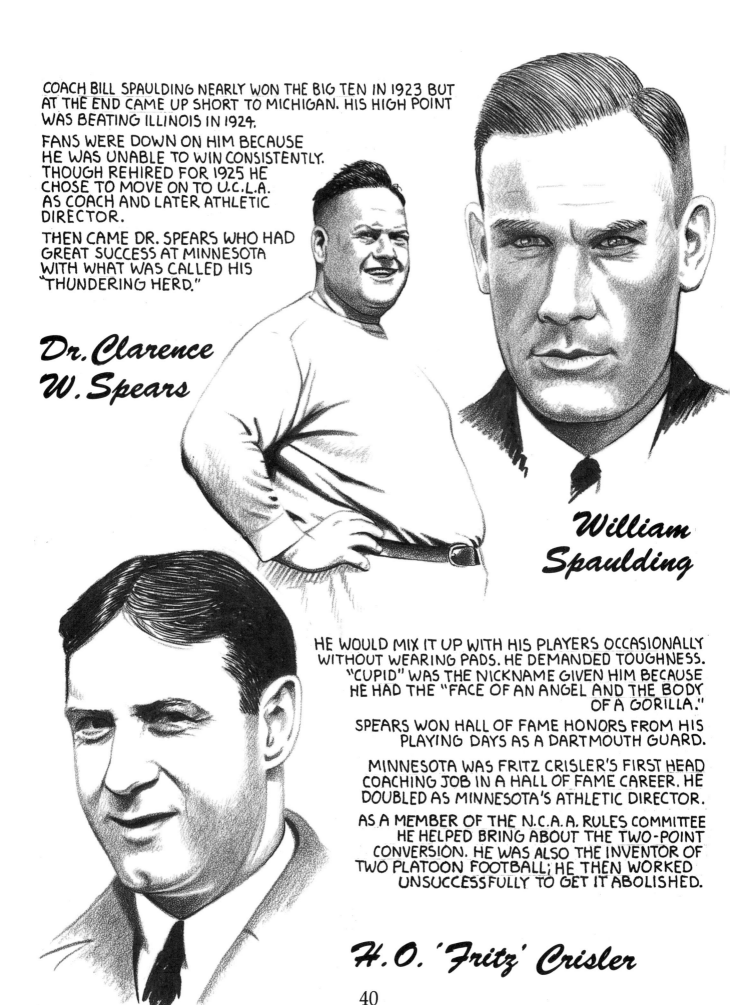

COACH BILL SPAULDING NEARLY WON THE BIG TEN IN 1923 BUT AT THE END CAME UP SHORT TO MICHIGAN. HIS HIGH POINT WAS BEATING ILLINOIS IN 1924.

FANS WERE DOWN ON HIM BECAUSE HE WAS UNABLE TO WIN CONSISTENTLY. THOUGH REHIRED FOR 1925 HE CHOSE TO MOVE ON TO U.C.L.A. AS COACH AND LATER ATHLETIC DIRECTOR.

THEN CAME DR. SPEARS WHO HAD GREAT SUCCESS AT MINNESOTA WITH WHAT WAS CALLED HIS "THUNDERING HERD."

Dr. Clarence W. Spears

William Spaulding

HE WOULD MIX IT UP WITH HIS PLAYERS OCCASIONALLY WITHOUT WEARING PADS. HE DEMANDED TOUGHNESS. "CUPID" WAS THE NICKNAME GIVEN HIM BECAUSE HE HAD THE "FACE OF AN ANGEL AND THE BODY OF A GORILLA."

SPEARS WON HALL OF FAME HONORS FROM HIS PLAYING DAYS AS A DARTMOUTH GUARD.

MINNESOTA WAS FRITZ CRISLER'S FIRST HEAD COACHING JOB IN A HALL OF FAME CAREER. HE DOUBLED AS MINNESOTA'S ATHLETIC DIRECTOR.

AS A MEMBER OF THE N.C.A.A. RULES COMMITTEE HE HELPED BRING ABOUT THE TWO-POINT CONVERSION. HE WAS ALSO THE INVENTOR OF TWO PLATOON FOOTBALL; HE THEN WORKED UNSUCCESSFULLY TO GET IT ABOLISHED.

H. O. 'Fritz' Crisler

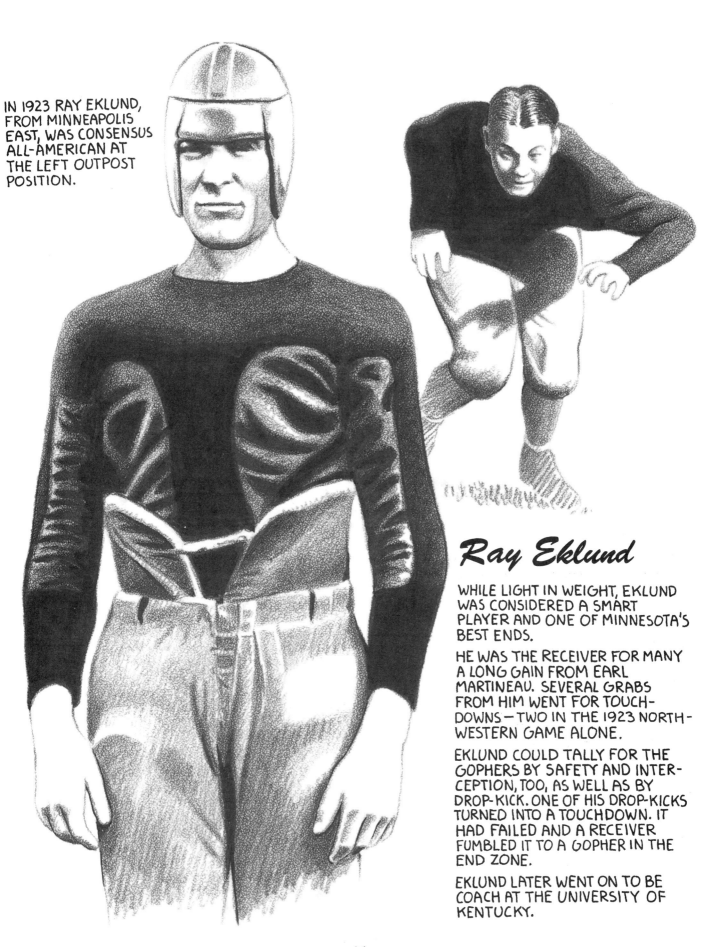

IN 1923 RAY EKLUND, FROM MINNEAPOLIS EAST, WAS CONSENSUS ALL-AMERICAN AT THE LEFT OUTPOST POSITION.

Ray Eklund

WHILE LIGHT IN WEIGHT, EKLUND WAS CONSIDERED A SMART PLAYER AND ONE OF MINNESOTA'S BEST ENDS.

HE WAS THE RECEIVER FOR MANY A LONG GAIN FROM EARL MARTINEAU. SEVERAL GRABS FROM HIM WENT FOR TOUCH-DOWNS — TWO IN THE 1923 NORTH-WESTERN GAME ALONE.

EKLUND COULD TALLY FOR THE GOPHERS BY SAFETY AND INTER-CEPTION, TOO, AS WELL AS BY DROP-KICK. ONE OF HIS DROP-KICKS TURNED INTO A TOUCHDOWN. IT HAD FAILED AND A RECEIVER FUMBLED IT TO A GOPHER IN THE END ZONE.

EKLUND LATER WENT ON TO BE COACH AT THE UNIVERSITY OF KENTUCKY.

41

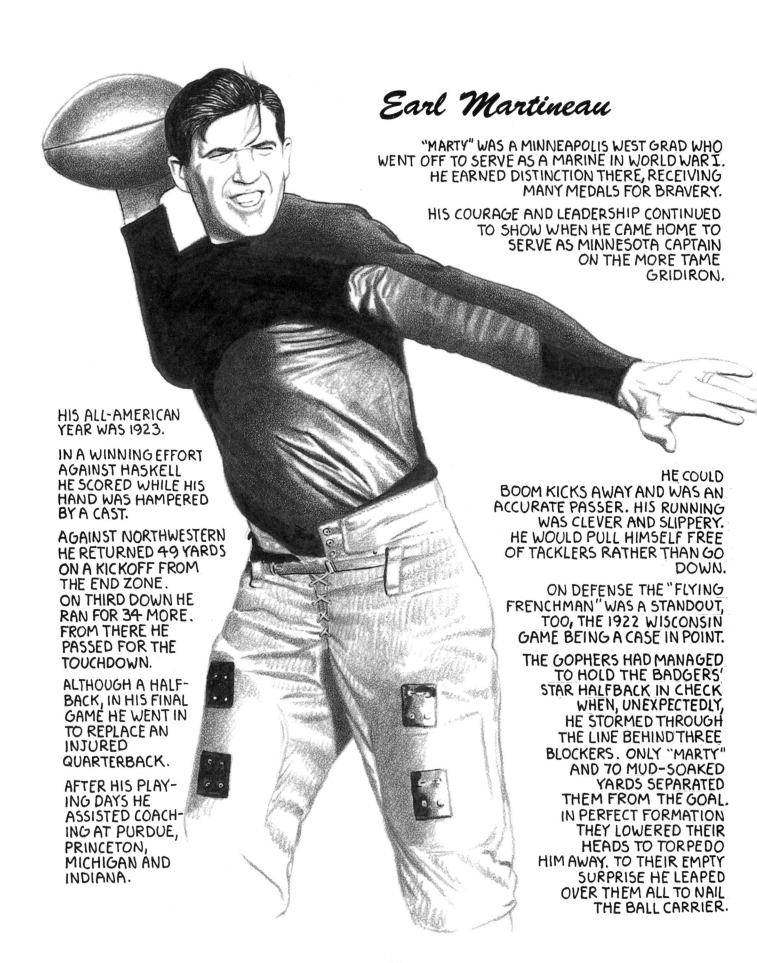

Earl Martineau

"MARTY" WAS A MINNEAPOLIS WEST GRAD WHO WENT OFF TO SERVE AS A MARINE IN WORLD WAR I. HE EARNED DISTINCTION THERE, RECEIVING MANY MEDALS FOR BRAVERY.

HIS COURAGE AND LEADERSHIP CONTINUED TO SHOW WHEN HE CAME HOME TO SERVE AS MINNESOTA CAPTAIN ON THE MORE TAME GRIDIRON.

HIS ALL-AMERICAN YEAR WAS 1923.

IN A WINNING EFFORT AGAINST HASKELL HE SCORED WHILE HIS HAND WAS HAMPERED BY A CAST.

AGAINST NORTHWESTERN HE RETURNED 49 YARDS ON A KICKOFF FROM THE END ZONE. ON THIRD DOWN HE RAN FOR 34 MORE. FROM THERE HE PASSED FOR THE TOUCHDOWN.

ALTHOUGH A HALF-BACK, IN HIS FINAL GAME HE WENT IN TO REPLACE AN INJURED QUARTERBACK.

AFTER HIS PLAY-ING DAYS HE ASSISTED COACH-ING AT PURDUE, PRINCETON, MICHIGAN AND INDIANA.

HE COULD BOOM KICKS AWAY AND WAS AN ACCURATE PASSER. HIS RUNNING WAS CLEVER AND SLIPPERY. HE WOULD PULL HIMSELF FREE OF TACKLERS RATHER THAN GO DOWN.

ON DEFENSE THE "FLYING FRENCHMAN" WAS A STANDOUT, TOO, THE 1922 WISCONSIN GAME BEING A CASE IN POINT.

THE GOPHERS HAD MANAGED TO HOLD THE BADGERS' STAR HALFBACK IN CHECK WHEN, UNEXPECTEDLY, HE STORMED THROUGH THE LINE BEHIND THREE BLOCKERS. ONLY "MARTY" AND 70 MUD-SOAKED YARDS SEPARATED THEM FROM THE GOAL. IN PERFECT FORMATION THEY LOWERED THEIR HEADS TO TORPEDO HIM AWAY. TO THEIR EMPTY SURPRISE HE LEAPED OVER THEM ALL TO NAIL THE BALL CARRIER.

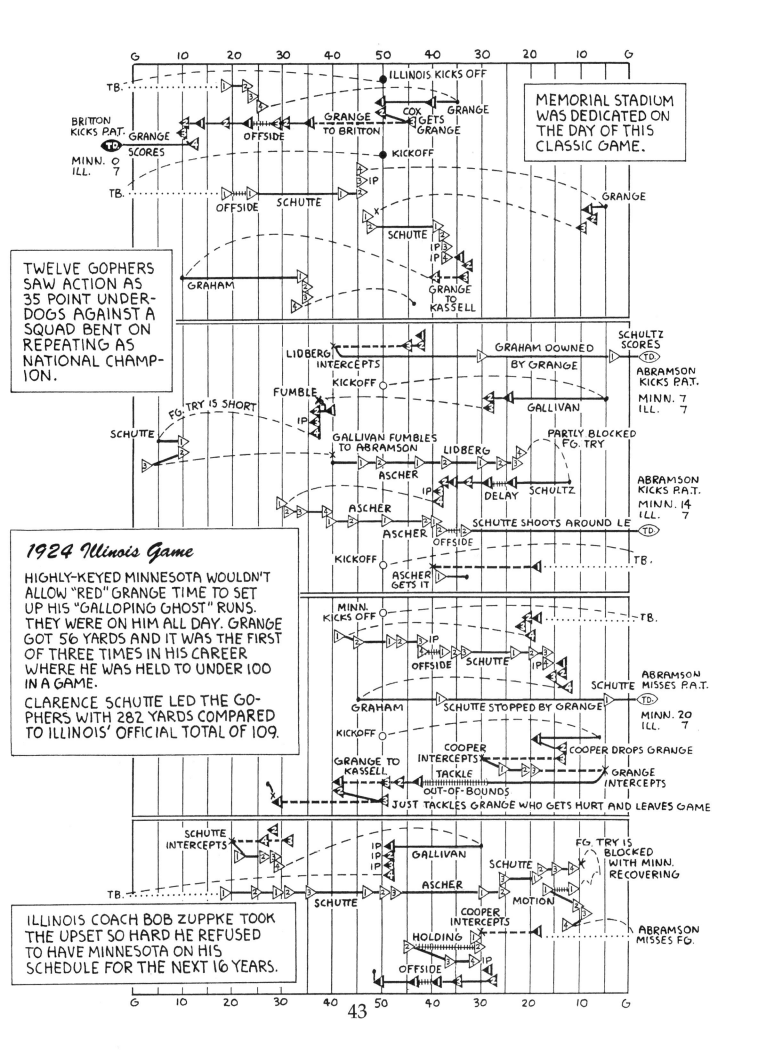

MEMORIAL STADIUM WAS DEDICATED ON THE DAY OF THIS CLASSIC GAME.

TWELVE GOPHERS SAW ACTION AS 35 POINT UNDER-DOGS AGAINST A SQUAD BENT ON REPEATING AS NATIONAL CHAMP-ION.

1924 Illinois Game

HIGHLY-KEYED MINNESOTA WOULDN'T ALLOW "RED" GRANGE TIME TO SET UP HIS "GALLOPING GHOST" RUNS. THEY WERE ON HIM ALL DAY. GRANGE GOT 56 YARDS AND IT WAS THE FIRST OF THREE TIMES IN HIS CAREER WHERE HE WAS HELD TO UNDER 100 IN A GAME.

CLARENCE SCHUTTE LED THE GO-PHERS WITH 282 YARDS COMPARED TO ILLINOIS' OFFICIAL TOTAL OF 109.

ILLINOIS COACH BOB ZUPPKE TOOK THE UPSET SO HARD HE REFUSED TO HAVE MINNESOTA ON HIS SCHEDULE FOR THE NEXT 16 YEARS.

Harold Hanson

AFTER ARRIVING FROM STEWART, MINNESOTA, HANSON ASKED COACH SPEARS IF HE WAS "ALLOWED" TO GO OUT FOR FOOTBALL. HE HAD NEVER PLAYED THE GAME BEFORE.

WITH HIS 185 POUNDS AND SIX FOOT STATURE HE STARTED AS A BACK AND THEN MOVED TO THE LINE AS A LEFT GUARD. HE EARNED HIS ALL-AMERICAN HONORS THERE IN 1927.

AFTER WATCHING HIM IN ACTION KNUTE ROCKNE PRAISED HIM AS THE "BEST GUARD" HE HAD "EVER SEEN."

Herb Joesting

ON THE SAME DAY AFTER LEAVING THE HOSPITAL THE "OWATONNA THUNDER-BOLT" STRUCK FOR 103 YARDS AGAINST IOWA.

HE ATTAINED CONSENSUS ALL-AMERICAN STATURE IN BOTH 1926 AND 27.

HE WAS LEAN AND SUPPLE, BUT HOW HE COULD POUND THAT LINE. THE HALL OF FAME FULL-BACK WAS ONE OF THE GREAT-EST LINE PULVERIZERS OF HIS ERA. THROUGH STRAIGHT-AHEAD BRUTE STRENGTH HE TIED A BIG TEN SEASON RECORD OF 13 TOUCHDOWNS. IN 1926 HE AVERAGED 130 YARDS PER GAME.

HE SERVED HIS PROFESSIONAL DAYS WITH THE MINNE-APOLIS RED JACKETS, PHILADELPHIA YELLOW JACKETS AND THE CHICAGO BEARS.

PASSING WAS ANOTHER FINE QUALITY OF HIS. HE THREW WHAT MAY HAVE BEEN HISTORY'S FIRST JUMP PASS IN THE 1927 NOTRE DAME GAME TO PRODUCE A BIG TOUCH-DOWN.

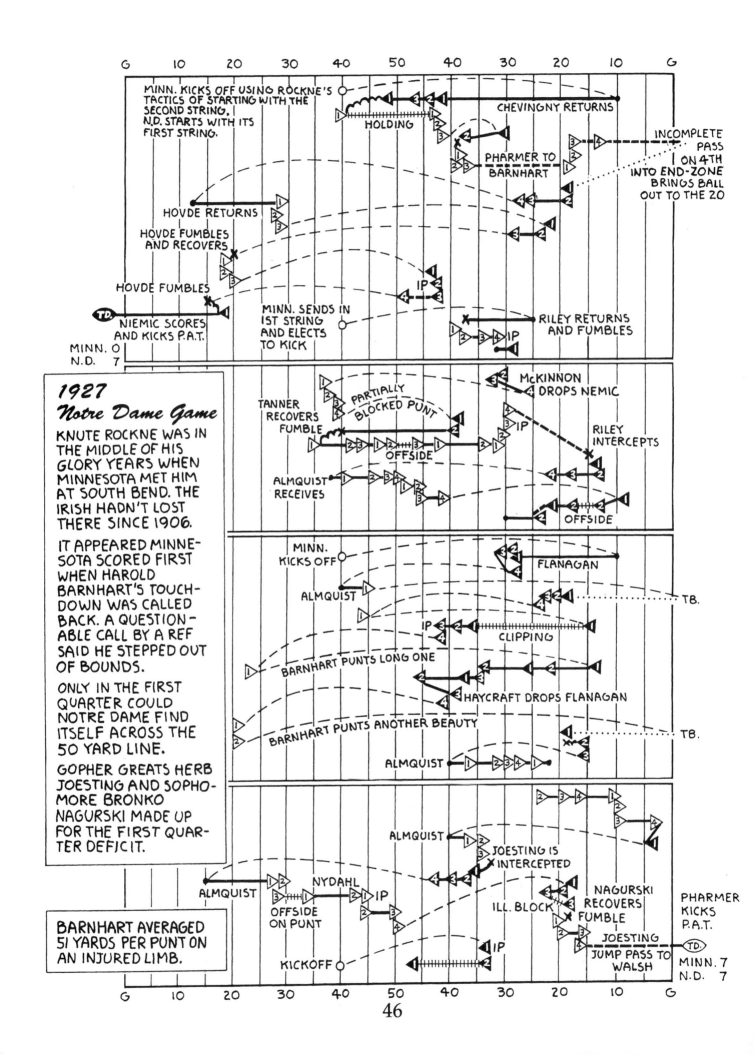

1927
Notre Dame Game

KNUTE ROCKNE WAS IN THE MIDDLE OF HIS GLORY YEARS WHEN MINNESOTA MET HIM AT SOUTH BEND. THE IRISH HADN'T LOST THERE SINCE 1906.

IT APPEARED MINNESOTA SCORED FIRST WHEN HAROLD BARNHART'S TOUCHDOWN WAS CALLED BACK. A QUESTIONABLE CALL BY A REF SAID HE STEPPED OUT OF BOUNDS.

ONLY IN THE FIRST QUARTER COULD NOTRE DAME FIND ITSELF ACROSS THE 50 YARD LINE.

GOPHER GREATS HERB JOESTING AND SOPHOMORE BRONKO NAGURSKI MADE UP FOR THE FIRST QUARTER DEFICIT.

BARNHART AVERAGED 51 YARDS PER PUNT ON AN INJURED LIMB.

46

George Gibson

THIS 1928 ALL-AMERICAN GUARD CAME NORTH FROM OKLAHOMA BECAUSE HE LIKED THE BIG TEN. HE PICKED MINNESOTA BECAUSE HIS FATHER, WHO WORKED FOR THE RAILROAD, COULD GET HIM FREE TICKETS HOME.

WHILE NOT CONSIDERED A FLASHY PLAYER HE WAS A LEADER WHO SHOWED HOW TO DO THE JOB. HE WAS A STOPPER ON DEFENSE AND ON OFFENSE COULD ALWAYS BE RELIED ON FOR OPENING GAPS.

GIBSON WAS A STRONG 195 POUNDS AND KNOWN TO OUT-WRESTLE HIS FRATERNITY ROOMMATE, BRONKO NAGURSKI.

HE SERVED AS GOPHER LINE COACH IN 1929 AND LATER AS HEAD COACH AT CARLETON. BETWEEN THESE JOBS HE PLAYED AND COACHED WITH THE MINNEAPOLIS RED JACKETS WHO WERE THE LOCAL ENTRY IN THE N.F.L.

47

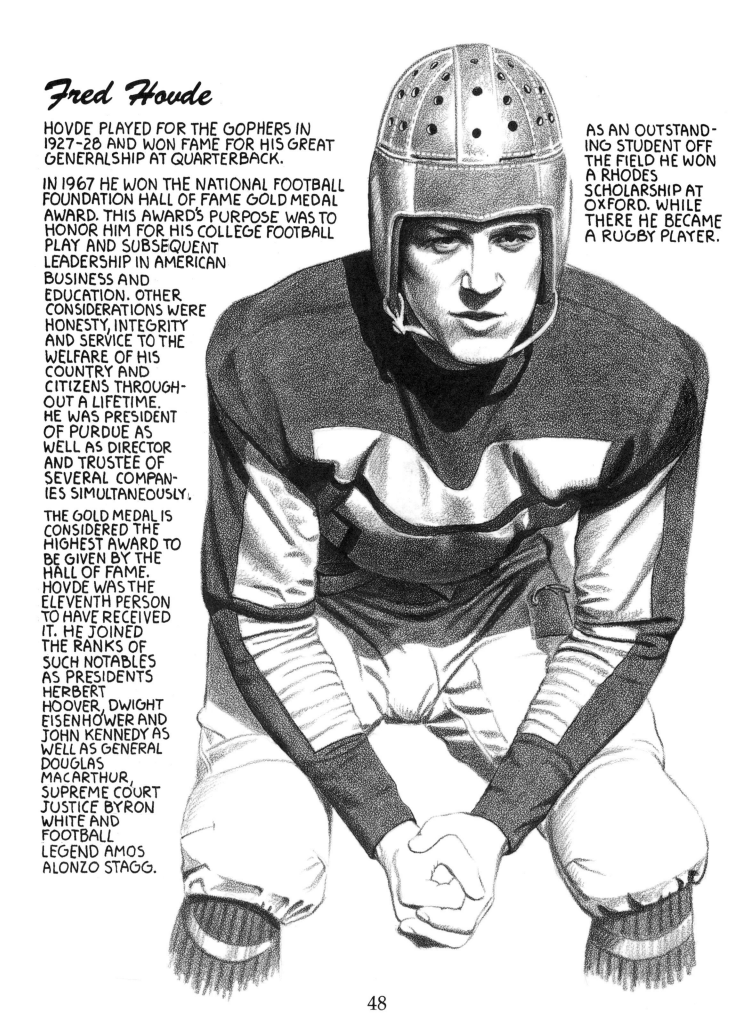

Fred Hovde

HOVDE PLAYED FOR THE GOPHERS IN 1927-28 AND WON FAME FOR HIS GREAT GENERALSHIP AT QUARTERBACK.

IN 1967 HE WON THE NATIONAL FOOTBALL FOUNDATION HALL OF FAME GOLD MEDAL AWARD. THIS AWARD'S PURPOSE WAS TO HONOR HIM FOR HIS COLLEGE FOOTBALL PLAY AND SUBSEQUENT LEADERSHIP IN AMERICAN BUSINESS AND EDUCATION. OTHER CONSIDERATIONS WERE HONESTY, INTEGRITY AND SERVICE TO THE WELFARE OF HIS COUNTRY AND CITIZENS THROUGH-OUT A LIFETIME. HE WAS PRESIDENT OF PURDUE AS WELL AS DIRECTOR AND TRUSTEE OF SEVERAL COMPAN-IES SIMULTANEOUSLY.

THE GOLD MEDAL IS CONSIDERED THE HIGHEST AWARD TO BE GIVEN BY THE HALL OF FAME. HOVDE WAS THE ELEVENTH PERSON TO HAVE RECEIVED IT. HE JOINED THE RANKS OF SUCH NOTABLES AS PRESIDENTS HERBERT HOOVER, DWIGHT EISENHOWER AND JOHN KENNEDY AS WELL AS GENERAL DOUGLAS MACARTHUR, SUPREME COURT JUSTICE BYRON WHITE AND FOOTBALL LEGEND AMOS ALONZO STAGG.

AS AN OUTSTAND-ING STUDENT OFF THE FIELD HE WON A RHODES SCHOLARSHIP AT OXFORD. WHILE THERE HE BECAME A RUGBY PLAYER.

48

Ken Haycraft

BORN IN BEMIDJI, HE MOVED TO MINNEAPOLIS WHERE HE ATTENDED EAST HIGH.

AFTER HIS GOPHER DAYS, HE WENT TO LAW SCHOOL AT MINNESOTA WHILE PLAYING FOR THE MINNEAPOLIS RED JACKETS AND GREEN BAY PACKERS.

HE SCORED THE WINNING TOUCHDOWN AGAINST MICHIGAN TO CONCLUDE AN UNDEFEATED 1927 SEASON. HIS SPECIALTY WAS SNATCHING LONG PASSES ON OR NEAR THE GOAL LINE. HERB JOESTING TOSSED TO HIM FOR MANY A SCORE. THOUGH RELATIVELY SMALL IN SIZE, HAYCRAFT MADE ALL-AMERICAN END IN 1928.

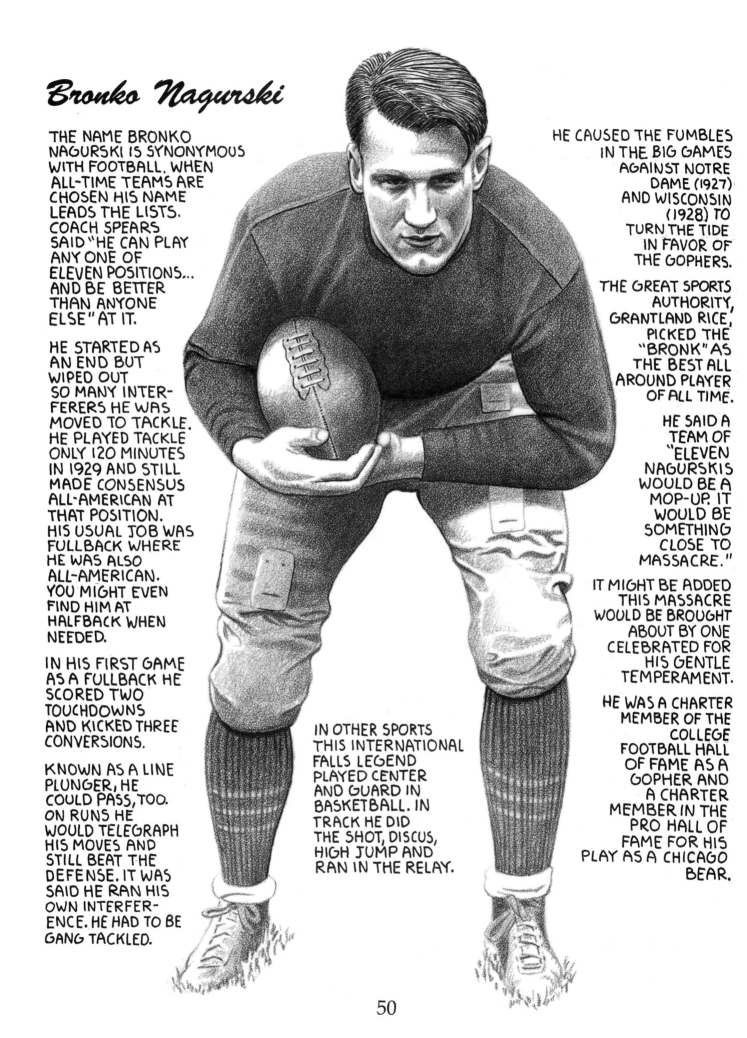

Bronko Nagurski

THE NAME BRONKO NAGURSKI IS SYNONYMOUS WITH FOOTBALL. WHEN ALL-TIME TEAMS ARE CHOSEN HIS NAME LEADS THE LISTS. COACH SPEARS SAID "HE CAN PLAY ANY ONE OF ELEVEN POSITIONS... AND BE BETTER THAN ANYONE ELSE" AT IT.

HE STARTED AS AN END BUT WIPED OUT SO MANY INTERFERERS HE WAS MOVED TO TACKLE. HE PLAYED TACKLE ONLY 120 MINUTES IN 1929 AND STILL MADE CONSENSUS ALL-AMERICAN AT THAT POSITION. HIS USUAL JOB WAS FULLBACK WHERE HE WAS ALSO ALL-AMERICAN. YOU MIGHT EVEN FIND HIM AT HALFBACK WHEN NEEDED.

IN HIS FIRST GAME AS A FULLBACK HE SCORED TWO TOUCHDOWNS AND KICKED THREE CONVERSIONS.

KNOWN AS A LINE PLUNGER, HE COULD PASS, TOO. ON RUNS HE WOULD TELEGRAPH HIS MOVES AND STILL BEAT THE DEFENSE. IT WAS SAID HE RAN HIS OWN INTERFERENCE. HE HAD TO BE GANG TACKLED.

IN OTHER SPORTS THIS INTERNATIONAL FALLS LEGEND PLAYED CENTER AND GUARD IN BASKETBALL. IN TRACK HE DID THE SHOT, DISCUS, HIGH JUMP AND RAN IN THE RELAY.

HE CAUSED THE FUMBLES IN THE BIG GAMES AGAINST NOTRE DAME (1927) AND WISCONSIN (1928) TO TURN THE TIDE IN FAVOR OF THE GOPHERS.

THE GREAT SPORTS AUTHORITY, GRANTLAND RICE, PICKED THE "BRONK" AS THE BEST ALL AROUND PLAYER OF ALL TIME.

HE SAID A TEAM OF "ELEVEN NAGURSKIS WOULD BE A MOP-UP. IT WOULD BE SOMETHING CLOSE TO MASSACRE."

IT MIGHT BE ADDED THIS MASSACRE WOULD BE BROUGHT ABOUT BY ONE CELEBRATED FOR HIS GENTLE TEMPERAMENT.

HE WAS A CHARTER MEMBER OF THE COLLEGE FOOTBALL HALL OF FAME AS A GOPHER AND A CHARTER MEMBER IN THE PRO HALL OF FAME FOR HIS PLAY AS A CHICAGO BEAR.

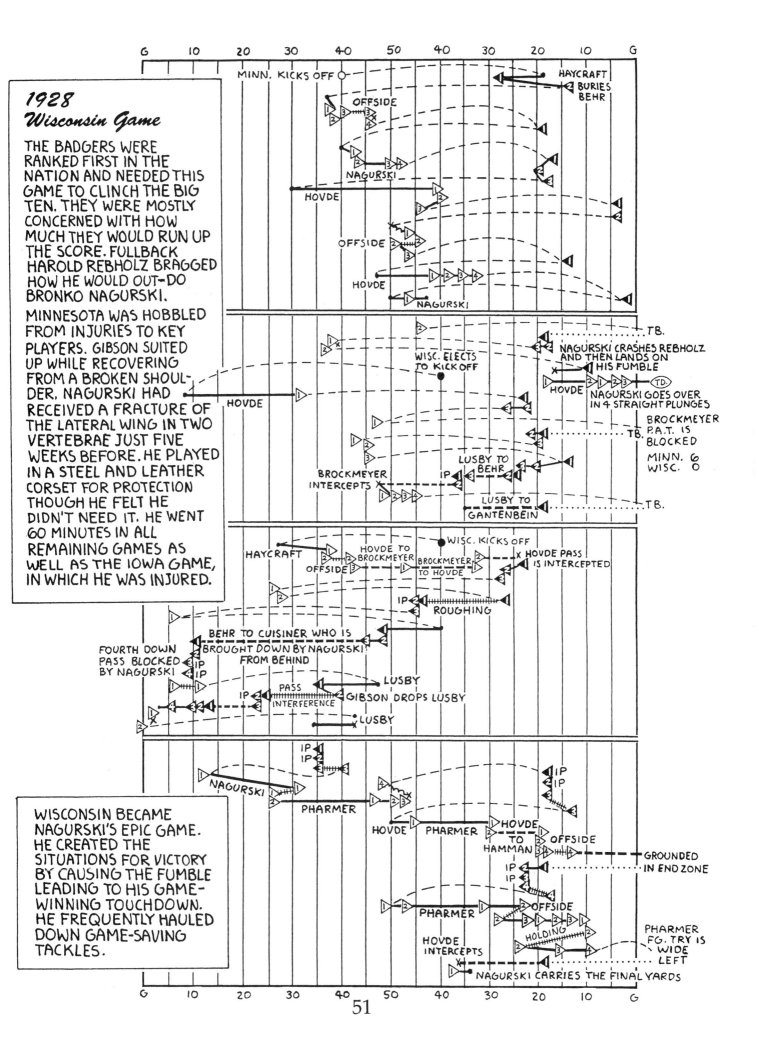

1928
Wisconsin Game

THE BADGERS WERE RANKED FIRST IN THE NATION AND NEEDED THIS GAME TO CLINCH THE BIG TEN. THEY WERE MOSTLY CONCERNED WITH HOW MUCH THEY WOULD RUN UP THE SCORE. FULLBACK HAROLD REBHOLZ BRAGGED HOW HE WOULD OUT-DO BRONKO NAGURSKI.

MINNESOTA WAS HOBBLED FROM INJURIES TO KEY PLAYERS. GIBSON SUITED UP WHILE RECOVERING FROM A BROKEN SHOULDER. NAGURSKI HAD RECEIVED A FRACTURE OF THE LATERAL WING IN TWO VERTEBRAE JUST FIVE WEEKS BEFORE. HE PLAYED IN A STEEL AND LEATHER CORSET FOR PROTECTION THOUGH HE FELT HE DIDN'T NEED IT. HE WENT 60 MINUTES IN ALL REMAINING GAMES AS WELL AS THE IOWA GAME, IN WHICH HE WAS INJURED.

WISCONSIN BECAME NAGURSKI'S EPIC GAME. HE CREATED THE SITUATIONS FOR VICTORY BY CAUSING THE FUMBLE LEADING TO HIS GAME-WINNING TOUCHDOWN. HE FREQUENTLY HAULED DOWN GAME-SAVING TACKLES.

MINN. KICKS OFF
OFFSIDE
NAGURSKI
HOVDE
HAYCRAFT BURIES BEHR
OFFSIDE
HOVDE
NAGURSKI

WISC. ELECTS TO KICK OFF
HOVDE
BROCKMEYER INTERCEPTS
LUSBY TO BEHR
LUSBY TO GANTENBEIN
TB.
NAGURSKI CRASHES REBHOLZ AND THEN LANDS ON HIS FUMBLE
HOVDE
NAGURSKI GOES OVER IN 4 STRAIGHT PLUNGES
TB.
BROCKMEYER P.A.T. IS BLOCKED
MINN. 6
WISC. 0
TB.

HAYCRAFT
OFFSIDE
HOVDE TO BROCKMEYER
BROCKMEYER TO HOVDE
WISC. KICKS OFF
X HOVDE PASS IS INTERCEPTED
IP
ROUGHING
FOURTH DOWN PASS BLOCKED BY NAGURSKI
BEHR TO CUISINER WHO IS BROUGHT DOWN BY NAGURSKI FROM BEHIND
LUSBY
PASS INTERFERENCE
GIBSON DROPS LUSBY
LUSBY

IP
IP
NAGURSKI
PHARMER
HOVDE
PHARMER
HOVDE TO HAMMAN
OFFSIDE
GROUNDED IN END ZONE
IP
IP
PHARMER
OFFSIDE
HOLDING
PHARMER FG. TRY IS WIDE LEFT
HOVDE INTERCEPTS
NAGURSKI CARRIES THE FINAL YARDS

51

Bob Tanner

THIS 1929 RIGHT END ALL-AMERICAN WAS BORN IN FAIRMOUNT AND LATER WENT TO HIGH SCHOOL AT MINNEAPOLIS EAST AND MARSHALL.

OTHER THAN FOOTBALL, HE PLAYED BASKETBALL AND WAS CAPTAIN OF THE BASEBALL TEAM. HE WON NINE LETTERS IN ALL.

HE PLAYED ONE YEAR OF PRO FOOTBALL FOR THE FRANKFORD YELLOWJACKETS.

Arthur Pharmer

HIS THREE FIELDGOALS IN 1929 WERE ENOUGH TO LEAD THE NATION FOR THAT YEAR.

HE PUNTED 11 TIMES AGAINST MICHIGAN FOR 592 TOTAL YARDS WHILE AVERAGING 54 YARDS PER BOOT.

Foot Notes (THE TWENTIES)

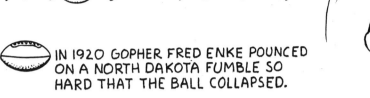

IN 1920 GOPHER FRED ENKE POUNCED ON A NORTH DAKOTA FUMBLE SO HARD THAT THE BALL COLLAPSED.

COACH BILL SPAULDING HAD SOME RATHER DEFINITE OPINIONS IN 1923. HE SAID THAT FOOTBALL "IS A WONDERFUL REMEDY FOR MALE EFFEMINACY WHICH ABOUNDS ON MANY A COLLEGE AND UNIVERSITY CAMPUS. IT TAKES BOYS OUT OF THE PARLORS AND POOL ROOMS AND MAKES MEN OF THEM IF SUCH A THING IS POSSIBLE. EVERY MINNESOTA MAN WHO IS PHYSICALLY ABLE SHOULD PLAY FOOTBALL."

FOOTBALL IS MEANT TO BE A FUN GAME. IT CAN ALSO END IN SERIOUS TRAGEDY. IN 1923 AN IOWA STATE TACKLE, JACK TRICE, WAS TAKEN FROM THE GAME IN THE THIRD QUARTER DUE TO INJURIES. UP TO THEN HE HAD PLAYED BRILLIANTLY. HIS INJURIES, NOT CONSIDERED SERIOUS AT THE TIME, ENDED HIS LIFE THE DAY AFTER THE GAME. IOWA STATE NAMED THEIR STADIUM AFTER HIM.

KNUTE ROCKNE PROMISED A NEW SUIT OF CLOTHES TO THE FIRST OF HIS PLAYERS WHO COULD THROW HERB JOESTING FOR A LOSS... BUT NEVER HAD TO PAY OFF.

GUARD LES PULKRABECK PLAYED IN THE EARLY 1920'S. DURING ONE PRACTICE HE STUFFED HIS NOSE SO FULL OF GRAVEL AND MUD TO STOP BLEEDING THAT IT TOOK A TRAINER AND AIDES OVER TWO HOURS TO CLEAR OUT HIS NOSTRILS, MOUTH AND THROAT.

THINGS MUST HAVE BEEN ROUGH FOR PLAYERS IN 1923-24. CARL LINDBERG RELATED, "ONCE I EVEN SOLD BLOOD SO I COULD EAT BEFORE A GAME."

MINNESOTA WOULD NOT COMPLY WITH BIG TEN "RECOMMENDATIONS" FOR PLAYERS TO WEAR NUMERALS IN 1914. BY 1921 THE BIG TEN "URGED" THAT THEY BE USED. COACH WILLIAMS DID NOT WANT HIS PLAYERS TO BE IDENTIFIED AND SO PUT FOUR-DIGIT NUMBERS ON THEM TO BE UNREADABLE.

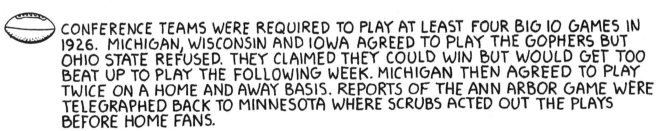

IN 1920 MINNESOTA LOST 225 YARDS TO NORTH DAKOTA IN PENALTIES. IT DIDN'T MAKE ANY DIFFERENCE, THOUGH, AS THEY MANAGED TO WIN ANYWAY... 41-3.

CONFERENCE TEAMS WERE REQUIRED TO PLAY AT LEAST FOUR BIG 10 GAMES IN 1926. MICHIGAN, WISCONSIN AND IOWA AGREED TO PLAY THE GOPHERS BUT OHIO STATE REFUSED. THEY CLAIMED THEY COULD WIN BUT WOULD GET TOO BEAT UP TO PLAY THE FOLLOWING WEEK. MICHIGAN THEN AGREED TO PLAY TWICE ON A HOME AND AWAY BASIS. REPORTS OF THE ANN ARBOR GAME WERE TELEGRAPHED BACK TO MINNESOTA WHERE SCRUBS ACTED OUT THE PLAYS BEFORE HOME FANS.

"GHOST BALL" WAS A NAME REFERRING TO NIGHT PRACTICE BEFORE THE 1911 CHICAGO GAME. THE LIGHTING TECHNIQUE WAS NOT MENTIONED BUT SEARCH LIGHTS WERE USED IN 1922 "GHOST BALL."

MINNESOTA BEAT WISCONSIN IN 1926 BY COMING FROM BEHIND IN AN UNUSUAL GAME. THE BADGERS STARTED BY SCORING ON AN 80 YARD RETURN OF A GOPHER FUMBLE. MINNESOTA FOUGHT BACK FOR A TOUCHDOWN WITH HERB JOESTING CARRYING FOUR DEFENDERS ON HIS BACK OVER THE GOAL LINE. THE CONVERSION FAILED. MINNESOTA THEN TOOK THE LEAD WITH A FIELD GOAL. ANOTHER GOPHER FUMBLE POSITIONED WISCONSIN FOR THEIR OWN THREE-POINTER. MINNESOTA DROPPED BEHIND AGAIN. LATE IN THE GAME, GOPHER MALLY NYDAHL RECEIVED A PUNT AND RETURNED IT 65 YARDS FOR A FINAL WINNING SCORE 16-10. ON THAT DAY MINNESOTA ALMOST LOST TO A TEAM THEY HAD OUT-FIRST-DOWNED 16-0 AND OUT-GAINED 353 YARDS TO 3.

IT TOOK $572,000 TO BUILD MEMORIAL STADIUM AND $568,000 TO TEAR IT DOWN.

MEMORIAL STADIUM 1924-1981

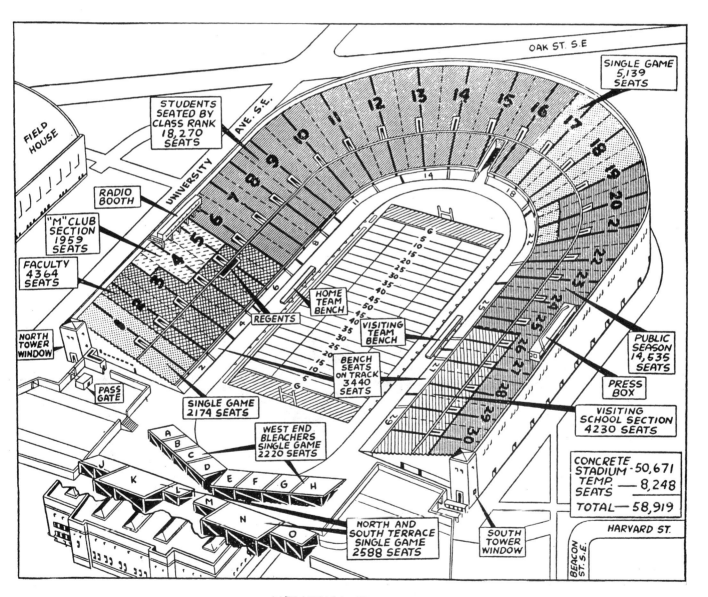

MEMORIAL STADIUM

Clarence 'Biggie' Munn

'BIGGIE' WAS QUICK AND AGILE FOR HIS SIZE. HE STARTED AT FULLBACK AND THEN TACKLE BUT, UNFORTUNATELY FOR HIM, SO DID NAGURSKI. GUARD EVENTUALLY BECAME HIS CONSENSUS ALL-AMERICAN AND BIG TEN M.V.P. SPOT IN 1931.

HE WAS BORN IN ANOKA BUT WENT TO SCHOOL AT MINNEAPOLIS NORTH. AT MINNESOTA HE WAS CAPTAIN FOR BOTH FOOTBALL AND TRACK TEAMS.

MUNN KICKED OFF AND WOULD OFTEN COME BEHIND THE LINE TO RUN OR PASS. HE WAS THE BEST GOPHER PUNTER UP TO HIS TIME AND WOULD USE THE THREAT TO RUN FROM THE PUNT FORMATION. HE RECEIVED PUNTS, TOO.

COACHING WAS HIS NEXT POSITION. HE WAS COACH OF THE YEAR IN 1952 WHILE HIS MICHIGAN STATE TEAM WON THE NATIONAL CHAMPIONSHIP. THE FIRST YEAR THEY WERE ELIGIBLE IN THE BIG TEN HE TOOK THEM TO THE TITLE AND A ROSE BOWL VICTORY. ONLY RETIREMENT AS COACH TO BE ATHLETIC DIRECTOR ENDED HIS 28 GAME WIN STRING. HE ENTERED THE HALL OF FAME AS A COACH, FROM THERE.

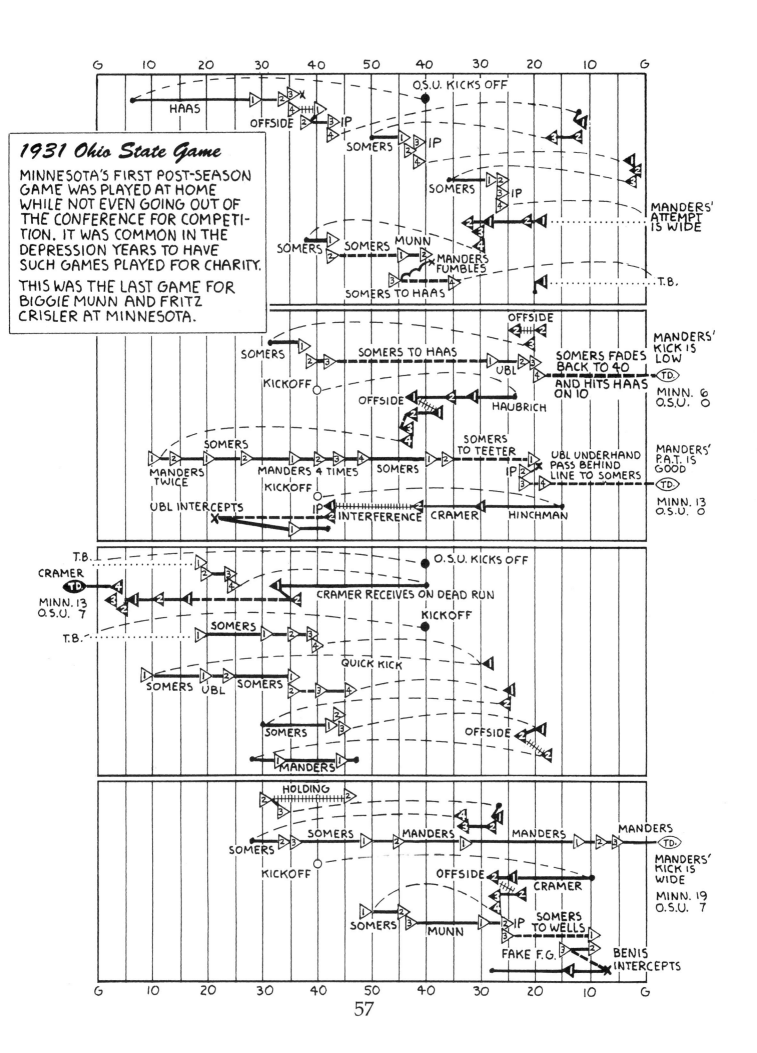

1931 Ohio State Game

MINNESOTA'S FIRST POST-SEASON GAME WAS PLAYED AT HOME WHILE NOT EVEN GOING OUT OF THE CONFERENCE FOR COMPETITION. IT WAS COMMON IN THE DEPRESSION YEARS TO HAVE SUCH GAMES PLAYED FOR CHARITY.

THIS WAS THE LAST GAME FOR BIGGIE MUNN AND FRITZ CRISLER AT MINNESOTA.

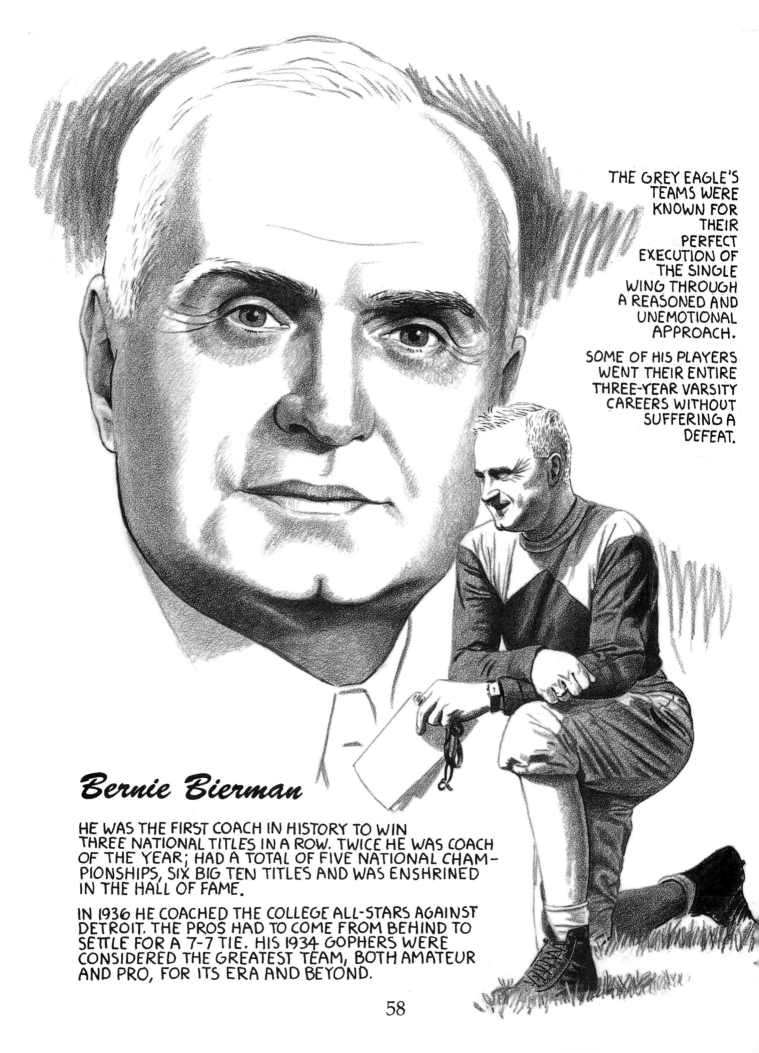

THE GREY EAGLE'S TEAMS WERE KNOWN FOR THEIR PERFECT EXECUTION OF THE SINGLE WING THROUGH A REASONED AND UNEMOTIONAL APPROACH.

SOME OF HIS PLAYERS WENT THEIR ENTIRE THREE-YEAR VARSITY CAREERS WITHOUT SUFFERING A DEFEAT.

Bernie Bierman

HE WAS THE FIRST COACH IN HISTORY TO WIN THREE NATIONAL TITLES IN A ROW. TWICE HE WAS COACH OF THE YEAR; HAD A TOTAL OF FIVE NATIONAL CHAMPIONSHIPS, SIX BIG TEN TITLES AND WAS ENSHRINED IN THE HALL OF FAME.

IN 1936 HE COACHED THE COLLEGE ALL-STARS AGAINST DETROIT. THE PROS HAD TO COME FROM BEHIND TO SETTLE FOR A 7-7 TIE. HIS 1934 GOPHERS WERE CONSIDERED THE GREATEST TEAM, BOTH AMATEUR AND PRO, FOR ITS ERA AND BEYOND.

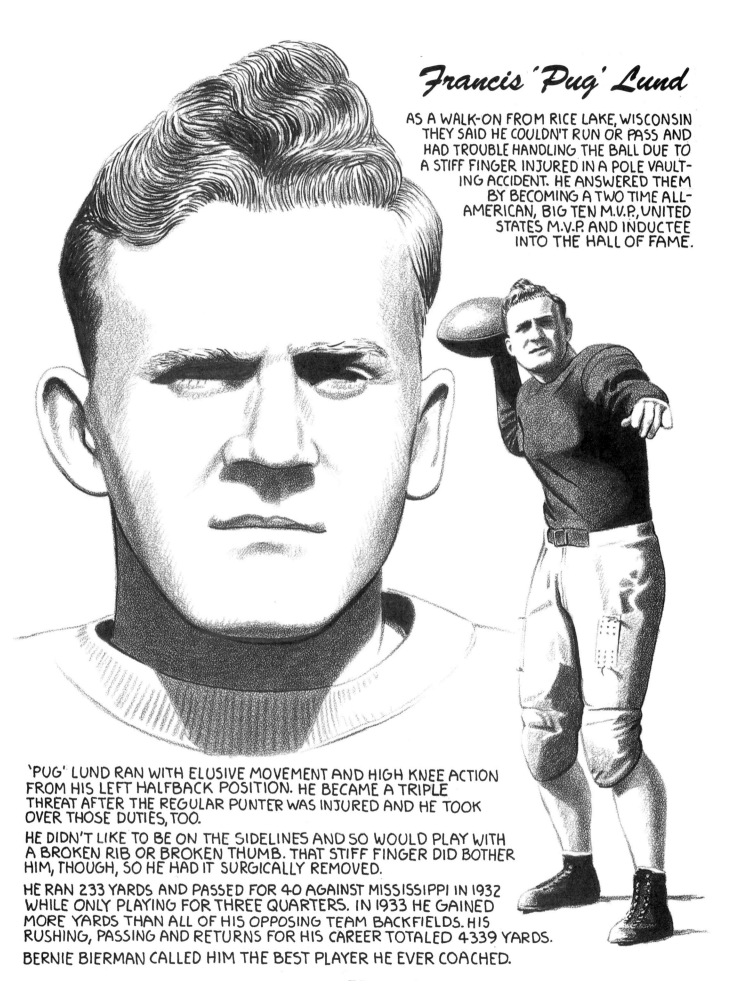

Francis 'Pug' Lund

AS A WALK-ON FROM RICE LAKE, WISCONSIN THEY SAID HE COULDN'T RUN OR PASS AND HAD TROUBLE HANDLING THE BALL DUE TO A STIFF FINGER INJURED IN A POLE VAULTING ACCIDENT. HE ANSWERED THEM BY BECOMING A TWO TIME ALL-AMERICAN, BIG TEN M.V.P., UNITED STATES M.V.P. AND INDUCTEE INTO THE HALL OF FAME.

'PUG' LUND RAN WITH ELUSIVE MOVEMENT AND HIGH KNEE ACTION FROM HIS LEFT HALFBACK POSITION. HE BECAME A TRIPLE THREAT AFTER THE REGULAR PUNTER WAS INJURED AND HE TOOK OVER THOSE DUTIES, TOO.

HE DIDN'T LIKE TO BE ON THE SIDELINES AND SO WOULD PLAY WITH A BROKEN RIB OR BROKEN THUMB. THAT STIFF FINGER DID BOTHER HIM, THOUGH, SO HE HAD IT SURGICALLY REMOVED.

HE RAN 233 YARDS AND PASSED FOR 40 AGAINST MISSISSIPPI IN 1932 WHILE ONLY PLAYING FOR THREE QUARTERS. IN 1933 HE GAINED MORE YARDS THAN ALL OF HIS OPPOSING TEAM BACKFIELDS. HIS RUSHING, PASSING AND RETURNS FOR HIS CAREER TOTALED 4339 YARDS.

BERNIE BIERMAN CALLED HIM THE BEST PLAYER HE EVER COACHED.

Frank 'Butch' Larson

IN THE OFF-SEASON 'BUTCH' WAS A BUTCHER. ON THE GRIDIRON HE WOULD SLICE THROUGH OPPOSITION. NOT WAITING FOR A BALL CARRIER TO COME TO HIM, HE WOULD CUT AND LEAP THROUGH THE INTERFERENCE, SOMETIMES KNOCKING THEM DOWN, TO GET AT HIS TACKLE VICTIM.

TWO GAMES IN A ROW HE FACED HALFBACKS WITH REPUTATIONS AS BEING AMONG THE BEST IN THE COUNTRY. HE HELD THEM FOR A COMBINED TWO YARDS LOSS.

THE RIGHT END FROM DULUTH DENFELD WAS ALL-AMERICAN IN 1933 AND CONSENSUS ALL-AMERICAN IN 1934.

IN THE LATTER YEAR HIS OFF-FIELD HIGH JINKS BUDDY, BOB TENNER, COMPLEMENTED THE OTHER END SPOT BY ATTAINING ALL-AMERICAN STATUS, TOO.

HE WAS ALL ARMS AND LEGS STRUNG TOGETHER WITH COORDINATION. HE WOULD SEEM TO LOAF AND THEN TAKE OFF TO SNATCH PASSES HIGH IN THE AIR.

60

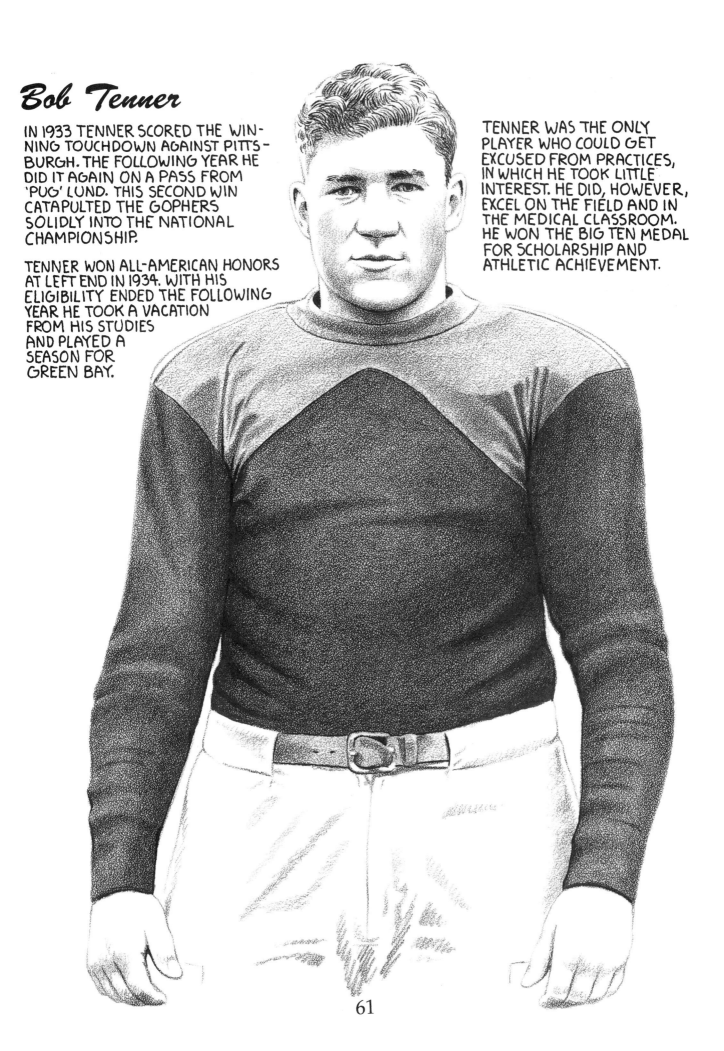

Bob Tenner

IN 1933 TENNER SCORED THE WIN- NING TOUCHDOWN AGAINST PITTS- BURGH. THE FOLLOWING YEAR HE DID IT AGAIN ON A PASS FROM 'PUG' LUND. THIS SECOND WIN CATAPULTED THE GOPHERS SOLIDLY INTO THE NATIONAL CHAMPIONSHIP.

TENNER WON ALL-AMERICAN HONORS AT LEFT END IN 1934. WITH HIS ELIGIBILITY ENDED THE FOLLOWING YEAR HE TOOK A VACATION FROM HIS STUDIES AND PLAYED A SEASON FOR GREEN BAY.

TENNER WAS THE ONLY PLAYER WHO COULD GET EXCUSED FROM PRACTICES, IN WHICH HE TOOK LITTLE INTEREST. HE DID, HOWEVER, EXCEL ON THE FIELD AND IN THE MEDICAL CLASSROOM. HE WON THE BIG TEN MEDAL FOR SCHOLARSHIP AND ATHLETIC ACHIEVEMENT.

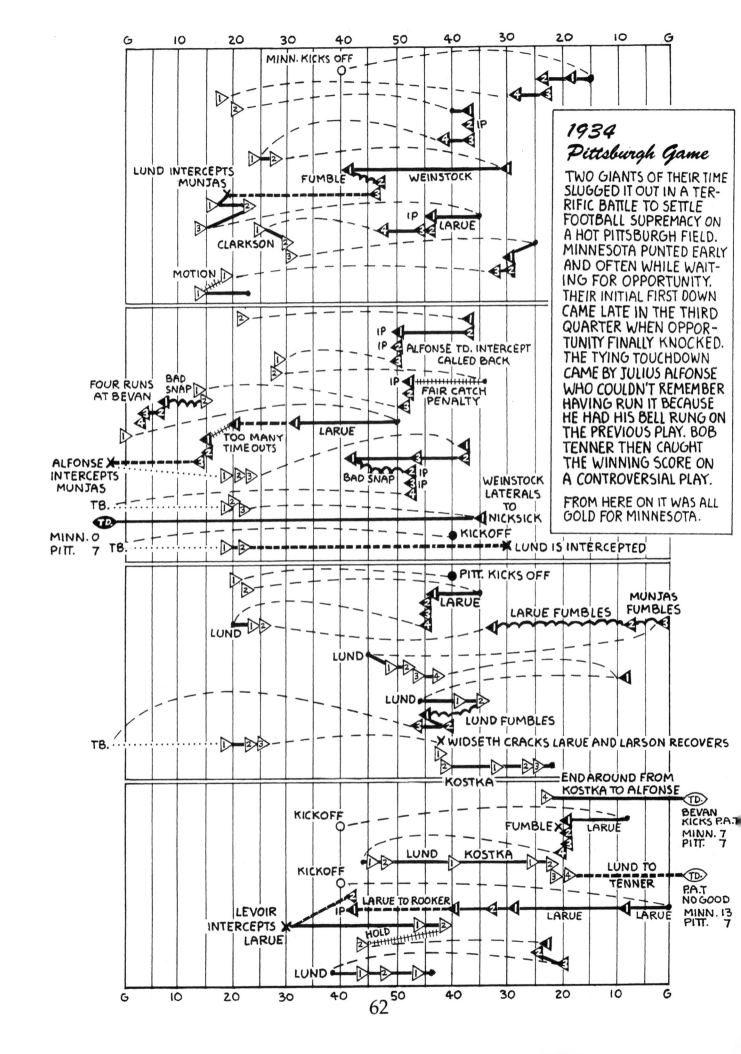

1934
Pittsburgh Game

TWO GIANTS OF THEIR TIME SLUGGED IT OUT IN A TERRIFIC BATTLE TO SETTLE FOOTBALL SUPREMACY ON A HOT PITTSBURGH FIELD. MINNESOTA PUNTED EARLY AND OFTEN WHILE WAITING FOR OPPORTUNITY. THEIR INITIAL FIRST DOWN CAME LATE IN THE THIRD QUARTER WHEN OPPORTUNITY FINALLY KNOCKED. THE TYING TOUCHDOWN CAME BY JULIUS ALFONSE WHO COULDN'T REMEMBER HAVING RUN IT BECAUSE HE HAD HIS BELL RUNG ON THE PREVIOUS PLAY. BOB TENNER THEN CAUGHT THE WINNING SCORE ON A CONTROVERSIAL PLAY.

FROM HERE ON IT WAS ALL GOLD FOR MINNESOTA.

MINN. KICKS OFF

LUND INTERCEPTS MUNJAS

FUMBLE

WEINSTOCK

IP

LARUE

CLARKSON

MOTION

FOUR RUNS AT BEVAN

BAD SNAP

TOO MANY TIME OUTS

LARUE

ALFONSE INTERCEPTS MUNJAS

IP IP ALFONSE T.D. INTERCEPT CALLED BACK

IP FAIR CATCH PENALTY

BAD SNAP IP IP

WEINSTOCK LATERALS TO NICKSICK

TB.

TD.

MINN. 0
PITT. 7   TB.

KICKOFF

LUND IS INTERCEPTED

PITT. KICKS OFF

LARUE

LARUE FUMBLES

MUNJAS FUMBLES

LUND

LUND

LUND

LUND FUMBLES

TB.

WIDSETH CRACKS LARUE AND LARSON RECOVERS

KOSTKA

END AROUND FROM KOSTKA TO ALFONSE

TD.
BEVAN KICKS P.A.T.
MINN. 7
PITT. 7

KICKOFF

FUMBLE

LARUE

KICKOFF

LUND

KOSTKA

LUND TO TENNER

TD.
P.A.T. NO GOOD
MINN. 13
PITT. 7

LEVOIR INTERCEPTS LARUE

IP LARUE TO ROOKER

LARUE

LARUE

HOLD

LUND

62

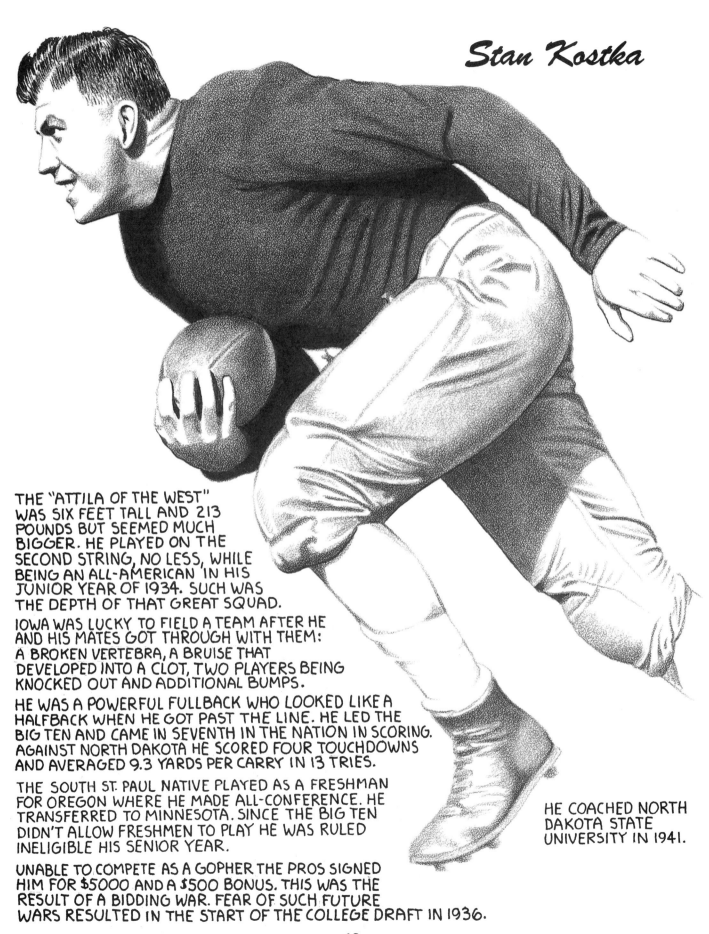

Stan Kostka

THE "ATTILA OF THE WEST" WAS SIX FEET TALL AND 213 POUNDS BUT SEEMED MUCH BIGGER. HE PLAYED ON THE SECOND STRING, NO LESS, WHILE BEING AN ALL-AMERICAN IN HIS JUNIOR YEAR OF 1934. SUCH WAS THE DEPTH OF THAT GREAT SQUAD.

IOWA WAS LUCKY TO FIELD A TEAM AFTER HE AND HIS MATES GOT THROUGH WITH THEM: A BROKEN VERTEBRA, A BRUISE THAT DEVELOPED INTO A CLOT, TWO PLAYERS BEING KNOCKED OUT AND ADDITIONAL BUMPS.

HE WAS A POWERFUL FULLBACK WHO LOOKED LIKE A HALFBACK WHEN HE GOT PAST THE LINE. HE LED THE BIG TEN AND CAME IN SEVENTH IN THE NATION IN SCORING. AGAINST NORTH DAKOTA HE SCORED FOUR TOUCHDOWNS AND AVERAGED 9.3 YARDS PER CARRY IN 13 TRIES.

THE SOUTH ST. PAUL NATIVE PLAYED AS A FRESHMAN FOR OREGON WHERE HE MADE ALL-CONFERENCE. HE TRANSFERRED TO MINNESOTA. SINCE THE BIG TEN DIDN'T ALLOW FRESHMEN TO PLAY HE WAS RULED INELIGIBLE HIS SENIOR YEAR.

HE COACHED NORTH DAKOTA STATE UNIVERSITY IN 1941.

UNABLE TO COMPETE AS A GOPHER THE PROS SIGNED HIM FOR $5000 AND A $500 BONUS. THIS WAS THE RESULT OF A BIDDING WAR. FEAR OF SUCH FUTURE WARS RESULTED IN THE START OF THE COLLEGE DRAFT IN 1936.

63

Bill Bevan

PLACE-KICKING MADE HIM ONE OF THE HIGHEST-SCORING LINEMEN IN THE COUNTRY. HE ALSO DID THE KICKOFF AND WAS ONE OF THE BEST DROP-KICKERS OF HIS TIME.

ROUGH AND TOUGH WAS HIS GAME. HE SLASHED AND HIT HARD TO CLEAR OPENINGS FOR RUNNERS. BERNIE BIERMAN SAID "HE NEVER HIT HIS STRIDE UNTIL HE WAS KICKED IN THE FACE." THIS MAY HAVE HAPPENED OFTEN BECAUSE HE WAS THE LAST IN THE BIG TEN TO NOT WEAR HEADGEAR.

IN THE 1934 PITTSBURGH GAME THE GOPHERS FOUND THEMSELVES DEFENDING ON THE SIX WITH GOAL TO GO. IT WAS PITT'S BELIEF THAT THEY MUST WIN BY GOING THROUGH THE BEST OPPOSITION. THEY RAN FOUR STRAIGHT TIMES AT BEVAN AS HE SLAMMED THE DOOR ON THEM.

THE ST. PAUL CENTRAL GUARD WAS ONE OF FOUR CONSENSUS ALL-AMERICANS ON THE GREAT 1934 GOPHER TEAM.

BEVAN MISSED PLAYING IN 1935 DUE TO THE FRESHMAN ELIGIBILITY RULE. THIS DIDN'T PREVENT HIM FROM BEING ELECTED AS ALTERNATE CAPTAIN, THOUGH.

BEISE PLAYED ON THE
NATIONAL CHAMP-
IONSHIP TEAMS OF
1934 AND 35.

HE WAS KNOWN
FOR HIS DEFENSIVE
PLAY AND AS A
STRONG BLOCKER.
HE WAS, PERHAPS,
THE BEST BLOCKING
BACK IN THE COUNTRY.
HE COULD ALSO SCORE,
AS HE PILED UP 54
POINTS HIS FINAL YEAR.

HE WAS ALL-BIG TEN
FOR THREE YEARS
AND WAS ALL-AMERICAN
IN 1935 TO CAP IT OFF.

Sheldon Beise

BY A VOTE OF THE FANS
THE MOUND NATIVE
WAS SELECTED TO
THE 1936 ALL-STAR
TEAM.

HE LETTERED IN
BASKETBALL AND TRACK,
AS WELL. AFTER HIS
PLAYING DAYS HE
SERVED AS AN
ASSISTANT GOPHER
FOOTBALL COACH.

65

Floyd of Rosedale

MINNESOTA REPRESENTATIVE TO THE BIG TEN, JAMES PAGE, PUSHED THE CAUSE TO SUSPEND IOWA FOR SLUSH FUND VIOLATIONS OCCURING IN 1929. HE SUCCEEDED BUT IOWA WAS RE-INSTATED AFTER HUMBLING ITSELF AND AGREEING TO CHANGES. A CLEAN UP OF THE PROGRAM BROUGHT OSSIE SOLEM IN AS NEW HEAD COACH. HE HAD BEEN A GOPHER ON THE 1915 TEAM.

BECAUSE OF THIS SUSPENSION EPISODE A GRUDGE WAS BORN AND FESTERED. THE 1934 GAME AT IOWA RAISED THE HAWKEYES' IRE EVEN MORE. THEIR STAR, OZZIE SIMMONS, WAS ALLEGEDLY GANGED UP ON AND HAD TO LEAVE THE GAME DUE TO INJURIES. MINNESOTA DENIED IT BECAUSE THEY DESTROYED EVERYONE CLEANLY WHO GOT IN THEIR WAY. THEY HAD NO REPUTATION FOR PLAYING DIRTY.

THE NEXT YEAR'S GAME WAS AGAIN AT IOWA AND THE FANS WERE STILL SIMMERING. IT REACHED FEVER PITCH WHEN IOWA GOVERNOR CLYDE HERRING SAID, "IF THE OFFICIALS STAND FOR ANY ROUGH TACTICS LIKE MINNESOTA USED LAST YEAR, I'M SURE THE CROWD WON'T." ALARMED, MINNESOTA GOVERNOR FLOYD OLSON TELEGRAPHED BACK, "MINNESOTA FOLKS EXCITED OVER YOUR STATEMENT ABOUT IOWA CROWD LYNCHING THE MINNESOTA FOOTBALL TEAM. I HAVE ASSURED THEM YOU ARE LAW-ABIDING GENTLEMAN AND ARE ONLY TRYING TO GET OUR GOAT... I WILL BET YOU A MINNESOTA PRIZE HOG AGAINST AN IOWA PRIZE HOG THAT MINNESOTA WINS." WITH THIS DIVERSION, THE FEVER BROKE.

MINNESOTA WON THE GAME AND THE FANS BEHAVED WITH RESTRAINT. THE IOWA HOG WAS PRESENTED TO OLSON IN GOOD HUMOR. CHARLES BRIOSCHI, OF ST. PAUL, DESIGNED A STATUE OF THE PIG TO BE A GAME TROPHY. IT WAS NAMED "FLOYD OF ROSEDALE" AFTER THE MINNESOTA GOVERNOR AND THE IOWA FARM IN WHICH THE PIG WAS BORN.

BACK IN IOWA SOMEONE TRIED TO HAVE GOVERNOR HERRING ARRESTED FOR GAMBLING.

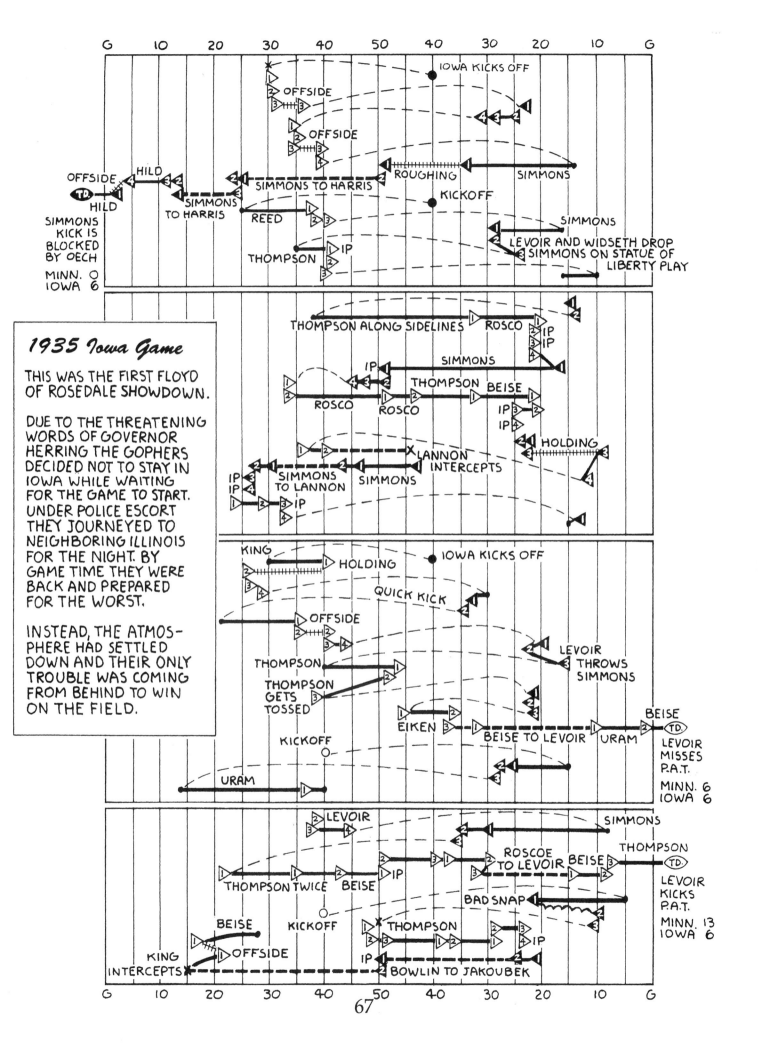

1935 Iowa Game

THIS WAS THE FIRST FLOYD OF ROSEDALE SHOWDOWN.

DUE TO THE THREATENING WORDS OF GOVERNOR HERRING THE GOPHERS DECIDED NOT TO STAY IN IOWA WHILE WAITING FOR THE GAME TO START. UNDER POLICE ESCORT THEY JOURNEYED TO NEIGHBORING ILLINOIS FOR THE NIGHT. BY GAME TIME THEY WERE BACK AND PREPARED FOR THE WORST.

INSTEAD, THE ATMOSPHERE HAD SETTLED DOWN AND THEIR ONLY TROUBLE WAS COMING FROM BEHIND TO WIN ON THE FIELD.

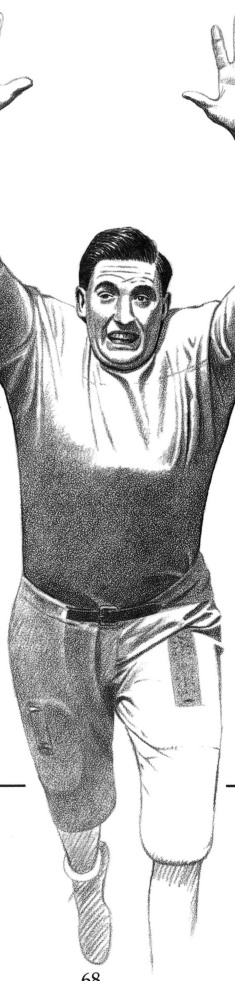

Dick Smith

HE WAS FAST FOR A BIG GUY. OPPONENTS WOULD FIND HIM IN THEIR BACKFIELDS BEFORE THEY COULD GET OUT.

HE COVERED PUNTS LIKE AN END AND WAS EVEN PUT IN THE END POSITION FOR THE 1934 WISCONSIN GAME. FROM THERE HE WAS ABLE TO SCORE A TOUCHDOWN.

FANS VOTED HIM TO PLAY IN THE 1936 ALL-STAR GAME.

SMITH CAME FROM ROCKFORD, ILLINOIS TO PLAY HOCKEY. AS A FRESHMAN HE INJURED HIS KNEE AND THEN DROPPED THE SPORT AT BERNIE BIERMAN'S REQUEST.

STILL WANTING SOMETHING TO DO IN THE WINTER, HE WENT OUT FOR BASKETBALL.

ON THE FOOTBALL FIELD SMITH WON THE ALL-AMERICAN SPOT AT TACKLE IN 1935.

Charles 'Bud' Wilkinson

IN 1935 THIS ALL-AMERICAN GUARD, FROM SOUTH MINNEAPOLIS AND SHATTUCK MILITARY ACADEMY, PROVED TO BE A GREAT DOWN-FIELD BLOCKER. HE COULD ALSO PUT POINTS ON THE BOARD BY KICKING CONVERSIONS.

THE GOPHERS NEEDED A QUARTERBACK IN 1936, AND SO HE WAS MOVED TO THAT POSITION. HE PRO-CEEDED TO WIN HONORABLE MENTION ALL-AMERICAN AT HIS NEW SPOT.

WILKINSON SERVED AS CAPTAIN OF THE 1935 HOCKEY TEAM, WHERE HE WAS AN ALL-AMERICAN GOALIE.

AS 18 YEAR HEAD COACH FOR OKLAHOMA HE FASHIONED AN INCREDIBLE RECORD: COACH OF THE YEAR FOR 1949; 14 CONFER-ENCE TITLES; 5 UNBEATEN TEAMS; 3 NATIONAL TITLES; 139-27-4 RECORD WITH AN .829 WINNING PERCENTAGE, THE LONGEST WINNING STRING IN COLLEGIATE HISTORY AT 47 GAMES, AND INDUCTION INTO THE HALL OF FAME.

Ed Widseth

ED WAS FROM CROOKSTON AND BECAME ALL-AMERICAN IN 1934 AND UNANIMOUS ALL-AMERICAN IN 1935 AND 36 AT TACKLE. THE U.P.I. NAMED HIM BIG-TEN M.V.P. HE WAS A BIG CHUNK IN THE "SEVEN BLOCKS OF GRANITE" AS THE GOPHER LINE WAS KNOWN.

HE HAD POWER, SIZE AND QUICK HANDS. GRANTLAND RICE CALLED HIM THE "FIFTH MAN IN THE OPPONENT'S BACKFIELD."

HIS BLOCKING OPENED BIG HOLES AND HE WAS THE FIRST ONE DOWN UNDER PUNTS. A SPECIAL TACKLE-ELIGIBLE PLAY WAS DEVISED TO UTILIZE HIS SPEED SO THIS HALL OF FAMER COULD RECEIVE PASSES.

WIDSETH WENT ON TO PLAY FIVE YEARS FOR THE NEW YORK GIANTS; WAS CAPTAIN OF THEIR WORLD CHAMPIONS; MADE ALL-PRO THREE TIMES AND WAS 1938 PLAYER OF THE YEAR.

70

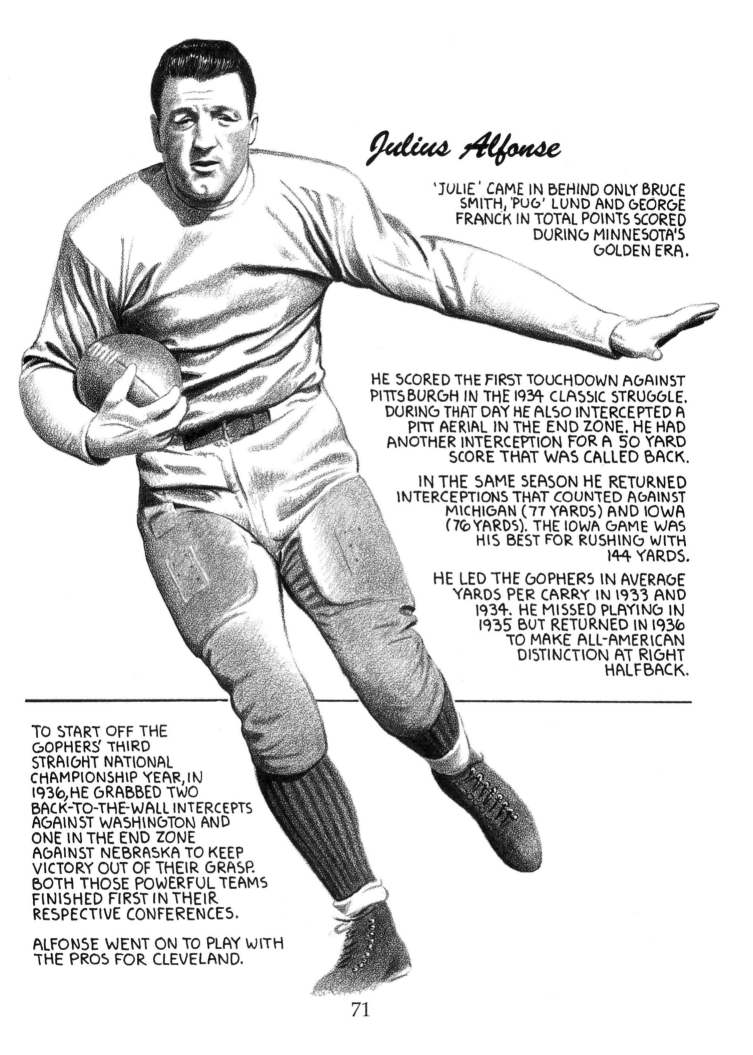

Julius Alfonse

'JULIE' CAME IN BEHIND ONLY BRUCE SMITH, 'PUG' LUND AND GEORGE FRANCK IN TOTAL POINTS SCORED DURING MINNESOTA'S GOLDEN ERA.

HE SCORED THE FIRST TOUCHDOWN AGAINST PITTSBURGH IN THE 1934 CLASSIC STRUGGLE. DURING THAT DAY HE ALSO INTERCEPTED A PITT AERIAL IN THE END ZONE. HE HAD ANOTHER INTERCEPTION FOR A 50 YARD SCORE THAT WAS CALLED BACK.

IN THE SAME SEASON HE RETURNED INTERCEPTIONS THAT COUNTED AGAINST MICHIGAN (77 YARDS) AND IOWA (76 YARDS). THE IOWA GAME WAS HIS BEST FOR RUSHING WITH 144 YARDS.

HE LED THE GOPHERS IN AVERAGE YARDS PER CARRY IN 1933 AND 1934. HE MISSED PLAYING IN 1935 BUT RETURNED IN 1936 TO MAKE ALL-AMERICAN DISTINCTION AT RIGHT HALFBACK.

TO START OFF THE GOPHERS' THIRD STRAIGHT NATIONAL CHAMPIONSHIP YEAR, IN 1936, HE GRABBED TWO BACK-TO-THE-WALL INTERCEPTS AGAINST WASHINGTON AND ONE IN THE END ZONE AGAINST NEBRASKA TO KEEP VICTORY OUT OF THEIR GRASP. BOTH THOSE POWERFUL TEAMS FINISHED FIRST IN THEIR RESPECTIVE CONFERENCES.

ALFONSE WENT ON TO PLAY WITH THE PROS FOR CLEVELAND.

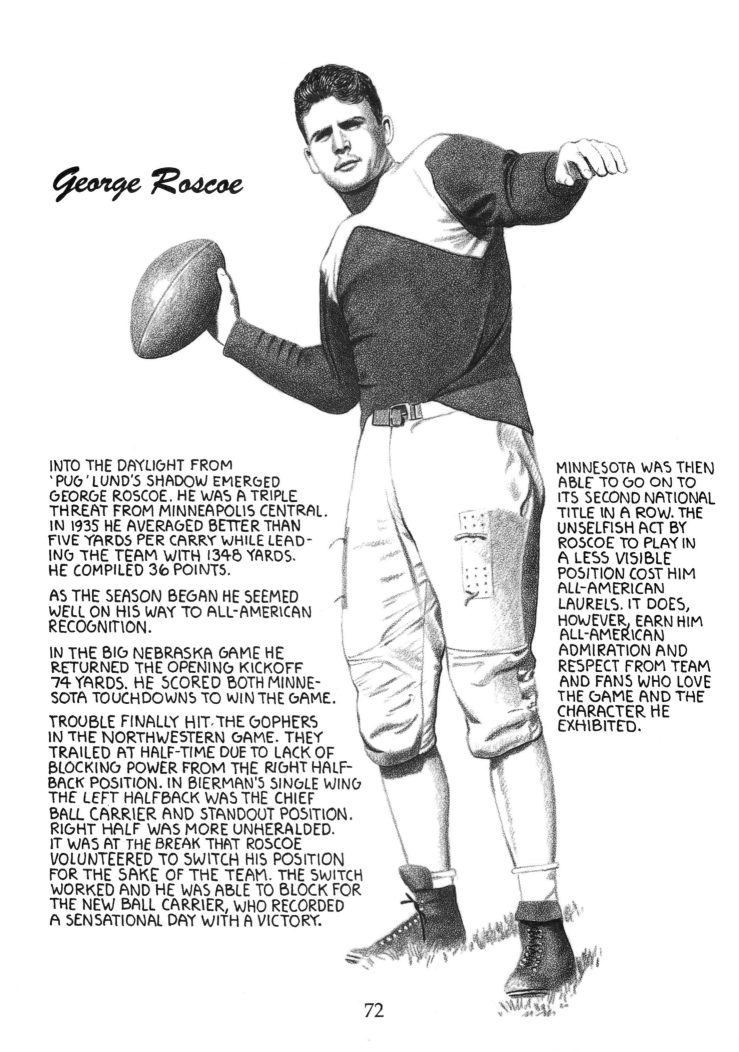

George Roscoe

INTO THE DAYLIGHT FROM 'PUG' LUND'S SHADOW EMERGED GEORGE ROSCOE. HE WAS A TRIPLE THREAT FROM MINNEAPOLIS CENTRAL. IN 1935 HE AVERAGED BETTER THAN FIVE YARDS PER CARRY WHILE LEADING THE TEAM WITH 1348 YARDS. HE COMPILED 36 POINTS.

AS THE SEASON BEGAN HE SEEMED WELL ON HIS WAY TO ALL-AMERICAN RECOGNITION.

IN THE BIG NEBRASKA GAME HE RETURNED THE OPENING KICKOFF 74 YARDS. HE SCORED BOTH MINNESOTA TOUCHDOWNS TO WIN THE GAME.

TROUBLE FINALLY HIT THE GOPHERS IN THE NORTHWESTERN GAME. THEY TRAILED AT HALF-TIME DUE TO LACK OF BLOCKING POWER FROM THE RIGHT HALFBACK POSITION. IN BIERMAN'S SINGLE WING THE LEFT HALFBACK WAS THE CHIEF BALL CARRIER AND STANDOUT POSITION. RIGHT HALF WAS MORE UNHERALDED. IT WAS AT THE BREAK THAT ROSCOE VOLUNTEERED TO SWITCH HIS POSITION FOR THE SAKE OF THE TEAM. THE SWITCH WORKED AND HE WAS ABLE TO BLOCK FOR THE NEW BALL CARRIER, WHO RECORDED A SENSATIONAL DAY WITH A VICTORY.

MINNESOTA WAS THEN ABLE TO GO ON TO ITS SECOND NATIONAL TITLE IN A ROW. THE UNSELFISH ACT BY ROSCOE TO PLAY IN A LESS VISIBLE POSITION COST HIM ALL-AMERICAN LAURELS. IT DOES, HOWEVER, EARN HIM ALL-AMERICAN ADMIRATION AND RESPECT FROM TEAM AND FANS WHO LOVE THE GAME AND THE CHARACTER HE EXHIBITED.

Vernal 'Babe' Le Voir

'BABE' PLAYED ALL POSITIONS IN THE BACKFIELD IN 1935. BEING A JACK OF ALL TRADES AND MASTER OF ALL EARNED HIM A SPECIAL DISTINCTION AS AN ALL-AMERICAN UTILITY PLAYER.

IN 1936 HE BECAME THE FIRST ALL-STAR TO EVER SCORE A POINT AGAINST A PRO TEAM.

73

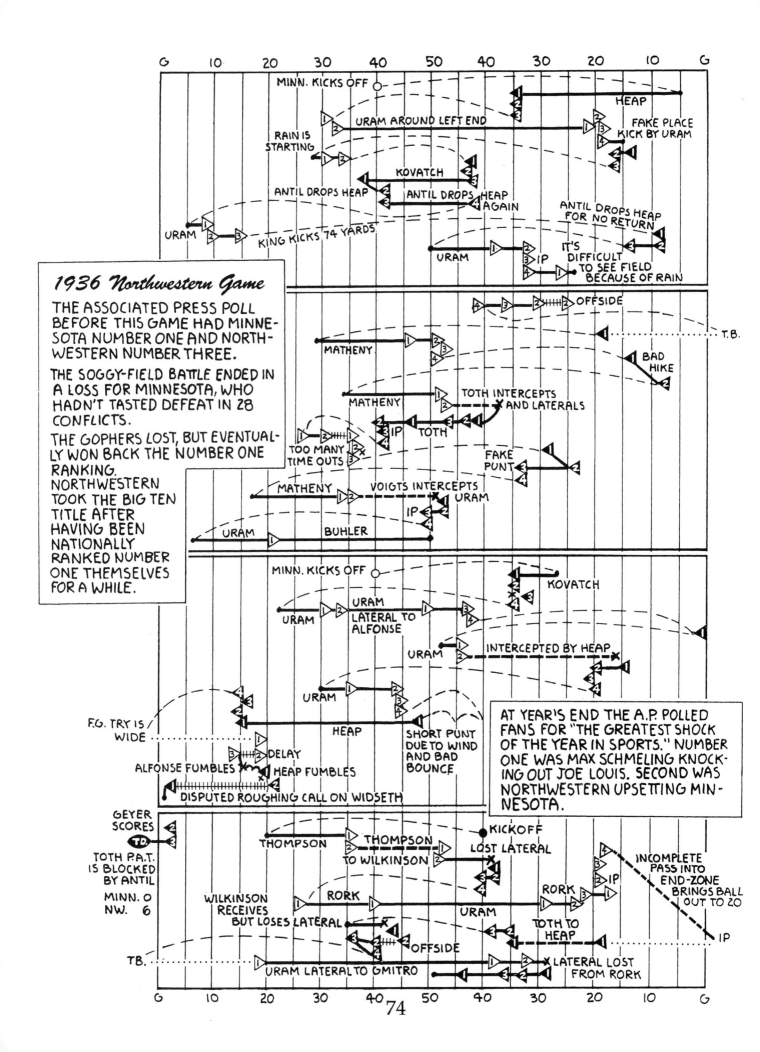

1936 Northwestern Game

THE ASSOCIATED PRESS POLL BEFORE THIS GAME HAD MINNESOTA NUMBER ONE AND NORTHWESTERN NUMBER THREE.

THE SOGGY-FIELD BATTLE ENDED IN A LOSS FOR MINNESOTA, WHO HADN'T TASTED DEFEAT IN 28 CONFLICTS.

THE GOPHERS LOST, BUT EVENTUALLY WON BACK THE NUMBER ONE RANKING. NORTHWESTERN TOOK THE BIG TEN TITLE AFTER HAVING BEEN NATIONALLY RANKED NUMBER ONE THEMSELVES FOR A WHILE.

AT YEAR'S END THE A.P. POLLED FANS FOR "THE GREATEST SHOCK OF THE YEAR IN SPORTS." NUMBER ONE WAS MAX SCHMELING KNOCKING OUT JOE LOUIS. SECOND WAS NORTHWESTERN UPSETTING MINNESOTA.

MINNEAPOLIS MARSHALL GAVE ANDY URAM TO MINNESOTA. HE WAS A TRIPLE THREAT WITH A FAST AND A LONG LOPING STRIDE. HE WAS ALL-AMERICAN FULLBACK IN 1936 BUT BROKE HIS WRIST EARLY IN 1937 TO END HIS COLLEGE CAREER.

HE HAD HIS SHARE OF LONG, EXCITING PLAYS. IN 1935, AGAINST MICHIGAN, HE REPLACED INJURED TUFFY THOMPSON AND RAN TOUCH-DOWNS OF 58 AND 73 YARDS. ALTOGETHER HE DASHED 187 YARDS ON 11 CARRIES THAT DAY.

AGAINST WISCONSIN HE TOOK A LATERAL ON A KICKOFF AND SCAMPERED FOR AN 83-YARD TOUCHDOWN.

AGAINST NORTH DAKOTA STATE, IN 1937, HE TOOK THE OPENING KICKOFF FOR 28 YARDS. ON THE FIRST PLAY HE WENT 29 MORE AND ON THE SECOND 29 AGAIN. TO SHOW FURTHER CONSISTENCY HE RAN FOR TWO 70-YARD TOUCHDOWNS.

HIS MOST HISTORIC RUN CAME WITH BETTER THAN A MINUTE TO GO AGAINST A POWERFUL NEBRASKA TEAM. A PUNT WENT TO BUD WILKINSON, WHO GOT BOTTLED UP. HE LATERALED TO URAM. INTERFERENCE FORMED IMMEDIATE-LY TO BLAST DOWNFIELD. ALONG THE WAY URAM DODGED TWO PLAYERS AND GOT A LITTLE HELP FROM HIS FRIENDS, WHO KNOCKED DOWN FIVE TACKLERS. HE THEN OUT RAN TWO PURSUERS TO PAY DIRT TO CLIMAX A 75 YARD TREK. MINNESOTA WON 7-0.

ANDY GOT HIS FIRST TASTE OF THE PROS WHILE ON THE 1938 ALL-STAR TEAM. HE SCORED ON AN INTERCEPTION IN THE CLOSING SECONDS OF A VICTORY OVER THE WASHINGTON REDSKINS. AFTER TURNING PRO HE SET THE N.F.L. RECORD, AT GREEN BAY, FOR THE LONGEST RUN FROM SCRIMMAGE. IT HELD FOR 40 YEARS.

Ray King

RAY KING ATTENDED DULUTH DENFELD WHERE HE WAS A STAR HURDLER.

ON THE GRIDIRON HE WAS ONE OF THE NATION'S FASTEST ENDS. IN 1937 HE SCAMPERED BACK A NORTHWESTERN INTERCEPTION 57 YARDS.

HE WAS A TERRIFIC PUNTER, TOO. ON ONE SOGGY FIELD HE LET ONE FLOAT FOR 74 YARDS.

HE WAS ALL-AMERICAN IN 1936 AND 37 AND WAS CAPTAIN OF THE 1937 ALL-AMERICAN TEAM.

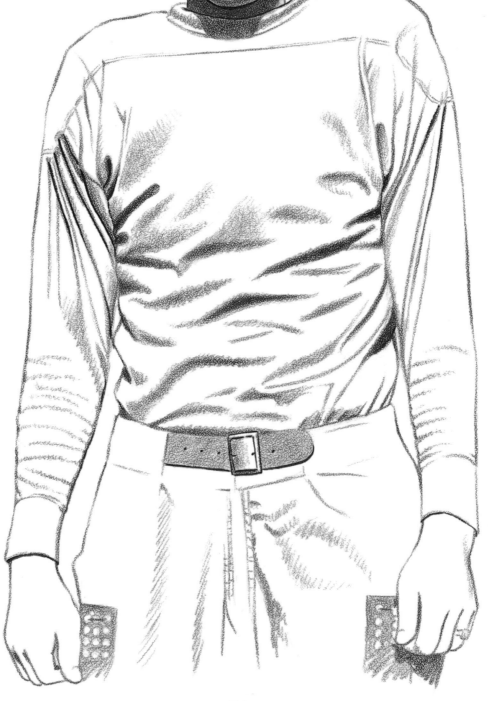

Harold Van Every

VAN EVERY CAME FROM WAYZATA HIGH SCHOOL. AS A SOPHOMORE, FOR THE GOPHERS, HE RECEIVED ALL-AMERICAN MENTION IN 1937. HE LED THE TEAM IN ALL CATEGORIES: PASSING, RUNNING, KICKOFF AND PUNT RETURNS FOR A TOTAL OF 1314 YARDS. HE PUNTED AN AVERAGE 34.9 YARDS AND SCORED SEVEN TOUCHDOWNS.

HIS LONGEST RUN WAS AGAINST NORTH DAKOTA STATE. HE WENT 76 YARDS WHILE FINISHING THE DAY WITH 147 YARDS IN FIVE ATTEMPTS.

INJURY CUT SHORT HIS PLAYING TIME THE NEXT SEASON. IN 1939 HE LED THE NATION IN INTERCEPTIONS WITH EIGHT.

SPORTS ILLUSTRATED NAMED VAN EVERY A SILVER ANNIVERSARY ALL-AMERICAN FOR HIS COMMUNITY WORK IN LATER YEARS.

HE LEAD HIS TEAM TO VICTORY OVER A POWERFUL MICHIGAN TEAM IN 1938. HE WAS JUST A FEW DAYS OUT OF THE HOSPITAL WITH A RUPTURED KIDNEY RECEIVED IN A PREVIOUS GAME.

AFTER RECEIVING THE BIG TEN SCHOLASTIC AND ATHLETIC ACHIEVEMENT AWARD, HE WAS DRAFTED BY GREEN BAY IN THE FIRST ROUND.

Lou Midler

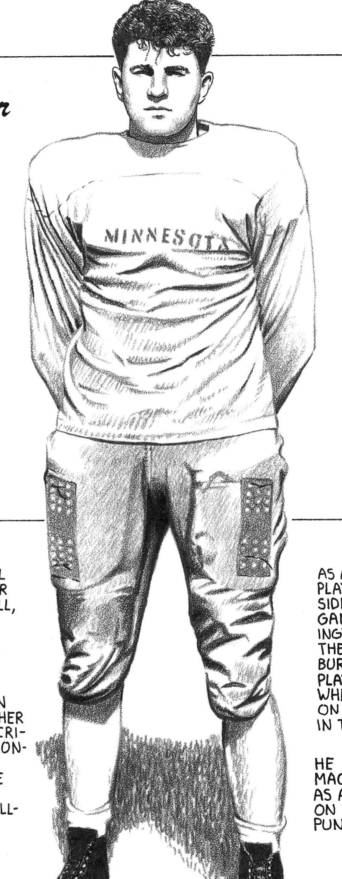

WHILE ATTENDING ST. PAUL WASHINGTON, LOU MIDLER WAS ALL-CITY IN FOOTBALL, BASKETBALL AND TRACK. THE ST. LOUIS CARDINALS TRIED SIGNING HIM FOR BASEBALL.

INSTEAD, HE BECAME AN IRON MAN FOR THE GOPHER GRIDDERS. BIERMAN SACRIFICED MIDLER'S EXCEPTIONAL KICKING ABILITY TO PLACE HIM AT THE MORE "IMPORTANT" TACKLE SPOT WHERE HE WON ALL-AMERICAN ACCLAIM IN 1937.

AS A COLLEGIAN HE PLAYED ON THE WINNING SIDE IN THE ALL-STAR GAME AGAINST WASHINGTON. HE WENT INTO THE PROS WITH PITTSBURGH AND FINALLY PLAYED FOR GREEN BAY WHERE HE WAS AGAIN ON THE WINNING SIDE IN THE ALL-STAR GAME.

HE LATER COACHED AT MACALESTER AS WELL AS AUTHORING A BOOK ON THE ART OF PUNTING.

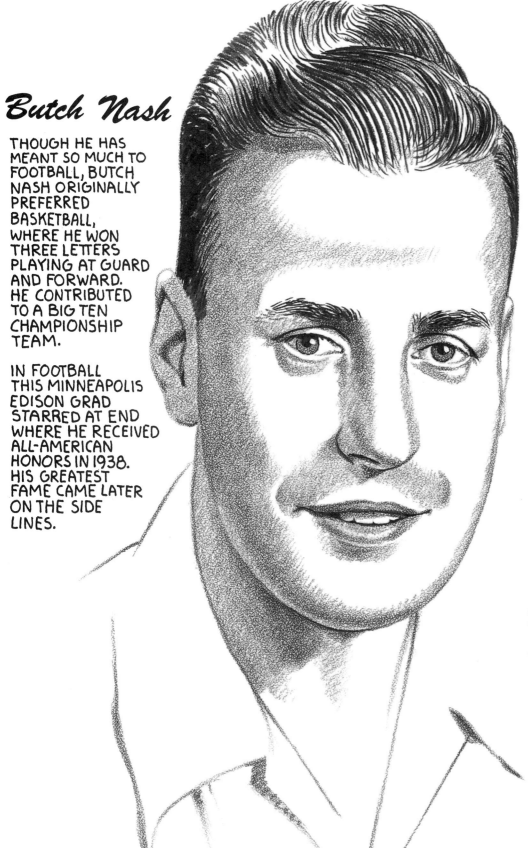

Butch Nash

THOUGH HE HAS MEANT SO MUCH TO FOOTBALL, BUTCH NASH ORIGINALLY PREFERRED BASKETBALL, WHERE HE WON THREE LETTERS PLAYING AT GUARD AND FORWARD. HE CONTRIBUTED TO A BIG TEN CHAMPIONSHIP TEAM.

IN FOOTBALL THIS MINNEAPOLIS EDISON GRAD STARRED AT END WHERE HE RECEIVED ALL-AMERICAN HONORS IN 1938. HIS GREATEST FAME CAME LATER ON THE SIDE LINES.

HE HAD EARLY SUCCESS AS A HIGH SCHOOL COACH BEFORE COMING HOME TO THE 'U' AS END COACH UNDER BERNIE BIERMAN. HE REMAINED AS A PERMANENT FIXTURE AFTER BIERMAN LEFT AND SERVED FESLER, WARMATH, STOLL AND SALEM.

NASH TAUGHT MANY GREAT GOPHER ENDS, SOME OF WHOM WENT INTO THE PRO RANKS.

HOLTZ CALLED HIM OUT OF RETIREMENT AND HE ALSO PUT IN PROFITABLE TIME FOR GUTEKUNST.

IN PREPARATION FOR MICHIGAN GAMES, HIS PEP TALKS REPLACED THOSE OF SIG HARRIS OF OLD. THESE TALKS WERE CREDITED FOR INSPIRING VICTORIES OVER NATIONALLY RANKED WOLVERINE TEAMS IN 1977 AND 1986.

Francis Twedell

TWEDELL CAME FROM AUSTIN, MINNESOTA TO LEAD
THE GOPHERS AS CAPTAIN IN 1938.

SOME THOUGHT THE GOPHERS' DAYS WERE NUMBERED
AS THEY "SLIPPED" TO TENTH IN THE NATION THAT
YEAR. THEY STILL WON THE BIG TEN, HOWEVER.
THOUGH THERE WAS CONCERN FOR THE BACKFIELD,
THERE WAS NOTHING WRONG IN THE MIDDLE OF
THE LINE, WHERE TWEDELL HELD THINGS DOWN AS
AN ALL-AMERICAN GUARD.

AFTER MINNESOTA HE PLAYED PRO FOR GREEN BAY.

80

Urban Odson

URBAN ODSON WAS A
CONSENSUS ALL-AMERICAN
TACKLE IN 1940. HE STOPPED
MICHIGAN WITHIN THE FIVE THAT
YEAR, AND THEN RECOVERED THEIR
FUMBLE. HE ALSO LED THE BLOCKING
IN THE FAMOUS TALKING PLAY THE
FOLLOWING YEAR.

HE WAS BIG AND WORE THE LARGEST
PAIR OF SHOULDER PADS IN THE NATION.

ON THE FIRST DAY OF PRACTICE IN 1941
HE SPRAINED HIS KNEE. IT HAMPERED HIM
FROM REPEATING AS ALL-AMERICAN. HE
WENT THROUGH THE YEAR WEARING A
METAL BRACE AND PLAYING IN PAIN.

Foot Notes (GOLDEN ERA)

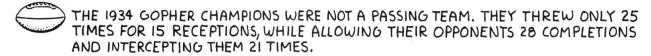

THE 1934 GOPHER CHAMPIONS WERE NOT A PASSING TEAM. THEY THREW ONLY 25 TIMES FOR 15 RECEPTIONS, WHILE ALLOWING THEIR OPPONENTS 28 COMPLETIONS AND INTERCEPTING THEM 21 TIMES.

ON OCTOBER 19, 1936, THE FIRST-EVER ASSOCIATED PRESS NATIONAL RANKING HAD MINNESOTA AT THE TOP.

FOR THREE STRAIGHT YEARS, 1934, 35 AND 36, THE GOPHERS CAME IN SECOND FOR BEING THE GREATEST TEAM IN ALL SPORTDOM BY THE ASSOCIATED PRESS.

THE CHAMPIONS OF 1934 HAD TEN ALL-AMERICANS AND FUTURE ALL-AMERICANS IN THEIR RANKS: BUTCH LARSON (1933 + 34), PUG LUND (1933 + 34), BILL BEVAN (1934), BOB TENNER (1934), STAN KOSTKA (1934), ED WIDSETH (1934, 35 + 36), SHELDON BEISE (1935), DICK SMITH (1935), BUD WILKINSON (1935) AND JULIUS ALFONSE (1936) WITH ADDITIONAL UNDERCLASSMEN ANDY URAM (1936) RAY KING (1936 + 37) AND LOU MIDLER (1937) INCREASING THE NUMBER TO 13.

ALMOST FIVE COMPLETE SEASONS HAD PASSED BEFORE A BIERMAN TEAM FIRST ATTEMPTED A FIELD GOAL. HORACE BELL THEN KICKED ONE, GOOD FROM 45 YARDS.

ART CLARKSON PLAYED ON THE 1934 TEAM. HE WAS BORN IN CHINA TO CANADIAN PARENTS, SPOKE CHINESE AND JAPANESE AND WAS AMBIDEXTROUS AT PASSING AND KICKING.

IN 1935 THE GOPHER BRUISER, STAN KOSTKA, WAS FEATURED ON AN EARLY DAY WHEATIES BOX.

A POST-SEASON GAME WAS OFFERED TO THE GOPHERS IN 1941. THE REGENTS RESPONDED THAT THEY WOULDN'T CONSIDER AN INVITATION FOR EITHER "COMMERCIAL OR CHARITABLE PURPOSES."

CLARK SHAUGHNESSY   BERNIE BIERMAN

FORMER GOPHER TEAMMATES, BERNIE BIERMAN AND CLARK SHAUGHNESSY, HAVE THE DISTINCTION OF BOTH COACHING NATIONAL CHAMPIONS AT THE SAME TIME FOR DIFFERENT TEAMS. IN 1940 BIERMAN'S MINNESOTA SQUAD WAS DECLARED CHAMPIONS WITH AN 8-0 RECORD. SHAUGHNESSY'S STANFORD TEAM RECEIVED THE SAME HONOR WITH A 9-0 RECORD, WHICH INCLUDED A VICTORY IN THE ROSE BOWL. SHAUGHNESSY TOOK OVER A TEAM THAT HAD A 1-7-1 RECORD THE PREVIOUS SEASON.

George 'Sonny' Franck

"SONNY" FRANCK WAS A WORLD CLASS SPRINTER FROM DAVENPORT, IOWA. HE WAS CAPTAIN OF THE GOPHER TRACK TEAM AND USED HIS SPEED AS AN EXCITING WEAPON ON THE GRIDIRON WHERE HE BECAME A HALL OF FAMER.

HE RETURNED TWO KICK-OFFS FOR TOUCHDOWNS IN HIS 1940 CONSENSUS ALL-AMERICAN YEAR. AMONG OTHER THINGS, HE RECEIVED TWO SCORING PASSES IN A FOUR-TOUCHDOWN DAY AGAINST IOWA. IN A THREE WEEK PERIOD HE THREW ONLY THREE PASSES... ALL GOOD FOR TOUCHDOWNS. AGAINST WISCONSIN HE WAS THE GAME DIFFERENCE THROUGH HIS SCORING AND PREVENTING A BADGER TALLY BY MAKING A CRITICAL PASS INTERCEPTION.

HE WAS ALSO WELL-KNOWN FOR HIS KICKING, BLOCKING AND TACKLING. HE BASHED INTO OPPOSITION WITH NO REGARD FOR HIS OWN BODILY STRUCTURE. IN ONE SUCH INSTANCE HE WAS THE LAST OBSTACLE OF A WASHINGTON BALL CARRIER. FRANCK RAMMED HIM SO HARD HE KNOCKED HIMSELF OUT. IT WAS A GAME-SAVING STOPPER THAT PROTECTED HIS EARLIER 98 YARD KICKOFF-RETURN SCORE.

THE A.P. COACHES' POLL RATED THIS HALFBACK, WHO CAME IN THIRD FOR THE HEISMAN TROPHY, HIGHER THAN THE ACTUAL HEISMAN WINNER.

HE WAS M.V.P. IN THE ALL-STAR GAME BEFORE JOINING THE N.Y. GIANTS.

Bruce Smith

THIS 1941 HEISMAN WINNER WAS AN EXAMPLE TO ALL FOR HIS INSPIRING AND HUMBLE LEADERSHIP. HE OFTEN PLAYED WELL WHILE INJURED. HIS VERY PRESENCE MEANT VICTORY ON THE FIELD AND IN THE HEARTS OF HIS TEAMMATES.

DEFENSIVELY THE FARIBAULT NATIVE WAS A HARD AND SURE TACKLER. ON OFFENSE HE WOULD THROW DEVASTATING BLOCKS WHEN NOT BEING DAZZLING WITH HIS RUNS.

SONNY FRANCK SAID OF HIM: "HE WAS A DECEPTIVE RUNNER WHO COULD FLY FOR 30 YARDS, DROP AN ANCHOR, SQUIRREL AROUND AND... BINGO! HE'D SHOOT FOR ANOTHER 30 YARDS."

SMITH WAS AN UNSURPASSED GAME BREAKING TRIPLE THREAT WHO WAS ENSHRINED IN THE HALL OF FAME. HIS PRO DAYS INCLUDED GREEN BAY AND LOS ANGELES.

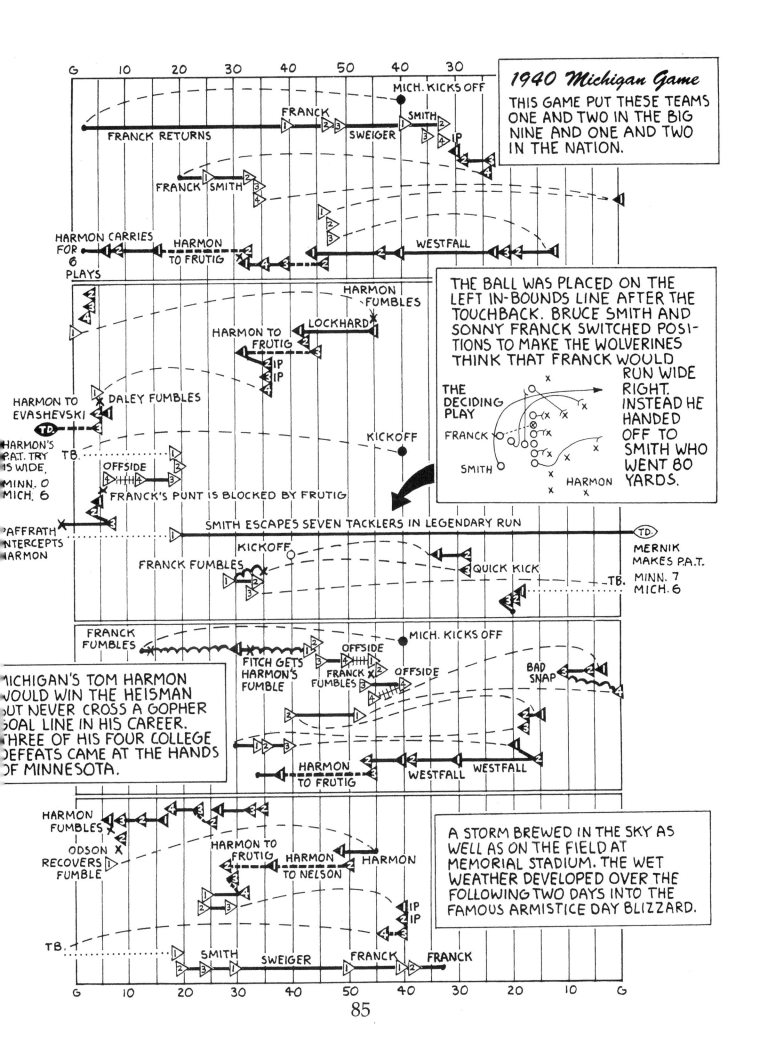

1940 Michigan Game

THIS GAME PUT THESE TEAMS ONE AND TWO IN THE BIG NINE AND ONE AND TWO IN THE NATION.

THE BALL WAS PLACED ON THE LEFT IN-BOUNDS LINE AFTER THE TOUCHBACK. BRUCE SMITH AND SONNY FRANCK SWITCHED POSITIONS TO MAKE THE WOLVERINES THINK THAT FRANCK WOULD RUN WIDE RIGHT. INSTEAD HE HANDED OFF TO SMITH WHO WENT 80 YARDS.

THE DECIDING PLAY
FRANCK
SMITH
HARMON

MICHIGAN'S TOM HARMON WOULD WIN THE HEISMAN BUT NEVER CROSS A GOPHER GOAL LINE IN HIS CAREER. THREE OF HIS FOUR COLLEGE DEFEATS CAME AT THE HANDS OF MINNESOTA.

A STORM BREWED IN THE SKY AS WELL AS ON THE FIELD AT MEMORIAL STADIUM. THE WET WEATHER DEVELOPED OVER THE FOLLOWING TWO DAYS INTO THE FAMOUS ARMISTICE DAY BLIZZARD.

The Talking Play

MINNESOTA WAS ON THE WAY TO THE NATIONAL TITLE IN 1941 WHILE MEETING UP WITH NORTHWESTERN. THE WILDCATS WERE PRIMED TO UPSET THE GOPHERS AS THEY HAD DONE IN 1936. THEY MADE A HABIT OF UPSETTING BIERMAN-COACHED TEAMS. WHEN BIERMAN WAS AT TULANE THEY ENDED A LONG WINNING STRING OF HIS THERE, TOO.

IN THIS GAME MINNESOTA OPENED THE SCORING WITH A SAFETY IN THE FIRST QUARTER. TOWARD THE END OF THE HALF THE GREAT PASSER, OTTO GRAHAM, TOSSED ONE TO THE END ZONE TO PUT NORTHWESTERN UP 7-2. TO MAKE MATTERS WORSE, BRUCE SMITH HAD BEEN TAKEN FROM THE GAME WITH A LEG INJURY.

MINNESOTA WAS PLAYING THE BETTER GAME BUT SIMPLY COULDN'T SCORE. FINALLY, IN THE THIRD QUARTER, A WILDCAT PUNT WAS PARTIALLY BLOCKED. THE GOPHERS LOOKED READY TO GET SOMETHING STARTED.

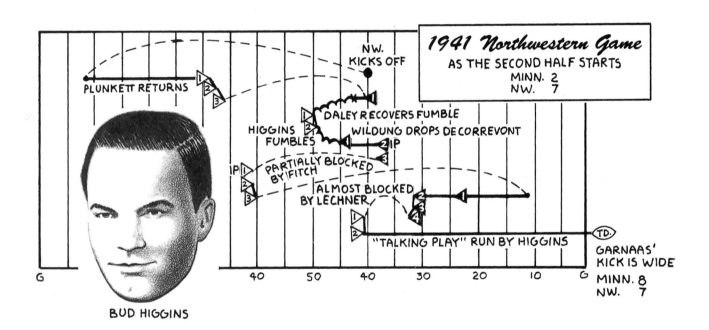

PLUNKETT RETURNS

NW. KICKS OFF

1941 Northwestern Game
AS THE SECOND HALF STARTS
MINN. 2
NW. 7

DALEY RECOVERS FUMBLE
HIGGINS FUMBLES
WILDUNG DROPS DE CORREVONT
PARTIALLY BLOCKED BY FITCH
ALMOST BLOCKED BY LECHNER
"TALKING PLAY" RUN BY HIGGINS

GARNAAS' KICK IS WIDE
MINN. 8
NW. 7

BUD HIGGINS

FIRST DOWN GOT NOWHERE AS BOB SWEIGERT RAN THE BALL BETWEEN THE OUT-OF-BOUNDS LINE AND HASH MARK. HE GOT A PUNCH FROM A WILDCAT ON THE PLAY AND BEGAN ARGUING OVER IT.

DURING THIS TIME THE GOPHER TEAM TOOK POSITION AND STOOD MOTIONLESS TO THE RIGHT OF THE BALL. AS SOON AS THE REF PLACED THE PIGSKIN DOWN ON THE HASH MARK, CENTER GENE FLICK GOT THINGS STARTED. HE WRAPPED HIS LEG AROUND THE REF'S AND FLIPPED THE BALL UNDERHAND TO BUD HIGGINS. SMITH WAS SUPPOSED TO BE THE BALL CARRIER, BUT HIGGINS HAD TAKEN OVER FOR HIM. HE WAS THE SMALLEST GUY ON THE TEAM. SUDDENLY HE WAS MAKING A BIG DASH AROUND RIGHT END FOR PAY DIRT. HE WAS LED BY URBAN ODSON, THE LARGEST PLAYER IN THE COUNTRY.

NO ONE NOTICED THE PLAY BEGIN, INCLUDING PHOTOGRAPHERS, BUT IT WAS GAINING ATTENTION NOW. ODSON DOWNED ONE AWAKENING DEFENDER AND THEN ANOTHER AS HIGGINS DODGED HIS WAY DOWN THE FIELD. TWO WILDCATS HAD A CHANCE FOR HIM AT THE GOAL BUT HE BULLDOZED HIS 155 POUNDS OVER FOR THE SCORE.

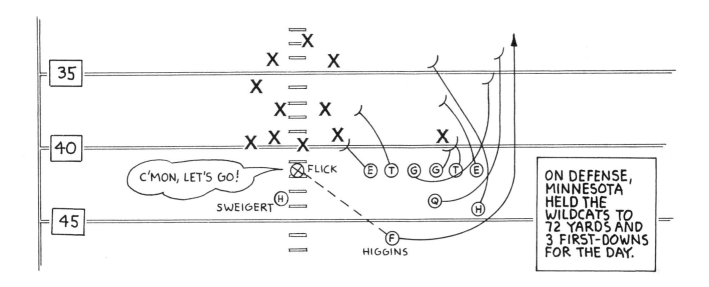

THIS WAS A CAREFULLY PREPARED QUICK ALIGNMENT PLAY. BIERMAN HAD EXPERIENCE AGAINST IT IN AN EAST-WEST GAME A COUPLE YEARS BEFORE. HE CONSIDERED USING IT THE PREVIOUS WEEK AGAINST MICHIGAN BUT DIDN'T FOLLOW THROUGH. THE SURPRISE ELEMENT WAS LOST BECAUSE THE WOLVERINES TRIED THEIR OWN QUICK PLAY FIRST.

IT WAS ONLY TO BE USED IN A MOST NECESSARY SITUATION. TO MAKE SURE IT WOULD COUNT THE GOPHERS EXPLAINED IT TO THE OFFICIALS BEFOREHAND AND WARNED THEM AS TO WHEN IT WOULD BEGIN. THE REFS PAID STRICT ATTENTION FOR ANYTHING WRONG.

THE ARGUMENT WAS NOT AN INTENTIONAL PART OF THE PLAN. FLICK THOUGHT IT MIGHT WRECK THINGS SO HE YELLED OUT "C'MON, LET'S GO!" THE DISPUTE WORKED TO GOOD ADVANTAGE AS IT FURTHER DISTRACTED THE WILDCATS. BECAUSE OF THIS IT BECAME KNOWN AS THE "TALKING PLAY."

NORTHWESTERN OBJECTED, TO NO AVAIL. CONTROVERSY CONTINUED IN THE NATIONAL NEWS.

PEARL HARBOR WAS ATTACKED A MONTH AFTER THE GAME. IT BROUGHT THIS COMMENT AS REPORTED IN THE MINNEAPOLIS TIMES: SEC. TAYLOR..."BERNIE BIERMAN'S EFFORTS TO CONCEAL THE FINE POINTS OF THAT FAST PLAY HIS TEAM PULLED TO DEFEAT NORTHWESTERN – THE PLAY NOBODY SAW – WERE IN VAIN. THE JAPANESE GOT THE IDEA ALL RIGHT. THEY ENGAGED US IN CONVERSATION AND SNAPPED THE BALL WHILE WE WEREN'T LOOKING."

Dick Wildung

DICK WILDUNG WAS
A CONSENSUS ALL-
AMERICAN IN BOTH
1941 AND 42. BERNIE
BIERMAN CALLED HIM HIS
BEST TACKLE.

HE WAS BORN IN ST. PAUL BUT
CAME TO THE GOPHERS BY WAY
OF LUVERNE HIGH SCHOOL.

THOUGH NOT BIG BY TODAY'S STANDARDS, JUST
OVER 200 POUNDS, HE HAD SAVVY WHICH WAS
PUT IN ACTION BY HIS AGILITY. HE SCORED
FOUR TOUCHDOWNS AGAINST PITTSBURGH IN 1942.
HE WAS NAMED TO THE HALL OF FAME.

WILDUNG SPENT HIS LONG PROFESSIONAL
CAREER WITH GREEN BAY.

88

GARNAAS CAME FROM NORTHFIELD BY WAY OF MINNEAPOLIS MARSHALL.

HE PLAYED QUARTERBACK AND DID THE PUNTING. AGAINST PITTSBURGH, IN HIS ALL-AMERICAN SOPHOMORE YEAR OF 1941, HE LET ONE FLY 75 YARDS WITH NO RETURN.

HE WAS THE LEADING GOPHER PASS RECEIVER AND MANAGED TO PICK OFF A COUPLE FROM MICHIGAN, TOO.

HE DID EXTRA DUTY BY SWITCHING FROM HIS REGULAR POSITION TO FILL IN FOR BRUCE SMITH AND HERMAN FRICKEY WHEN THEY WERE INJURED.

Bill Garnaas

IN HIS JUNIOR YEAR GARNAAS WAS UNABLE TO REPEAT AS ALL-AMERICAN DUE TO MISSING TOO MANY GAMES BECAUSE OF INJURY. AGAIN IN HIS LAST YEAR HE MISSED BECAUSE HE WAS CALLED INTO THE MILITARY AT MID-SEASON.

AFTER WORLD WAR II HE PLAYED PRO FOR PITTSBURGH.

IN THE 1942 OPENER GARNAAS GOT A TORN KNEE LIGAMENT. IT PUT HIM OUT OF THE LINE-UP FOR THREE GAMES. HE CAME BACK IN TIME FOR MICHIGAN TO KICK THE LAST EVER DROP-KICK SCORED IN THE BIG TEN. IT CAME DURING THE HURRY OF THE CLOCK RUNNING OUT IN THE FIRST HALF. IT PROVED TO BE THE GAME WINNER.

Charles W. Schultz

THIS TACKLE, FROM ST. PAUL, PLAYED FOR THE GOPHERS FROM 1935-37.

AFTER LEAVING MINNESOTA HE WENT ON TO PLAY FOR GREEN BAY.

WHEN WAR BROKE OUT HE ENLISTED AND WAS "ASSIGNED" TO PLAY FOOTBALL FOR IOWA PRE-FLIGHT AND HIS FORMER COACH, BERNIE BIERMAN.

PROFESSIONAL AND COLLEGE PLAYERS LINED UP TOGETHER ON THIS TEAM. THEY COULDN'T BE AWAY FROM CAMP MORE THAN 48 HOURS SO THEY PLAYED AGAINST COLLEGE TEAMS NEARBY. IT WAS UNDER THIS CIRCUMSTANCE HE WAS NAMED BY LOOK MAGAZINE TO THE ALL-SERVICE TEAM IN 1942.

90

George Svendsen

SVENDSEN WAS A CENTER HAILING FROM MINNEAPOLIS MARSHALL.

IN 1935 HE WAS ANOTHER VICTIM OF THE FRESHMAN ELIGIBILITY RULE AND WAS FORCED TO MISS HIS SENIOR YEAR.

HE BECAME THE FIRST IN A LONG STRING OF GOPHERS TO PLAY FOR GREEN BAY. EVENTUALLY HE WAS INDUCTED INTO THE PACKER HALL OF FAME.

UPON PLAYING FOR IOWA PREFLIGHT IN 1942, HE WON ACCLAIM BY COLLIERS AND LOOK MAGAZINES ON THEIR ALL-SERVICE TEAM. THIS SOMEWHAT MADE UP FOR THE ALL-AMERICAN RECOGNITION HE SURELY WOULD HAVE MADE IN 1935.

AFTER THE WAR HE CAME HOME TO COACH THE GOPHER LINE FROM 1945-50.

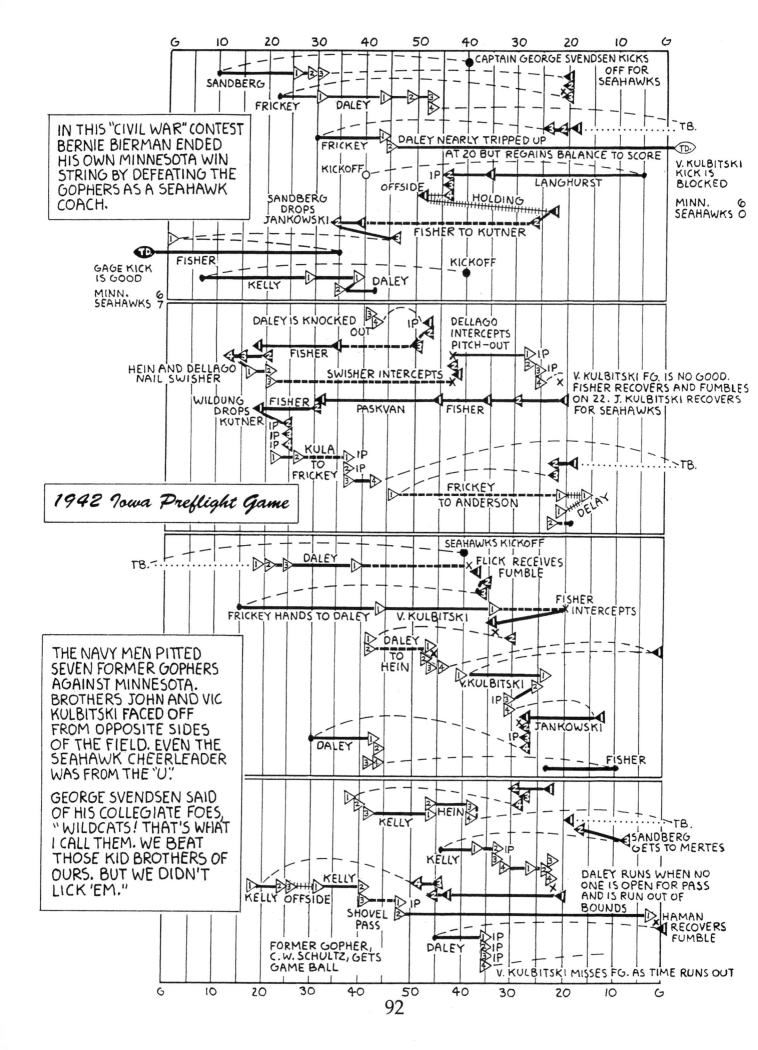

IN THIS "CIVIL WAR" CONTEST BERNIE BIERMAN ENDED HIS OWN MINNESOTA WIN STRING BY DEFEATING THE GOPHERS AS A SEAHAWK COACH.

1942 Iowa Preflight Game

THE NAVY MEN PITTED SEVEN FORMER GOPHERS AGAINST MINNESOTA. BROTHERS JOHN AND VIC KULBITSKI FACED OFF FROM OPPOSITE SIDES OF THE FIELD. EVEN THE SEAHAWK CHEERLEADER WAS FROM THE "U".

GEORGE SVENDSEN SAID OF HIS COLLEGIATE FOES, "WILDCATS! THAT'S WHAT I CALL THEM. WE BEAT THOSE KID BROTHERS OF OURS. BUT WE DIDN'T LICK 'EM."

SANDBERG

CAPTAIN GEORGE SVENDSEN KICKS OFF FOR SEAHAWKS

FRICKEY   DALEY

T.B.

FRICKEY   DALEY NEARLY TRIPPED UP AT 20 BUT REGAINS BALANCE TO SCORE   TD.

V. KULBITSKI KICK IS BLOCKED

KICKOFF   IP   LANGHURST

OFFSIDE   HOLDING

SANDBERG DROPS JANKOWSKI   FISHER TO KUTNER

MINN.   6
SEAHAWKS 0

GAGE KICK IS GOOD   FISHER   KICKOFF

MINN.   6
SEAHAWKS 7

KELLY   DALEY

DALEY IS KNOCKED OUT   IP   DELLAGO INTERCEPTS PITCH-OUT

FISHER   IP

HEIN AND DELLAGO NAIL SWISHER   SWISHER INTERCEPTS

V. KULBITSKI FG. IS NO GOOD. FISHER RECOVERS AND FUMBLES ON 22. J. KULBITSKI RECOVERS FOR SEAHAWKS

WILDUNG DROPS KUTNER   FISHER   PASKVAN   FISHER

IP
IP
IP

KULA TO FRICKEY   IP
IP   T.B.

FRICKEY TO ANDERSON   DELAY

SEAHAWKS KICKOFF

T.B.   DALEY   FLICK RECEIVES FUMBLE

FRICKEY HANDS TO DALEY   V. KULBITSKI   FISHER INTERCEPTS

DALEY TO HEIN

V. KULBITSKI   IP

JANKOWSKI   IP

DALEY   FISHER

KELLY   HEIN

KELLY   T.B.

SANDBERG GETS TO MERTES

KELLY OFFSIDE   KELLY

SHOVEL PASS   IP

DALEY RUNS WHEN NO ONE IS OPEN FOR PASS AND IS RUN OUT OF BOUNDS

HAMAN RECOVERS FUMBLE

FORMER GOPHER, C.W. SCHULTZ, GETS GAME BALL

DALEY   IP
IP
IP

V. KULBITSKI MISSES FG. AS TIME RUNS OUT

Foot Notes (THE FORTIES)

- BECAUSE OF WAR-TIME MANEUVERING OF MILITARY MEN FROM ONE SCHOOL TO ANOTHER, BOB HANZLIK LETTERED FOR THREE BIG TEN TEAMS: WISCONSIN (1942 AND 43) AS AN END, MICHIGAN (1943) AS A TACKLE AND, AFTER HIS RELEASE FROM THE MARINES, MINNESOTA (1945) AS A GUARD.

- BOB BERG SUBSTITUTED FOR A BALL AND FLEW OVER THE GOAL POSTS FOR A FIELD GOAL IN 1942. THE CHEERLEADER DID IT WITH THE HELP OF A TEETER BOARD AND WOULD SOAR 15 FEET ABOVE THE GROUND.

- A SECOND TIER WAS PROPOSED FOR MEMORIAL STADIUM IN 1946 TO INCREASE SEATING TO 80,000.

- THE 1949 GOPHER SQUAD PRODUCED SIX FIRST ROUND DRAFT PICKS: BUD GRANT, FLOYD JASZEWSKI, LEO NOMELLINI, WAYNE ROBINSON, GORDIE SOLTAU AND CLAYTON TONNEMAKER.

- THIS WAS THE BREAD AND BUTTER FORMATION OF THE GOLDEN ERA... THE SINGLE WING WITH THE UNBALANCED LINE TO THE RIGHT.

  ITS STRENGTH WAS MASS POWER AND BLOCKING POSITION. BIERMAN BELIEVED THAT THE TEAM THAT BLOCKED BEST WOULD WIN. THE PASS, REVERSE AND QUICK KICK WERE USED TO KEEP THE DEFENSE HONEST.

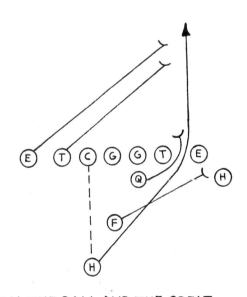

  THE LEFT HALFBACK WAS THE CHIEF BALL CARRIER WHILE THE FULLBACK AND QUARTERBACK WERE KEY BLOCKERS. THE RIGHT HALFBACK FOLLOWED THE BALL CARRIER TO RECEIVE A POSSIBLE LATERAL AFTER GOING BEYOND THE LINE OF SCRIMMAGE. THE WEAK LEFT SIDE PLAYERS WERE DEFINITE DOWNFIELD BLOCKERS. IN TIMES PAST DOWNFIELD BLOCKING WAS A MERE HAPPENING RATHER THAN A DELIBERATE ASSIGNMENT.

  DISADVANTAGES OF THE FORMATION WERE IN HIDING THE BALL AND THE GREAT LENGTH OF TIME IT TOOK TO SET UP THE PLAY. THAT'S WHY, IN BLOCKING, IT WAS IMPORTANT TO KNOCK DEFENDERS COMPLETELY ON THEIR BACKS.

  THE FORMATION WAS DESIGNED TO SCORE A TOUCHDOWN ON EVERY PLAY. BIERMAN STRESSED DISCIPLINE AND PERFECTION, WHICH IS WHAT THE SINGLE WING REQUIRED. HE WAS THE MOST CAPABLE COACH AT GETTING IT.

- INDIANA FUMBLED 12 TIMES AGAINST THE GOPHERS IN 1946. MINNESOTA GOBBLED UP SEVEN OF THEM.

- IN 1947 LEO NOMELLINI WAS SENT DOWN TO THE SECOND TEAM AFTER TURNING IN HIS "WORST" PERFORMANCE OF THE SEASON AGAINST IOWA. IOWA, HOWEVER, VOTED HIM ON THEIR ALL-OPPONENTS TEAM OF THE SEASON.

DALEY WAS A THREE YEAR IRON MAN FROM MELROSE WHO PERFORMED FOR TWO GOPHER NATIONAL CHAMPIONSHIP TEAMS.

HE SET A NATIONAL RECORD FOR MOST CAREER YARDS AT 2301.

AFTER COLLEGE HE PLAYED PROFESSIONALLY FOR MIAMI, BROOKLYN AND CHICAGO.

IN 1941, VS. MICHIGAN, DALEY MADE TWO INTERCEPTIONS; ONE IN THE END ZONE AND THE OTHER ON HIS OWN 12 TO HALT THE WOLVERINES AT THE END. MINNESOTA WON 7-0.

AS ONE OF THE FASTEST MEN ON THE SQUAD HE RAN A 73 YARD OPEN FIELD SCORE AGAINST ILLINOIS WITH BRUCE SMITH BLOCKING. BY THE END OF THE SEASON HE ACTUALLY RUSHED MORE YARDS IN MORE TRIES WITH A HIGHER YARDS PER CARRY AVERAGE THAN HIS HEISMAN TEAMMATE.

HE REPORTED TO MINNESOTA IN 1943 BUT WITH THE OUTBREAK OF WORLD WAR II HE HAD TO TRANSFER TO MICHIGAN WHERE THERE WAS A MILITARY UNIT. THIS WAS SO HE COULD FINISH HIS SCHOOLING BEFORE GOING INTO THE SERVICE. HE EARNED CONSENSUS ALL-AMERICAN HONORS THERE. HE PLAYED ON BOTH WINNING SIDES OF THE LITTLE BROWN JUG GAME. BOTH TEAMS CLAIM HIM AS THEIR OWN.

94

UNDER THE SAME CIRCUMSTANCES AS DALEY, HERB HEIN WON HIS ALL-AMERICAN HONORS WHILE AWAY FROM MINNESOTA.

Herb Hein

HE WAS ALL-AMERICAN END FOR NORTH-WESTERN IN 1943.

AS A WILDCAT, HEIN SCORED FROM A PASS FOR THE FIRST TOUCHDOWN AGAINST HIS MINNESOTA TEAMMATES. 36 OF NORTHWESTERN'S 42 POINTS, THAT DAY, WERE SCORED BY GOPHERS IN MILITARY UNITS.

HEIN RETURNED TO MINNESOTA AFTER THE WAR TO PLAY OUT HIS SENIOR YEAR. INJURIES PREVENTED HIS REPEATING AS ALL-AMERICAN.

95

Wayne 'Red' Williams

THIS MINNEAPOLIS ROOSEVELT PRODUCT HAD A BIG DAY AGAINST IOWA IN 1943 BY SCORING FOUR TOUCHDOWNS. HE THEN HAD A BIG YEAR AGAINST EVERYBODY IN 1944 BY LEADING THE NATION IN OVER-ALL OFFENSE. HE RUSHED AND RETURNED PUNTS AND KICKS FOR 1467 YARDS WHILE AVERAGING 163 YARDS PER GAME. HE DID IT ALL WHILE RECEIVING NO PASSES.

AFTER A BACK INJURY HE CONTINUED PLAY WHILE WEARING A HARNESS.

Paul Bunyan Ax

WISCONSIN **MINNESOTA**

Paul Bunyan
FOOTBALL TROPHY
Presented by The
NATIONAL W CLUB
1948

THE SLAB OF BACON TROPHY ORIGINALLY WENT TO THE WINNER OF THE MINNESOTA-WISCONSIN GAME. IT WAS CREATED BY DR. R.B. FOUCH OF MINNEAPOLIS. IT HAD A BACON SLAB DONE IN BLACK WALNUT. DEPENDING ON HOW IT WAS DISPLAYED IT SHOWED AN "M" OR "W." THE BALL ON IT WAS GOLD AND RED.

IN 1948 THE WISCONSIN "W" CLUB REPLACED IT WITH THE PAUL BUNYAN AX. THE GAME SCORES FROM 1890 TO THE PRESENT ARE RECORDED ON THE LONG HANDLE.

THE SERIES BETWEEN THESE TEAMS IS THE LONGEST IN DIVISION I-A FOOTBALL. IT'S THE THIRD LONGEST CONTINUOUS SERIES. ITS ONLY INTERRUPTION CAME IN 1906. THE REASON WAS DUE TO PRESIDENT THEODORE ROOSEVELT'S DESIRE TO COOL OFF HOT RIVALRIES. THERE HAD BEEN A RASH OF GRID INJURIES IN THE LAND AND THIS WAS ONE ACTION THOUGHT TO HELP END THEM.

THE MINNESOTA-WISCONSIN SERIES HAS BASICALLY BEEN PLAYED UNDER GOOD FEELINGS, THOUGH IT DIDN'T START THAT WAY. IN 1890 AN OVERCONFIDENT TEAM FROM MADISON CAME FOR THE LURE OF $250. THEY REFUSED TO SET FOOT ON THE MINNESOTA CAMPUS, HOWEVER. THIS RILED THE GOPHERS WHO PROMISED ONE ANOTHER TO GIVE A GOOD SHOWING. THEY DID JUST THAT TO THE TUNE OF 63-0. GENE PATTERSON CHALKED UP SEVEN TOUCHDOWNS.

THOUGH MINNESOTA HAS WON MOST OF THE GAMES, WISCONSIN CAN BE A PAIN IN THE FOOT; THE FOOT OF PAT O'DAY, THE KICKER FROM AUSTRALIA, THAT IS.

IN 1897 O'DAY MADE AN ALL-TIME RECORD PUNT OF 110 YARDS AGAINST THE GOPHERS. TWO YEARS LATER, AS MINNESOTA PUNTED TO HIM, HE RECEIVED AND DROP-KICKED IT RIGHT BACK FOR A 50 YARD FIELD GOAL WHILE ON THE RUN. THE ACT DEVASTATED MINNESOTA. THE BADGERS ROMPED 19-0.

WISCONSIN WON AGAIN IN 1908 WITH AN END LYING ON THE GROUND BY THE SIDELINE AND THEN DASHING FOR AN UNEXPECTED PASS. MINNESOTA MUST HAVE LEARNED FROM IT BECAUSE THEY USED THE SAME PLAY THE FOLLOWING WEEK TO BEAT CARLISLE.

MINNESOTA'S FIRST HOMECOMING GAME WAS PLAYED AGAINST THE BADGERS IN 1914. THE BADGERS' FIRST HOMECOMING WAS AGAINST THE GOPHERS IN 1919. MINNESOTA WON BOTH CONTESTS.

TIES SEEM TO COME IN BUNCHES BETWEEN THESE TWO TEAMS. THE YEARS 1923-24-25 WERE ALL TIES AS WELL AS 1952 AND 53. THE LATTER TWO GAMES WERE BY IDENTICAL SCORES 21-21. MINNESOTA HAS TIED WITH WISCONSIN MORE THAN ANY OF ITS OTHER OPPONENTS. THE FIRST OVERTIME GAME THE GOPHERS EVER PLAYED WAS AGAINST THE BADGERS IN 1999.

Leo Nomellini

LEO "THE LION" NOMELLINI CAME FROM ITALY BY WAY OF CHICAGO. HE REPORTED AS A FULLBACK BUT BECAME A CONSENSUS ALL-AMERICAN TACKLE IN 1948 AND 49.

A STARTER BROKE HIS LEG ON THE FIRST PLAY OF THE 1946 SEASON AND THE FRESH-MAN, NOMELLINI, REPLACED HIM. HE HAD NEVER SO MUCH AS PLAYED HIGH SCHOOL BEFORE. HE STAYED IN THE LINEUP FOR FOUR YEARS. HIS CONTINUOUS PLAYING STRING WENT INTO THE PROS ANOTHER 174 GAMES. HE WAS ONE OF THE FASTEST PLAYERS ON THE GOPHER TEAM AS HE DEVELOPED INTO ALL-TIME ALL-BIG TEN CALIBER. EVERY MINNESOTA FOE PICKED HIM ON THEIR ALL-OPPONENT TEAM IN 1948.

"GIUSEPPI" WAS A FIRST ROUND DRAFT PICK IN THE N.F.L. AND WAS ALL-PRO HIS FIRST YEAR. HE MADE THE HALL OF FAME AS A GOPHER AND AS A PRO.

"TWO-TON TONNY" WAS A UNANIMOUS ALL-AMERICAN AT CENTER IN 1949 WHO BECAME A MEMBER OF THE HALL OF FAME.

SOME COLLEGE SCOUTS SOUGHT THE MINNEAPOLIS EDISON ATHLETE TO PLAY BASKETBALL AND NOT FOOTBALL.

Clayton Tonnemaker

HE CAME IN THIRD ON THE HEISMAN TROPHY BALLOTING.

NATIONAL CHAMPION MICHIGAN COULD GAIN ONLY 22 YARDS RUSHING AGAINST TONNEMAKER AND NOMELLINI IN 1948. THE FOLLOWING WEEK THIS DUO HELD INDIANA TO MINUS 23 YARDS RUSHING AND 73 YARDS OVER-ALL.

IN THE EAST-WEST GAME TONNEMAKER INTERCEPTED A PASS AND RETURNED 67 YARDS FOR A SCORE.

HE WAS DRAFTED BY GREEN BAY IN THE FIRST ROUND AND PLAYED IN THE PRO BOWL HIS FIRST SEASON.

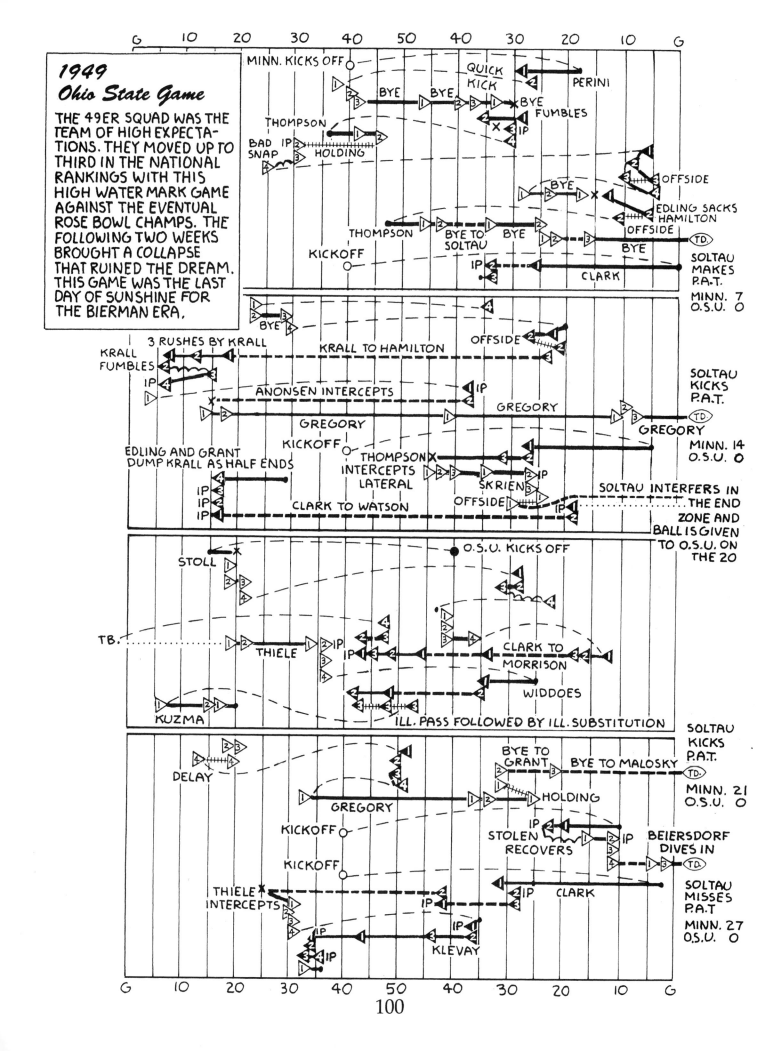

1949
Ohio State Game

THE 49ER SQUAD WAS THE TEAM OF HIGH EXPECTATIONS. THEY MOVED UP TO THIRD IN THE NATIONAL RANKINGS WITH THIS HIGH WATER MARK GAME AGAINST THE EVENTUAL ROSE BOWL CHAMPS. THE FOLLOWING TWO WEEKS BROUGHT A COLLAPSE THAT RUINED THE DREAM. THIS GAME WAS THE LAST DAY OF SUNSHINE FOR THE BIERMAN ERA.

MINN. KICKS OFF
QUICK KICK
PERINI
BYE   BYE   BYE   FUMBLES
THOMPSON
BAD SNAP   HOLDING   IP
OFFSIDE
BYE
EDLING SACKS HAMILTON
OFFSIDE
THOMPSON   BYE TO SOLTAU   BYE   BYE
KICKOFF
IP   CLARK
SOLTAU MAKES P.A.T.
MINN. 7
O.S.U. 0

BYE
3 RUSHES BY KRALL   KRALL TO HAMILTON   OFFSIDE
KRALL FUMBLES
IP
ANONSEN INTERCEPTS   IP
GREGORY
GREGORY   GREGORY
SOLTAU KICKS P.A.T.
KICKOFF
THOMPSON INTERCEPTS LATERAL
SKRIEN
EDLING AND GRANT DUMP KRALL AS HALF ENDS
IP   IP   IP   CLARK TO WATSON   OFFSIDE   IP   SOLTAU INTERFERS IN THE END ZONE AND BALL IS GIVEN TO O.S.U. ON THE 20
MINN. 14
O.S.U. 0

O.S.U. KICKS OFF
STOLL
TB.
THIELE   IP   CLARK TO MORRISON
IP
WIDDOES
KUZMA
ILL. PASS FOLLOWED BY ILL. SUBSTITUTION

DELAY
BYE TO GRANT   BYE TO MALOSKY
GREGORY   HOLDING
KICKOFF
STOLEN RECOVERS   IP   BEIERSDORF DIVES IN
KICKOFF
THIELE INTERCEPTS   IP   CLARK
IP   KLEVAY   IP
IP

SOLTAU KICKS P.A.T.
MINN. 21
O.S.U. 0

SOLTAU MISSES P.A.T
MINN. 27
O.S.U. 0

100

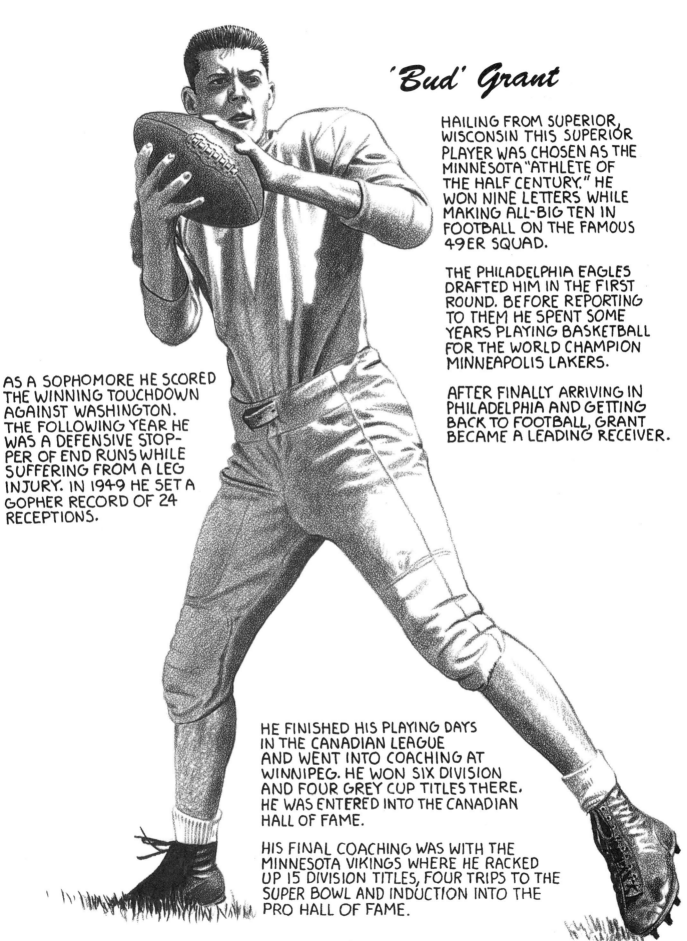

'Bud' Grant

HAILING FROM SUPERIOR, WISCONSIN THIS SUPERIOR PLAYER WAS CHOSEN AS THE MINNESOTA "ATHLETE OF THE HALF CENTURY." HE WON NINE LETTERS WHILE MAKING ALL-BIG TEN IN FOOTBALL ON THE FAMOUS 49ER SQUAD.

THE PHILADELPHIA EAGLES DRAFTED HIM IN THE FIRST ROUND. BEFORE REPORTING TO THEM HE SPENT SOME YEARS PLAYING BASKETBALL FOR THE WORLD CHAMPION MINNEAPOLIS LAKERS.

AFTER FINALLY ARRIVING IN PHILADELPHIA AND GETTING BACK TO FOOTBALL, GRANT BECAME A LEADING RECEIVER.

AS A SOPHOMORE HE SCORED THE WINNING TOUCHDOWN AGAINST WASHINGTON. THE FOLLOWING YEAR HE WAS A DEFENSIVE STOPPER OF END RUNS WHILE SUFFERING FROM A LEG INJURY. IN 1949 HE SET A GOPHER RECORD OF 24 RECEPTIONS.

HE FINISHED HIS PLAYING DAYS IN THE CANADIAN LEAGUE AND WENT INTO COACHING AT WINNIPEG. HE WON SIX DIVISION AND FOUR GREY CUP TITLES THERE. HE WAS ENTERED INTO THE CANADIAN HALL OF FAME.

HIS FINAL COACHING WAS WITH THE MINNESOTA VIKINGS WHERE HE RACKED UP 15 DIVISION TITLES, FOUR TRIPS TO THE SUPER BOWL AND INDUCTION INTO THE PRO HALL OF FAME.

Paul Giel

GIEL WAS AN ALL-AMERICAN BASEBALL PITCHER. IN HIS JUNIOR YEAR HE TURNED DOWN A PRO OFFER SO HE COULD FINISH HIS FOOTBALL CAREER.

THE WINONA GREAT DID IT ALL: CALL PLAYS, PASS, CATCH, RUSH, KICK, BLOCK, HOLD FOR CONVERSIONS AND BE A TEAM MAN. HE BEGAN AS A QUARTERBACK BUT MADE ALL-AMERICAN HALFBACK IN 1952 AND WAS UNANIMOUS IN 1953. BOTH YEARS HE WAS BIG TEN M.V.P.

HE SCORED 212 OF HIS TEAM'S 443 POINTS IN THREE YEARS. HE NARROWLY MISSED THE HEISMAN BUT WAS STILL VOTED PLAYER OF THE YEAR AND BACK OF THE YEAR.

GIEL WAS INDUCTED INTO THE HALL OF FAME AND SERVED MINNESOTA AS ATHLETIC DIRECTOR LONGER THAN ANY OTHER.

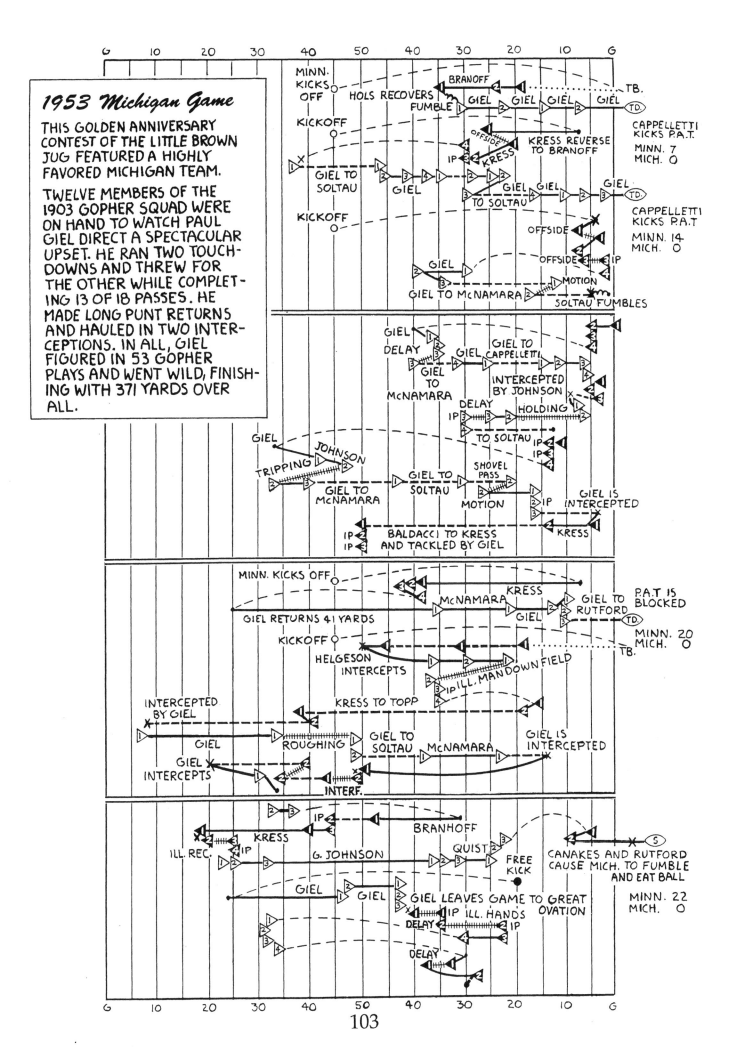

1953 Michigan Game

THIS GOLDEN ANNIVERSARY CONTEST OF THE LITTLE BROWN JUG FEATURED A HIGHLY FAVORED MICHIGAN TEAM.

TWELVE MEMBERS OF THE 1903 GOPHER SQUAD WERE ON HAND TO WATCH PAUL GIEL DIRECT A SPECTACULAR UPSET. HE RAN TWO TOUCHDOWNS AND THREW FOR THE OTHER WHILE COMPLETING 13 OF 18 PASSES. HE MADE LONG PUNT RETURNS AND HAULED IN TWO INTERCEPTIONS. IN ALL, GIEL FIGURED IN 53 GOPHER PLAYS AND WENT WILD, FINISHING WITH 371 YARDS OVERALL.

103

Dr. George Hauser

THE FORMER MINNESOTA ALL-AMERICAN SERVED AS LINE COACH FROM THE EARLY 1930'S. WITH THE OUTBREAK OF WORLD WAR II THE TEAM WAS BROKEN UP FOR MILITARY EXPEDIENCY. 17 PLAYERS WERE LOST. EVEN BIERMAN WAS SENT OFF. HAUSER TOOK OVER FOR THE DURATION. ABOUT 350 OTHER COLLEGES SUSPENDED FOOTBALL ALTOGETHER DURING THIS TIME.

ALTHOUGH BEING VICTORIOUS OVER WISCONSIN, HAUSER TOLD THE BADGERS TO HOLD THE "SLAB OF BACON" GAME TROPHY UNTIL COMPLETION OF THE WAR.

Wes Fesler

AFTER SUCCESS AS AN OHIO STATE ALL-AMERICAN AND COACH, WES FESLER DECIDED TO RETIRE FROM THE PRESSURE OF THE GAME. MINNESOTA TALKED HIM INTO GIVING COACHING ANOTHER TRY.

HIS SECOND YEAR WAS HIS MOST SUCCESSFUL AS A GOPHER. HIS RATHER AVERAGE TEAM HEADED BY AN OUTSTANDING LEADER, PAUL GIEL, ALMOST SNATCHED THE BIG TEN TITLE.

HIS HIGHLIGHT, HOWEVER, WAS THE STUNNING UPSET OF MICHIGAN IN HIS FINAL SEASON OF 1953.

WARMATH HAD BEEN AN END AT TENNESSEE IN THE 1930'S. HE HELD SEVERAL COACHING POSITIONS BEFORE COMING TO MINNESOTA IN 1954.

Murray Warmath

WHILE BEING A DRIVING PERFECTIONIST HE KEPT HIS PLAYERS LOOSE WITH HIS HUMOR AND WARM SMILE.

HE BELIEVED IN DEFENSE TO WIN GAMES BY CAPITALIZING WHEN OPPONENTS MADE MISTAKES.

WARMATH RECEIVED SEVERE TESTING IN 1958 AND 59. HE HELD HIS COURSE, WITH FAITH IN HIS PLAYERS AND HIMSELF, TO GO FROM LAST IN THE BIG TEN TO FIRST IN THE NATION. IN THIS RAGS TO RICHES ERA HE RECEIVED COACH OF THE YEAR RECOGNITION AND TOOK THE GOPHERS TO THE ROSE BOWL. OVER HIS CAREER HE DEVELOPED MANY PLAYERS WHO WENT ON INTO THE PROS.

AT DIFFERENT TIMES HE COACHED BOTH SIDES IN THE BLUE AND GREY GAME.

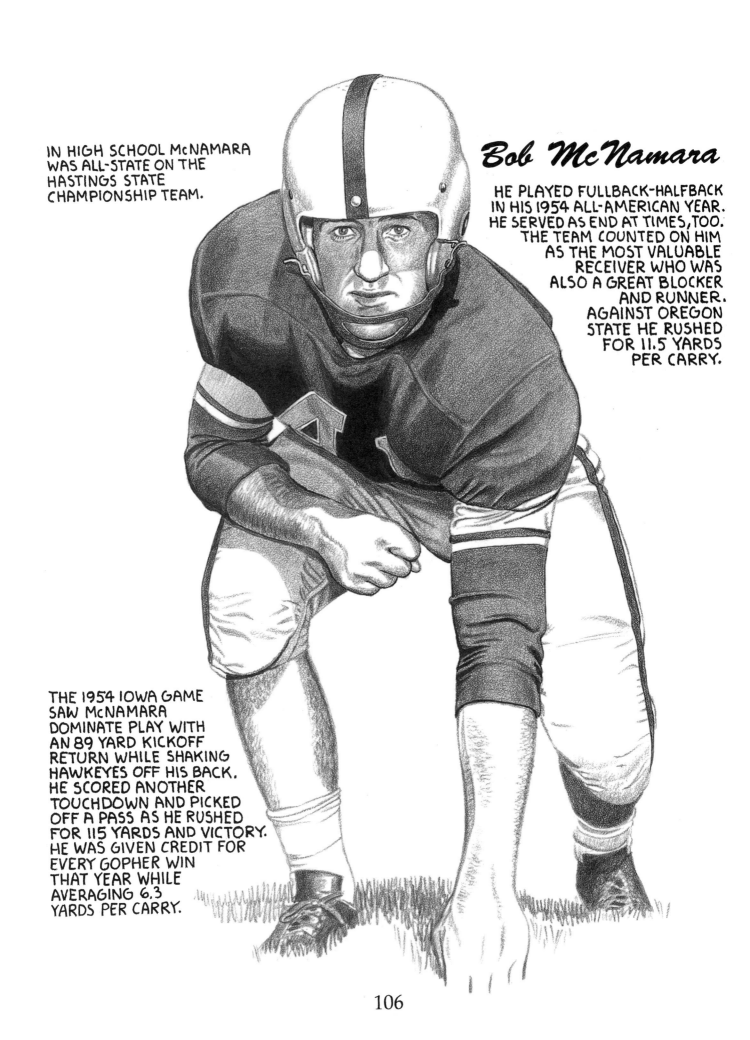

IN HIGH SCHOOL McNAMARA WAS ALL-STATE ON THE HASTINGS STATE CHAMPIONSHIP TEAM.

Bob McNamara

HE PLAYED FULLBACK-HALFBACK IN HIS 1954 ALL-AMERICAN YEAR. HE SERVED AS END AT TIMES, TOO. THE TEAM COUNTED ON HIM AS THE MOST VALUABLE RECEIVER WHO WAS ALSO A GREAT BLOCKER AND RUNNER. AGAINST OREGON STATE HE RUSHED FOR 11.5 YARDS PER CARRY.

THE 1954 IOWA GAME SAW McNAMARA DOMINATE PLAY WITH AN 89 YARD KICKOFF RETURN WHILE SHAKING HAWKEYES OFF HIS BACK. HE SCORED ANOTHER TOUCHDOWN AND PICKED OFF A PASS AS HE RUSHED FOR 115 YARDS AND VICTORY. HE WAS GIVEN CREDIT FOR EVERY GOPHER WIN THAT YEAR WHILE AVERAGING 6.3 YARDS PER CARRY.

Bob Hobert

HE WAS A TWIN WHO CAME
FROM MINNEAPOLIS WEST.

76

IN 1956 HE MADE ALL-AMERICAN AS A TACKLE
AFTER HAVING STARTED EVERY GAME
FROM HIS SOPHOMORE YEAR ON. HE ALSO
MADE THE ALL-ACADEMIC ALL-AMERICA
TEAM AND BECAME THE FIRST GOPHER
GRIDDER TO EARN PHI BETA KAPPA.

IN THE PROS HE PLAYED ON A VICTORIOUS
WINNIPEG TEAM FOR THE GREY CUP
UNDER BUD GRANT.

Tom Brown

COACH WARMATH CALLED "BROWNIE" A "ONE MAN INTERIOR LINE."

HE CAME IN SECOND FOR THE HEISMAN TROPHY, BUT TOOK ALL OTHER POSSIBLE HONORS: BIG TEN M.V.P., UNANIMOUS ALL-AMERICAN, OUTLAND AWARD AND LEADER OF THE GOPHERS TO THE 1960 NATIONAL CHAMPIONSHIP.

A KNEE INJURY HOBBLED THE GUARD FROM MINNEAPOLIS CENTRAL IN 1959, BUT THE FOLLOWING YEAR HE SETTLED IN AS THE "HUMAN ROCK OF GIBRALTAR" AND BECAME A MEMBER OF THE HALL OF FAME.

IN THE KEY GAME OF 1960 HE TRASHED THE IOWA LINE. THE HAWKEYE CENTER, EVER MIND-FUL OF BROWN THROWING HIM AROUND, HIKED THE BALL SIX FEET OVER HIS PUNTER'S HEAD TO SET UP THE GOPHERS' FIRST SCORE. A LITTLE LATER BROWN BOWLED AN IOWA LINEMAN INTO THE BACKFIELD, TOPPLING THE INTERFERENCE BLOCKER AND BALL CARRIER IN ONE MOTION. HE DOMINATED THE GAME WITHOUT TOUCHING THE BALL.

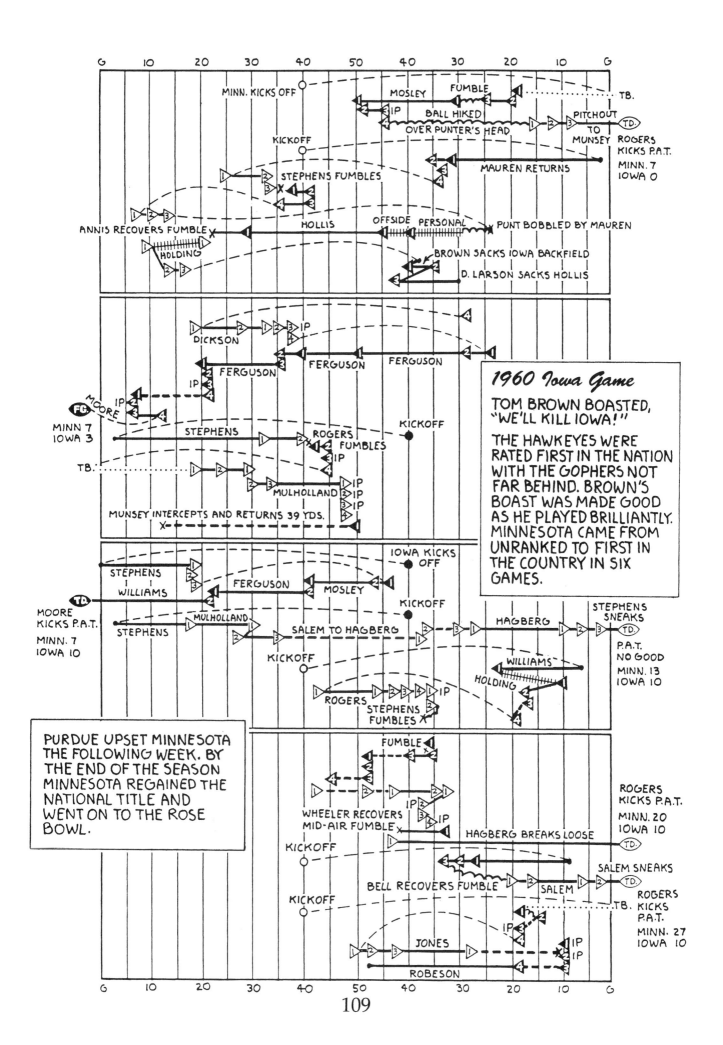

1960 Iowa Game

TOM BROWN BOASTED, "WE'LL KILL IOWA!"

THE HAWKEYES WERE RATED FIRST IN THE NATION WITH THE GOPHERS NOT FAR BEHIND. BROWN'S BOAST WAS MADE GOOD AS HE PLAYED BRILLIANTLY. MINNESOTA CAME FROM UNRANKED TO FIRST IN THE COUNTRY IN SIX GAMES.

PURDUE UPSET MINNESOTA THE FOLLOWING WEEK. BY THE END OF THE SEASON MINNESOTA REGAINED THE NATIONAL TITLE AND WENT ON TO THE ROSE BOWL.

Sandy Stephens

SANDY STEPHENS WAS A HIGH SCHOOL ALL-AMERICAN AT UNION TOWN, PENNSYLVANIA. HE WAS RECRUITED BY 53 SCHOOLS, OF WHICH MINNESOTA WAS THE BIG WINNER.

HIS START WAS SHAKY, WITH THE POOREST PASSING RECORD IN THE BIG TEN... BUT ENDED UP WITH A THREE YEAR AVERAGE OF 16.2 YARDS PER PASS.

HE WAS A TRIPLE THREAT, AND MORE, WHO MASTERED THE OPTION. IN 1961 HE RAN FOR A TOUCHDOWN AGAINST ILLINOIS AND TOSSED FOR FOUR MORE. AGAINST MICHIGAN HE LED THE GOPHERS FROM A 13-0 DEFICIT BY RUNNING A 63 YARD TOUCHDOWN AND THROWING A TWO-POINT CONVERSION. A 43 YARD PASS ADDED ANOTHER SCORE AND HE LATER SET UP ANOTHER. ON DEFENSE HE BLOCKED A SURE MICHIGAN DEEP PASS AND ENDED THE GAME BY INTERCEPTING ON HIS OWN TWO TO CLINCH VICTORY. THE NEXT WEEK, WITH SIMILAR HEROICS, HE LED TO THE DEFEAT OF MICHIGAN STATE AS SHOWN IN THE GAME CHART ON THE NEXT PAGE.

STEPHENS CAPPED OFF HIS CAREER AS M.V.P. IN A ROSE BOWL WIN; M.V.P. IN THE BIG TEN; FOURTH IN HEISMAN VOTING AND CONSENSUS QUARTERBACK ALL-AMERICAN FOR 1961.

110

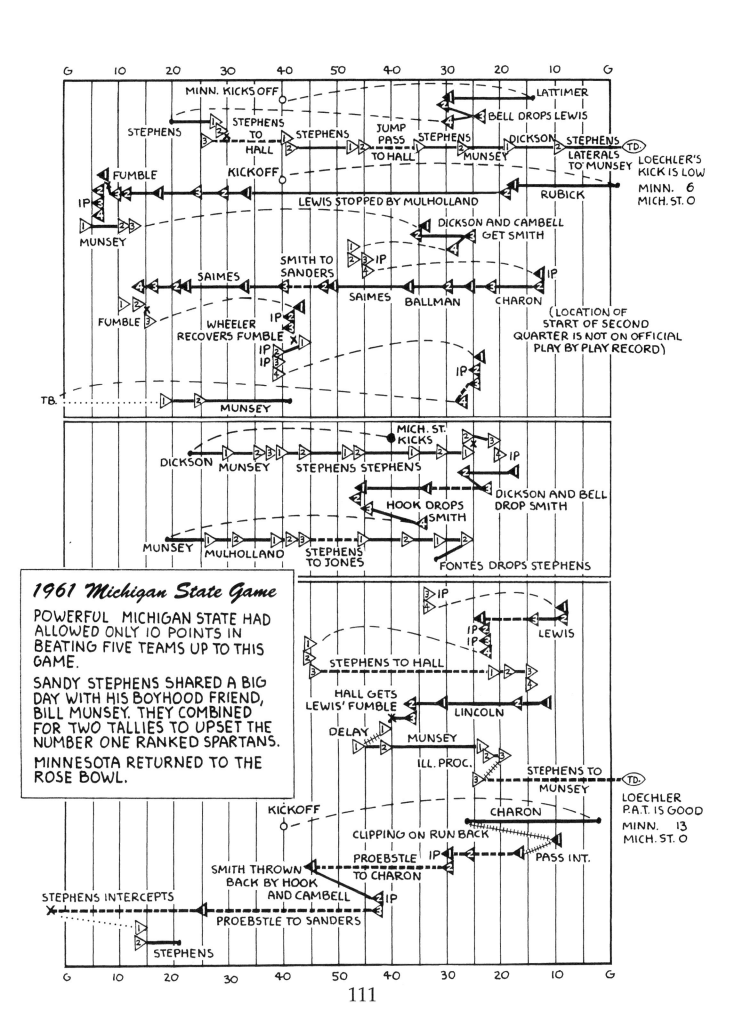

1961 Michigan State Game

POWERFUL MICHIGAN STATE HAD ALLOWED ONLY 10 POINTS IN BEATING FIVE TEAMS UP TO THIS GAME.

SANDY STEPHENS SHARED A BIG DAY WITH HIS BOYHOOD FRIEND, BILL MUNSEY. THEY COMBINED FOR TWO TALLIES TO UPSET THE NUMBER ONE RANKED SPARTANS.

MINNESOTA RETURNED TO THE ROSE BOWL.

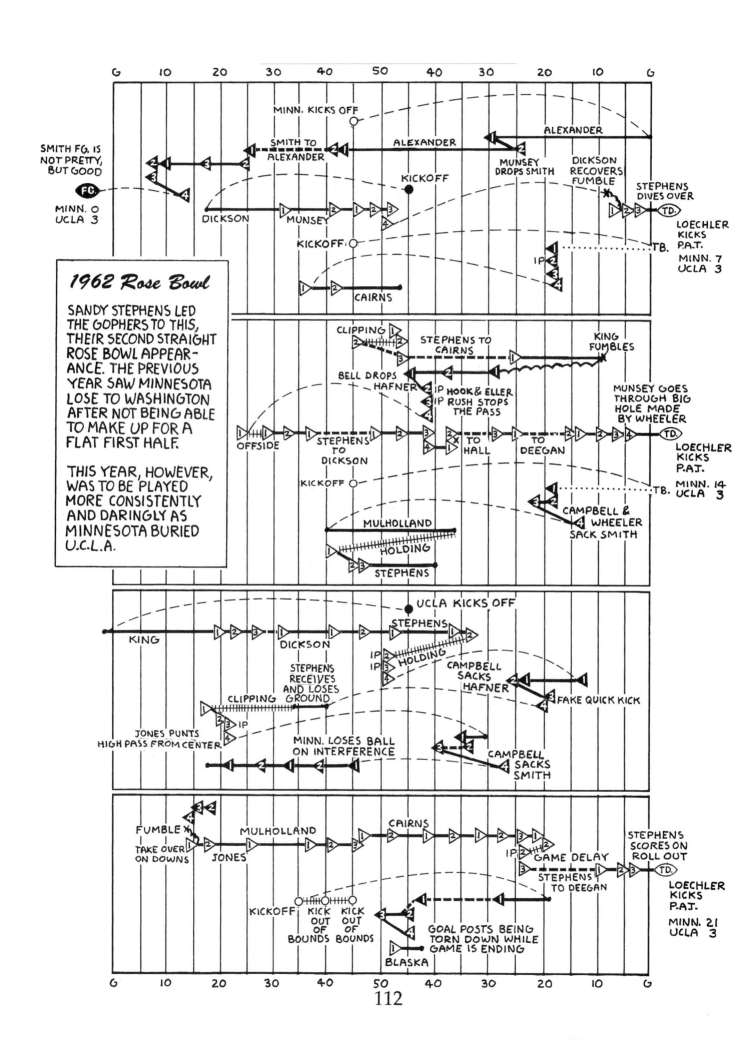

1962 Rose Bowl

SANDY STEPHENS LED THE GOPHERS TO THIS, THEIR SECOND STRAIGHT ROSE BOWL APPEARANCE. THE PREVIOUS YEAR SAW MINNESOTA LOSE TO WASHINGTON AFTER NOT BEING ABLE TO MAKE UP FOR A FLAT FIRST HALF.

THIS YEAR, HOWEVER, WAS TO BE PLAYED MORE CONSISTENTLY AND DARINGLY AS MINNESOTA BURIED U.C.L.A.

MINN. KICKS OFF

SMITH TO ALEXANDER

ALEXANDER

ALEXANDER

SMITH FG. IS NOT PRETTY, BUT GOOD

MUNSEY DROPS SMITH

DICKSON RECOVERS FUMBLE

STEPHENS DIVES OVER

KICKOFF

MINN. 0
UCLA 3

DICKSON

MUNSEY

LOECHLER KICKS P.A.T.

KICKOFF

TB.

MINN. 7
UCLA 3

CAIRNS

CLIPPING

STEPHENS TO CAIRNS

KING FUMBLES

BELL DROPS HAFNER

IP HOOK & ELLER
IP RUSH STOPS THE PASS

MUNSEY GOES THROUGH BIG HOLE MADE BY WHEELER

OFFSIDE

STEPHENS TO DICKSON

TO HALL

TO DEEGAN

LOECHLER KICKS P.A.T.

KICKOFF

TB.

MINN. 14
UCLA 3

CAMPBELL & WHEELER SACK SMITH

MULHOLLAND

HOLDING

STEPHENS

UCLA KICKS OFF

KING

STEPHENS

DICKSON

IP HOLDING
IP

CAMPBELL SACKS HAFNER

STEPHENS RECEIVES AND LOSES GROUND

FAKE QUICK KICK

CLIPPING

JONES PUNTS HIGH PASS FROM CENTER

MINN. LOSES BALL ON INTERFERENCE

CAMPBELL SACKS SMITH

FUMBLE

MULHOLLAND

CAIRNS

STEPHENS SCORES ON ROLL OUT

TAKE OVER ON DOWNS

JONES

IP

GAME DELAY

STEPHENS TO DEEGAN

LOECHLER KICKS P.A.T.

KICKOFF

KICK OUT OF BOUNDS

KICK OUT OF BOUNDS

GOAL POSTS BEING TORN DOWN WHILE GAME IS ENDING

MINN. 21
UCLA 3

BLASKA

112

Bobby Bell

BELL CAME TO MINNESOTA FROM SHELBY, NORTH CAROLINA TO BE A QUARTERBACK. IT TURNED OUT HE WAS GREAT AT WHATEVER HE DID AND WAS NEEDED AT TACKLE MORE. HE COULDN'T BELIEVE THEY WOULD REALLY PUT HIM THERE, BUT HE DID ALL RIGHT. HE MADE ALL-AMERICAN IN 1961 AND UNANIMOUS ALL-AMERICAN IN 1962. IN ADDITION, HE WAS THIRD IN HEISMAN VOTING AND WON THE OUTLAND AWARD FOR BEST INTERIOR LINEMAN. HE WON THE OUTSTANDING LINEMAN AWARD FOR THE ALL-AMERICAN BOWL GAME AND BECAME A MEMBER OF THE HALL OF FAME.

TO HIS TEAMMATES BELL WAS POPULAR, WITH A GREAT SENSE OF HUMOR. TO OPPONENTS HE WAS UNPOPULAR FOR USING HIS GREAT MIXTURE OF STRENGTH, AGILITY, SAVVY AND DESIRE AGAINST THEM. ALTHOUGH DOUBLE-TEAMED BY BIGGER PLAYERS, HE WOULD ESCAPE THEM TO MAKE HIS TACKLE. HE WAS ALSO ONE OF THE FASTEST GOPHERS ON THE SQUAD. AT 6'4", WITH LONG ARMS AND BIG HANDS, BELL WAS THE MAJOR REASON MINNESOTA HAD ONE OF THE BEST PASS DEFENSES IN THE COUNTRY. THOSE BIG HANDS HELPED HIM AS THE TEAM CENTER ON PUNTS AND KICKS, TOO.

IN THE 1961 WISCONSIN GAME HE GOT TWO RIBS CRACKED IN THE FIRST HALF. WITH A LITTLE TAPE AND BANDAGING, HE PLAYED A GREAT SECOND HALF AND LATER WENT ON TO WIN IN THE ROSE BOWL.

BELL BECAME AN ALL-PRO FOR KANSAS CITY AND EARNED A SUPER BOWL RING BY DEFEATING THE MINNESOTA VIKINGS.

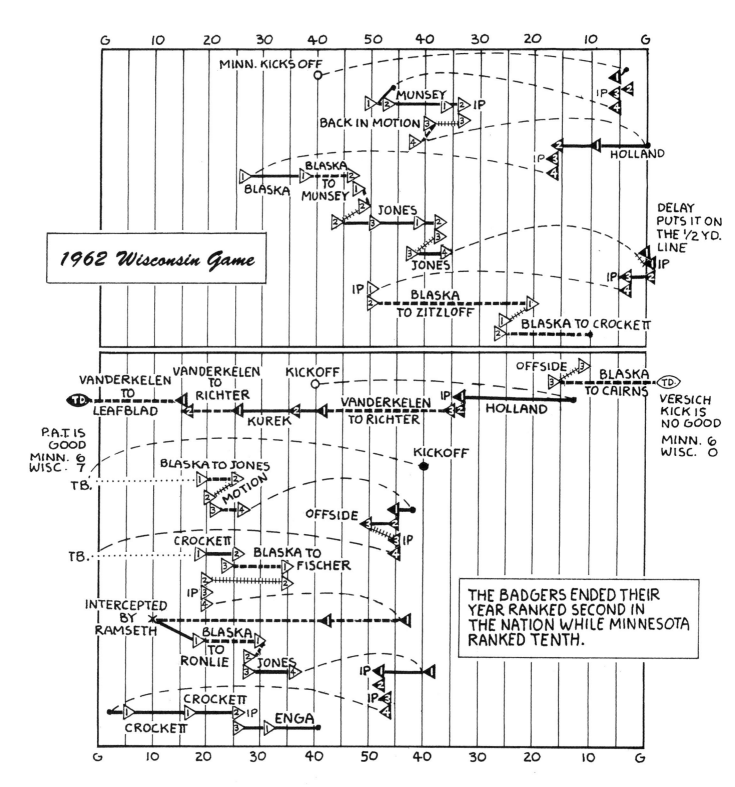

1962 Wisconsin Game

THE BADGERS ENDED THEIR
YEAR RANKED SECOND IN
THE NATION WHILE MINNESOTA
RANKED TENTH.

THE BIG TEN CHAMPIONSHIP AND A THIRD TRIP IN A ROW TO THE ROSE BOWL WERE AT STAKE.
IT WAS NOT TO BE, THOUGH. THE HIGH STAKES AND HEATED MANNER IN WHICH THIS GAME WAS
LOST IS WHAT MADE IT SO MEMORABLE. PLAYERS ON BOTH SIDES WERE SUBJECTED TO ERRATIC
OFFICIATING. AFTER SNATCHING GAME-WINNING PLAYS AWAY FROM MINNESOTA IT APPEARED THE
REFS TRIED TO REPENT AND GIVE THEM BACK AGAIN DURING A LATE GOPHER MARCH.
WISCONSIN HUNG TOUGH AND WENT ON TO THE ROSE BOWL.

THE HEARTBREAKING PLAYS STARTED Ⓐ WHEN BILL MUNSEY CLAIMED TO HAVE BARELY GOTTEN
OVER FOR A SCORE. HE WAS DRIVEN BACK BUT THERE WAS NO WHISTLE. DUANE BLASKA, THE
PASSER ON THE PLAY, CAME DOWN FIELD AND PUSHED MUNSEY OVER AGAIN. THE PENALTY FOR
AIDING A BALL CARRIER IN THIS MANNER PUT A TOUCHDOWN OUT OF REACH AT THE 15. THE

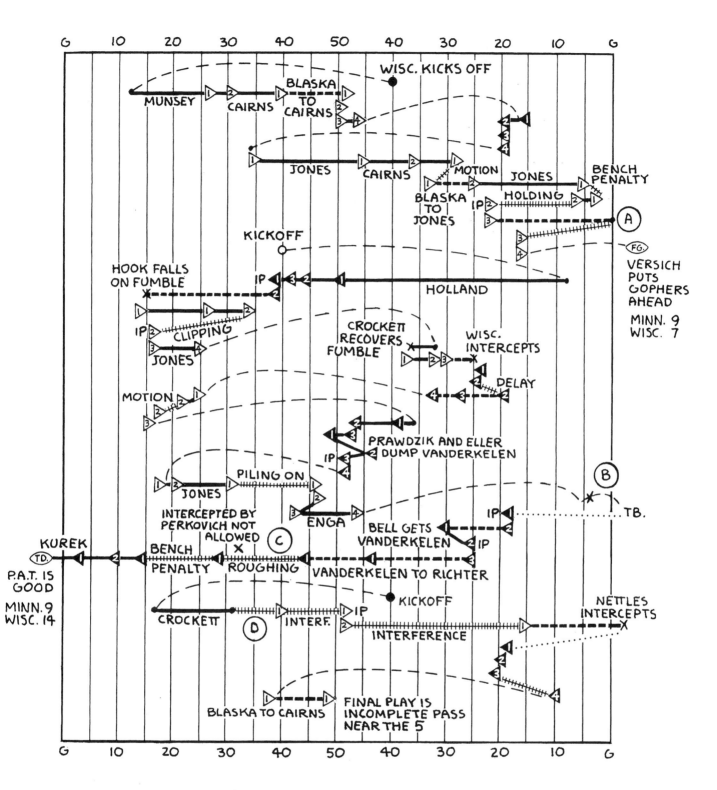

GOPHERS HAD TO SETTLE FOR A FIELD GOAL.
LATER A PUNT BOUNCED OFF A BADGER RECEIVER'S LEG INTO THE END ZONE Ⓑ. IT WAS
JUMPED ON BY THE GOPHERS FOR WHAT SEEMED TO BE A TOUCHDOWN BUT POSSESSION WAS
GIVEN TO WISCONSIN AT THE 20 INSTEAD.

TEMPERS BOILED OVER AFTER BOBBY BELL MADE HIS MOST TIMELY AND BRILLIANT PLAY Ⓒ OF
THE GAME. WHILE COMING DOWN ON THE PASSER HE DEFLECTED THE BALL INTO THE ARMS OF
TEAMMATE JOHN PERKOVICH. THE GAME SEEMED ON ICE, BUT INSTEAD, BELL WAS MIRACULOUSLY
CALLED FOR ROUGHING. WITH THE ADDITION OF A BENCH PENALTY, WISCONSIN WAS PUT DEEP IN
MINNESOTA TERRITORY WHERE IT MADE THE DECISIVE SCORE. LATE INTERFERENCE CALLS Ⓓ TO
MINNESOTA'S ADVANTAGE COULDN'T CHANGE THE FINAL TALLY.

Carl Eller

HAILING FROM SALEM, NORTH CAROLINA, THE "GENTLEMANLY GIANT" HAD A FONDNESS FOR ANCIENT GREEK DRAMA. ON THE FIELD HE WAS DRAMATIC TRAGEDY TO OPPONENTS.

HE IS IN THE COLLEGE AND PRO HALLS OF FAME.

EVEN WITH HIS LARGE SIZE, ELLER WAS QUICK TO RUSH ENEMY BACKFIELDS AND STOP PLAY WITH A CRACKLING TACKLE. IN 1962 HE LED MINNESOTA IN THROWING NAVY FOR A MINUS 31 YARDS RUSHING.

ON OFFENSE HE WAS AN OUTSTANDING BLOCKER AND EVEN RECEIVED ON A TACKLE ELIGIBLE PASS PLAY.

HE WAS RUNNER-UP FOR THE OUTLAND TROPHY AND MADE CONSENSUS ALL-AMERICAN IN 1963. HE WAS DRAFTED IN THE FIRST ROUND BY TWO LEAGUES AND PLAYED IN FOUR SUPER BOWLS WITH THE MINNESOTA VIKINGS.

116

BROWN CAME FROM PORT ARTHUR, TEXAS WHERE HE PLAYED FOOTBALL ONLY ONE YEAR. HE WAS A FULL-BACK WHO HAD NEVER CAUGHT A PASS. HIS FIRST SPORT WAS BASKETBALL.

Aaron Brown

AFTER COMING TO MINNESOTA HE WAS MADE INTO AN END, WHERE HE PLAYED BOTH WAYS.

TWO-PLATOON FOOTBALL CREATED TEAM SPECIALISTS IN OFFENSE AND DEFENSE, AND SO ALL-AMERICAN ROSTERS CHANGED TO SHOW THIS IN 1965. IT WAS AT THIS TIME BROWN BECAME CONSENSUS ALL-AMERICAN AT DEFENSIVE END.

HE PREFERRED DEFENSE MOST FOR ITS HITTING, FREEDOM AND INITIATIVE.

ON OFFENSE HE WAS NO SLOUCH EITHER. HE HAULED IN 27 PASSES, TO SET A SCHOOL RECORD IN 1964.

IN THE SECOND GAME OF 1965 HE SUFFERED A BROKEN JAW AFTER BEING CLOTHSLINED. HE CONTINUED PLAY WHILE OCCASIONALLY GOING TO THE SIDELINE TO SPIT BLOOD. HE FINISHED THE SEASON WITH HIS MOUTH WIRED SHUT. DEFENSE WAS HIS MAIN DUTY AFTER THE INJURY, BUT HE MANAGED TO PULL DOWN 24 PASSES ON OFFENSE ANYWAY.

HE WAS DRAFTED IN THE FIRST ROUND BY KANSAS CITY AND LATER PLAYED FOR GREEN BAY.

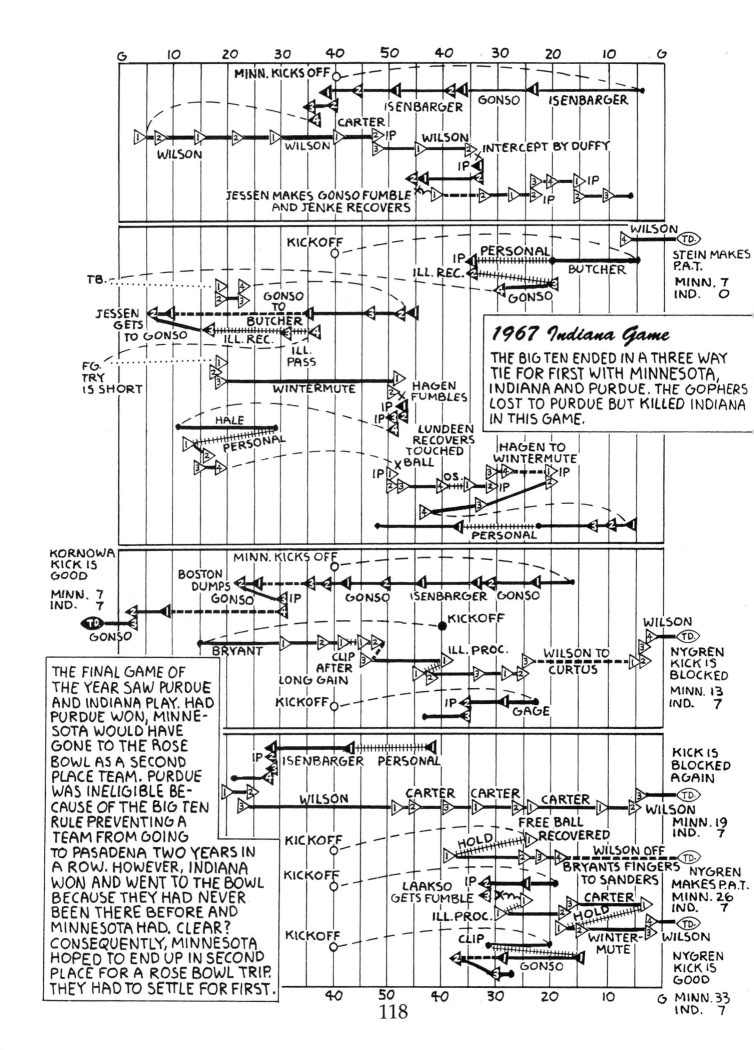

MINN. KICKS OFF
ISENBARGER GONSO ISENBARGER
CARTER
WILSON WILSON IP WILSON INTERCEPT BY DUFFY
IP
JESSEN MAKES GONSO FUMBLE IP
AND JENKE RECOVERS IP

KICKOFF WILSON
PERSONAL TD.
IP STEIN MAKES
ILL. REC. BUTCHER P.A.T.
GONSO MINN. 7
TB. IND. 0
GONSO
JESSEN TO
GETS BUTCHER
TO GONSO ILL. REC. ILL.
PASS
FG. **1967 Indiana Game**
TRY HAGEN THE BIG TEN ENDED IN A THREE WAY
IS SHORT WINTERMUTE FUMBLES TIE FOR FIRST WITH MINNESOTA,
IP INDIANA AND PURDUE. THE GOPHERS
IP LOST TO PURDUE BUT KILLED INDIANA
HALE LUNDEEN IN THIS GAME.
PERSONAL RECOVERS
TOUCHED HAGEN TO
X BALL WINTERMUTE
IP O.S. IP
IP
PERSONAL

KORNOWA MINN. KICKS OFF
KICK IS BOSTON
GOOD DUMPS IP
GONSO GONSO ISENBARGER GONSO
MINN. 7 GONSO
IND. 7 WILSON
TD. KICKOFF TD.
GONSO BRYANT ILL. PROC. NYGREN
CLIP WILSON TO KICK IS
AFTER CURTUS BLOCKED
LONG GAIN
KICKOFF MINN. 13
IP IND. 7
GAGE

THE FINAL GAME OF
THE YEAR SAW PURDUE IP KICK IS
AND INDIANA PLAY. HAD ISENBARGER PERSONAL BLOCKED
PURDUE WON, MINNE- AGAIN
SOTA WOULD HAVE
GONE TO THE ROSE CARTER CARTER CARTER TD.
BOWL AS A SECOND WILSON WILSON
PLACE TEAM. PURDUE MINN. 19
WAS INELIGIBLE BE- FREE BALL IND. 7
CAUSE OF THE BIG TEN KICKOFF HOLD RECOVERED
RULE PREVENTING A WILSON OFF TD.
TEAM FROM GOING KICKOFF BRYANTS FINGERS NYGREN
TO PASADENA TWO YEARS IN LAAKSO IP TO SANDERS MAKES P.A.T.
A ROW. HOWEVER, INDIANA GETS FUMBLE CARTER MINN. 26
WON AND WENT TO THE BOWL HOLD IND. 7
BECAUSE THEY HAD NEVER ILL. PROC.
BEEN THERE BEFORE AND WINTER- TD.
MINNESOTA HAD. CLEAR? KICKOFF CLIP MUTE WILSON
CONSEQUENTLY, MINNESOTA NYGREN
HOPED TO END UP IN SECOND GONSO KICK IS
PLACE FOR A ROSE BOWL TRIP. GOOD
THEY HAD TO SETTLE FOR FIRST.
MINN. 33
IND. 7

118

John Williams

JOHN WILLIAMS GREW UP IN OHIO. ALONG WITH FOOTBALL HE PLAYED BASKETBALL, BASEBALL AND SET HIS HIGH SCHOOL'S RECORD IN THE SHOT PUT. HIS GRID PROWESS WAS DISCOVERED BY SCOUTS WHO CAME TO SEE A NATIONALLY-RANKED OPPOSING TEAM.

HE HAD ALWAYS INTENDED TO GO TO OHIO STATE BUT BECAME IMPRESSED WITH MINNESOTA.

HE SERVED HIS FIRST TWO YEARS WITH THE GOPHERS AS A FULLBACK. FOR HIS THIRD YEAR HE MOVED TO DEFENSIVE END. AS A SENIOR HE BE-CAME A STANDOUT OFFENSIVE RIGHT TACKLE WHERE HE WON ALL-AMERICAN HONORS ON THE 1967 BIG TEN CHAMPION-SHIP TEAM.

BALTIMORE DRAFTED HIM IN THE FIRST ROUND. FOR THEM HE PLAYED IN TWO SUPER BOWLS. HE ENDED HIS PRO CAREER WITH THE L.A. RAMS.

Charlie Sanders

SANDERS MOVED TO A NEW
POSITION IN EACH OF HIS YEARS AT
MINNESOTA: RUNNING BACK,
DEFENSIVE BACK, DEFENSIVE END
AND TIGHT END. HIS FINAL YEAR,
1967, SAW A BIG TEN CHAMPIONSHIP.

HE WENT ON TO PLAY HIS PRO
CAREER FOR THE DETROIT LIONS
WHERE HE WAS IN THE PRO
BOWL AS A ROOKIE. HE PLAYED
IN SEVEN ALL TOTALED.

AS A TIGHT END HE ENTERED
THE PRO HALL OF FAME.

THIS ALL-STATER FROM
ST. LOUIS PARK WAS A GOPHER
ALL-AMERICAN AT DEFENSIVE
END IN 1967 AND 68.

Bob Stein

AMONG HIS BEST ABILITIES
WAS HIS RUSH ON THE
PASSER AS WELL AS BEING
A LEADING FIELD GOAL
KICKER.

IN HIS SOPHOMORE YEAR
HE WAS INJURED AFTER ONLY
TWO GAMES. UP TO THAT
POINT HE WAS LEADING
THE BIG TEN IN THROWING
THE MOST NUMBER OF
OPPONENTS FOR A LOSS,
WITH EIGHT. THOUGH HE
WAS OUT FOR THE REST
OF THE SEASON, HE STILL
TIED FOR THIRD IN THAT
DEPARTMENT FOR THE
YEAR.

HE MADE THE ALL-AMERICAN
SCHOLASTIC TEAM IN 1968
AND POST GRADUATE TEAM
IN 1969.

HE WENT ON TO PLAY FOR
THE KANSAS CITY CHIEFS
AND BECOME PRESIDENT
OF THE MINNESOTA
TIMBERWOLVES BASKETBALL
TEAM OF THE N.B.A.

121

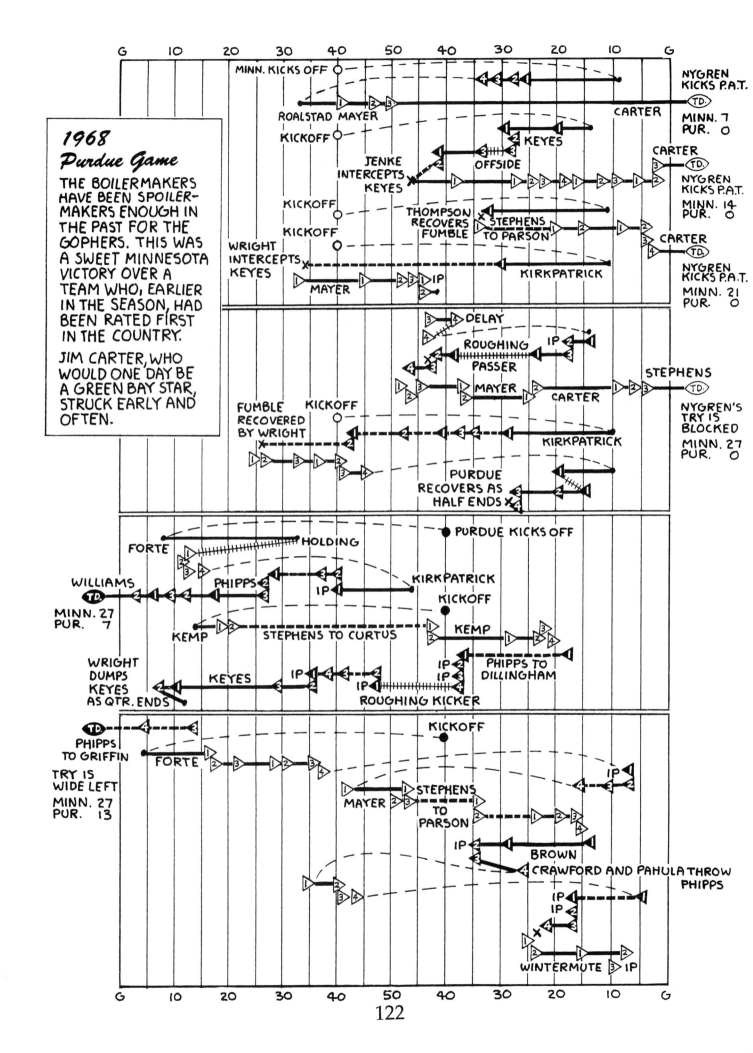

1968

Purdue Game

THE BOILERMAKERS HAVE BEEN SPOILERMAKERS ENOUGH IN THE PAST FOR THE GOPHERS. THIS WAS A SWEET MINNESOTA VICTORY OVER A TEAM WHO, EARLIER IN THE SEASON, HAD BEEN RATED FIRST IN THE COUNTRY.

JIM CARTER, WHO WOULD ONE DAY BE A GREEN BAY STAR, STRUCK EARLY AND OFTEN.

MINN. KICKS OFF

NYGREN KICKS P.A.T.

ROALSTAD MAYER

CARTER

MINN. 7
PUR. 0

KICKOFF

KEYES

CARTER

JENKE INTERCEPTS KEYES

OFFSIDE

NYGREN KICKS P.A.T.

MINN. 14
PUR. 0

KICKOFF

THOMPSON RECOVERS FUMBLE

STEPHENS TO PARSON

CARTER

KICKOFF

NYGREN KICKS P.A.T.

WRIGHT INTERCEPTS KEYES

KIRKPATRICK

MINN. 21
PUR. 0

MAYER

IP

DELAY

ROUGHING PASSER

IP

MAYER

CARTER

STEPHENS

NYGREN'S TRY IS BLOCKED

FUMBLE RECOVERED BY WRIGHT

KICKOFF

KIRKPATRICK

MINN. 27
PUR. 0

PURDUE RECOVERS AS HALF ENDS

PURDUE KICKS OFF

FORTE

HOLDING

WILLIAMS

PHIPPS

IP

KIRKPATRICK

KICKOFF

MINN. 27
PUR. 7

KEMP

STEPHENS TO CURTUS

KEMP

WRIGHT DUMPS KEYES AS QTR. ENDS

KEYES

IP

IP
IP

PHIPPS TO DILLINGHAM

ROUGHING KICKER

KICKOFF

PHIPPS TO GRIFFIN

FORTE

IP

TRY IS WIDE LEFT

MAYER

STEPHENS TO PARSON

MINN. 27
PUR. 13

IP

BROWN

CRAWFORD AND PAHULA THROW PHIPPS

IP
IP

WINTERMUTE
IP

122

AT RICHFIELD, KINGSRITER WAS PREP ATHLETE OF THE YEAR. AT MINNESOTA HE USED HIS ABILITY TO PITCH ON THE BASEBALL TEAM AS WELL AS CATCH ON THE FOOTBALL TEAM.

Doug Kingsriter

QUARTERBACK IS WHERE HE EXPECTED TO PLAY, BUT WAS SOON MOVED TO CENTER AND FINALLY TIGHT END, WHERE HE EARNED ALL-AMERICAN STATUS IN 1971.

AS A FRESHMAN HE BROKE HIS WRIST AND HAD TO SIT OUT A YEAR. WHEN HE GOT HIS CHANCE, IN THE MIDDLE OF THE FOLLOWING YEAR, HE GRABBED A 20 YARD PASS ON HIS FIRST PLAY. IN ALL, HE GOT SIX RECEPTIONS THAT DAY AND WENT ON TO LEAD THE TEAM FOR THE SEASON WITH 26.

THOUGH HE WAS A GOOD RUNNER WITH THE BALL, HE WAS A MASTER AT THE ONE-HANDED GRAB.

HE WAS DRAFTED BY THE MINNESOTA VIKINGS.

Cal Stoll

CAL STOLL'S FIRST STINT WITH MINNESOTA WAS AS A DEFENSIVE END ON THE TALENTED 1949 TEAM. HE RETURNED AS HEAD COACH IN 1972. IN BETWEEN HE SERVED AS END COACH AT MICHIGAN STATE IN THE CHAMPIONSHIP YEARS OF DUFFY DAUGHERTY. HE HAD HEAD COACHING SUCCESS HIMSELF, AT WAKE FOREST.

1977 WAS HIS BIG YEAR WITH GOPHER WINS OVER BOTH ROSE BOWL PARTICIPANTS, WASHINGTON AND MICHIGAN. MICHIGAN HAD BEEN RATED FIRST IN THE COUNTRY AS STOLL'S BOYS SHUT THEM DOWN TO THE TUNE OF 16-0. IT WAS THE FIRST SKUNK MICHIGAN HAD RECEIVED IN 113 GAMES. MINNESOTA WENT ON TO PLAY IN THE HALL OF FAME BOWL.

Joe Salem

ANOTHER FORMER GOPHER TO RETURN AS COACH WAS JOE SALEM. HE WAS CALLED "SMOKEY" JOE BY MURRAY WARMATH. IT HAD TO DO WITH THE EXCITING WAY HE WOULD COME INTO THE GAME AS A RESERVE QUARTERBACK IN THE NATIONAL CHAMPIONSHIP YEAR OF 1960.

SALEM WAS A SUCCESSFUL COACH AT SOUTH DAKOTA AND NORTHERN ARIZONA BUT RAN INTO HARD TIMES AT HIS ALMA MATER.

Lou Holtz

LOU HOLTZ PICKED UP A SAGGING FOOTBALL PROGRAM WITH HIS OPTIMISM AND DRIVE. AT HIS PRODDING THE NEW INDOOR FACILITIES WERE BUILT AND NICKNAMED THE TAJ-MA-HOLTZ.

RECRUITING IMPROVED AND HIS 1984 BUILDING YEAR WAS CLIMAXED WITH AN UPSET OVER IOWA. IN 1985 HIS SQUAD ALMOST TIPPED THE SCALE AGAINST NATIONAL CHAMPION OKLAHOMA BY GOING DOWN TO THE FINAL PLAY OF THE GAME.

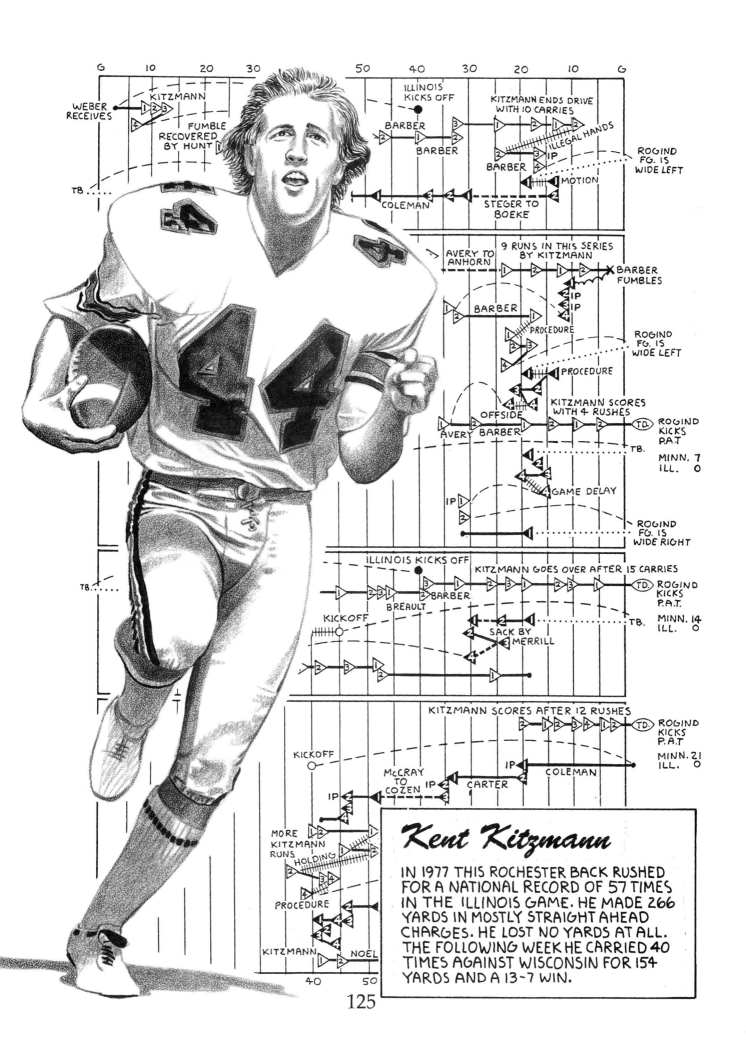

Kent Kitzmann

IN 1977 THIS ROCHESTER BACK RUSHED FOR A NATIONAL RECORD OF 57 TIMES IN THE ILLINOIS GAME. HE MADE 266 YARDS IN MOSTLY STRAIGHT AHEAD CHARGES. HE LOST NO YARDS AT ALL. THE FOLLOWING WEEK HE CARRIED 40 TIMES AGAINST WISCONSIN FOR 154 YARDS AND A 13-7 WIN.

A HIGH SCHOOL ALL-STATER FROM MICHIGAN, DUNGY CAME TO MINNESOTA TO BE QUARTERBACK AND STUDENT OF THE GAME.

HE THREW FOUR TOUCHDOWNS AGAINST NORTH DAKOTA IN 1974 AND ENDED WITH A CAREER 25 TOUCHDOWN PASSES.

HE PLAYED FOR THE PITTSBURGH STEELERS AS A DEFENSIVE BACK AND TOOK PART IN THEIR SUPER BOWL XIII VICTORY.

HE RETURNED TO MINNESOTA AS GOPHER DEFENSIVE COORDINATOR AND LATER WAS DEFENSIVE COORDINATOR FOR THE MINNESOTA VIKINGS. HIS VIKING DEFENSE RANKED NUMBER ONE.

Tony Dungy

AS HEAD COACH, HIS INDIANAPOLIS COLTS WON SUPER BOWL XLI IN 2007. WHILE DOING THIS, HIS OFFENSIVE COORDINATOR WAS TOM MOORE, WHO RECRUITED HIM AS A PLAYER FOR THE GOPHERS. TWO FORMER GOPHERS, DARRELL REID AND STARTER BEN UTECHT WERE ON THE SQUAD.

Lloyd Stein

CENTERS WERE KNOWN AS "SNAPPERS" IN CANADA WHERE LLOYD STEIN PLAYED SOME EARLY FOOTBALL. HE BECAME KNOWN AS "SNAPPER" THE REST OF HIS LIFE. THE TWO HARBORS NATIVE WAS STARTING GOPHER CENTER IN THE LATE 1920'S. HE WAS ONCE KNOWN TO OUT-PLAY AN ALL-AMERICAN ON THE OTHER SIDE OF THE BALL FROM HIM.

AFTER HIS PLAYING DAYS HE SERVED AS TEAM TRAINER FOR 42 YEARS. HE GUESSED HE HAD TAPED AROUND 700,000 ANKLES IN HIS TIME.

"SNAPPER'S" CONTRIBUTIONS IN METHODS, THEORIES AND TECHNIQUES TO HIS ART EARNED HIM ENTRY INTO THE HALL OF FAME AS A TRAINER.

MANY PLAYERS HOLD THE NATIONAL RECORD
OF 100 YARDS FOR A KICKOFF RETURN.
MINNESOTA HAS TWO BEARERS OF THIS
DISTINCTION. RICK UPCHURCH DID HIS
PART AGAINST WISCONSIN IN 1974.

Bobby Weber

Rick Upchurch

IN 1977 BOBBY WEBER RETURNED
THE 100 AGAINST OHIO STATE.

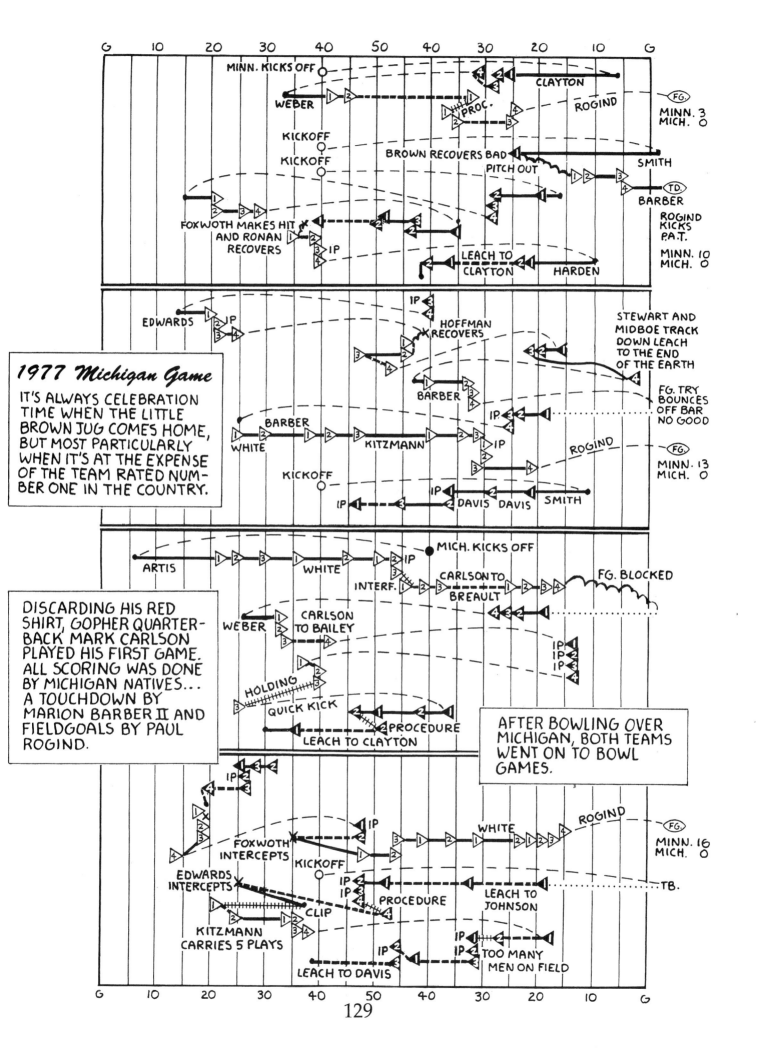

G   10   20   30   40   50   40   30   20   10   G

MINN. KICKS OFF

CLAYTON

WEBER   PROC.   ROGIND

FG.
MINN. 3
MICH. 0

KICKOFF

KICKOFF

BROWN RECOVERS BAD
PITCH OUT   SMITH

FOXWOTH MAKES HIT
AND RONAN
RECOVERS   IP

TD.
BARBER

ROGIND
KICKS
P.A.T.

MINN. 10
MICH. 0

LEACH TO
CLAYTON   HARDEN

IP

EDWARDS   IP

HOFFMAN
RECOVERS

STEWART AND
MIDBOE TRACK
DOWN LEACH
TO THE END
OF THE EARTH

1977 Michigan Game

IT'S ALWAYS CELEBRATION
TIME WHEN THE LITTLE
BROWN JUG COMES HOME,
BUT MOST PARTICULARLY
WHEN IT'S AT THE EXPENSE
OF THE TEAM RATED NUM-
BER ONE IN THE COUNTRY.

BARBER

WHITE   BARBER
KITZMANN

IP

IP

FG. TRY
BOUNCES
OFF BAR
NO GOOD

ROGIND

FG.
MINN. 13
MICH. 0

KICKOFF

IP   IP   DAVIS   DAVIS   SMITH

MICH. KICKS OFF

ARTIS   WHITE   IP

CARLSON TO
BREAULT

FG. BLOCKED

INTERF.

DISCARDING HIS RED
SHIRT, GOPHER QUARTER-
BACK MARK CARLSON
PLAYED HIS FIRST GAME.
ALL SCORING WAS DONE
BY MICHIGAN NATIVES...
A TOUCHDOWN BY
MARION BARBER II AND
FIELDGOALS BY PAUL
ROGIND.

WEBER   CARLSON
TO BAILEY

IP
IP
IP

HOLDING

QUICK KICK

PROCEDURE

LEACH TO CLAYTON

AFTER BOWLING OVER
MICHIGAN, BOTH TEAMS
WENT ON TO BOWL
GAMES.

IP

FOXWOTH
INTERCEPTS

KICKOFF

WHITE   ROGIND

FG.
MINN. 16
MICH. 0

EDWARDS
INTERCEPTS

IP
IP
PROCEDURE

LEACH TO
JOHNSON

TB.

CLIP

KITZMANN
CARRIES 5 PLAYS

IP
IP   TOO MANY
MEN ON FIELD

IP

LEACH TO DAVIS

G   10   20   30   40   50   40   30   20   10   G

129

John Gutekunst

AS DEFENSIVE COORDI-NATOR, JOHN GUTEKUNST GUIDED VIRGINIA TECH TO LEAD THE NATION IN LEAST POINTS ALLOWED IN 1983. MINNESOTA WAS LEADING THE NATION IN MOST POINTS ALLOWED DURING THE SAME PERIOD.

WHEN "GUTE" CAME TO MINNESOTA THE FOLLOWING YEAR, HE TURNED THE DEFENSE AROUND FOR THE GOPHERS. IN TWO YEARS THE GOPHERS WERE WINNING IN THE INDEPENDENCE BOWL WITH HIM IN HIS FIRST GAME AS HEAD COACH.

HIS FIRST FULL SEASON AT THE HELM SAW THE RETURN OF THE LITTLE BROWN JUG AND A TRIP TO THE LIBERTY BOWL.

130

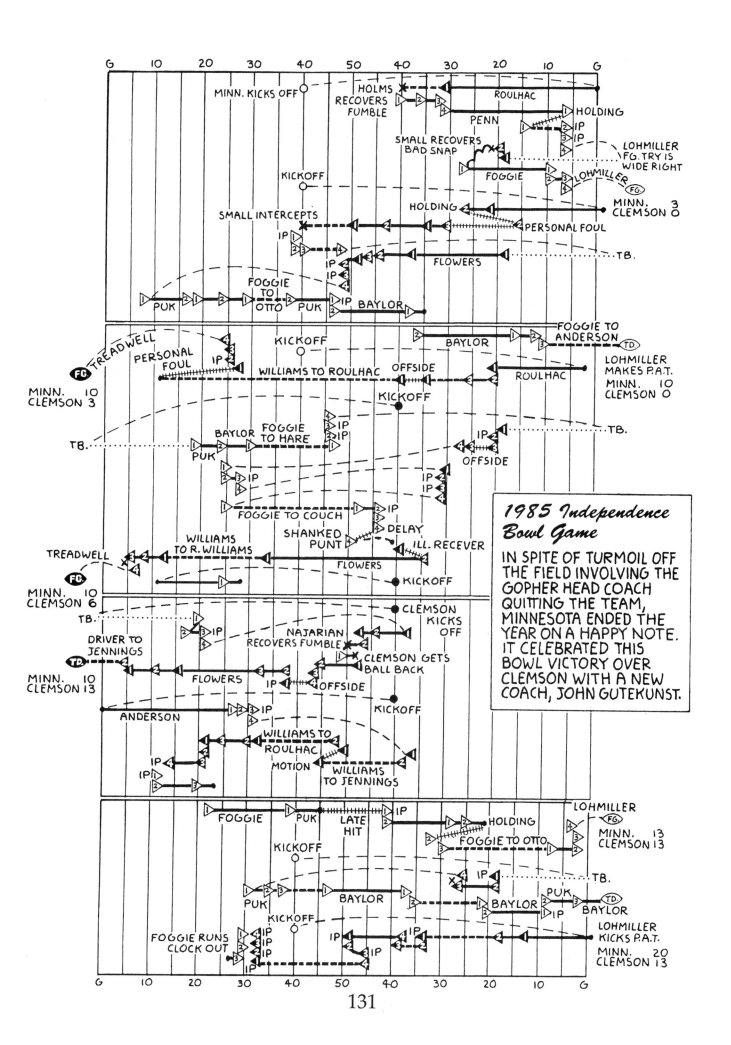

1985 Independence Bowl Game

IN SPITE OF TURMOIL OFF THE FIELD INVOLVING THE GOPHER HEAD COACH QUITTING THE TEAM, MINNESOTA ENDED THE YEAR ON A HAPPY NOTE. IT CELEBRATED THIS BOWL VICTORY OVER CLEMSON WITH A NEW COACH, JOHN GUTEKUNST.

Rickey Foggie

BEFORE ENDING HIS DAYS FOR THE MAROON AND GOLD IN 1987, RICKEY FOGGIE WAS A THREAT EVERY TIME HE TOUCHED THE BALL. PLAYING FROM THE OPTION, HE BECAME ONLY THE THIRD QUARTERBACK IN COLLEGE HISTORY TO RUN OVER 2,000 YARDS AND PASS FOR OVER 4,000.

132

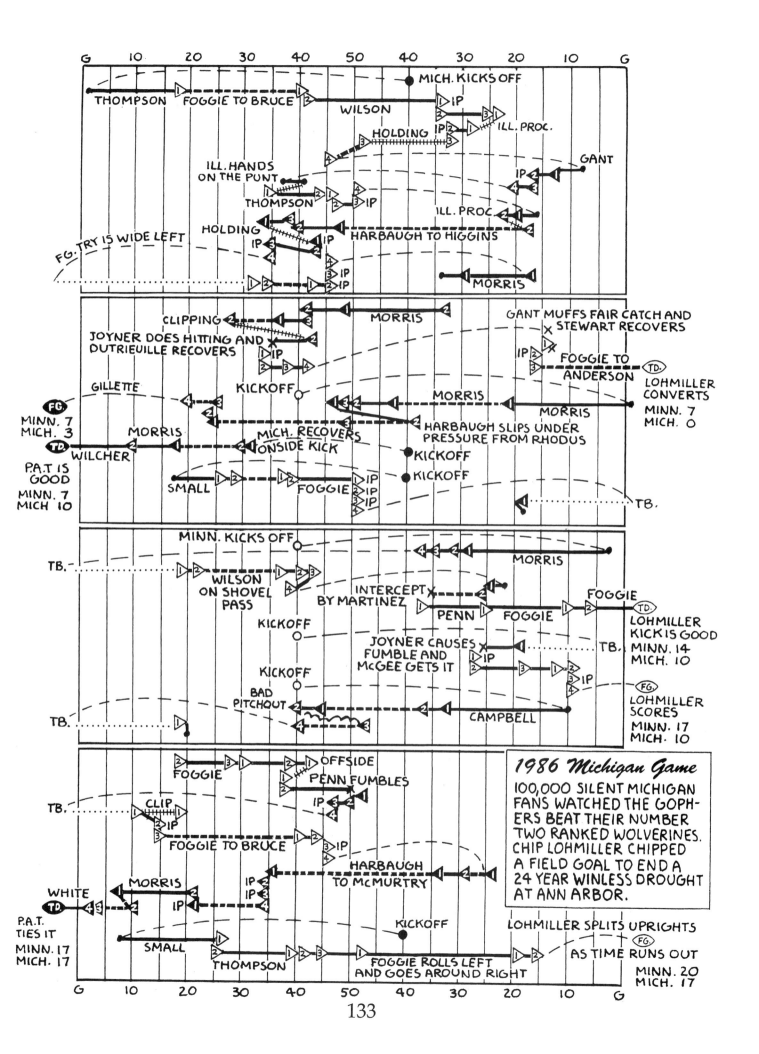

1986 Michigan Game

100,000 SILENT MICHIGAN FANS WATCHED THE GOPHERS BEAT THEIR NUMBER TWO RANKED WOLVERINES. CHIP LOHMILLER CHIPPED A FIELD GOAL TO END A 24 YEAR WINLESS DROUGHT AT ANN ARBOR.

Darrell Thompson

AS A ROOKIE THIS POPULAR RUNNING BACK, FROM ROCHESTER JOHN MARSHALL, WAS ELECTED M.V.P. BY HIS TEAMMATES. HE PERSONALLY BOUGHT AND PRESENTED TROPHIES TO HIS LINEMEN IN GRATITUDE FOR HELPING HIM GET THROUGH THE LINE.

HE SET A NATIONAL RECORD FOR MOST YARDS (205) RUSHING BY A FRESHMAN IN A FIRST GAME.

AGAINST MICHIGAN HE SET A BIG TEN MARK IN 1987 WITH A 98 YARD RUN. HIS OVER 200 YARDS FOR THE DAY IS THE HIGHEST TOTAL ANYONE HAS EVER MADE AGAINST A MICHIGAN TEAM.

THOMPSON CHALKED UP THREE 1000 YARD SEASONS IN RUSHING AND BARELY MISSED THE FOURTH, DUE TO INJURY. HE RAN FARTHER (4518 YARDS) THAN ANY GOPHER IN HISTORY AND SCORED THE MOST TOUCHDOWNS (43) FOR THE MOST POINTS (260).

HE ATTEMPTED TWO PASSES IN HIS MINNESOTA CAREER... BOTH GOOD FOR TOUCHDOWNS.

GREEN BAY DRAFTED HIM IN THE FIRST ROUND.

Chip Lohmiller

SUREFOOTED KICKER FROM WOODBURY, MINNESOTA.

HE LAUNCHED A 62 YARD FIELDGOAL AGAINST IOWA IN 1986 TO SET A NATIONAL INDOOR RECORD.

IN 1992 HE RETURNED TO THE DOME AS A WASHINGTON REDSKIN TO MAKE THREE FIELDGOALS IN A WINNING SUPER BOWL EFFORT.

Jim Wacker

CARRYING A SPARKLING RESUME FOR REBUILDING, JIM WACKER ARRIVED WITH HIS WIDE OPEN PASSING ATTACK.

EXCITING HEART ATTACKS BEGAN IN HIS SECOND GAME WHICH WAS AGAINST HIGHLY RATED COLORADO. THE GOPHERS SUCCESSFULLY FAKE PUNTED FROM THE END ZONE TO MARCH DOWN FIELD. THE FIELD GOAL TRY MISSED BY A FOOT AS TIME RAN OUT IN A ONE POINT LOSS. THE NEXT YEAR PRODUCED A WILD VICTORY OVER PURDUE, 59-56, AS WELL AS DEFEATING ROSE BOWL-BOUND WISCONSIN.

THOUGH BEATING A RANKED SYRACUSE TEAM AND ALMOST UPSETTING NORTHWESTERN IN HIS FIFTH YEAR, HE COULDN'T TURN THE WIN-LOSS COLUMN AROUND.

Governor's Victory Bell

THE GOPHERS PLAYED PENN STATE IN THE NITTANY LIONS' FIRST GAME AS A BIG TEN MEMBER ON SEPTEMBER 4, 1993.

THE GAME TROPHY SIGNIFYING THIS EVENT WAS INAUGURATED BY THE ACTING GOVERNOR MARK SINGEL OF PENNSYLVANIA AND GOVERNOR ARNIE CARLSON OF MINNESOTA.

THE GOPHERS PLAY FOR MORE GAME TROPHIES- FOUR-THAN ANY OTHER TEAM.

Marquel Fleetwood

THE LONGEST TOUCHDOWN
PASS PLAY IN THE NATION FOR
1992 WAS FROM MARQUEL
FLEETWOOD TO JOHN LEWIS.
IT WENT AGAINST MICHIGAN
FOR 94 YARDS.

John Lewis

Bronko Nagurski Trophy

PERHAPS THE GREATEST PLAYER OF THEM ALL, MINNESOTA'S BRONKO NAGURSKI, INSPIRES THE NAME OF THIS TROPHY.

THE "COLLEGE FOOTBALL DEFENSIVE PLAYER OF THE YEAR AWARD" WAS BEGUN IN 1993 BY THE FOOTBALL WRITERS ASSOCIATION OF AMERICA.

BRONKO NAGURSKI TROPHY

COLLEGE FOOTBALL DEFENSIVE PLAYER OF THE YEAR AWARD

IN 1999 GLEN MASON WAS RECOGNIZED AS BIG TEN AND NATIONAL COACH OF THE YEAR. HE WAS ALSO COACH OF THE YEAR IN TWO PREVIOUS CONFERENCES. 2002 SAW HIM ELECTED PRESIDENT OF THE AMERICAN FOOTBALL COACHES ASSOCIATION.

Glen Mason

HE BROUGHT WINNING BACK WITH THE GOPHERS' HIGHEST SCORING OFFENSE SINCE HENRY WILLIAMS. HIS TEN WINS IN 2003 WERE THE MOST SINCE 1905. THAT SAME TEAM ALSO SET A BIG TEN RECORD IN TOTAL OFFENSE.

HIS 1000 YARD DUO RUSHING CLUB STRETCHED TO A RECORD THREE YEARS. SEVEN OF HIS TEN TEAMS WENT TO BOWLS.

HIGLIGHTS WERE BEATING SECOND RANKED PENN STATE AND FIFTH RANKED OHIO STATE IN THEIR OWN BACK-YARDS.

140

Lamanzer Williams

COACH MASON SAID, "IF THEY DON'T DOUBLE-TEAM HIM, HE SACKS THE QUARTERBACK."

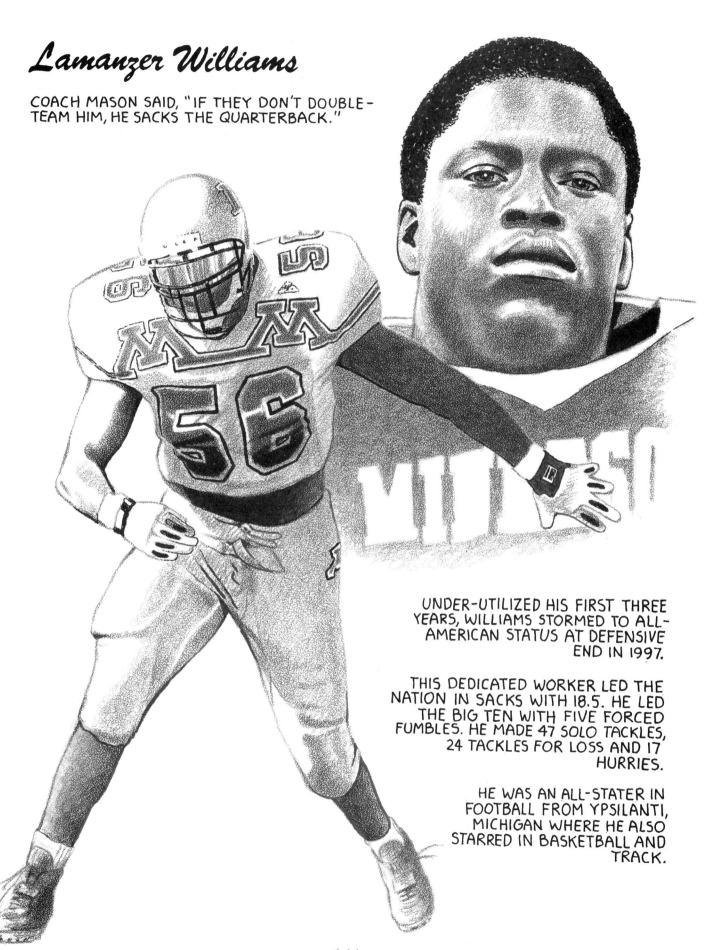

UNDER-UTILIZED HIS FIRST THREE YEARS, WILLIAMS STORMED TO ALL-AMERICAN STATUS AT DEFENSIVE END IN 1997.

THIS DEDICATED WORKER LED THE NATION IN SACKS WITH 18.5. HE LED THE BIG TEN WITH FIVE FORCED FUMBLES. HE MADE 47 SOLO TACKLES, 24 TACKLES FOR LOSS AND 17 HURRIES.

HE WAS AN ALL-STATER IN FOOTBALL FROM YPSILANTI, MICHIGAN WHERE HE ALSO STARRED IN BASKETBALL AND TRACK.

141

Tutu Atwell

IOWA STATE SHOULDN'T HAVE KICKED ANYWHERE NEAR TUTU ATWELL IN 1997.

THE 53-29 GOPHER VICTORY EXTENDED TO 99 YEARS SINCE IOWA STATE HAD BEATEN MINNESOTA.

IN THIS GAME HE SET A NATIONAL RECORD FOR MOST YARDS RETURNED FROM KICKS... 59 YARDS FROM PUNTS AND 225 YARDS FROM KICKOFFS. TWO OF HIS RUNBACKS TIED THE NATIONAL RECORD FOR MOST TOUCHDOWNS ON KICKOFF RETURNS IN A GAME. THEY WENT 89 AND 93 YARDS.

142

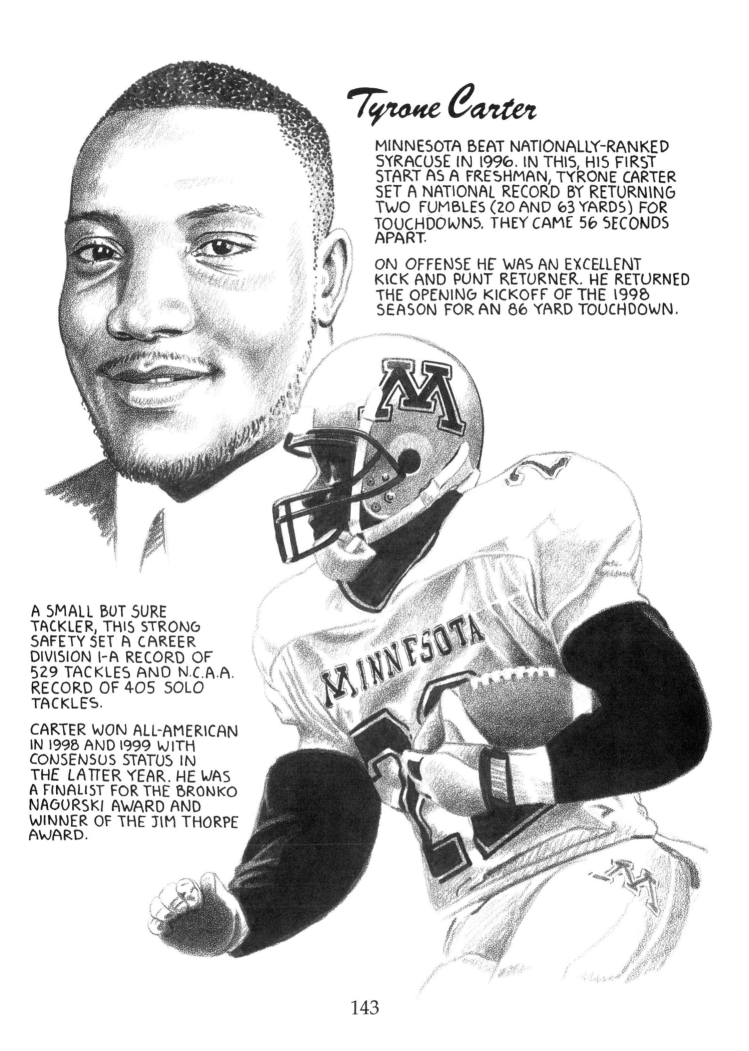

Tyrone Carter

MINNESOTA BEAT NATIONALLY-RANKED SYRACUSE IN 1996. IN THIS, HIS FIRST START AS A FRESHMAN, TYRONE CARTER SET A NATIONAL RECORD BY RETURNING TWO FUMBLES (20 AND 63 YARDS) FOR TOUCHDOWNS. THEY CAME 56 SECONDS APART.

ON OFFENSE HE WAS AN EXCELLENT KICK AND PUNT RETURNER. HE RETURNED THE OPENING KICKOFF OF THE 1998 SEASON FOR AN 86 YARD TOUCHDOWN.

A SMALL BUT SURE TACKLER, THIS STRONG SAFETY SET A CAREER DIVISION I-A RECORD OF 529 TACKLES AND N.C.A.A. RECORD OF 405 SOLO TACKLES.

CARTER WON ALL-AMERICAN IN 1998 AND 1999 WITH CONSENSUS STATUS IN THE LATTER YEAR. HE WAS A FINALIST FOR THE BRONKO NAGURSKI AWARD AND WINNER OF THE JIM THORPE AWARD.

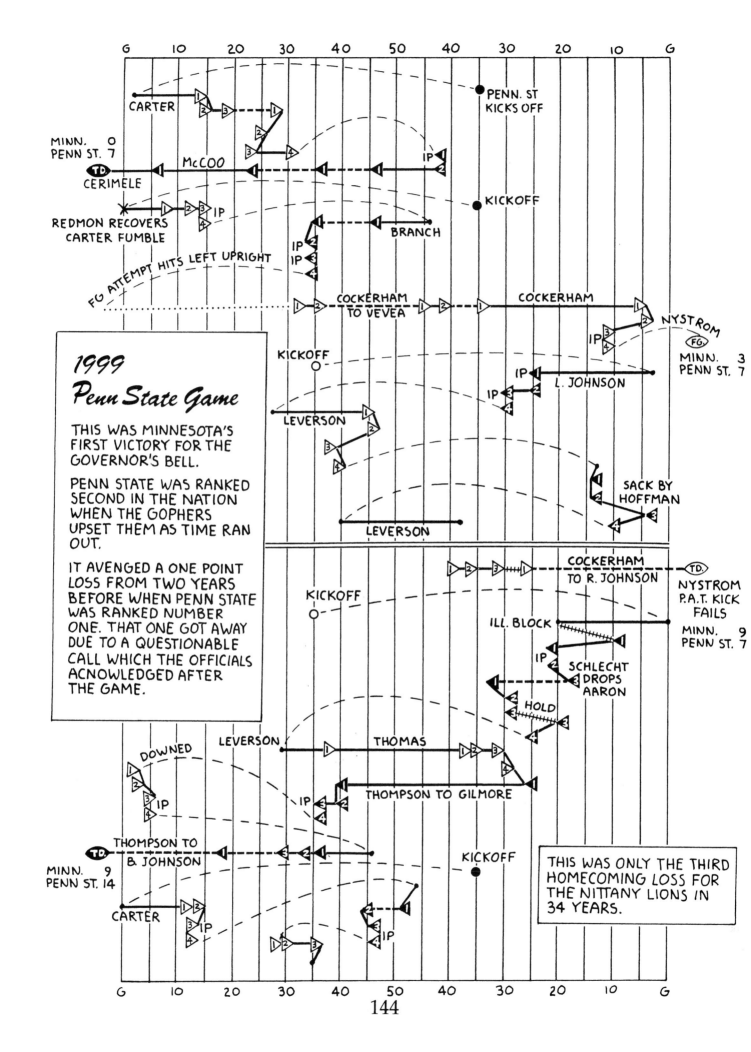

G 10 20 30 40 50 40 30 20 10 G

● PENN. ST
KICKS OFF

CARTER

MINN. 0
PENN ST. 7
TD CERIMELE

McCOO

IP

● KICKOFF

REDMON RECOVERS
CARTER FUMBLE

IP

IP
IP

BRANCH

FG ATTEMPT HITS LEFT UPRIGHT

COCKERHAM
TO VEVEA

COCKERHAM

NYSTROM
FG

MINN. 3
PENN ST. 7

1999
Penn State Game

THIS WAS MINNESOTA'S
FIRST VICTORY FOR THE
GOVERNOR'S BELL.

PENN STATE WAS RANKED
SECOND IN THE NATION
WHEN THE GOPHERS
UPSET THEM AS TIME RAN
OUT.

IT AVENGED A ONE POINT
LOSS FROM TWO YEARS
BEFORE WHEN PENN STATE
WAS RANKED NUMBER
ONE. THAT ONE GOT AWAY
DUE TO A QUESTIONABLE
CALL WHICH THE OFFICIALS
ACNOWLEDGED AFTER
THE GAME.

KICKOFF ○

LEVERSON

LEVERSON

IP
IP
L. JOHNSON

SACK BY
HOFFMAN

COCKERHAM
TO R. JOHNSON

TD NYSTROM
P.A.T. KICK
FAILS

MINN. 9
PENN ST. 7

KICKOFF ○

ILL. BLOCK

IP
SCHLECHT
DROPS
AARON

HOLD

DOWNED

IP

LEVERSON THOMAS

THOMPSON TO GILMORE

IP

THOMPSON TO
B. JOHNSON

MINN. 9
PENN ST. 14

TD

CARTER

IP

KICKOFF
●

IP

THIS WAS ONLY THE THIRD
HOMECOMING LOSS FOR
THE NITTANY LIONS IN
34 YEARS.

G 10 20 30 40 50 40 30 20 10 G

144

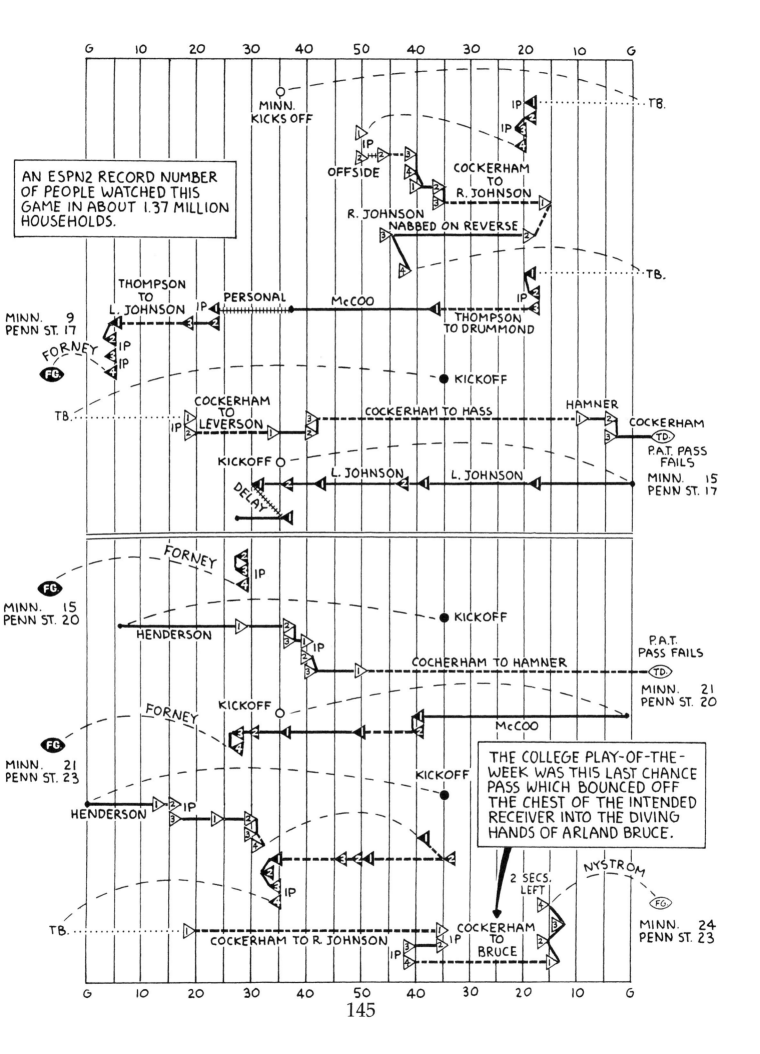

AN ESPN2 RECORD NUMBER OF PEOPLE WATCHED THIS GAME IN ABOUT 1.37 MILLION HOUSEHOLDS.

MINN. KICKS OFF

OFFSIDE

IP

COCKERHAM TO R. JOHNSON

R. JOHNSON NABBED ON REVERSE

TB.

TB.

THOMPSON TO L. JOHNSON

PERSONAL

McCOO

THOMPSON TO DRUMMOND

MINN. 9
PENN ST. 17

FORNEY

IP
IP

FG

TB.

COCKERHAM TO LEVERSON

COCKERHAM TO HASS

HAMNER

COCKERHAM

TD.

P.A.T. PASS FAILS

KICKOFF

KICKOFF

DELAY

L. JOHNSON

L. JOHNSON

MINN. 15
PENN ST. 17

FORNEY

IP

FG

MINN. 15
PENN ST. 20

KICKOFF

HENDERSON

IP

COCHERHAM TO HAMNER

P.A.T. PASS FAILS

TD.

MINN. 21
PENN ST. 20

FORNEY

KICKOFF

McCOO

FG

MINN. 21
PENN ST. 23

THE COLLEGE PLAY-OF-THE-WEEK WAS THIS LAST CHANCE PASS WHICH BOUNCED OFF THE CHEST OF THE INTENDED RECEIVER INTO THE DIVING HANDS OF ARLAND BRUCE.

HENDERSON

IP

KICKOFF

2 SECS. LEFT

NYSTROM

FG

IP

COCKERHAM TO BRUCE

MINN. 24
PENN ST. 23

TB.

COCKERHAM TO R. JOHNSON

IP

IP

BEN HAMILTON CAME FROM PLYMOUTH, MINNESOTA WHERE HE WAS ALL-STATE FOR WAYZATA HIGH. HE ALWAYS WANTED TO PLAY FOR THE GOPHERS BUT HIS LEAN SIZE CAST DOUBTS.

HE OVERCAME THEM TO BE THE TEAM ANCHOR AT CENTER WHERE HE WON ALL-AMERICAN RECOGNITION IN 1999 AND 2000.

HE WAS FOUR TIMES ON THE BIG TEN ALL-ACADEMIC TEAM.

Ben Hamilton

TWICE HE WAS TEAM CAPTAIN. ONLY ONE SACK WAS RECORDED AGAINST HIM IN 1999 AND HE HAD NO PENALTIES IN TWO YEARS.

146

Tellis Redmon

IN THE MICRONPC.COM BOWL OF 2000 TELLIS REDMON TIED A NATIONAL BOWL RECORD FOR MOST ALL PURPOSE PLAYS.

HE HAD 42 RUSHES, 3 RECEPTIONS AND 2 PUNT RETURNS FOR A TOTAL OF 47.

Ron Johnson

RESISTING TEMPTATION TO TURN PRO AFTER HIS JUNIOR YEAR, RON JOHNSON STAYED A GOPHER TO PUT HIS ACCOMPLISHMENTS IN THE RECORD BOOKS.

HE BECAME RANKED AS ONE OF THE BEST RECEIVERS IN BIG TEN HISTORY BY PLACING SEVENTH IN ALL-TIME YARDS, FIFTH IN TOUCHDOWNS AND THIRD IN CAREER CATCHES. HE TOOK OVER FIVE OF SIX GOPHER RECEIVING RECORDS.

IN PRACTICE, BEFORE THE FINAL GAME OF HIS LAST YEAR IN 2001, HE DISLOCATED TWO FINGERS. ONE BONE BROKE THROUGH THE SKIN. IT DIDN'T STOP HIM FROM CATCHING A 45 YARD PASS FOR A GAME-CLINCHING TOUCHDOWN. HE TIED A NATIONAL RECORD FOR HAVING RECEIVED PASSES IN 46 CONSECUTIVE GAMES.

Preston Gruening

FROM THE FIRST PUNT OF THE 2000 SEASON TO ITS END, PRESTON GRUENING LED THE NATION IN PUNTING AVERAGE. THAT OPENING BOOT WENT 65 YARDS.

HIS 45.2 YARDS AVERAGE FOR THE YEAR WON HIM ALL-AMERICAN RECOGNITION AS WELL AS BEING A FINALIST FOR THE RAY GUY AWARD.

ONLY 21 OF HIS 50 KICKS WERE RETURNED.

HE WAS ALSO KNOWN TO PASS ON FAKE PUNTS. ONE OF HIS TOUCHDOWN TOSSES SEALED A WIN OVER WISCONSIN, HIS HOME STATE, IN 2001.

149

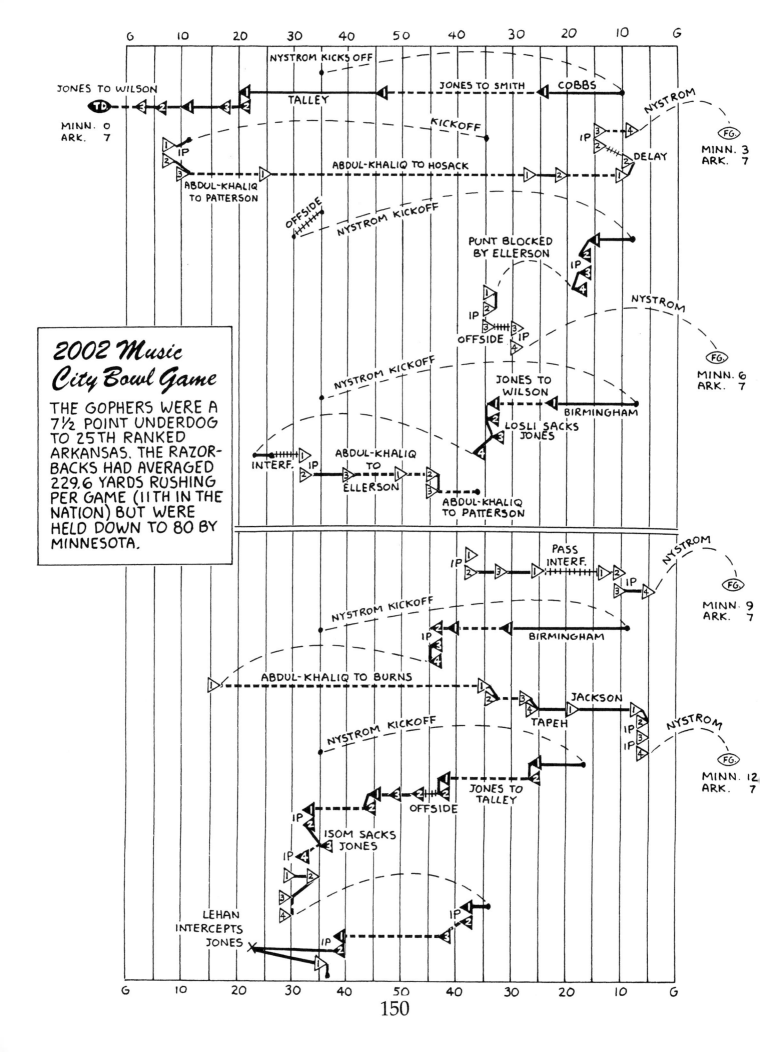

2002 Music City Bowl Game

THE GOPHERS WERE A 7½ POINT UNDERDOG TO 25TH RANKED ARKANSAS. THE RAZORBACKS HAD AVERAGED 229.6 YARDS RUSHING PER GAME (11TH IN THE NATION) BUT WERE HELD DOWN TO 80 BY MINNESOTA.

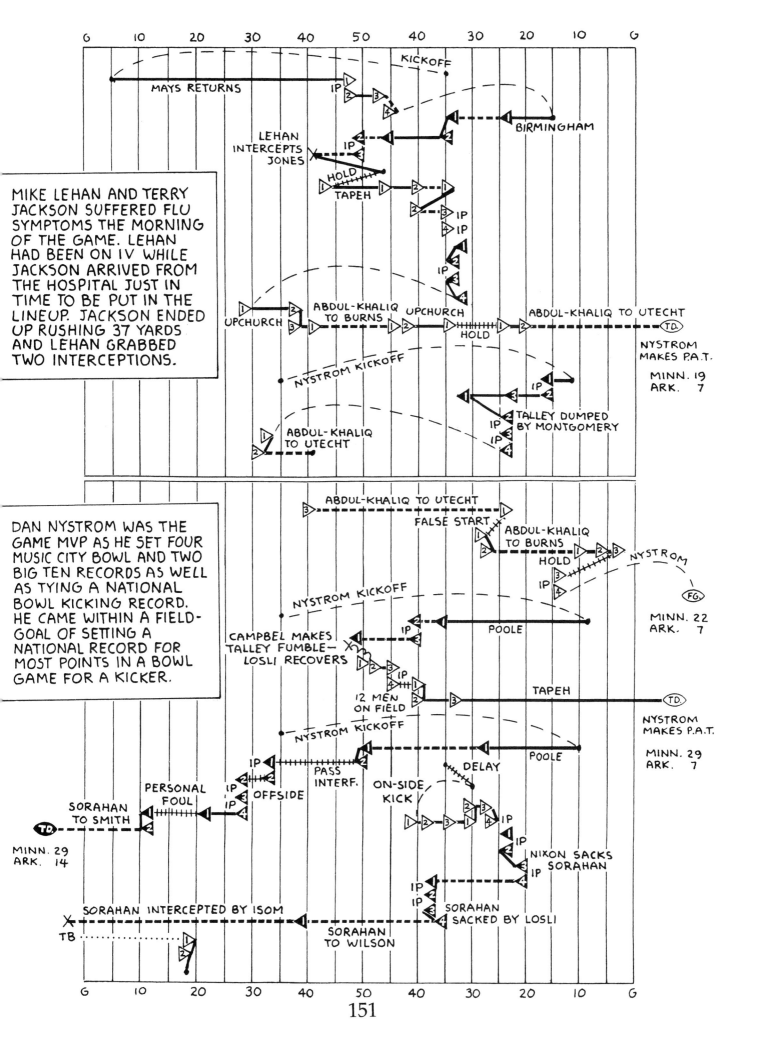

MIKE LEHAN AND TERRY JACKSON SUFFERED FLU SYMPTOMS THE MORNING OF THE GAME. LEHAN HAD BEEN ON IV WHILE JACKSON ARRIVED FROM THE HOSPITAL JUST IN TIME TO BE PUT IN THE LINEUP. JACKSON ENDED UP RUSHING 37 YARDS AND LEHAN GRABBED TWO INTERCEPTIONS.

DAN NYSTROM WAS THE GAME MVP AS HE SET FOUR MUSIC CITY BOWL AND TWO BIG TEN RECORDS AS WELL AS TYING A NATIONAL BOWL KICKING RECORD. HE CAME WITHIN A FIELD-GOAL OF SETTING A NATIONAL RECORD FOR MOST POINTS IN A BOWL GAME FOR A KICKER.

151

Dan Nystrom

DAN NYSTROM CAME FROM COOPER HIGH SCHOOL IN NEW HOPE AS A TWO-TIME ALL-STATER.

AS A GOPHER HE SET RECORDS FOR MOST CAREER POINTS IN BIG TEN HISTORY (367) AND MOST FIELDGOALS (71).

HE KICKED THE WINNING POINTS IN THE 1999 PENN STATE GAME AS TIME RAN OUT AND MADE BIG TEN PLAYER OF THE WEEK FOR TWO CONSECUTIVE WEEKS... AS A FRESHMAN.

HIS NEARLY PERFECT FINAL YEAR SAW HIM MAKE 20 OF 21 FIELDGOALS AND 42 OF 42 CONVERSION KICKS. HIS LAST GAME EARNED HIM M.V.P. RECOGNITION IN THE 2002 MUSIC CITY BOWL AGAINST ARKANSAS. HE EQUALED A NATIONAL RECORD FIVE FIELDGOALS FOR A BOWL GAME.

HIS GOPHER CAREER ENDED WITH A STRING OF 87 CONVERSION KICKS AND HE BECAME THE FIRST PLAYER TO LEAD MINNESOTA IN MOST POINTS FOR FOUR STRAIGHT YEARS.

152

THIS SPEEDSTER WAS MISSOURI STATE HIGH SCHOOL CHAMPION IN THE 4X400. HE PROCEEDED TO RUN CIRCLES AROUND GOPHER OPPONENTS. HIS BIG DAY WAS AS CO-BIG TEN PLAYER OF THE WEEK BY CARRYING 46 TIMES FOR 217 YARDS AND 333 ALL-PURPOSE YARDS. HE RUSHED OVER 1000 YARDS IN EACH OF HIS THREE YEARS. 21 OF HIS GAMES WENT OVER 100 YARDS. A FEW OF THEM WERE ATTAINED IN NEARLY ONE PLAY OF 80 YARDS OR MORE. THREE TIMES HE RAN OVER 200 AND HAD A CAREER AVERAGE OF 5.96 YARDS PER RUSH.

HE TEAMED WITH MARION BARBER III OR GARY RUSSELL TEN TIMES IN GAMES WHERE TWO PLAYERS RAN 100 YARDS.

Lawrence Maroney

A LATE SEASON FOOT INJURY TRIPPED HIS CHANCES FOR THE HEISMAN BUT HE RECEIVED RECOGNITION AS ALL-AMERICAN IN 2005. HE WAS TAKEN IN THE N.F.L. FIRST ROUND DRAFT BY THE NEW ENGLAND PATRIOTS.

153

Marion Barber III

Lawrence Maroney

Gary Russell

UNCHARTED HISTORY WAS MADE BY
THESE THREE GOPHERS. THEY SET
A NATIONAL RECORD FOR HAVING
TWO PLAYERS ON THE SAME
TEAM RUSH OVER 1000 YARDS
FOR THREE CONSECUTIVE SEASONS.

2003	BARBER	1196
	MARONEY	1121
2004	BARBER	1348
	MARONEY	1269
2005	MARONEY	1355
	RUSSELL	1045

154

Mark Setterstrom

HE HAILED FROM NORTHFIELD, MINNESOTA WHERE HE WAS AN ALL-STATER.

FROM THEIR TRUE FRESHMEN SEASON, HE AND GREG ESLINGER STARTED EVERY GAME OF THEIR FOUR YEARS SIDE-BY-SIDE. THEY WERE A BIG REASON FOR THE RECORD EXPLOSION OF 1000 YARD TANDEM RUSHERS FOR THREE OF THOSE YEARS. DURING THAT TIME THE OVERALL RUSH AVERAGE WAS 274 YARDS PER GAME.

SETTERSTROM, KNOWN FOR HIS TOUGHNESS, WAS THOUGHT TO "MAUL" HIS OPPONENTS. HE SAID, "YOU HAVE TO TREAT PRACTICE LIKE GAMES. YOU CAN'T TAKE PLAYS OFF OR TAKE PRACTICE OFF." HE WON ALL-AMERICAN HONORS AS GUARD IN 2004.

MINNESOTA WAS THE ONLY DIVISION I-A
TEAM TO OFFER ESLINGER A
SCHOLARSHIP. HE CAME FROM
BISMARCK, N.D.

HE HAD NEVER PLAYED CENTER
BEFOREHAND, BUT GOT THE
JOB BECAUSE HE "UNDERSTOOD
LEVERAGE... HE NEVER
SEEMED OFF-BALANCE."
THAT WENT FOR ON AND
OFF THE FIELD. AN IOWA
OPPONENT SAID, "THERE'S
NOT A BETTER REPRESENT-
ATIVE FOR OUR LEAGUE
AS FAR AS TALENT AND
SPORTSMANSHIP AND
PLAYING THE GAME THE
RIGHT WAY."

Greg Eslinger

HE WAS RECOGNIZED AS ALL-AMERICAN IN 2004. HIS
CAREER WAS TOPPED OFF IN 2005 AS A THREE-TIME
ALL-BIG TEN, CONFERENCE LINEMAN OF THE YEAR,
CONSENSUS ALL-AMERICAN, OUTLAND AND RIMINGTON
TROPHY WINNER AND FINALIST FOR THE GRADDY TROPHY
(THE ACADEMIC HEISMAN). THE STAR-TRIBUNE
NAMED HIM SPORTSMAN OF THE YEAR.

156

SPAETH WAS ON THE ALL-METRO TEAM WHILE PLAYING FOR ST. MICHAEL-ALBERTVILLE. HE CONTINUED ON TO EARN ALL-AMERICAN AND MACKEY AWARDS FOR MINNESOTA IN 2006.

DEFENSIVE END WAS HIS POSITION BEFORE HE WAS MOVED TO TIGHT END. FROM THERE HE SET A GOPHER RECORD FOR RECEPTIONS AND RECEIVING YARDAGE, BUT WAS MOSTLY KNOWN FOR HIS BLOCKING.

Matt Spaeth

NEVER COMPLAINING, HE PLAYED WITH A WORSENING SPORTS HERNIA IN 2004. IN HIS FINAL YEAR, HE SUFFERED A SHOULDER SEPARATION WHICH NEEDED SURGERY. HE PUT IT OFF TO HELP HIS TEAM WIN ITS FINAL THREE GAMES TO QUALIFY FOR A BOWL.

STARTING AS AN ALL-BIG TEN PLAYER FOR ILLINOIS, TIM BREWSTER WENT INTO COACHING WHERE HE BUILT A REPUTATION AS A STRONG COLLEGE RECRUITER. IT HAS BEEN A MISSING INGREDIENT FOR THE GOPHERS WHICH HAVE LACKED DEPTH WHILE FIELDING SOME GREAT STARS.

Tim Brewster

HE TURNED AROUND A FIRST YEAR LOSING SEASON INTO A WINNING SECOND WHICH INCLUDED A BOWL APPEARANCE.

HIS LAST STINT WAS IN THE PRO RANKS AS DENVER'S TIGHT ENDS COACH BEFORE COMING TO BUILD A NEW OFFENSE FROM SCRATCH. IT HAS BEEN UP AND DOWN, SO FAR. HE HAS UNTIRING ENERGY AND CAN-DO FOCUS. WITH THE SETTLING IN OF HIS RECRUITS AND NEW STADIUM, IT IS HOPED THAT SUCCESS LOOMS NEAR.

158

Halsey Hall

OVER THE LONG STRETCH THE MOST FAMILIAR VOICES TO MINNESOTA FANS WERE HALSEY "HOLY COW" HALL AND JULES PERLT.

HALSEY'S FRIENDLY VOICE AND INFECTIOUS LAUGHTER, COUPLED WITH HIS DEEP KNOWLEDGE OF THE GAME, WERE A JOY TO LISTEN TO. HE WAS A SPORTS WRITER AS WELL AS SPORTSCASTER.

IN 1934 HE WAS CREDITED WITH GIVING THE GOPHERS THE NICKNAME "GOLDEN GOPHERS." THIS WAS DUE TO THEIR ALL-GOLD UNIFORMS. COACH BIERMAN DECIDED ON THE ALL-GOLD LOOK BECAUSE HE THOUGHT THE COLOR WOULD BEST HIDE THE BALL.

Jules Perlt

JULES PERLT'S DISTINCTIVE AND DRAMATIC VOICE WAS "THE" VOICE OF U OF M SPORTS FOR OVER 50 YEARS. FROM BRONKO NAGURSKI TO DARRELL THOMPSON, HE KEPT STADIUM FANS INFORMED OF WHAT WAS HAPPENING ON THE FIELD. SOMEHOW THINGS WEREN'T OFFICIAL UNTIL HE SPOKE.

Minnesota's Home Fields

THESE FIELD LOCATIONS ARE
SHOWN ON PRESENT DAY STREETS.

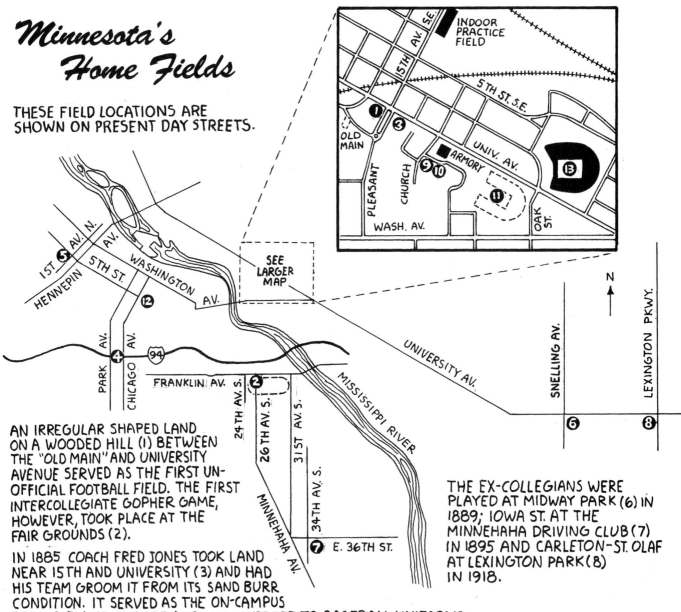

AN IRREGULAR SHAPED LAND
ON A WOODED HILL (1) BETWEEN
THE "OLD MAIN" AND UNIVERSITY
AVENUE SERVED AS THE FIRST UN-
OFFICIAL FOOTBALL FIELD. THE FIRST
INTERCOLLEGIATE GOPHER GAME,
HOWEVER, TOOK PLACE AT THE
FAIR GROUNDS (2).

IN 1885 COACH FRED JONES TOOK LAND
NEAR 15TH AND UNIVERSITY (3) AND HAD
HIS TEAM GROOM IT FROM ITS SAND BURR
CONDITION. IT SERVED AS THE ON-CAMPUS
FIELD. A FIX-UP COST OF $70 WAS DIVERTED TO BASEBALL UNIFORMS.

THE EX-COLLEGIANS WERE
PLAYED AT MIDWAY PARK (6) IN
1889; IOWA ST. AT THE
MINNEHAHA DRIVING CLUB (7)
IN 1895 AND CARLETON-ST. OLAF
AT LEXINGTON PARK (8)
IN 1918.

IN 1886 OFF-CAMPUS FIELDS WERE LEASED. THE FIRST CHARGED ADMISSION TOOK PLACE AT THE
PARK AVENUE GROUNDS (4). LATER ATHLETIC PARK (5) WAS RENTED AND SERVED AS THE MOST USED
HOME. IT SEATED 4000 FANS. NORTHWESTERN PROTESTED THE FIELD IN 1892 BECAUSE IT WASN'T
REGULATION SIZE. A FEW FEET WERE ADDED TO MAKE IT RIGHT.

THE CAMPUS ARMORY WAS BUILT IN 1896 AND SERVED AS TRAINING QUARTERS. AT THE SAME TIME A
FIELD WAS MADE JUST SOUTH OF IT (9). THIS FIELD HAD ONLY CHAIRS ALONG THE SIDELINE WITH NO
ENCLOSED FENCE. BEING INADEQUATE, GAMES WERE CONTINUED AT ATHLETIC PARK UNTIL 1899.
THE ARMORY SITE WAS FIXED WITH A GRANDSTAND SEATING 3000 AND THE STUDENTS BUILT A
FENCE. IT BECAME THE FIRST NORTHROP FIELD.

THE GREATER NORTHROP FIELD (10) WAS BUILT UNDER FRED JONES' DIRECTION. IT WAS THE FINEST
IN THE COUNTRY WITH A SEATING OF 10,000. ANOTHER 10,000 COULD BE ADDED IN BLEACHERS
AND STANDING ROOM. THOUGH USED THROUGHOUT THE SEASON, IT WASN'T COMPLETED
UNTIL THE HISTORIC 1903 MICHIGAN GAME.

THEN CAME MEMORIAL STADIUM (11) WHICH WAS READY FOR THE 1924 SEASON. FUNDS
WERE RAISED IN AN OVERWHELMING MANNER BY SUBSCRIPTION AND IT WAS DEDICATED TO THE
MINNESOTANS WHO DIED IN WORLD WAR I. ITS BIGGEST CROWD WAS 66,284 AGAINST
PURDUE IN 1961. THE GOPHERS MOVED TO THE METRODOME (12) IN 1982 AND BACK TO THE
CAMPUS (13) IN 2009.

Extra Points

MINNESOTA, MICHIGAN AND NORTHWESTERN FORMED THE "INTERCOLLEGIATE ATHLETIC ASSOCIATION OF THE NORTHWEST" IN 1892. IT COVERED FOOTBALL, BASEBALL AND TRACK. THE ASSOCIATION DISBANDED AFTER ITS SECOND SEASON WITH MINNESOTA WINNING THE ONLY TWO FOOTBALL CHAMPIONSHIPS.

THE 1933 TEAM HAD A 4-WIN 4-TIE SEASON WHILE SCORING ONLY 64 POINTS TO THEIR OPPONENTS' 32. STILL, THEY WERE RATED THIRD NATIONALLY BEHIND MICHIGAN AND NEBRASKA.

GOPHER M.J. LUBY WAS ONE OF THE FOUNDERS OF A PUBLICATION CALLED "FOOTBALL" IN 1899. "FOOTBALL" EVOLVED INTO THE "MINNESOTA DAILY" WITH LUBY AS ITS FIRST MANAGER.

MINNESOTA MAY HAVE PLAYED IN THE DOME, BUT THE FIRST INDOOR GAME HAD PENN PLAYING RUTGERS IN 1887 AT MADISON SQUARE GARDEN, N.Y.

THE MINNEAPOLIS PARK BOARD, IN 1933, RECEIVED A SUGGESTION THAT IT BUILD A COVERED FIELD-HOUSE FOR PROFESSIONAL FOOTBALL DURING THE WINTER MONTHS.

ALF PILLSBURY WON 14 LETTERS AT THE 'U', SEVEN IN FOOTBALL AND SEVEN MORE IN BASEBALL.

THE FOLLOWING WAS THE MINNESOTA FANS' RETALIATION FOR WISCONSIN'S "OLE" CHEER IN 1909:

OLE OLSON! YON YONSON!
VE SKIN VISKONSIN!
YAH-H-H!

MINNESOTA WON THE CHEERS AND THE GAME.

FORMER GOPHER, PUDGE HEFFELFINGER, INVENTED THE FIRST SHIN GUARDS WHILE AT YALE. WHEN THIS PROTECTIVE EQUIPMENT SHOWED UP AT MINNESOTA THE FIRST PLAYER SEEN WEARING THEM WAS CALLED A "BABY."

THE FIRST HOMECOMING BONFIRE AT MINNESOTA DATES BACK TO 1915.

IN 1889 MICHIGAN WAS CHALLENGED TO A GAME. THEY INSISTED ON $200 TRAVEL EXPENSES TO COME. THIS IDEA WAS DECLINED AND THE GAME WAS NOT PLAYED.

THE FIRST OUT-OF-STATE GAME FOR MINNESOTA WAS IN 1890 AGAINST GRINNELL COLLEGE IN IOWA (MINNESOTA 18 – GRINNELL 13).

HALL OF FAMER ED ROGERS PLAYED END IN THE DAYS BEFORE THE FORWARD PASS. SINCE HIS OUTPOST POSITION WAS CONSIDERED TOO FAR AWAY TO RUN AND GET THE BALL HE NEVER BECAME A BALL CARRIER.

CLARK SHAUGHNESSY WOULD BECOME AN ALL-AMERICAN AND ENTER THE HALL OF FAME AS A COACH, BUT MINNESOTA COACHES THOUGHT HIM TOO "CLUMSY" WHEN HE CAME TO TRY OUT. HENRY WILLIAMS ORDERED, "HEY RUBE! TRY IT AT GUARD." SHAUGHNESSY THEN PROCEEDED TO RIP THE VETERAN LINE TO SHREDS.

COACH BIERMAN ORDERD BOB FITCH TO START RUNNING AND THEN FORGOT TO TELL HIM TO STOP. FITCH WAS STILL RUNNING HOURS LATER.

MINNESOTA'S WINNINGEST COACH, HENRY WILLIAMS, RECRUITED PLAYERS BY WALKING THE CAMPUS AND ASKING BIG STUDENTS TO COME OUT FOR THE TEAM.

THE CHICAGO COLLEGE OF PHYSICIANS & SURGEONS CAME TO PLAY IN 1901. THE "GOPHER" YEARBOOK SAID OF THE FUTURE DOCTORS OF OUR HEALTH..."THE CHICAGO TEAM WAS A HEAVY ONE, BUT IN SUCH POOR PHYSICAL CONDITION THAT THE VARSITY WERE GIVEN BUT POOR PRACTICE."

THE 1898 ILLINOIS GAME WAS PLAYED IN MINUS 20° WEATHER. A KICK OUT OF BOUNDS LANDED IN A SNOW BANK. BOTH TEAMS BURIED THEMSELVES IN THE SNOW TO FIND THE BALL SO THEY COULD CONTINUE PLAY.

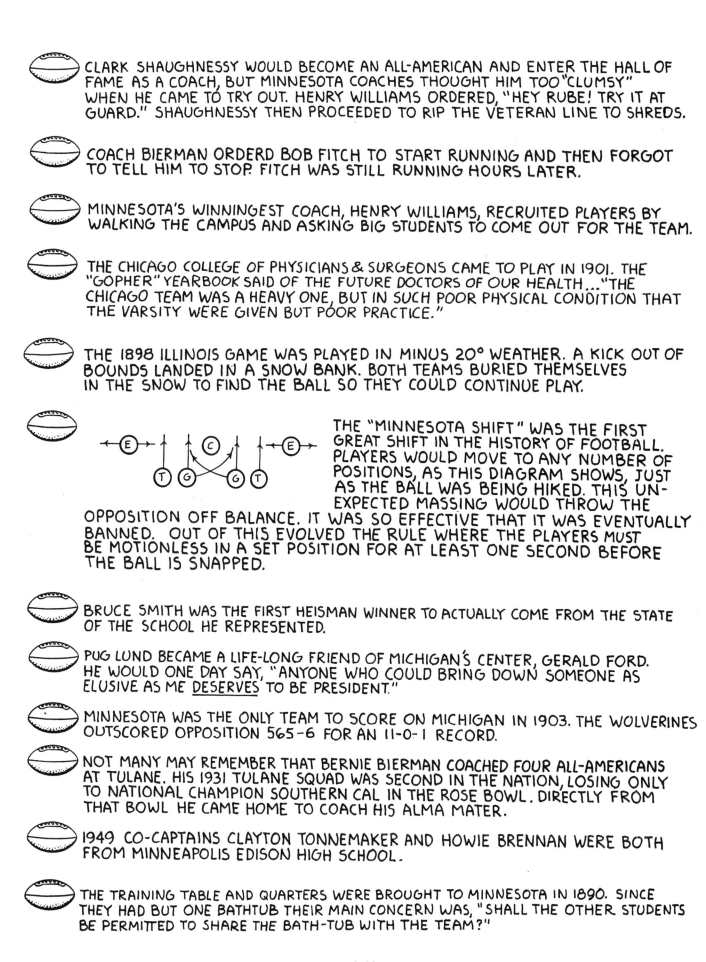

THE "MINNESOTA SHIFT" WAS THE FIRST GREAT SHIFT IN THE HISTORY OF FOOTBALL. PLAYERS WOULD MOVE TO ANY NUMBER OF POSITIONS, AS THIS DIAGRAM SHOWS, JUST AS THE BALL WAS BEING HIKED. THIS UN- EXPECTED MASSING WOULD THROW THE OPPOSITION OFF BALANCE. IT WAS SO EFFECTIVE THAT IT WAS EVENTUALLY BANNED. OUT OF THIS EVOLVED THE RULE WHERE THE PLAYERS MUST BE MOTIONLESS IN A SET POSITION FOR AT LEAST ONE SECOND BEFORE THE BALL IS SNAPPED.

BRUCE SMITH WAS THE FIRST HEISMAN WINNER TO ACTUALLY COME FROM THE STATE OF THE SCHOOL HE REPRESENTED.

PUG LUND BECAME A LIFE-LONG FRIEND OF MICHIGAN'S CENTER, GERALD FORD. HE WOULD ONE DAY SAY, "ANYONE WHO COULD BRING DOWN SOMEONE AS ELUSIVE AS ME DESERVES TO BE PRESIDENT."

MINNESOTA WAS THE ONLY TEAM TO SCORE ON MICHIGAN IN 1903. THE WOLVERINES OUTSCORED OPPOSITION 565-6 FOR AN 11-0-1 RECORD.

NOT MANY MAY REMEMBER THAT BERNIE BIERMAN COACHED FOUR ALL-AMERICANS AT TULANE. HIS 1931 TULANE SQUAD WAS SECOND IN THE NATION, LOSING ONLY TO NATIONAL CHAMPION SOUTHERN CAL IN THE ROSE BOWL. DIRECTLY FROM THAT BOWL HE CAME HOME TO COACH HIS ALMA MATER.

1949 CO-CAPTAINS CLAYTON TONNEMAKER AND HOWIE BRENNAN WERE BOTH FROM MINNEAPOLIS EDISON HIGH SCHOOL.

THE TRAINING TABLE AND QUARTERS WERE BROUGHT TO MINNESOTA IN 1890. SINCE THEY HAD BUT ONE BATHTUB THEIR MAIN CONCERN WAS, "SHALL THE OTHER STUDENTS BE PERMITTED TO SHARE THE BATH-TUB WITH THE TEAM?"

AGAINST MICHIGAN, IN 1935, TUFFY THOMPSON RETURNED KICKOFFS FOR 93 AND 95 YARDS.

ROBERT LIGGETT SCORED SEVEN TOUCHDOWNS AGAINST GRINNELL IN 1902.

HOWARD T. ABBOTT WAS CAPTAIN IN 1885 THOUGH NO GAMES WERE PLAYED THAT YEAR.

ALL-BIG TEN PLAYER CHUCK ORTMANN OF MICHIGAN SET A BIG TEN RECORD BY LOSING AN OVERALL 38 YARDS TO MINNESOTA IN 1950.

TULANE MADE GOOD USE OF FORMER GOPHER PLAYERS BY HAVING THEM AS THEIR HEAD COACHES: CLARK SHAUGHNESSY, BERNIE BIERMAN AND TED COX.

ADAM KELLY GOT OFF A PUNT OF 83 YARDS AGAINST IOWA IN 1984.

MINNESOTA ADVANCED THE BALL 1,183 YARDS IN THE 1904 WISCONSIN GAME.

IN THEIR FIRST EVER GAME WITH MICHIGAN, IN 1892, THE GOPHERS CAME OUT THE VICTOR. THIS ELEVATED MINNESOTA FROM A SMALL COLLEGE TO ONE OF THE BIGGIES BECAUSE THEY HAD DEFEATED SUCH A PRESTIGIOUS COLLEGE. THE CELEBRATIONS LASTED INTO THE SPRING. IT WAS THE ONLY TIME THE GOPHERS HELD THE EDGE IN THIS SCHOOL SERIES.

MINNESOTA HAS HAD MORE THAN ALL-AMERICAN PLAYERS. GEORGE AAGAARD WAS AN ALL-AMERICAN DRUM MAJOR. FROM 1932-36 HE WOULD KICK OFF THE HALFTIME CEREMONIES BY TOSSING HIS BATON OVER THE GOAL POST.

AFTER THE PRESEASON PRACTICE FOR THE 1918 SEASON WAS ENDED THE ENTIRE BACKFIELD WAS CALLED INTO THE ARMED SERVICES.

GEORGE AAGAARD

MINNESOTA'S BEST 5-YEAR RECORD IS 54-3-3 (.925%) FROM 1900-1904.

IN 1903 MINNESOTA OUT SCORED ITS OPPONENTS 661-12. THE 1904 SEASON IMPROVED TO 725-12. THESE BACK-TO-BACK SEASONS TOTALED 1,386-24.

IN 1962 MICHIGAN STATE WAS RANKED NUMBER ONE IN THE COUNTRY IN RUSHING. THE GOPHERS HELD THEM TO 30 YARDS AFTER THROWING BACK MICHIGAN TO A MINUS 46 THE WEEK BEFORE.

MIKE HOHENSEE, IN 1981, ATTEMPTED 67 PASSES AGAINST OHIO STATE. FIVE OF THEM WERE FOR TOUCHDOWNS IN THE VICTORY.

WHEN THE TRAINING TABLE BEGAN IT WAS CONSIDERED A "PHENOMENAL ENTERPRISE."

1886 WAS THE FIRST YEAR MINNESOTA USED SIGNALS. THEY WERE MILITARY TYPE COMMANDS.

THE 1962 MAROON AND GOLD VICTORY IN THE ROSE BOWL WAS THE FIRST COLLEGE FOOTBALL GAME TO BE TELEVISED NATIONALLY IN COLOR.

THE FORWARD PASS WAS LEGALIZED IN 1906. IF AN ATTEMPTED PASS HIT THE GROUND WITHOUT IT BEING TOUCHED BY A PLAYER ON EITHER TEAM, THE BALL WAS TURNED OVER TO THE DEFENDING TEAM AT THE POINT WHERE IT WAS THROWN. IN THE MEAN TIME THE DEFENSE HAD THE RIGHT TO INTERFERE WITH THE OFFENSIVE RECEIVER.

DURING THE FIRST YEAR OF THE PASS, IN THE NEBRASKA GAME, WILLIAM DOANE BECAME THE FIRST GOPHER TO RECORD AN INTERCEPTION.

 BECAUSE OF THE WORLD WAR, ATHLETICS WERE TAKEN OVER BY THE MILITARY IN 1918. THERE WAS LITTLE INTEREST SHOWN BY UNIVERSITY FANS BUT THERE WERE ENOUGH PLAYERS TO FIELD 16 COMPANY TEAMS.

 A SHOULDER INJURY RESULTED IN ED WIDSETH HAVING HIS ARM STRAPPED TO HIS SIDE FOR THE LAST HALF OF HIS FINAL SEASON. HE STILL MADE CONSENSUS ALL-AMERICAN.

 MINNESOTA WAS THE FIRST TEAM EVER TO BE SEEN ON TELEVISION. THIS HAPPENED ON SEPTEMBER 10, 1939 WHEN KSTP EXPERIMENTED ON A PRACTICE SESSION.

 MINNESOTA'S FIRST GAME APPEARANCE ON TELEVISION WAS AGAINST PITTSBURGH IN 1953.

 OF PRESENT DIVISION I-A FOOTBALL TEAMS, ONLY MICHIGAN AND NAVY HAVE PLAYED LONGER THAN MINNESOTA.

 BOBBY BELL WAS THE FIRST OUTSIDE LINEBACKER EVER INDUCTED INTO THE PRO FOOTBALL HALL OF FAME.

MINNESOTA BECAME AMONG THE FIRST TEAMS TO WEAR HEAD TELEMETRY (HIT) SYSTEMS IN 2007. ITS SENSORS RECORD WHERE AND HOW HARD CONCUSSION BLOWS ARE TO WARN OF INJURY.

1892 SAW HARVARD INVENT THE FLYING WEDGE AND MINNESOTA THE REVOLVING WEDGE. ROUGHNESS AND INJURY BECAME SO PREVALENT THAT THESE MASS PLAYS WERE ABOLISHED IN 1894 TO SAVE THE GAME.

OSSIE SOLEM WAS A GOPHER UNDER HENRY WILLIAMS. AFTERWARD HE COACHED 299 GAMES OVER 37 YEARS. THIS RANKS HIGH IN THE ALL-TIME GAMES AND YEARS-COACHED LIST. ONE OF THE FIVE TEAMS HE DIRECTED WAS IOWA. WHILE THERE HE FOUGHT THE GOPHERS IN THE FIRST EVER FLOYD OF ROSEDALE GAME.

THE MINNEAPOLIS JOURNAL REPORTED AFTER THE 1906 SEASON THAT, "THE TEN YARD RULE HAS PROVED A FAILURE, THE FAILURE IT WAS EXPECTED TO BE." THEY CLAIMED IT CAUSED MORE KICKING AND FEWER TOUCHDOWNS WHILE SUGGESTING ADDING ANOTHER DOWN.

HAROLD VAN EVERY AND VIC SPADACCINI WERE FORMER GOPHERS WHO PLAYED FOR THE WARTIME SECOND AIR FORCE BOMBERS. IN THE 1943 SUN BOWL THEY TEAMED UP TO SCORE BOTH TOUCHDOWNS IN A WIN (13-7) OVER PREVIOUSLY UNBEATEN HARDIN-SIMMONS.

LAWRENCE MARONEY PLANTED THE MINNESOTA FLAG IN MICHIGAN'S MIDFIELD AFTER VICTORY IN 2005.

MINNESOTA IS THE FIRST SCHOOL TO HAVE THREE RUNNING BACKS NAMED BIG TEN PLAYER OF THE WEEK IN THE SAME YEAR (2005): LAWRENCE MARONEY AGAINST PURDUE, GARY RUSSELL AGAINST INDIANA AND AMIR PINNIX AGAINST MICHIGAN STATE.

BRUCE SMITH'S HEISMAN TROPHY WAS SOLD AT AUCTION IN 2005 FOR $336,375. SMITH JOKED HE HAD ONCE USED IT FOR A DOOR STOP.

BERNIE BIERMAN BELIEVED EVERY PLAY WAS DESIGNED TO BE A TOUCHDOWN IF EACH PLAYER DID HIS JOB. A CAMERA GOT A PICTURE OF SHELDON BEISE SCORING AGAINST WISCONSIN IN 1935. IT ALSO SHOWED 11 BADGERS ON THE GROUND AFTER THE GOPHERS MOWED THEM DOWN.

BOBBY BELL WAS ELECTED TO THE A.F.L. ALL-TIME TEAM.

W. R. SMITH, HEAD OF UNIVERSITY INTRAMURAL SPORTS IN 1920, NOTICED STUDENTS PLAYING FOOTBALL WITHOUT TACKLING. HE THOUGHT IT A GOOD IDEA FOR HIS PROGRAM. FROM THIS TOUCH FOOTBALL WAS BORN.

LEO NOMELLINI WENT ON TO BE A SIX TIME ALL-PRO, TWO TIMES FOR HIS DEFENSIVE WORK AND FOUR TIMES FOR OFFENSE.

A QUOTE FROM JIM WACKER: "IT'S ABOUT THE FOUR F'S. IT'S ABOUT FAITH. IT'S ABOUT FAMILY. IT'S ABOUT FRIENDS AND IT'S ABOUT FOOTBALL."

BERNIE BIERMAN COACHED ONE YEAR OF HIGH SCHOOL FOOTBALL. HE DIRECTED BUTTE, MONTANA TO THE STATE TITLE.

IKE ARMSTRONG WAS MINNESOTA ATHLETIC DIRECTOR FROM 1950-1963. BEFORE COMING TO MINNESOTA HE COACHED UTAH FOR 25 YEARS AND LEFT A 140-55-15 RECORD, FOR A WINNING PERCENTAGE OF .702. IT EARNED HIM ENTRANCE INTO THE HALL OF FAME AS A COACH.

FLOYD OF ROSEDALE WASN'T JUST ANY HOG. HE WAS THE BROTHER OF A MOVIE STAR WHO APPEARED IN THE 1933 MOVIE "STATE FAIR" WITH WILL ROGERS. FAME DIDN'T SAVE POOR FLOYD, THOUGH. HE WAS GIVEN TO AN AUSTIN LAD WHO WON HIM IN AN ESSAY CONTEST AND WAS PROBABLY LAST SEEN ON A DINNER TABLE.

IKE ARMSTRONG

AT ONE TIME ROCKET DISPLAYS WOULD FOLLOW GOPHER TOUCHDOWNS.

AFTER HIS GOPHER CAREER BOB McNAMARA PLAYED IN THE PROS FOR WINNIPEG. IN 1956 HE SCORED SIX TOUCHDOWNS AGAINST VANCOUVER. HE MADE THE ALL-PRO AND ALL-CANADIAN TEAMS.

A MOVIE, "SMITH OF MINNESOTA" WAS MADE OF THE LIFE OF HEISMAN TROPHY WINNER BRUCE SMITH.

PANT... WHEEZE

SMITH ONCE COLLAPSED FROM EXHAUSTION AFTER BREAKING FREE FOR A SURE TOUCHDOWN. HE HAD BEEN RUNNING CIRCLES AROUND THE OPPOSITION ALL DAY, UNTIL HE DROPPED.

THE MOST GOLDEN OF GOPHERS HAVE HAD THEIR NUMERALS RETIRED: BRUCE SMITH (54), BRONKO NAGURSKI (72) AND PAUL GIEL (10).

IN 1951 PAUL GIEL SET A THEN-BIG TEN RECORD BY RUSHING AND PASSING FOR 1,078 YARDS. WHAT'S MORE AMAZING IS HE DID IT ON A TEAM WITH A 1-4-1 RECORD. AGAINST WISCONSIN HE MADE 106 YARDS, THOUGH THE BADGERS LED THE NATION IN DEFENSE.

THE HEISMAN MEMORIAL TROPHY

ALL-AMERICAN BOB McNAMARA AND HIS BROTHER PINKY GANGED UP ON MICHIGAN STATE IN 1954. THEY BOTH PLAYED THE FULL GAME AND COMBINED FOR OVER 100 YARDS RUSHING. THEY CAUGHT ALL THE GOPHER PASSES ON THE DAY FOR 91 YARDS. BOB SCORED ON AN INTERCEPTION AS THEY SETTLED FOR A SATISFYING WIN.

SOME TIME AFTER HIS PLAYING DAYS GEORGE HAUSER RAN INTO WALTER CAMP, THE MOST RECOGNIZED AUTHORITY IN NAMING ALL-AMERICANS. IT SEEMED CAMP HAD STARTED TO PUT HAUSER ON HIS ALL-AMERICAN TEAM OF 1916 BUT WITHDREW HIM AT THE REQUEST OF COACH WILLIAMS. WILLIAMS DIDN'T WANT A JUNIOR TO WIN THE HONOR BECAUSE IT MIGHT NOT GIVE HIM SOMETHING TO "SHOOT AT" IN HIS SENIOR YEAR. IN 1917, IN RESPECT TO THOSE WHO WENT TO WAR, CAMP DIDN'T MAKE ALL-AMERICAN SELECTIONS. HE DID HAVE AN HONOR ROLL. HE TOLD HAUSER HE WAS RETHINKING THIS AND WOULD MAKE A RETROACTIVE TEAM FOR THAT YEAR WHICH WOULD INCLUDE HIM. BEFORE CAMP OFFICIALLY HAD A CHANCE TO DO IT, HE DIED. GEORGE HAUSER WAS A TWO-TIME WALTER CAMP ALL-AMERICAN WHO NEVER GOT CREDIT FOR IT.

166

THE INDIANA GAME OF 1906 WAS PLAYED ON A SLIPPERY FIELD. EACH TEAM PUNTED 28 TIMES FOR A GAME TOTAL OF 56! INDIANA SCORED ON A MISJUDGED PUNT OVER A GOPHER RECEIVER. MINNESOTA CAME BACK ON A PUNT WHERE THE INDIANA RECEIVER WAS CARRIED OVER THE GOAL FOR A SAFETY (LEGAL THEN). AFTER A GOPHER FIELD GOAL, INDIANA WAS HELD DEEP NEAR THEIR OWN GOAL. A BAD SNAP ON A PUNT TRY HAD INDIANA COUGHING UP ANOTHER SAFETY, AS WELL AS THE GAME 8-6.

MINNESOTA PLAYED IN DOUBLE HEADERS IN 1899 AND 1905.

ED ROGERS ALMOST COMPLETELY MISSED THE 1903 BELOIT GAME. HE WAS LOCKED UP WITH JURY DUTY.

A DEDICATED AND TRUE LEADER WAS CAPTAIN BOLES ROSENTHAL OF THE 1914 TEAM. DUE IN LARGE PART TO HIS EFFORTS, 11 OF 12 SCHOLASTICALLY INELIGIBLE PLAYERS WERE ABLE TO PASS EXAMINATIONS WHEN THEY WENT BEFORE THE ELIGIBILITY COMMITTEE.

JOHN PHILIP SOUSA CAME TO TOWN IN 1926 TO GIVE A CONCERT. A UNIVERSITY COMMITTEE ASKED HIM TO COMPOSE A TUNE FOR THE U OF M. HE ANSWERED BY WRITING THE STIRRING "MINNESOTA MARCH." THE WORDS WERE THEN ADDED TO IT BY MICHAEL M. JALMA, DIRECTOR OF THE MINNESOTA BAND.

JOHN PHILIP SOUSA

TRUMAN E. RICKARD COMPOSED "HAIL MINNESOTA" IN 1904 FOR A SENIOR CLASS PLAY. ADDITIONS TO ITS LYRICS BY ARTHUR UPSON HAVE MADE IT AN ENDURING SCHOOL SONG. IN 1945 IT WAS ADOPTED BY THE LEGISLATURE AS THE MINNESOTA STATE SONG.

THE "MINNESOTA ROUSER" (SEE NEXT PAGE FOR ORIGINAL VERSION) WAS WRITTEN BY FLOYD M. HUTSELL IN 1909. IT WAS THE WINNER OF A CONTEST SPONSORED BY THE MINNEAPOLIS TRIBUNE. THE AWARD WAS $100. A COUPLE OF THE CONTEST JUDGES WERE U OF M PRESIDENT CYRUS W. NORTHROP AND MINNESOTA GOVERNOR A. O. EBERHART.

HUNGRY FOR THAT SAME $100 WAS A SONG WRITER NAMED WILLIAM PURDY. HE CAME UP WITH A TUNE STARTING WITH THE WORDS "MINNESOTA! MINNESOTA!" HIS ROOMMATE, CARL BECK, CONVINCED HIM TO GIVE UP THE CONTEST AND CHANGE THE WORDS TO SUIT A UNIVERSITY THAT BECK HAD PREVIOUSLY ATTENDED. THE TUNE BECAME REBORN AS "ON, WISCONSIN!"

167

THE U. OF M. ROUSER.

Dedicated to B. A. Rose, Band Master, U. of M.

Allegro moderato.

Words and music by FLOYD M. HUTSELL.

Rah, rah, - - - - - - - Hon-or to our col-lege Min-ne-so-ta U.

Loy-al to thy stand-ards We'll nev-er be un-true. Un-der-neath thy pen-nant

Pul-ses beat with pride And vic-to-ry e'er shall be our aim O'er the na-tion wide, (Yell)

REFRAIN.

Min - ne - so - ta, hats off to thee, To your col - ors

true we shall ev - er be...... Firm and strong, u - ni - ted are we.

Rah, rah, rah, for Ski - U - Ma, Rah, rah, rah, rah, rah, rah, rah, Rah, for the U of

M. Ah................... Rah for the U. of M...............

169

THE FEWEST YARDS THE GOPHERS HAVE ALLOWED IN A MODERN ERA GAME IS MINUS ONE AGAINST WESTERN MICHIGAN IN 1977.

 TWO GAMES OF THE 1918 SEASON WERE PLAYED UNDER QUARANTINE DUE TO AN INFLUENZA EPIDEMIC.

 THE COLLEGE SPORTS INFORMATION DIRECTORS OF AMERICA STARTED THE ALL-ACADEMIC ALL-AMERICA TEAM IN 1952. IT REQUIRES AT LEAST A 3.2 GRADE POINT AVERAGE TO QUALIFY. GOPHERS WHO HAVE MADE THE GRADE ARE:

1956 – BOB HOBERT (T)   1970 – BARRY MAYER (RB)
1960 – FRANK BRIXIUS (T)   1989 – BRENT HERBEL (P)
1968 – BOB STEIN (DE)   1994 – JUSTIN CONZEMIUS (DB)

JIM WACKER DIRECTED HIS GOPHER SQUADS THREE YEARS IN A ROW TO LEAD IN ACADEMIC ALL-BIG TEN TEAM SELECTIONS.

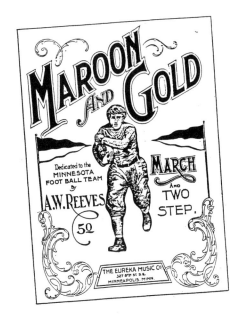

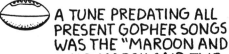 A TUNE PREDATING ALL PRESENT GOPHER SONGS WAS THE "MAROON AND GOLD MARCH AND TWO STEP" OF 1903.

THE STAR-TRIBUNE PICKED ITS "100 MOST IMPORTANT SPORTS FIGURES OF THE (20TH) CENTURY." THOUGH NOT ALL STRICTLY KNOWN FOR FOOTBALL, HERE ARE THOSE THAT WERE: BRONKO NAGURSKI (2); BUD GRANT (4); BERNIE BIERMAN (12); BRUCE SMITH (17); VERN GAGNE (26); PAUL GIEL (27); CARL ELLER (29); SANDY STEPHENS (30); MURRY WARMATH (37); BOBBY MARSHALL (51); PUG LUND (58); BOBBY BELL (63); ED WIDSETH (75).

THE GOPHERS WERE LEADING NEBRASKA 16-12 IN THEIR 1904 CONTEST. DARKNESS WAS FALLING ON THE FINAL MOMENTS AS THE CORNHUSKERS ADVANCED TO THE GOPHER

THREE. THERE WAS TIME FOR ONLY ONE MORE PLAY TO DECIDE THE OUTCOME.

MINNESOTA END USHER BURDICK NOTICED HOW SIMILAR HIS SOCKS WERE TO HIS OPPONENTS'. IN THE EXCITEMENT, BETWEEN PLAYS, HE SNEAKED INTO THE NEBRASKA BACKFIELD. AMAZINGLY, NO ONE NOTICED HIM AS THEY LOOKED TO THE GROUND

WHILE RECEIVING INSTRUCTIONS. AFTER ALL, DIDN'T THEY ALL LOOK LIKE TEAMMATES FROM THE KNEES DOWN? HE GOT THE PLAY DIRECTLY FROM THE CAPTAIN.

AS THEY LINED UP, BURDICK WAITED AN ETERNITY FOR THE BALL TO BE HIKED. AT LONG LAST IT CAME AND HE CHARGED THE BALL CARRIER. THERE BEING NO FORWARD PROGRESS RULES THEN, HE PICKED HIM UP AND STARTED CARRYING HIM TOWARD THE OPPOSITE GOAL. THE CORNHUSKER WAS BEATING HIM ON THE NECK ALL THE WAY WHILE YELLING "DOWN!" TO STOP THE PLAY. BY THE TIME HE WAS HEARD HE HAD BEEN TAKEN FOR A 12 YARD LOSS. THE GUN SOUNDED TO END THE GAME.

 RUSSELL RATHBUN WAS TOO SMALL TO PLAY FOOTBALL BUT STILL MANAGED TO MAKE A UNIQUE CONTRIBUTION. THE 5'5" BIG TEN CHAMPION IN THE MILE RUN WAS VOTED BY THE STUDENT BODY TO BE TEAM CHEERLEADER, OR "ROOTER KING" AS THEY WERE CALLED BACK IN 1910.

HE DIDN'T REALLY WANT THE JOB BUT DECIDED TO DO IT "RIGHT," ANYWAY. TO GET ATTENTION ON THE SIDELINES HE GOT THE IDEA OF WEARING A UNIFORM. HE DRESSED IN ALL WHITE AND PUT AN "M" ON HIS CHEST.

RATHBUN, WHO WAS WELL KNOWN AS "BUNNY" BECAUSE HE RAN AROUND THE TRACK LIKE A RABBIT, DID FLIPS AND GYMNASTICS TO EXCITE THE CROWDS. HIS CHEERLEADING STYLE AND USE OF A UNIFORM WAS HIS INNOVATION HANDED DOWN TO THIS DAY.

TERRITORIAL SETTLERS LOOKED FOR A PROPER ANIMAL TO SYMBOLIZE THE NEW GREAT STATE OF MINNESOTA. OTHER STATES HAD THEM AND MINNESOTA CERTAINLY POSSESSED AMPLE CREATURES TO CHOOSE FROM FOR ITSELF. THE BEAVER WAS THE MOST FAVORED CHOICE, BUT IN THE END IT LOST TO CIRCUMSTANCES THAT MADE THE CHOICE FOR THEM.

ABOVE IS THE CARTOON THAT DECIDED IT ALL. IT WAS WIDELY DISTRIBUTED AND WAS CRITICAL OF A $5,000,000 BOND ISSUE SUPPORTING A RAILROAD CONSTRUCTION PROPOSAL. THE BOND CAME TO THE LEGISLATURE TWO WEEKS BEFORE STATEHOOD IN 1858. THE CARTOON FEATURED THE LOWLY, DESTRUCTIVE GOPHER WITH HEADS OF PROMINENT PRO-BOND PEOPLE ON THEM. THESE "LOW LIFES" WERE REPRESENTED AS TAKING BRIBES, SUPPORTING CORRUPTION AND CLAIMING POLITICAL POWER TO DO AS THEY PLEASED.

THE BOND WON IN SPITE OF THE MUCH-TALKED-ABOUT CARTOON. BEING MUCH TALKED ABOUT, THOUGH, THE NAME "GOPHER" BECAME LINKED TO MINNESOTA... THE GOPHER STATE.

TWINS PLAYED ON THE GOPHER LINE IN 1931. THEY WERE ALLEN AND ALVIN TEETER WHO WERE NICKNAMED "NIP" AND "TUCK."

THE 1918 CARLETON TEAM PUNTED 50 TIMES TO MINNESOTA.

IN 1916 WISCONSIN WAS HELD FOR NO GAINS DURING THE FIRST QUARTER. THEN THE GOPHERS THREW THEM BACK FOR A MINUS 30 YARDS FOR THE DAY.

172

THE HIGHEST SCORE BY A LOSING TEAM WITHIN THE BIG TEN WAS 43 BY INDIANA AGAINST MINNESOTA IN 1973. PURDUE RAISED IT TO 56 AGAINST THE GOPHERS IN 1993.

A QUESTIONNAIRE TO FORMER PLAYERS WAS SENT OUT IN 1914. MOST RETURNED COMMENTS WERE POSITIVE BUT THERE WERE A COUPLE OF COMPLAINTS. ONE WAS, "SECRET PRACTICE AND THE PAID PROFESSIONAL COACH MUST GO IF FOOTBALL IS TO REMAIN A COLLEGE AND AN AMATEUR SPORT."

CAPTAINS OF TWO GOPHER NATIONAL CHAMPIONSHIP TEAMS, GLENN SEIDEL-1935 AND GREG LARSON-1960, WERE GRADS OF THE SAME HIGH SCHOOL, MINNE-APOLIS ROOSEVELT.

EARL PICKERING WAS TAKEN OUT OF THE NEBRASKA GAME IN 1910 WHILE SUFFERING AN ACUTE APPENDIX ATTACK. AFTER A RUPTURE AND INFECTION HE RECOVERED FROM HIS CRITICAL CONDITION TO HELP BEAT WISCONSIN A FEW WEEKS LATER.

BRONKO NAGURSKI AND CLAYTON TONNEMAKER WERE NAMED TO THE CHICAGO TRIBUNE'S CENTENNIAL BIG TEN TEAM.

ALL-AMERICAN JAMES WALKER WAS 6'3" TALL AND WEIGHED BETWEEN 230-250 POUNDS. HIS FOLKS OBJECTED TO HIS PLAYING, SO HE QUIT AFTER HIS SOPHOMORE YEAR AND WENT OUT EAST TO CONTINUE THERE.

IN 1978 WASHINGTON TURNED OVER FIVE INTERCEPTIONS AND FOUR FUMBLES TO MINNESOTA.

AL BROSKY, OF ILLINOIS, SET A NATIONAL RECORD OF INTERCEPTING A PASS IN 15 STRAIGHT GAMES. THE STRING WAS ENDED BY MINNESOTA IN 1952.

THE INDIAN WAR DRUM WAS A GIFT FROM ED ROGERS. HE SAID IT WAS USED IN TIME OF DANGER AND SHOULD BE BEATEN WHEN THE TEAM NEEDED EXTRA ENCOURAGEMENT TO PULL A GAME OUT. CHIPPEWA FROM LEECH LAKE WORE FULL CEREMONIAL COSTUMES WHEN IT WAS PRESENTED AT HOMECOMING IN 1917. UNIVERSITY STUDENTS WORE SIMILAR COSTUMES LATER ON AND USED THE DRUM WHEN OPPONENTS ENTERED MINNESOTA TERRITORY. IT WENT OUT OF USE IN THE 1930'S.

BIG SCHOOLS HAD OFFICIAL CHEERS. MINNESOTA LACKED SUCH AN IDENTITY. ADDING INSULT TO INJURY, GOPHER COACHES CHEERED FOR THEIR OWN ALMA MATERS RATHER THAN MINNESOTA WHEN THEIR RESPECTIVE PLAYERS SCORED IN INTRASQUAD GAMES. CAPTAIN JOHN ADAMS DECIDED TO CHANGE THAT BY INVENTING A UNIQUE HOME CHEER.

SOMETHING HAD TO GO WITH "RAH, RAH, RAH," HE THOUGHT. THE EXPRESSION "SKI-OO" WENT THROUGH HIS MIND AS A START. HE HAD HEARD IT THE PREVIOUS SUMMER FROM SOME SOUIX INDIANS WHO WERE VICTORIOUS IN CANOE RACES ON THE RIVER. HE MISHEARD THE PRONUNCIATION, THOUGH, WHICH SHOULD HAVE BEEN "SKOO-YA." IT MEANS "SWEET." TO MAKE IT RHYME WITH "RAH," HE INVENTED THE WORD "MAH." THEN HE TOOK THE "E" OUT OF "MINNESOTA." THE CHEER HAD A DRUMBEAT RHYTHM... "RAH-RAH-RAH, SKI-OO-MAH, MINN-SO-TA!"

PLEASED, ADAMS AND HIS ROOMMATE TRIED IT OUT IN THE EARLY HOURS ON THE CORNER WHERE THEY LIVED (1401 S.E. 6TH ST.) TO SEE IF ANYONE ELSE WAS IMPRESSED. THEY WERE ANSWERED WITH, "SHUT UP AND GO TO BED!" THE CHEER BEGAN ITS USE IN THE FALL OF 1884.

 THE BIG TEN HAS HAD THE ROSE BOWL CONTRACT SINCE 1947 WITH THE EXCEPTION OF 1961 AND 1962. MINNESOTA WENT BY INVITATION THOSE TWO YEARS.

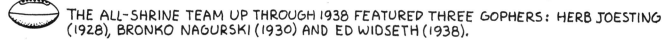 THE ALL-SHRINE TEAM UP THROUGH 1938 FEATURED THREE GOPHERS: HERB JOESTING (1928), BRONKO NAGURSKI (1930) AND ED WIDSETH (1938).

IF JOHN McGOVERN HAD QUIT PLAYING AT MID-SEASON BECAUSE OF A BROKEN COLLAR BONE, HE WOULD HAVE LOST HIS CHANCE FOR ALL-AMERICAN HONORS IN 1909. HE CONVINCED COACH WILLIAMS TO LET HIM CONTINUE.

MICHIGAN COACH FIELDING YOST ADMIRED THE SPUNKY McGOVERN. HE ORDERED HIS PLAYERS NOT TO HURT HIM.

AT ONE POINT, DURING THE ENSUING GAME, McGOVERN GOT AWAY A PUNT AS THREE WOLVERINES WERE CLOSING IN ON HIM. THE FIRST BOWLED HIM TO THE GROUND. INSTEAD OF ROLLING OVER McGOVERN AND POSSIBLY AGGRAVATING HIS INJURY, HE MANAGED TO STOP SHORT AND BRIDGE HIMSELF OVER HIS BODY. AT THAT POINT THE OTHER TWO WOLVERINES WERE UNABLE TO STOP THEIR COLLISION COURSE. THE WOLVERINE ON THE GROUND PROCEEDED TO BLOCK HIS OWN PLAYERS OUT OF THE WAY. McGOVERN WAS SAVED AND WENT ON TO ALL-AMERICAN DISTINCTION.

MINNESOTA ◻◻ **MINUTES TO PLAY** ◻◻ **SECONDS** ◻◻
◻ **VISITORS** ◻◻ **PERIOD**◻ **DOWN** ◻ **YARDS TO GO** ◻◻

PHIL BRAIN WAS THE 'U' TENNIS COACH WHO DOUBLED AS FOOTBALL GAME MOVIE PHOTOGRAPHER. SEEING A NEED FOR FANS TO KEEP TRACK OF THE GAME'S RUNNING TIME AND SCORE HE USED THE TALENTS FROM HIS ELECTRONICS HOBBY TO INVENT THE ELECTRIC SCOREBOARD. IT WAS READY FOR THE 1937 SEASON. THE 52'x6' BOARD BECAME A FAMILIAR SIGHT ATOP COOK HALL AT THE OPEN END OF MEMORIAL STADIUM. OHIO STATE AND WISCONSIN HAD HIM BUILD THEIR SCOREBOARDS IN 1939. HE ADAPTED HIS CREATION FOR OTHER SPORTS AND IT IS NOW USED EVERY-WHERE.

THE GOPHERS COULD HAVE USED BRAIN'S CLOCK IN 1896. THEY THOUGHT THEY HAD 18 SECONDS LEFT SO THE TEAM VOTED TO USE IT UP ON A FOURTH DOWN RUN RATHER THAN PUNT. THEY HAD LOST THE WEEK BEFORE IN THE SAME SITUATION BY PUNTING. THIS TIME, FROM DEEP IN THEIR OWN TERRITORY, THEY SUCCEEDED IN CROSSING THE FIRST DOWN MARKER BUT WERE PUSHED BACK. WISCONSIN TOOK POSSESSION. OOPS! THERE WAS ANOTHER MINUTE TO GO. THE BADGERS WENT ON TO SCORE AND THE GOPHERS DROPPED ANOTHER ONE.

THE NATIONAL CHAMPION GOPHERS OF 1960 WERE NOT RANKED IN THE TOP 20 BY THE ASSOCIATED PRESS UNTIL THE THIRD GAME OF THE SEASON.

OHIO STATE AND NEBRASKA WERE CO-NATIONAL CHAMPIONS IN 1970. MINNESOTA HAD THE DISTINCTION OF PLAYING THEM EACH WITHIN 14 DAYS.

IN 1970, AGAINST MICHIGAN STATE, WALTER BOWSER RAN BACK 140 YARDS OF INTERCEPTIONS AND JEFF WRIGHT INTERCEPTED THREE OF HIS OWN.

PURDUE HAD SCORED ITS MOST POINTS IN A BIG TEN GAME AGAINST MINNESOTA IN 1993. UNFORTUNATELY FOR THEM, IT WAS ALSO THE MOST POINTS FOR A LOSING TEAM IN A DIVISION I GAME. PURDUE GAINED 559 YARDS TO THE GOPHERS' 625. MINNESOTA AVERAGED EIGHT YARDS PER PLAY AS THEY OUTLASTED THE BOILERMAKERS 59-56.

MINNESOTA'S FIRST TWO-TIME ALL-AMERICAN, BERT BASTON, DIDN'T MAKE THE SQUAD IN HIS FRESHMAN YEAR DUE TO HIS "LACK OF BLOCKING."

UNFORTUNATELY, THE LONGEST TOUCHDOWN FROM A RECOVERED FUMBLE IS 105 YARDS BY H.M. COLEMAN, OF WISCONSIN, AGAINST MINNESOTA IN 1891. IT CAN NEVER BE BEATEN BECAUSE MODERN RECORDS DON'T RECOGNIZE A PLAY OVER 100 YARDS.

OUTSIDE OF FOOTBALL HENRY WILLIAMS MADE HIS MARK IN TRACK AS WELL. UPON GRADUATION FROM YALE HE HELD THE COLLEGE RECORD IN THE LOW HURDLES AND WORLD RECORD IN THE HIGH HURDLES.

WILLIAMS' 1903 GOPHERS WERE KNOWN AS THE "GIANTS OF THE NORTH." THEY AVERAGED, HOWEVER, ONLY 185 POUNDS. GUARD JOHN FLYNN WAS 6'3½" AND 183 POUNDS BUT WAS REPORTED TO BE 240 POUNDS. THEY WERE ALSO KNOWN AS "SWEDES" THOUGH THERE WEREN'T ANY ON THE TEAM. EGIL BOECKMANN WAS THE CLOSEST, HAVING BEEN BORN IN NORWAY.

DR. WILLIAMS' TEAMS OF 1903-04 SKUNKED 13 STRAIGHT OPPONENTS.

AFTER HIS OFFICIAL COACHING DAYS WERE OVER, WILLIAMS WOULD STILL SIT ON THE GOPHER BENCH DURING GAMES AND ASSIST HIS SUCCESSOR, BILL SPAULDING.

DR. HENRY WILLIAMS

YOU COULD SAY THAT THE GOPHERS WERE UPSET FROM BEING UPSET BY NEBRASKA IN 1902. A COUPLE OF WEEKS AFTER THAT GAME THEY TOOK ON GRINNELL WHO HAD LOST TO THE CORNHUSKERS 17-0. MINNESOTA PROCEEDED TO SCORE 17 TOUCHDOWNS ON THEM; ONE FOR EVERY POINT MADE BY NEBRASKA. THE GRINNELL CAPTAIN PLEADED, "LET UP ON US, CAN'T YOU; WE'LL TAKE YOUR WORD FOR IT THAT YOU COULD LICK NEBRASKA."

STANFORD INVITED THE SUCCESSFUL 1903 GOPHERS TO PLAY IN THE SECOND-EVER ROSE BOWL GAME. AFTER THE CONTRACT WAS SET ADDITIONAL CONCESSIONS WERE PUT TO MINNESOTA. THE GOPHERS WOULDN'T AGREE TO THEM AND SO THE 1904 ROSE BOWL CONTEST WAS CANCELLED. THE NEW YEAR'S DAY GAMES WEREN'T TAKEN UP AGAIN UNTIL 1916.

HOW THINGS HAVE CHANGED. THE QUARTERBACK WAS A BLOCKING BACK AND NOT A BALL CARRIER ON THE 1934 TEAM. GLENN SEIDEL CARRIED ONLY FIVE TIMES IN SIX GAMES.

IN THE 1965 INDIANA GAME THERE WERE NO PUNTS BY EITHER THE GOPHERS OR HOOSIERS.

MINNESOTA SKUNKED 12 TEAMS IN 1903. THE ONLY TEAMS TO SCORE IN RETURN WERE MICHIGAN AND MINNEAPOLIS CENTRAL HIGH SCHOOL. THEY SKUNKED 12 MORE THE FOLLOWING YEAR. ONLY NEBRASKA COULD SCORE. FROM 1900-1905 THE GOPHERS HELD 59 TEAMS SCORELESS.

IN 1910 MINNESOTA'S RECORD WAS 6-1-0. ALL GAMES ENDED WITH THE LOSING TEAM BEING UNABLE TO SCORE.

MINNESOTA HAS PLAYED IN TEN GAMES ENDING IN A SCORELESS TIE:
1890 - EX-GOLLEGIANS
1900 - MINNEAPOLIS CENTRAL H.S.
1908 - NEBRASKA
1918 - ALL-STARS
1923 - WISCONSIN
1930 - STANFORD
1933 - NORTHWESTERN
1933 - MICHIGAN
1956 - NORTHWESTERN
1962 - MISSOURI

WHO SAYS A TIE IS LIKE KISSING YOUR SISTER?

MINNESOTA BOTH RUSHED AND PASSED FOR 2000 YARDS IN SEVEN STRAIGHT YEARS (1999-2005)

THE GOPHER CHAMPS OF 1934 FUMBLED 12 TIMES AGAINST NEBRASKA.

IN 1928 BRONKO NAGURSKI HAD BOTH HIS WRISTS BROKEN AGAINST PURDUE. HE CAME BACK TO PLAY TWO WEEKS LATER.

THREE GOPHER COACHES HAVE BEEN ELECTED TO THE PRESIDENCY OF THE AMERICAN FOOTBALL COACHES ASSOCIATION: BERNIE BIERMAN (1935), MURRAY WARMATH (1968) AND GLEN MASON (2002).

SINCE MINNESOTA CLAIMED ITS FIRST ALL-AMERICAN IN 1903 THE LONGEST DROUGHT FOR HAVING SUCH HONOR IS 25 SEASONS (1972-1996). PREVIOUS TO THAT IT WAS FIVE SEASONS (1918-1922).

THE MOST CONSECUTIVE SEASONS MINNESOTA HAS HAD ALL-AMERICANS IS SIX (1933-1938) WITH 17 DIFFERENT PLAYERS.

MAYOR BAINBRIDGE, OF MINNEAPOLIS, GAVE EACH PLAYER A RABBIT'S FOOT BEFORE THE 1934 PITTSBURGH GAME. THEY HAD THEM SEWED INTO THEIR UNIFORMS.

EIGHT GOPHERS LED A BALANCED TEAM FOR INTERCEPTIONS IN 2005 WITH ONE.

13 GOPHERS WENT INTO THE N.F.L. DRAFT IN 1950; 11 IN 1944.

THE BROTHER OF GOPHER ALL-AMERICAN LAMANZER WILLIAMS, DAN, WAS AN ALL-AMERICAN FOR TOLEDO.

STUDENT, O.L. WINT, ORGANIZED MINNESOTA'S FIRST HOMECOMING IN 1914. TEDDY ROOSEVELT ATTENDED IT IN 1919.

THE FOUR HORSEMEN, OF NOTRE DAME, STARTED THE KNUTE ROCKNE TROPHY IN 1931 TO HONOR THEIR LATE COACH. MINNESOTA TOOK PERMANENT POSSESSION OF THE NATIONAL AWARD IN 1940 AFTER HAVING WON IT FOR THE THIRD TIME. IT WAS REPLACED BY THE HENRY WILLIAMS TROPHY WHICH CAME INTO PERMANENT POSSESSION OF NOTRE DAME IN 1948.

SECOND TEAM ALL-AMERICAN BOBBY MARSHALL NOT ONLY STARRED IN SEVERAL OTHER SPORTS BUT WAS FEATURED IN RIPLEY'S "BELIEVE-IT-OR-NOT" FOR ICE SKATE JUMPING OVER BARRELS.

CLARK SHAUGHNESSY AND BERNIE BIERMAN WERE COACHING TULANE WHEN THEY WERE VISITED BY HENRY WILLIAMS. WHILE HE HELPED OUT FOR SEVERAL WEEKS THE TULANE TEAM HAD THE DISTINCTION OF BEING DIRECTED BY THREE EVENTUAL HALL OF FAME COACHES FROM MINNESOTA.

GOPHER, TED COX (1922-24), COACHED TULANE TO VICTORY IN THE FIRST EVER SUGAR BOWL IN 1935.

GOPHER GREAT, BIGGIE MUNN, COACHED MICHIGAN STATE TO VICTORY IN THE FIRST EVER TV BROADCAST ROSE BOWL IN 1953.

AS COACHES, THESE GOPHERS WON 100 GAMES IN THE FEWEST TRIES:

NAME	NATL' RANK	TOTAL GAMES	RECORD W-L-T	SEASONS TO ACCOMPLISH	TEAMS COACHED	PLAYED AT MINN.	COACHED AT MINN.
GIL DOBIE	1	108	100-5-3	16	NO. DAK. ST. WASHINGTON NAVY CORNELL	1899-1901	—
BUD WILKINSON	3	111	100-8-3	10	OKLAHOMA	1934-36	—
HENRY WILLIAMS	9	122	100-13-9	11	ARMY MINNESOTA	—	1900-21

GOPHER AND PRO HALL OF FAMER, CHARLIE SANDERS, WROTE THIS SENTIMENT ABOUT THE GAME:

"SO GIVE YOUR ALL AND NOTHING LESS,
TODAY WE WIN, TOMORROW WE REST.
YOU ARE NOT JUST MY TEAMMATE,
BUT MY VERY BEST FRIEND.
LET'S PLAY TOGETHER TO THE VERY END."

BRONKO NAGURSKI IS FAMOUS FOR BEING ALL-AMERICAN AT TWO POSITIONS IN THE SAME POLL. ANOTHER GOPHER DID IT ALSO, BUT IN DIFFERENT POLLS. LORIN SOLIN DID IT AS A BACK AND END IN 1915.

WHEN DARRELL THOMPSON RUSHED 205 YARDS IN HIS FIRST APPEARANCE AS A GOPHER, HE HAD STARTED THE GAME ON THE THIRD STRING.

IT WAS THE STYLE OF GRANTLAND RICE, DEAN OF AMERICAN SPORTS WRITERS, TO EXPRESS HIMSELF IN POETRY. THE FOLLOWING WAS WRITTEN TO HONOR PAUL GIEL:

AROUND THE ENDS, OR THROUGH THE LINE,
  ALONG THE GROUND OR IN THE AIR,

YOU SET A TINGLE IN THE SPINE.
  YOU TRAVEL WHERE THE TOUCHDOWNS FARE.

YOUR FLYING FEET ALL SEEM TO SAY—
  WE'RE HEADED FOR THE WINNING CLOVER —

FOR WE STILL SING UPON OUR WAY
  "ON TO THE GOAL AGAIN—AND OVER."

IN RAGING BATTLE ROUT AND REEL.
  WHILE DRIVING ONWARD FOR THAT GOAL.

SKOAL TO MINNESOTA'S GIEL.
  AND ONCE AGAIN ANOTHER SKOAL.

THE NORTH STAR SHINES IN FAME AND FLAME.
  FOR THOSE WHO TURN TO FIGHT AND LIVE

JUST ADD THIS LINE — HE PLAYED THE GAME—
  HE GAVE THE BEST HE HAD TO GIVE.

FOR OTHERS LET THE WELKIN RING
  HIGH-ANSWERED UP TO THE HILLS OF GOD.

BUT HERE TONIGHT WE CROWN HIM KING
  OF ALL WHOSE CLEATS RIPPED UP THE SOD.

                    GRANTLAND RICE
                    1953

MINNESOTA OUTSCORED ALL 16 OPPONENTS IN THEIR SIX NATIONAL CHAMPION-SHIP YEARS 1254 – 282 WITH 17 SHUTOUTS IN 50 GAMES. THEY BEAT FOUR OF THE SAME TEAMS IN EACH OF THOSE SEASONS:

IOWA	208 – 47	WITH 1 SHUTOUT
MICHIGAN	124 – 6	WITH 5 SHUTOUTS
NEBRASKA	87 – 28	WITH 2 SHUTOUTS
WISCONSIN	160 – 33	WITH 2 SHUTOUTS

AFTER HIS MINNESOTA DAYS, MIKE HOHENSEE MADE THE FIRST EVER ARENA LEAGUE TOUCHDOWN PASS IN 1987.

THE GOPHERS SCORED ON THEIR FIRST DRIVE IN SIX OF SEVEN GAMES IN-A-ROW STARTING WITH VIRGINIA IN THE 2005 MUSIC CITY BOWL INTO THE NEXT SEASON WITH KENT STATE, CALIFORNIA, TEMPLE, PURDUE, MISSING MICHIGAN AND FINISHING WITH PENN STATE.

ON FRESHMAN TEAM PICTURE DAY, FRANCIS LUND WAS ASKED FOR SOMETHING MORE MANLY TO BE NICKNAMED FOR THE NEWSPAPER. THEY CALLED HIM 'FRANCIE' IN HIGH SCHOOL SO HE HELD HIS TONGUE. FELLOW TEAMMATE AL PAPAS, SR. CHIMED IN, "CALL HIM 'PUG'". THIS WAS BECAUSE HE THOUGHT LUND WAS ALREADY "EVERY BIT AS GOOD" AS ALL-AMERICAN 'PUG' RENTNER OF NORTHWESTERN.

MINNESOTA'S TANDEM 1000 YARD RUSHING RECORD FOR THREE STRAIGHT SEASONS (2003, 04, 05) CAME WITHIN 94 YARDS OF A FOURTH. TERRY JACKSON II HAD 1317 YARDS WHILE THOMAS TAPEH HAD 906 THE YEAR BEFORE (2002) THE RECORD SETTING YEARS.

ACCORDING TO BERNIE BIERMAN, THE PROPER ATTITUDE OF A PLAYER IS TO BELIEVE HE WILL WIN AND FEAR HE WON'T.

The Golden Honor Roll

THE BIG TEN STARTED ITS ALL-CONFERENCE TEAM IN 1947. BEFORE THAT SELECTIONS WERE MADE BY PRESTIGIOUS SPORTS WRITERS AND NEWS SERVICES. PLAYERS IN EARLY TIMES WERE CALLED "ALL-WESTERN." THIS WAS EVEN BEFORE THE BIG TEN WAS CREATED. ALL-AMERICAN SELECTIONS STARTED IN 1889, HEISMAN IN 1935 AND OUTLAND IN 1946.

FORMER GOPHERS MAKING ARMED SERVICE TEAMS DURING WORLD WAR II ARE NOT SHOWN ON THIS CHART. HOWEVER, THOSE PLAYERS INCLUDE BILL DALEY, HERB HEIN, URBAN ODSON, CHARLES W. SCHULTZ, BRUCE SMITH AND GEORGE SVENDSEN.

Key to Symbols

	AT MINN.	AWAY FROM MINN.*
PLAYER	●	○
CONFERENCE MVP	⬢	
CONSENSUS ALL-AMERICAN	●	○
HEISMAN AWARD	H	
OUTLAND AWARD	Ot	
RIMINGTON AWARD	R	
MACKEY AWARD	M	
GOLD MEDAL AWARD		G
THORPE AWARD	T	
COACH	■	□
TRAINER	Tr	
ALL-WESTERN (BEFORE BIG 10)	◑	

* THESE GOPHERS ARE RECOGNIZED FOR THEIR ACCOMPLISHMENTS AS PLAYERS AND COACHES AFTER LEAVING MINNESOTA AND SERVING OTHER TEAMS. THE GOLD MEDAL AWARD IS FOR LIFETIME ACHIEVEMENTS AFTER FOOTBALL DAYS.

MARKS IN THE HALL OF FAME COLUMN FALL IN THE INDIVIDUAL'S LAST YEAR AT MINNESOTA RATHER THAN THE ACTUAL YEAR OF INDUCTION INTO THE HALL.

Columns: ALL-CONF. · ALL-AMER. · MISC. AWARD · HALL/FAME

Year / Player	ALL-CONF.	ALL-AMER.	MISC. AWARD	HALL/FAME
1887				
PUDGE HEFFELFINGER-G	-	-	-	○
1889				
PUDGE HEFFELFINGER-G	-	○	-	-
1890				
PUDGE HEFFELFINGER-G	-	○	-	-
1891				
PUDGE HEFFELFINGER-G	-	○	-	-
JOHN W. ADAMS-C	-	○	-	-
1894				
EVERHART HARDING-RG	◑	-	-	-
JOHN HARRISON-LE	◑	-	-	-
JOHN DALRYMPLE-LT	◑	-	-	-
WILLIAM DALRYMPLE-RE	◑	-	-	-
1895				
JOHN HARRISON-LE	◑	-	-	-
1896				
EVERHART HARDING-LG	●	-	-	-
GEORGE FINLAYSON-RG	●	-	-	-
JOHN HARRISON-RE	●	-	-	-
1897				
JOHN HARRISON-LE	●	-	-	-
1900				
BEYER AUNE-LE	●	-	-	-
JOHN FLYNN-LG	●	-	-	-
L.A. PAGE, JR.-C	●	-	-	-
1901				
GILMORE DOBIE-QB	-	-	-	□
JOHN FLYNN-LG	●	-	-	-
L.A. PAGE, JR.-C	●	-	-	-
1903				
EARL CURRENT-FB	●	-	-	-
SIG HARRIS-QB	●	-	-	-
JAMES IRSFELD-RHB	●	-	-	-
ED ROGERS-LE	●	-	-	●
FRED SCHACHT-RT	●	●	-	-
MOSE STRATHERN-C				
1904				
MOSE STRATHERN-C	●	●	-	-
WALTON THORP-LG	●	-	-	-
1905				
WILLIAM ITTNER-LT	●	-	-	-
BOBBY MARSHALL-LE	●	-	-	-

1906

Name	ALL-CONF.	ALL-AMER.	MISC. AWARD	HALL/FAME
GEORGE CASE-RT	●	-	-	-
WILLIAM DOANE-LE	●	-	-	-
WILLIAM ITTNER-LHB	●	-	-	-
BOBBY MARSHALL-LE,RE	●	-	-	●
ORREN SAFFORD-C	●	-	-	-
J.R. SCHUKNECHT-RHB	●	-	-	-
DAN SMITH-RG	●	-	-	-
THEODORE VITA-LG,LT	●	-	-	-

1907

Name	ALL-CONF.	ALL-AMER.	MISC. AWARD	HALL/FAME
HARRY CAPRON-E	●	-	-	-
GEORGE CASE-T	●	-	-	-

1908

Name	ALL-CONF.	ALL-AMER.	MISC. AWARD	HALL/FAME
ORREN SAFFORD-C				

1909

Name	ALL-CONF.	ALL-AMER.	MISC. AWARD	HALL/FAME
EARL FARNAM-C	●	-	-	-
LISLE JOHNSTON-LHB	●	-	-	-
JOHN McGOVERN-QB	●	●	-	-
EARL PICKERING-FB	●	-	-	-
RUBE ROSENWALD-LHB	●	-	-	-
JAMES WALKER-LT	●	-	-	-

1910

Name	ALL-CONF.	ALL-AMER.	MISC. AWARD	HALL/FAME
LISLE JOHNSTON-FB	●	●	-	-
JOHN McGOVERN-QB	●	-	-	●
RUBE ROSENWALD-LHB	●	-	-	-
JAMES WALKER-LT	●	●	-	-

1911

Name	ALL-CONF.	ALL-AMER.	MISC. AWARD	HALL/FAME
RALPH CAPRON-QB	●	-	-	-
LUCIUS SMITH-LG	●	-	-	-
CLIFFORD MORRELL-C	●	-	-	-
RUBE ROSENWALD-LHB	●	-	-	-

1912

Name	ALL-CONF.	ALL-AMER.	MISC. AWARD	HALL/FAME
WILLIAM McALMON-HB	●	-	-	-
BOLESLAUS ROSENTHAL-T,G	●	-	-	-
CLARK SHAUGHNESSY-RT	●	-	-	-

1913

Name	ALL-CONF.	ALL-AMER.	MISC. AWARD	HALL/FAME
CLARK SHAUGHNESSY-FB	●	●	-	□
LORIN SOLON-LE	●	●	-	-

1914

Name	ALL-CONF.	ALL-AMER.	MISC. AWARD	HALL/FAME
LORIN SOLON-FB	●	-	-	-

1915

Name	ALL-CONF.	ALL-AMER.	MISC. AWARD	HALL/FAME
BERT BASTON-LE	●	●	-	-
BERNIE BIERMAN-LHB,FB	●	●	-	-
MERTON DUNNIGAN-RG,C	●	●	-	-

1916

Name	ALL-CONF.	ALL-AMER.	MISC. AWARD	HALL/FAME
BERT BASTON-LE	●	●	-	●
CONRAD EKLUND-G	●	-	-	-
GEORGE HAUSER-RT	●	-	-	-
SHORTY LONG-QB	-	●	-	-
FRANK MAYER-T	●	-	-	-
GILBERT SINCLAIR-LG	●	-	-	-
JACK TOWNLEY-C	●	-	-	-
ARNOLD WYMAN-FB	●	-	-	-

1917

Name	ALL-CONF.	ALL-AMER.	MISC. AWARD	HALL/FAME
GEORGE HAUSER-RT	●	●	-	-

1918

Name	ALL-CONF.	ALL-AMER.	MISC. AWARD	HALL/FAME
NORMAN KINGSLEY-FB	●	-	-	-

1919

Name	ALL-CONF.	ALL-AMER.	MISC. AWARD	HALL/FAME
ROBERT BUTLER-G	●	-	-	-
ARNOLD OSS-HB,FB	●	-	-	-
EDMOND RUBEN-FB	●	-	-	-
VERN WILLIAMS-C	●	-	-	-

1920

Name	ALL-CONF.	ALL-AMER.	MISC. AWARD	HALL/FAME
GUS ECKBERG-E	●	-	-	-
ARNOLD OSS-FB	●	-	-	-
FESTUS TIERNEY-RG	●	-	-	-

1921

Name	ALL-CONF.	ALL-AMER.	MISC. AWARD	HALL/FAME
DR. HENRY WILLIAMS-COACH	-	-	-	■

1922

Name	ALL-CONF.	ALL-AMER.	MISC. AWARD	HALL/FAME
EARL MARTINEAU-LHB,RHB	●	-	-	-

1923

Name	ALL-CONF.	ALL-AMER.	MISC. AWARD	HALL/FAME
RAY ECKLUND-LE	●	●	-	-
EARL MARTINEAU-RHB,QB	●	●	-	-

1924

Name	ALL-CONF.	ALL-AMER.	MISC. AWARD	HALL/FAME
GEORGE ABRAMSON-G	●	-	-	-
TED COX-T	●	-	-	-

1925

Name	ALL-CONF.	ALL-AMER.	MISC. AWARD	HALL/FAME
LEN WALSH-G	●	-	-	-

1926

Name	ALL-CONF.	ALL-AMER.	MISC. AWARD	HALL/FAME
HAROLD ALMQUIST-QB	●	-	-	-
MITCHELL GARY-RT	●	-	-	-
HAROLD HANSON-T,G	●	●	-	-
HERB JOESTING-FB	●	●	-	-
GEORGE MAC KINNON-C	●	-	-	-
MALLY NYDAHL-QB	●	-	-	-
ROGER WHEELER-E	●	-	-	-

1927

Name	ALL-CONF.	ALL-AMER.	MISC. AWARD	HALL/FAME
HAROLD ALMQUIST-QB	●	-	-	-
MITCHELL GARY-RT	●	-	-	-
HAROLD HANSON-LG	●	●	-	-
KENNETH HAYCRAFT-E	●	-	-	-
HERB JOESTING-FB	●	●	-	●

1928

Name	ALL-CONF.	ALL-AMER.	MISC. AWARD	HALL/FAME
GEORGE GIBSON-LG	●	●	-	-
KENNETH HAYCRAFT-E	●	●	-	-
FRED HOVDE-QB	●	-	-	G
BRONKO NAGURSKI-FB,T	●	-	-	-

1929

Name	ALL-CONF.	ALL-AMER.	MISC. AWARD	HALL/FAME
BRONKO NAGURSKI-FB,T	●	●	-	●
ROBERT TANNER-RE	●	●	-	-

1930

Name	ALL-CONF.	ALL-AMER.	MISC. AWARD	HALL/FAME
BIGGIE MUNN-LG	●	-	-	-

1931

Name	ALL-CONF.	ALL-AMER.	MISC. AWARD	HALL/FAME
FRITZ CRISLER-COACH	-	-	-	□
JACK MANDERS-FB	●	-	-	-
BIGGIE MUNN-LG	●	●	-	□

Player	ALL-CONF.	ALL-AMER.	MISC. AWARD	HALL/FAME
1932				
MARSHALL WELLS - T	●	-	-	-
1933				
SHELDON BEISE - FB	●	●	-	-
BUTCH LARSON - RE	●	●	-	-
PUG LUND - LHB	●	●	-	-
1934				
SHELDON BEISE - FB	●	-	-	-
PHIL BENGTSON - RT	●	-	-	-
BILL BEVAN - RG	●	●	-	-
STAN KOSTKA - FB	-	●	-	-
BUTCH LARSON - RE	●	●	-	-
PUG LUND - LHB	●	●	-	●
BOB TENNER - LE	●	-	-	-
ED WIDSETH - LT	●	●	-	-
1935				
SHELDON BEISE - FB	●	●	-	-
BABE LEVOIR - QB	●	●	-	-
DICK SMITH - RT	●	●	-	-
ED WIDSETH - LT	●	●	-	-
BUD WILKINSON - LG	●	●	-	-
1936				
JULIUS ALFONSE - RHB	-	●	-	-
RAYMOND ANTIL - LE	●	-	-	-
RAY KING - RE	-	●	-	-
ANDY URAM - FB, HB	●	●	-	-
ED WIDSETH - LT	●	●	-	●
BUD WILKINSON - QB	-	-	-	□
1937				
RUDY GMITRO - RHB	●	-	-	-
RAY KING - RE	●	●	-	-
LOU MIDLER - RT	●	●	-	-
FRANCIS TWEDELL - RG	●	-	-	-
ANDY URAM - FB	-	●	-	-
HAROLD VAN EVERY - LHB	-	●	-	-
1938				
WILBER MOORE - HB, QB	●	-	-	-
BUTCH NASH - RE	●	●	-	-
FRANCIS TWEDELL - RG	●	●	-	-
1939				
GEORGE FRANCK - LHB	●	-	-	-
WIN PEDERSON - LT	●	-	-	-
HAROLD VAN EVERY - RHB	●	-	-	-
1940				
GEORGE FRANCK - LHB	●	●	-	●
URBAN ODSON - RT	●	●	-	-
HELGE PUKEMA - RG	●	-	-	-
1941				
BILL DALEY - FB, HB	●	-	-	-
ROBERT FITCH - LE	●	-	-	-
BILL GARNAAS - QB, HB	-	●	-	-
LEONARD LEVY - LG	●	-	-	-
URBAN ODSON - RT	●	-	-	-
BRUCE SMITH - LHB	●	●	H	●
DICK WILDUNG - RT	●	●	-	-
1942				
DICK WILDUNG - RT	●	●	-	●
1943				
BILL DALEY - FB	○	○	-	-
HERB HEIN - RE	○	○	-	-
PAUL MITCHELL - RT	●	-	-	-
1947				
LEO NOMELLINI - RG, LT	●	-	-	-
1948				
BUD GRANT - LE	●	-	-	-
LEO NOMELLINI - RG, LT	●	●	-	-
1949				
BUD GRANT - LE	●	-	-	-
LEO NOMELLINI - RG, LT	●	●	-	●
CLAYTON TONNEMAKER - C	●	●	-	●
1950				
BERNIE BIERMAN - COACH	-	-	-	■
1952				
PAUL GIEL - LHB	●	●	-	-
BOB McNAMARA - RHB, FB	●	●	-	-
PERCY ZACHARY - G	●	-	-	-
1953				
PAUL GIEL - LHB	●	●	-	●
1954				
BOB McNAMARA - RHB, FB	●	●	-	-
1956				
BOB HOBERT - RT	●	●	-	-
1958				
MIKE SVENDSON - C	●	-	-	-
1960				
TOM BROWN - RG	●	●	Ot	●
GREG LARSON - C	●	-	-	-
1961				
BOBBY BELL - RT	●	●	-	-
TOM HALL - RE	●	-	-	-
SANDY STEPHENS - QB	●	●	-	-
1962				
BOBBY BELL - RT	●	●	Ot	●
JOHN CAMPBELL - RE	●	-	-	-
JULIAN HOOK - LG	●	-	-	-
1963				
CARL ELLER - LT	●	●	-	-
1964				
AARON BROWN - RE	●	-	-	-
KRAIG LOFQUIST - LHB	●	-	-	-
1965				
AARON BROWN - ORE, DLE	●	●	-	-

Year / Player	ALL-CONF.	ALL-AMER.	MISC. AWARD	HALL/FAME
1967				
McKINLEY BOSTON – DRT	●	-	-	-
TOM SAKAL – RHB	●	-	-	-
BOB STEIN – DLE	●	●	-	-
JOHN WILLIAMS – ORT	●	●	-	-
1968				
DICK ENDERLE – ORG	●	-	-	-
NOEL JENKE – DLB	●	-	-	-
BOB STEIN – DRE	●	●	-	-
1969				
RAY PARSON – ORE	●	-	-	-
1970				
BILL LIGHT – DLB	●	-	-	-
JEFF WRIGHT – DRB	●	-	-	-
1971				
DOUG KINGSRITER – TE	●	●	-	-
BILL LIGHT – DLB	●	-	-	-
1972				
JOHN KING – FB	●	-	-	-
1973				
KEITH FAHNHORST – ORE	●	-	-	-
STEVE NEILS – DLE	●	-	-	-
1974				
KEITH SIMONS	●	-	-	-
1975				
RON KULLAS – WR	●	-	-	-
KEITH SIMONS – DRT	●	-	-	-
LLOYD STEIN – TRAINER	-	-	-	Tr
1976				
GEORGE ADZICK – SS	●	-	-	-
1977				
STEVE MIDBOE – DLT	●	-	-	-
PAUL ROGIND – K	●	-	-	-
1978				
MARION BARBER – TB	●	-	-	-
KEITH BROWN – DB	●	-	-	-
PAUL ROGIND – K	●	-	-	-
STAN SYTSMA – DRE	●	-	-	-
1979				
ELMER BAILEY – ORE	●	-	-	-
MARION BARBER – TB	●	-	-	-
1980				
MARION BARBER – TB	●	-	-	-
JEFF SCHUH – DRE	●	-	-	-
GARRY WHITE – FB	●	-	-	-
1981				
KEN DALLAFIOR – OLT	●	-	-	-
JIM FAHNHORST – DLB	●	-	-	-
1986				
BRUCE HOLMES – DLB	●	-	-	-
CHIP LOHMILLER – PK	●	-	-	-
DARRELL THOMPSON – TB	●	-	-	-
1987				
JON LEVERENZ – DLB	●	-	-	-
TROY WOLKOW – ORG	●	-	-	-
1990				
CHRIS THOME – C	●	-	-	-
1991				
PATT EVANS – TE	●	-	-	-
SEAN LUMPKIN – DB	●	-	-	-
1994				
CHRIS DARKINS – RB	●	-	-	-
ED HAWTHORNE – DT	●	-	-	-
1997				
LAMANZER WILLIAMS – DE	●	●	-	-
1998				
TYRONE CARTER – DB	●	●	-	-
1999				
TYRONE CARTER – DB	●	●	T	-
BEN HAMILTON – C	●	●	-	-
THOMAS HAMNER – RB	●	-	-	-
KARON RILEY – DE	●	-	-	-
2000				
PRESTON GRUENING – P	-	●	-	-
BEN HAMILTON – C	●	●	-	-
RON JOHNSON – WR	●	-	-	-
WILLIE MIDDLEBROOKS – CB	●	-	-	-
KARON RILEY – DE	●	-	-	-
2001				
JACK BREWER – FS	●	-	-	-
2003				
MARION BARBER III – RB	●	-	-	-
GREG ESLINGER – C	●	-	-	-
BEN UTECHT – TE	●	-	-	-
2004				
UKEE DOZIER – CB	●	-	-	-
GREG ESLINGER – C	●	●	-	-
LAURENCE MARONEY – RB	●	-	-	-
RIAN MELANDER – LT	●	-	-	-
MARK SETTERSTROM – OG	●	-	-	-
2005				
GREG ESLINGER – C	●	●	OtR	-
LAWRENCE MARONEY – RB	●	●	-	-
MARK SETTERSTROM – OG	●	-	-	-
MATT SPAETH – TE	●	-	-	-
2006				
MATT SPAETH – TE	●	●	M	-
2008				
ERIC DECKER – WR	●	-	-	-
WILLIE VAN DE STEEG – DE	●	-	-	-

We're Number One!

- **#1** SELF-PROCLAIMED CHAMPIONS OF THE NORTHWEST: 1890, 1891

- **#1** CHAMPIONS OF THE INTERCOLLEGIATE ATHLETIC ASSOCIATION OF THE NORTHWEST: 1892, 1893

- **#1** SELF-PROCLAIMED CHAMPIONS OF THE MIDWEST: 1900, 1903, 1911, 1915

- **#1** BIG TEN CHAMPIONS: 1900, 1903, 1904, 1906, 1909, 1910, 1911, 1915, 1927, 1933, 1934, 1935, 1937, 1938, 1940, 1941, 1960, 1967

- **#1** NATIONAL CHAMPIONS: 1934, 1935, 1936, 1940, 1941, 1960

- **#1** UNDEFEATED SEASONS: 1892 (5-0-0), 1893 (6-0-0), 1900 (10-0-2), 1903 (13-0-1), 1904 (13-0-0), 1911 (6-0-1), 1927 (6-0-2), 1933 (4-0-4), 1934 (8-0-0), 1935 (8-0-0), 1940 (8-0-0), 1941 (8-0-0)

- **#1** LONGEST UNDEFEATED STRINGS: 1903-05 (33-0-1), 1933-36 (24-0-4), 1900-01 (17-0-2), 1939-42 (18-0-0), 1891-94 (17-0-1), 1914-16 (12-0-1)

- **#1** ALL-AMERICANS: 64 PLAYERS

- **#1** HEISMAN AWARD: 1 PLAYER

- **#1** OUTLAND AWARD: 3 PLAYERS

- **#1** RIMINGTON AWARD: 1 PLAYER

- **#1** ALL-BIG TEN: 175 PLAYERS

- **#1** BIG TEN MVP: 6 PLAYERS

- **#1** ALL-TIME ALL-BIG TEN: 2 PLAYERS

- **#1** THORPE AWARD: 1 PLAYER

- **#1** MACKEY AWARD: 1 PLAYER

- **#1** COLLEGE FOOTBALL HALL OF FAME: 16 PLAYERS, 2 COACHES, 1 TRAINER

- **#1** GOPHERS TO ENTER THE COLLEGE FOOTBALL HALL OF FAME FOR SERVICES RENDERED AT OTHER SCHOOLS AFTER THEIR PLAYING DAYS AT MINNESOTA: 1 PLAYER, 5 COACHES

- **#1** NATIONAL FOOTBALL FOUNDATION GOLD MEDAL AWARD: 1 PLAYER

- **#1** 20TH CENTURY COLLEGE RECORD FOR MOST POINTS SCORED IN A SEASON: 725 IN 1904

- **#1** NATIONAL LEADER FOR HIGH SCORING IN A GAME FOR 1904: 146 AGAINST GRINNELL

- **#1** NATIONAL LEADER OF FIELD GOALS FOR 1907: GEORGE CAPRON WITH 11

- **#1** NATIONAL LEADER OF FIELD GOALS FOR 1929: ARTHUR PHARMER WITH 3

- **#1** THE ONLY PLAYER IN HISTORY TO BE NAMED ALL-AMERICAN AT TWO POSITIONS AT THE SAME TIME: BRONKO NAGURSKI AT FULLBACK AND TACKLE IN 1929

- **#1** NATIONAL LEADER IN INTERCEPTIONS FOR 1939: HAROLD VAN EVERY WITH 8

- **#1** NATIONAL RECORD IN KICKOFF RETURN AVERAGE: 36.4 YARDS IN 1940

(#1) NATIONAL LEADER IN YARDS GAINED FOR 1944: WAYNE "RED" WILLIAMS RUSHED 911 YARDS IN 136 CARRIES; RETURNED PUNTS 242 YARDS; RETURNED KICKOFFS FOR 314 YARDS AND AVERAGED 163 YARDS PER GAME FOR A TOTAL 1467 YARDS

(#1) NATIONAL LEADER IN PUNT RETURNS FOR 1953: PAUL GIEL WITH 17 RETURNS FOR 288 YARDS AND A 16.9 YARD PER RETURN AVERAGE

(#1) NATIONAL LEADING TEAM IN RUSH DEFENSE FOR 1962: 52.2 YARDS PER GAME

(#1) NATIONAL RECORD FOR MOST RUSHES IN A GAME: 57 BY KENT KITZMANN AGAINST ILLINOIS IN 1977

(#1) NATIONAL RECORD FOR LONGEST KICKOFF RETURN: 100 YARDS BY RICK UPCHURCH AGAINST WISCONSIN IN 1974 AND BY BOBBY WEBER AGAINST OHIO STATE IN 1977

(#1) NATIONAL RECORD FOR MOST YARDS GAINED BY A FRESHMAN FOR THE FIRST GAME IN HIS CAREER: 205 YARDS BY DARRELL THOMPSON AGAINST BOWLING GREEN IN 1986

(#1) BIG TEN RECORD FOR FEWEST TEAM PASS ATTEMPTS IN A GAME: 0 IN 1940 AGAINST OHIO STATE.

(#1) BIG TEN RECORD FOR MOST YARDS RETURNED ON KICKOFFS IN A GAME: 203 YARDS BY RON ENGEL AGAINST MICHIGAN IN 1951

(#1) NATIONAL RECORD FOR THE LONGEST INDOOR FIELDGOAL: 62 YARDS BY CHIP LOHMILLER IN 1968.

(#1) BIG TEN RECORD FOR MOST YARDS RETURNED IN A GAME BY INTERCEPTION: 140 BY WALTER BOWSER AGAINST MICHIGAN STATE IN 1970.

(#1) BIG TEN RECORD FOR MOST YARDS RETURNED IN A SEASON BY INTERCEPTION: 203 YARDS BY WALTER BOWSER ON 5 INTERCEPTIONS IN 1970

(#1) BIG TEN RECORD FOR FEWEST TEAM FUMBLES IN A SEASON: 8 IN 1976

(#1) BIG TEN RECORD FOR MOST SCORES IN A GAME BY SAFETY: 2 VS. INDIANA IN 1981

(#1) NATIONAL LEADER FOR LONGEST RUN FROM SCRIMMAGE FOR 1987: 98 YARDS BY DARRELL THOMPSON AGAINST MICHIGAN.

(#1) BIG TEN RECORD FOR GAINING OVER 1000 YARDS BY RUSHING IN EACH OF HIS FIRST TWO YEARS OF PLAY: DARRELL THOMPSON IN 1986 (1240 YARDS) AND 1987 (1229 YARDS)

(#1) NATIONAL LEADER FOR LONGEST TOUCHDOWN PASS PLAY FOR 1992: MARQUEL FLEETWOOD TO JOHN LEWIS FOR 94 YARDS AGAINST MICHIGAN.

(#1) BIG TEN RECORD FOR MOST TOUCHDOWN RECEPTIONS IN A GAME: 5 BY OMAR DOUGLAS AGAINST PURDUE IN 1993

(#1) NATIONAL RECORD FOR MOST TOUCHDOWNS IN A GAME OFF FUMBLE RECOVERIES: 2 BY TYRONE CARTER AGAINST SYRACUSE IN 1996

(#1) NATIONAL LEADER IN QUARTERBACK SACKS FOR 1997: 18.5 BY LAMANZER WILLIAMS

(#1) BIG TEN LEADER IN FORCED FUMBLES FOR 1997: 5 BY LAMANZER WILLIAMS

#1 NATIONAL RECORD FOR MOST YARDS ON KICK RETURNS IN A GAME: 284 YARDS (59 ON PUNT RETURNS AND 225 ON KICKOFF RETURNS) BY TUTU ATWELL AGAINST IOWA STATE IN 1997.

#1 NATIONAL RECORD FOR MOST TOUCHDOWNS SCORED ON KICKOFF RETURNS IN A GAME: 2 BY TUTU ATWELL AGAINST IOWA STATE IN 1997.

#1 NATIONAL RECORD FOR CAREER SOLO TACKLES: 405 BY TYRONE CARTER IN 1999

#1 DIVISION I CAREER LEADING TACKLER BY A DEFENSIVE BACK: 529 BY TYRONE CARTER IN 1999

#1 NATIONAL LEADER IN PUNTING AVERAGE FOR 2000: 45.5 YARDS BY PRESTON GRUENING.

#1 NATIONAL RECORD FOR MOST ALL-PURPOSE PLAYS IN A BOWL GAME: 47 BY TELLIS REDMON (42 RUSH, 3 RECEPTIONS, 2 PUNT RETURNS) IN THE 2000 MICRONPC.COM BOWL.

#1 NATIONAL RECORD FOR CATCHING A PASS IN CONSECUTIVE GAMES: 46 BY RON JOHNSON FROM 1998-2001.

#1 NATIONAL RECORD FOR THE MOST FIELDGOALS IN A BOWL GAME: 5 BY DAN NYSTROM IN 2002.

#1 BIG TEN RECORD FOR MOST CAREER POINTS BY KICKING: 367 BY DAN NYSTROM 1999-2002.

#1 BIG TEN RECORD FOR MOST CAREER FIELDGOALS MADE: 71 BY DAN NYSTROM 1999-2002.

#1 NATIONAL RECORD FOR TWO PLAYERS ON THE SAME TEAM TO RUSH OVER 1,000 YARDS IN BACK-TO-BACK SEASONS: BY MARION BARBER III (1,196 & 1,348 YARDS) AND LAWRENCE MARONEY (1,121 & 1,269 YARDS) IN 2003 & 2004.

#1

MINNESOTA AND OTHER NATIONAL CHAMPIONSHIP TEAMS WHOSE COACHES HAVE A GOPHER CONNECTION:

YEAR	CHAMPION TEAM	COACH / GOPHER CONNECTION
1921 1922	CORNELL	GILMORE DOBIE / GOPHER PLAYER 1899-1901
1934 1935 1936 1940 1941	MINNESOTA	BERNIE BIERMAN / GOPHER PLAYER 1913-15 AND COACH 1932-41, 1945-50
1940	STANFORD	CLARK SHAUGHNESSY / GOPHER PLAYER 1912-13
1947	MICHIGAN	FRITZ CRISLER / GOPHER COACH 1930-31
1950 1955 1956	OKLAHOMA	BUD WILKINSON / GOPHER PLAYER 1934-36
1951 1952	MICHIGAN STATE	BIGGIE MUNN / GOPHER PLAYER 1929-31
1960	MINNESOTA	MURRAY WARMATH / GOPHER COACH 1954-71
1968	NOTRE DAME	LOU HOLTZ / GOPHER COACH 1984-85

#1 NATIONAL RECORD FOR TWO PLAYERS ON THE SAME TEAM TO RUSH OVER 1000 YARDS IN THREE CONSECUTIVE SEASONS. 2003: MARION BARBER III, 1196 YARDS, LAWRENCE MARONEY, 1121 YARDS. 2004: MARION BARBER III, 1348 YARDS, LAWRENCE MARONEY, 1269 YARDS. 2006: LAWRENCE MARONEY, 1355 YARDS, GARY RUSSELL, 1045 YARDS.

#1 NATIONAL LEADER IN FAVORABLE TURNOVERS FROM INTERCEPTIONS AND FUMBLES FOR 2006: +18 (14 TURNOVERS BY MINNESOTA TO 32 BY OPPONENTS) +1.38 AVERAGE PER GAME.

For the Record

THE GAME AND ITS STATISTICS HAVE CHANGED OVER TIME. TWO PRINCIPAL RECORD BOOKS WERE SPALDING, IN THE EARLY DAYS, AND BARNES, LATER ON. NOW THEY HAVE OFFICIAL STATS DONE BY THE N.C.A.A.

EARLY BOOKS HAD THE HEADING, "FAMOUS RUNS." THEY LUMPED TOGETHER KICKOFF RETURNS, RUNS FROM SCRIMMAGE, FUMBLES AND PUNTS. YOU HAD TO SEPARATE THEM YOURSELF IF YOU WANTED TO COMPARE EACH TYPE. FIELD GOALS HAD DROPKICKS AND PLACE KICKS INDIVIDUALLY LABLED, BUT MIXED TOGETHER, TOO. IN A 1913 BOOK THESE STATS DATED BACK TO 1873.

"PRINCIPAL TOUCHDOWNS SCORED FROM COMPLETED FORWARD PASS" WERE RECORDED AS (1)"LONGEST AIRBORNE PASS RESULTING IN A TD," (2)"LONGEST RUN AFTER RECEIVING A PASS FOR TD" AND (3)"LONGEST COMPLETE PASS FOR TD." THERE WASN'T A GREAT VARIETY OF RECORDS. THEY HAD RUNDOWNS OF THE PREVIOUS YEAR AND SOME PICTURES WITH A LIST FOR THE NEXT YEAR. INDIVIDUAL HONORS WERE ALSO NOTED.

BY 1980 THE N.C.A.A. STARTED TO INCREASE THEIR INFORMATION. YOU COULD EVEN FIND PAST ACCOMPLISHMENTS THAT HADN'T FOUND THEIR WAY INTO THE OLDER BOOKS. IN 1990 A BOOM OF INFORMATION STARTED TO MAKE THE STATISTICAL BOOK BIG AND THICK, LIKE BASEBALL'S.

Final Score

IN ORDER TO RECORD THE FOLLOWING GAME STATISTICS; OLD GOPHER YEARBOOKS, HISTORICAL BIOGRAPHIES, PROGRAMS, PRESS GUIDES ETC. HAVE BEEN STUDIED. IF THERE WAS A DISCREPANCY IN ANYTHING A SEARCH WAS MADE FOR THAT GAME THROUGH OLD NEWSPAPERS. HUNDREDS OF PAPERS, MAINLY FROM THE MINNEAPOLIS STAR, JOURNAL AND TRIBUNE, WERE CONSULTED.

ADDED IS ONE GAME NORMALLY NOT INCLUDED IN OFFICIAL RECORDS. IT WAS AGAINST THE MINNEAPOLIS FOOTBALL ASSOCIATION IN 1883. A STUDENT NEWSPAPER ACCOUNT DIDN'T REPORT THE SCORE, BUT DID MENTION THAT THE UNIVERSITY TEAM BEAT THEM "IGNOMINIOUSLY."

SEPARATELY RECORDED ARE THE SPRING GAMES (1956-60) AGAINST THE ALUMNI. ALTHOUGH NOT OFFICIAL, THEY WERE TRUE BATTLES JUST AS THE ALUMNI AND COLLEGIATE GAMES WERE BEFORE 1900. THE ALUMS OF THE 1950'S WEREN'T ENTIRELY OLD MEN USING THEIR SCRAPBOOKS FOR PADDING. SOME WERE STILL ACTIVE IN PRO BALL AND WON THREE OF FIVE GAMES. ONE OF THOSE VICTORIES WAS AGAINST A NATIONALLY RANKED GOPHER SQUAD. ANOTHER GAME SAW THE AGING BRONKO NAGURSKI CARRY NATIONAL CHAMPION LINEMEN ON HIS BACK FOR FIVE YARD GAINS.

Key to Symbols

MINNESOTA SCORE IS ALWAYS SHOWN FIRST

- **H** HOME GAME
- **HC** HOMECOMING GAME
- **A** AWAY GAME
- **▼** OPPONENT WAS CONFERENCE CHAMPION
- **★** OPPONENT WAS RANKED FIRST NATIONALLY WHILE GOING AGAINST MINNESOTA BUT DIDN'T NECESSARILY FINISH THE SEASON SO RANKED
- **☆** OPPONENT WAS RANKED FIRST NATIONALLY SOMETIME DURING THE SEASON BUT NOT WHILE GOING AGAINST MINNESOTA
- **[ ]** OPPONENT NATIONAL RANKING AT SEASON END
- **[ ]** GOPHER NATIONAL RANKING FOLLOWS OVERALL W-L-T RECORD
- **[u]** UNRANKED
- **( )** GOPHER CONFERENCE RANKING FOLLOWS CONFERENCE W-L-T RECORD

COACH: NONE

1882
SEP. 30	H	4 - 0	HAMLINE
OCT. 16	A	0 - 2	HAMLINE
		4 - 2	1-1-0 [?]

COACH: THOMAS PEEBLES

1883
?	A	2 - 4	CARLETON
OCT. 29	?	W - L	MPLS. FOOTBALL ASSN.
NOV. 3	A	5 - 0	HAMLINE
?	?	2 - 4	EX-COLLEGIANS
		9 - 8	2-2-0 [?]

1884
NO INTERCOLLEGIATE GAMES PLAYED

1885
NO INTERCOLLEGIATE GAMES PLAYED

COACH: FREDERICK S. JONES

1886
OCT. 25	A	5 - 9	SHATTUCK
NOV. ?	H	8 - 18	SHATTUCK
		13 - 27	0-2-0 [?]

1887
OCT. ?	H	8 - 0	MINNEAPOLIS HIGH
OCT. ?	H	14 - 0	ALUMNI
		22 - 0	2-0-0 [?]

1888
OCT. 27	A	8 - 16	SHATTUCK
OCT. 31	H	14 - 0	SHATTUCK
		22 - 16	1-1-0 [?]

COACH: D.W. & AL McCORD, FRANK HEFFELFINGER & "BILLY" MORSE

1889
OCT. 5	H	2 - 0	EX-COLLEGIATES
OCT. 26	H	10 - 0	EX-COLLEGIATES
NOV. 11	A	8 - 28	SHATTUCK
NOV. 20	H	26 - 0	SHATTUCK
		46 - 28	3-1-0 [?]

COACH: TOM ECK

1890
OCT. 27	?	44 - 0	HAMLINE
NOV. 3	A	58 - 0	SHATTUCK
NOV. 5	H	0 - 0	EX-COLLEGIATES
NOV. 8	H	18 - 13	GRINNELL
NOV. 15	H	63 - 0	WISCONSIN
NOV. 19	H	11 - 14	EX-COLLEGIATES
NOV. 29	H	14 - 6	EX-COLLEGIATES
		208 - 33	5-1-1 [?]

(CHAMPIONS OF THE NW)

COACH: EDWARD MOULTON

1891
OCT. 17	H	0 - 4	EX-COLLEGIATES
OCT. 24	H	26 - 12	WISCONSIN
OCT. 31	A	12 - 12	GRINNELL
NOV. 2	A	42 - 4	IOWA
NOV. 14	H	22 - 14	GRINNELL
		102 - 46	3-1-1 [?]

(CHAMPIONS OF THE NW)

COACH: NONE

1892
OCT. 1   H   18-10   EX-COLLEGIATES
OCT. 17   H   14- 6   MICHIGAN
OCT. 22   H   40-24   GRINNELL
OCT. 29   A   32- 4   WISCONSIN
NOV. 8   H   18-12   NORTHWESTERN
             122-56   5-0-0 [?]
                      3-0-0 (1)

COACH: "WALLIE" WINTER

1893
OCT. 14   H   12- 6   KANSAS
OCT. 21   H   36- 6   GRINNELL
OCT. 24   A   10- 6   HAMLINE
OCT. 28   A   34-20   MICHIGAN
OCT. 30   A   16- 0   NORTHWESTERN
NOV. 11   H   40- 0   WISCONSIN
             148-38   6-0-0 [?]
                      3-0-0 (1)

COACH: THOMAS COCHRANE, JR.

1894
OCT. 13   H   10- 2   GRINNELL
OCT. 27   H   24- 0   PURDUE
NOV. 10   H   40- 0   BELOIT
NOV. 17   A   0- 6   WISCONSIN
              74- 8   3-1-0 [?]

COACH: WALTER "PUDGE" HEFFELFINGER

1895
SEP. 29   H   20- 0   MPLS. CENTRAL
OCT. 5   H   4- 6   GRINNELL
OCT. 12   A   6- 0   MINN. BOAT CLUB
OCT. 19   H   24- 0   IOWA ST.
OCT. 25   A   10- 6   CHICAGO
OCT. 29   A   4-16   PURDUE
NOV. 2   H   40- 0   MACALESTER
NOV. 16   H   14-10   WISCONSIN
NOV. 23   A   0-20   MICHIGAN
NOV. 28   H   14- 0   EX-COLLEGIANS
             136-58   7-3-0 [?]

COACH: ALEXANDER N. JERREMS

1896
SEP. 19   H   34- 0   MPLS. SOUTH
SEP. 26   H   50- 0   MPLS. CENTRAL
OCT. 3   H   16- 6   CARLETON
OCT. 10   H   12- 0   GRINNELL
OCT. 17   H   14- 0   PURDUE
OCT. 24   H   18- 6   IOWA ST.
OCT. 31   H   8- 0   EX-COLLEGIATES
NOV. 7   H   4- 6   MICHIGAN
NOV. 21   A   0- 6   WISCONSIN▼
NOV. 28   A   12- 0   KANSAS
             168-24   8-2-0 [?]
                      1-2-0 (5)

1897
SEP. 25   H   22- 0   MPLS. SOUTH
OCT. 2   H   26- 0   MACALESTER
OCT. 9   H   48- 6   CARLETON
OCT. 16   H   6- 0   GRINNELL
OCT. 23   H   10-12   IOWA ST.
OCT. 30   H   0-39   WISCONSIN▼
NOV. 13   A   0-14   MICHIGAN
NOV. 26   A   0- 6   PURDUE
             112-77   4-4-0 [?]
                      0-3-0 (6)

"WALLIE" WINTER

"PUDGE" HEFFELFINGER

COACH: JACK MINDS

1898
OCT. 1   H   32- 0   CARLETON
OCT. 5   H   0- 5   ALUMNI
OCT. 8   H   12- 0   RUSH MED. COL. OF CHI.
OCT. 15   H   6-16   GRINNELL
OCT. 22   H   0- 6   IOWA ST.
OCT. 29   A   0-28   WISCONSIN
NOV. 5   H   15- 0   NO. DAKOTA
NOV. 12   H   17- 6   NORTHWESTERN
NOV. 24   H   10-11   ILLINOIS
              92-72   4-5-0 [?]
                      1-2-0 (5)

COACH: WILLIAM C. LEARY &
       JOHN M. HARRISON

1899
SEP. 26   H   20- 0   MPLS. CENTRAL
OCT. 3   H   29- 0   MACALESTER
OCT. 7   H   40- 0   SHATTUCK
OCT. 14   H   35- 5   CARLETON
OCT. 21   H   6- 0   IOWA ST.
OCT. 28   H   5- 5   GRINNELL
NOV. 4   H   5-11   NORTHWESTERN
NOV. 4   H   6- 5   ALUMNI
NOV. 11   H   5- 5   BELOIT
NOV. 18   H   0-19   WISCONSIN
NOV. 25   A   0-29   CHICAGO▼
             151-79   6-3-2 [?]
                      0-3-0 (6)

COACH: DR. HENRY L. WILLIAMS

1900
SEP. 15   H   0- 0   MPLS. CENTRAL
SEP. 22   H   26- 0   ST. PAUL CENTRAL
SEP. 26   H   66- 0   MACALESTER
SEP. 29   H   44- 0   CARLETON
OCT. 6   H   27- 0   IOWA ST.
OCT. 13   H   6- 6   CHICAGO
OCT. 20   H   26- 0   GRINNELL
OCT. 27   H   34- 0   NO. DAKOTA
NOV. 3   H   6- 5   WISCONSIN
NOV. 10   H   23- 0   ILLINOIS
NOV. 12   H   21- 0   NORTHWESTERN
NOV. 29   A   20-12   NEBRASKA
             299-23   10-0-2 [?]
                      3-0-1 (1)

1901
SEP. 21   H   0- 0   MPLS. CENTRAL
SEP. 21   H   16- 0   ST. P. CENTRAL
SEP. 28   H   35- 0   CARLETON
OCT. 5   H   27- 0   CHICAGO COLLEGE
OCT. 12   H   19- 0   NEBRASKA
OCT. 26   H   16- 0   IOWA
NOV. 4   H   28- 0   HASKELL
NOV. 9   H   10- 0   NO. DAKOTA
NOV. 16   A   0-18   WISCONSIN▼
NOV. 23   A   16- 0   NORTHWESTERN
NOV. 28   A   16- 0   ILLINOIS
             183-18   9-1-1 [?]
                      3-1-0 (3)

WILLIAM C. LEARY

JOHN HARRISON

188

1902
SEP. 22	H	0-0	ST. P. CENTRAL
SEP. 22	H	28-0	MPLS. CENTRAL
SEP. 27	H	33-0	CARLETON
SEP. 30	H	59-0	HAMLINE
OCT. 4	H	16-0	IOWA ST.
OCT. 11	H	29-0	BELOIT
OCT. 18	H	0-6	NEBRASKA
OCT. 25	A	34-0	IOWA
NOV. 1	H	102-0	GRINNELL
NOV. 8	H	17-5	ILLINOIS
NOV. 15	H	11-0	WISCONSIN
NOV. 27	A	6-23	MICHIGAN▼[1]

335-34 9-2-1 [15]
3-1-0 (3)

1903
SEP. 19	H	21-6	MPLS. CENTRAL
SEP. 19	H	36-0	ST. P. CENTRAL
SEP. 23	H	37-0	MPLS. EAST
SEP. 26	H	29-0	CARLETON
SEP. 30	H	112-0	MACALESTER
OCT. 3	H	39-0	GRINNELL
OCT. 7	H	65-0	HAMLINE
OCT. 10	H	46-0	IOWA ST.
OCT. 17	H	75-0	IOWA
OCT. 24	H	46-0	BELOIT
OCT. 31	H	6-6	MICHIGAN▼★
NOV. 7	A	46-0	LAWRENCE
NOV. 14	A	32-0	ILLINOIS
NOV. 21	A	49-0	N.D. STATE
NOV. 26	A	17-0	WISCONSIN

656-12 14-0-1 [?]
3-0-1 (1)

1904
SEP. 17	H	{75-0	MPLS. CENTRAL (1ST ½)
		{32-0	ST. P. CENTRAL (2ND ½)
SEP. 24	H	77-0	SO. DAKOTA
SEP. 28	H	75-0	SHATTUCK
OCT. 1	H	65-0	CARLETON
OCT. 5	H	47-0	ST. THOMAS
OCT. 8	H	35-0	NO. DAKOTA
OCT. 15	H	32-0	IOWA ST.
OCT. 22	H	146-0	GRINNELL
OCT. 29	H	16-12	NEBRASKA
NOV. 5	H	69-0	LAWRENCE
NOV. 12	H	28-0	WISCONSIN
NOV. 19	A	17-0	NORTHWESTERN
NOV. 24	A	11-0	IOWA

725-12 13-0-0 [?]
3-0-0 (1)

1905
SEP. 23	H	{35-0	MPLS. CENTRAL (1ST ½)
		{39-0	ST. P. CENTRAL (2ND ½)
SEP. 30	H	{33-0	SHATTUCK (1ST ½)
		{21-0	PILLSBURY (2ND ½)
SEP. 30	H	42-0	ST. THOMAS
OCT. 7	H	45-0	NO. DAKOTA
OCT. 14	H	42-0	IOWA ST.
OCT. 21	H	39-0	IOWA
OCT. 28	H	46-0	LAWRENCE
NOV. 4	H	12-16	WISCONSIN
NOV. 11	H	81-0	SO. DAKOTA
NOV. 18	H	35-0	NEBRASKA
NOV. 25	H	72-6	NORTHWESTERN

542-22 10-1-0 [?]
2-1-0 (2)

1906
OCT. 27	H	22-4	IOWA ST.
NOV. 3	H	13-0	NEBRASKA
NOV. 10	A	4-2	CHICAGO
NOV. 17	H	0-17	CARLISLE
NOV. 24	H	8-6	INDIANA

47-29 4-1-0 [?]
2-0-0 (1)

1907
OCT. 12	H	8-0	IOWA ST.
OCT. 19	H	8-5	NEBRASKA
NOV. 2	H	12-18	CHICAGO▼
NOV. 16	H	10-12	CARLISLE
NOV. 23	A	17-17	WISCONSIN

55-52 2-2-1 [?]
0-1-1 (5)

1908
OCT. 3	H	6-0	LAWRENCE
OCT. 10	H	15-10	IOWA ST.
OCT. 17	H	0-0	NEBRASKA
OCT. 31	A	0-29	CHICAGO▼
NOV. 7	H	0-5	WISCONSIN
NOV. 21	H	11-6	CARLISLE

32-50 3-2-1 [?]
0-2-0 (7)

1909
SEP. 25	H	25-0	LAWRENCE
OCT. 2	H	41-0	IOWA
OCT. 9	H	18-0	IOWA ST.
OCT. 16	A	14-0	NEBRASKA
OCT. 30	A	20-6	CHICAGO
NOV. 13	A	34-6	WISCONSIN
NOV. 20	H	6-15	MICHIGAN

158-27 6-1-0 [?]
3-0-0 (1)

1910
SEP. 24	H	34-0	LAWRENCE
OCT. 1	H	17-0	SO. DAKOTA
OCT. 8	H	49-0	IOWA ST.
OCT. 15	H	27-0	NEBRASKA
OCT. 29	H	24-0	CHICAGO
NOV. 12	H	28-0	WISCONSIN
NOV. 19	A	0-6	MICHIGAN

179-6 6-1-0 [8]
2-0-0 (1)

1911
SEP. 30	H	5-0	IOWA ST.
OCT. 7	H	5-0	SO. DAKOTA
OCT. 21	H	21-3	NEBRASKA
OCT. 28	H	24-6	IOWA
NOV. 4	H	30-0	CHICAGO
NOV. 18	A	6-6	WISCONSIN
NOV. 25	A	11-0	ILLINOIS

102-15 6-0-1 [?]
3-0-1 (1)

Free Souvenir

Foot Ball

Program

Carlisle vs Minnesota

Saturday,
November 21st

University of Minnesota

1908

A FRESHLY PAINTED "LITTLE BROWN JUG" COMES HOME AFTER A STAY IN MICHIGAN

Souvenir Program

Minnesota-Michigan

Foot-Ball Game

Nov. 20, 1909

CAPT. McGOVERN

1912
SEP. 28	H	0 – 10	SO. DAKOTA
OCT. 5	H	5 – 0	IOWA ST.
OCT. 19	H	13 – 0	NEBRASKA
OCT. 26	H	56 – 7	IOWA
NOV. 2	H	13 – 0	ILLINOIS
NOV. 16	H	0 – 14	WISCONSIN ▼
NOV. 23	A	0 – 7	CHICAGO

87 – 38 4-3-0 [?]
2-2-0 (3)

1913
SEP. 27	H	14 – 0	SO. DAKOTA
OCT. 4	H	25 – 0	IOWA ST.
OCT. 18	A	0 – 7	NEBRASKA
OCT. 25	H	30 – 0	NO. DAKOTA
NOV. 1	A	21 – 3	WISCONSIN
NOV. 15	H	7 – 13	CHICAGO ▼
NOV. 22	A	19 – 9	ILLINOIS

116 – 32 5-2-0 [?]
2-1-0 (2)

1914
OCT. 3	H	28 – 6	NO. DAKOTA
OCT. 10	H	26 – 0	IOWA ST.
OCT. 17	H	29 – 7	SO. DAKOTA
OCT. 24	A	7 – 0	IOWA
OCT. 31	H	6 – 21	ILLINOIS ▼
NOV. 14	HC	14 – 3	WISCONSIN
NOV. 21	A	13 – 7	CHICAGO

123 – 44 6-1-0 [?]
3-1-0 (2)

1915
OCT. 2	H	41 – 0	NO. DAKOTA
OCT. 9	H	34 – 6	IOWA ST.
OCT. 16	H	19 – 0	SO. DAKOTA
OCT. 23	H	51 – 13	IOWA
OCT. 30	A	6 – 6	ILLINOIS ▼
NOV. 13	HC	20 – 7	CHICAGO
NOV. 20	A	20 – 3	WISCONSIN

191 – 35 6-0-1 [?]
3-0-1 (1)

1916
OCT. 7	H	41 – 7	SO. DAKOTA ST.
OCT. 14	H	47 – 7	NO. DAKOTA
OCT. 21	H	81 – 0	SO. DAKOTA
OCT. 28	H	67 – 0	IOWA
NOV. 4	H	9 – 14	ILLINOIS
NOV. 18	HC	54 – 0	WISCONSIN
NOV. 25	A	49 – 0	CHICAGO

348 – 28 6-1-0 [?]
3-1-0 (3)

1917
OCT. 13	H	64 – 0	SO. DAKOTA ST.
OCT. 20	H	33 – 9	INDIANA
NOV. 3	A	7 – 10	WISCONSIN
NOV. 17	HC	33 – 0	CHICAGO
NOV. 24	A	27 – 6	ILLINOIS

164 – 25 4-1-0 [?]
3-1-0 (2)

1918
OCT. 5	H	0 – 0	ALL STARS
OCT. 19	H	30 – 0	OVERLAND STATION
OCT. 26	A	25 – 7	ST. THOMAS
NOV. 2	H	59 – 6	CARLETON-ST. OLAF
NOV. 9	A	0 – 6	IOWA
NOV. 16	HC	6 – 0	WISCONSIN
NOV. 23	A	6 – 20	CHI. MUNICIPAL PIER
NOV. 30	A	7 – 0	CHICAGO

133 – 39 5-2-1 [?]
2-1-0 (4)

1919
OCT. 4	H	39 – 0	NO. DAKOTA
OCT. 11	H	6 – 6	NEBRASKA
OCT. 18	A	20 – 6	INDIANA
OCT. 25	H	6 – 9	IOWA
NOV. 1	A	19 – 7	WISCONSIN
NOV. 8	HC	6 – 10	ILLINOIS ▼
NOV. 22	A	34 – 7	MICHIGAN

130 – 45 4-2-1 [?]
3-2-0 (4)

1920
OCT. 2	H	41 – 3	NO. DAKOTA
OCT. 9	A	0 – 17	NORTHWESTERN
OCT. 16	H	7 – 21	INDIANA
OCT. 30	A	7 – 17	ILLINOIS
NOV. 6	H	0 – 3	WISCONSIN
NOV. 13	A	7 – 28	IOWA
NOV. 20	HC	0 – 3	MICHIGAN

62 – 92 1-6-0 [?]
0-6-0 (9)

1921
OCT. 1	H	19 – 0	NO. DAKOTA
OCT. 8	H	28 – 0	NORTHWESTERN
OCT. 15	A	0 – 27	OHIO ST.
OCT. 22	H	6 – 0	INDIANA
OCT. 29	A	0 – 35	WISCONSIN
NOV. 5	HC	7 – 41	IOWA ▼
NOV. 19	A	0 – 38	MICHIGAN

60 – 141 3-4-0 [?]
2-4-0 (6)

COACH: WILLIAM SPAULDING

1922
OCT. 7	H	22 – 0	NO. DAKOTA
OCT. 14	A	20 – 0	INDIANA
OCT. 21	A	7 – 7	NORTHWESTERN
OCT. 28	H	9 – 0	OHIO ST.
NOV. 4	HC	0 – 14	WISCONSIN
NOV. 11	A	14 – 28	IOWA ▼
NOV. 25	H	7 – 16	MICHIGAN ▼

79 – 65 3-3-1 [?]
2-3-1 (5)

1923
OCT. 6	H	20 – 17	IOWA ST
OCT. 13	H	13 – 12	HASKELL
OCT. 20	H	27 – 0	NO. DAKOTA
OCT. 27	A	0 – 0	WISCONSIN
NOV. 3	H	34 – 14	NORTHWESTERN
NOV. 17	HC	20 – 7	IOWA
NOV. 24	A	0 – 10	MICHIGAN ▼

114 – 60 5-1-1 [?]
2-1-1 (4)

1924
OCT. 4	H	14 – 0	NO. DAKOTA
OCT. 11	H	20 – 0	HASKELL
OCT. 18	A	7 – 7	WISCONSIN
OCT. 25	A	0 – 13	IOWA
NOV. 1	HC	0 – 13	MICHIGAN
NOV. 8	H	7 – 7	IOWA ST. [6]
NOV. 15	H	20 – 7	ILLINOIS ★ [4]
NOV. 22	H	0 – 16	VANDERBILT

68 – 63 3-3-2 [U]
1-2-1 (6)

LINEUP AND SCORE CARD

MINNESOTA
vs.
SOUTH DAKOTA

OCTOBER 1, 1932
— at —
MINNESOTA STADIUM

	First	Second	Third	Fourth
Minnesota				
South Dakota				

NOTRE DAME
vs.
MINNESOTA

DAD'S DAY
MEMORIAL STADIUM
October 9, 1926

...ERSITY of MINNESOTA

...AL PROGRAM

COACH: DR. CLARENCE W. SPEARS

1925
OCT. 3	H	25 – 6	NO. DAKOTA
OCT. 10	H	34 – 6	GRINNELL
OCT. 17	H	32 – 6	WABASH
OCT. 24	H	7 – 19	NOTRE DAME
OCT. 31	H	12 – 12	WISCONSIN [8]
NOV. 7	H	33 – 7	BUTLER
NOV. 14	H	33 – 0	IOWA
NOV. 21	A	0 – 35	MICHIGAN ▼ [2]
		176 – 91	5-2-1 [U]
			1-1-1 (4)

1926
OCT. 2	H	51 – 0	NO. DAKOTA
OCT. 9	H	7 – 20	NOTRE DAME [3]
OCT. 16	A	0 – 20	MICHIGAN ▼ [3]
OCT. 23	H	67 – 7	WABASH
OCT. 30	A	16 – 10	WISCONSIN
NOV. 6	A	41 – 0	IOWA
NOV. 13	H	81 – 0	BUTLER
NOV. 20	HC	6 – 7	MICHIGAN ▼
		269 – 64	5-3-0 [U]
			2-2-0 (6)

1927
OCT. 1	H	57 – 10	NO. DAKOTA U.
OCT. 8	H	40 – 0	OKLAHOMA A&M
OCT. 15	A	14 – 14	INDIANA
OCT. 22	HC	38 – 0	IOWA
OCT. 29	H	13 – 7	WISCONSIN
NOV. 5	A	7 – 7	NOTRE DAME [4]
NOV. 12	H	27 – 6	DRAKE
NOV. 19	A	13 – 7	MICHIGAN [7]
		209 – 51	6-0-2 [3]
			3-0-1 (1)

1928
OCT. 6	H	40 – 0	CREIGHTON
OCT. 13	H	15 – 0	PURDUE
OCT. 20	HC	33 – 7	CHICAGO
OCT. 27	A	6 – 7	IOWA
NOV. 3	A	9 – 10	NORTHWESTERN
NOV. 10	H	21 – 12	INDIANA
NOV. 17	H	52 – 0	HASKELL
NOV. 24	A	6 – 0	WISCONSIN ★ [4]
		182 – 36	6-2-0 [U]
			4-2-0 (3)

1929
OCT. 5	H	39 – 0	COE
OCT. 12	H	15 – 6	VANDERBILT
OCT. 19	A	26 – 14	NORTHWESTERN
OCT. 26	H	54 – 0	RIPON
NOV. 2	H	19 – 7	INDIANA
NOV. 9	A	7 – 9	IOWA
NOV. 16	HC	6 – 7	MICHIGAN
NOV. 23	H	13 – 12	WISCONSIN
		179 – 55	6-2-0 [U]
			3-2-0 (3)

COACH: FRITZ CRISLER

1930
SEP. 27	H	48 – 0	SO. DAKOTA ST.
OCT. 4	H	7 – 33	VANDERBILT
OCT. 11	H	0 – 0	STANFORD [7]
OCT. 18	H	6 – 0	INDIANA
NOV. 1	HC	6 – 27	NORTHWESTERN ▼ [4]
NOV. 8	H	59 – 0	SO. DAKOTA
NOV. 15	A	0 – 7	MICHIGAN ▼ [5]
NOV. 22	A	0 – 14	WISCONSIN
		126 – 81	3-4-1 [U]
			1-3-0 (6)

1931
SEP. 26	H	13 – 7	NO. DAKOTA ST.
SEP. 26	H	30 – 0	RIPON
OCT. 3	H	20 – 0	OKLAHOMA A&M
OCT. 10	A	0 – 13	STANFORD
OCT. 24	H	34 – 0	IOWA
OCT. 31	HC	14 – 0	WISCONSIN
NOV. 7	A	14 – 32	NORTHWESTERN ▼ [4]
NOV. 14	H	47 – 7	CORNELL (IOWA)
NOV. 21	A	0 – 6	MICHIGAN ▼ (POST
NOV. 28	H	19 – 7	OHIO ST. – SEASON)
		191 – 72	7-3-0 [U]
			3-2-0 (5)

COACH: BERNIE BIERMAN

1932
OCT. 1	H	12 – 0	SO. DAKOTA ST.
OCT. 8	H	0 – 7	PURDUE ▼ [4]
OCT. 15	H	7 – 6	NEBRASKA
OCT. 22	A	21 – 6	IOWA
OCT. 29	HC	7 – 0	NORTHWESTERN
NOV. 5	H	26 – 0	MISSISSIPPI
NOV. 12	A	13 – 20	WISCONSIN [11]
NOV. 19	H	0 – 3	MICHIGAN ▼ [1]
		86 – 42	5-3-0 [U]
			2-3-0 (5)

1933
SEP. 30	H	19 – 6	SO. DAKOTA ST.
OCT. 7	H	6 – 6	INDIANA
OCT. 14	H	7 – 7	PURDUE [10]
OCT. 21	H	7 – 3	PITTSBURGH [4]
OCT. 28	HC	19 – 7	IOWA
NOV. 4	A	0 – 0	NORTHWESTERN
NOV. 18	A	0 – 0	MICHIGAN ▼ [1]
NOV. 25	H	6 – 3	WISCONSIN
		64 – 32	4-0-4 [3]
			2-0-4 (1)

1934
SEP. 29	H	56 – 12	NO. DAKOTA ST.
OCT. 6	H	20 – 0	NEBRASKA
OCT. 20	A	13 – 7	PITTSBURGH ★ [2]
OCT. 27	A	48 – 12	IOWA
NOV. 3	HC	34 – 0	MICHIGAN
NOV. 10	H	30 – 0	INDIANA
NOV. 17	H	35 – 7	CHICAGO
NOV. 24	A	34 – 0	WISCONSIN
		270 – 38	8-0-0 [1]
			5-0-0 (1)

1935
SEP. 28	H	26 – 6	NO. DAKOTA ST.
OCT. 12	A	12 – 7	NEBRASKA
OCT. 19	H	20 – 0	TULANE
OCT. 26	HC	21 – 13	NORTHWESTERN
NOV. 2	H	29 – 7	PURDUE
NOV. 9	A	13 – 6	IOWA
NOV. 16	A	40 – 0	MICHIGAN
NOV. 23	H	33 – 7	WISCONSIN
		194 – 46	8-0-0 [1]
			5-0-0 (1)

1936
SEP. 26	A	14 – 7	WASHINGTON [4]
OCT. 10	H	7 – 0	NEBRASKA [9]
OCT. 17	H	26 – 0	MICHIGAN
OCT. 24	H	33 – 0	PURDUE
OCT. 31	A	0 – 6	NORTHWESTERN ▼ ☆ [6
NOV. 7	HC	52 – 0	IOWA
NOV. 14	H	47 – 19	TEXAS
NOV. 21	A	24 – 0	WISCONSIN
		203 – 32	7-1-0 [1]
			4-1-0 (2)

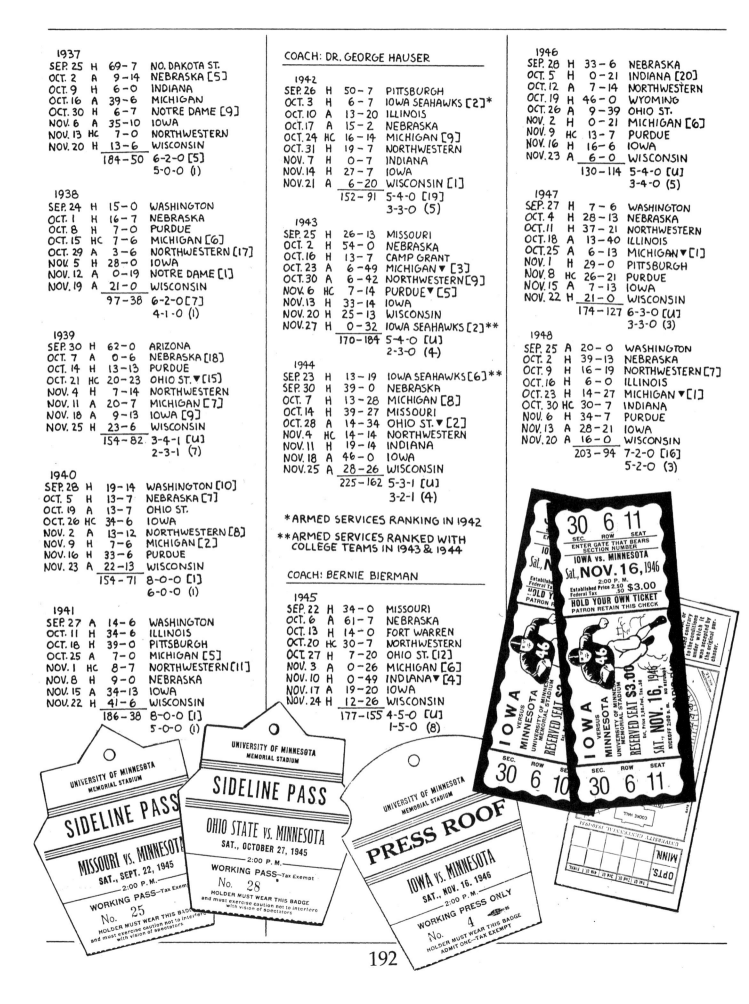

1937
SEP. 25 H 69-7 NO. DAKOTA ST.
OCT. 2 A 9-14 NEBRASKA [5]
OCT. 9 H 6-0 INDIANA
OCT. 16 A 39-6 MICHIGAN
OCT. 30 H 6-7 NOTRE DAME [9]
NOV. 6 A 35-10 IOWA
NOV. 13 HC 7-0 NORTHWESTERN
NOV. 20 H 13-6 WISCONSIN
184-50 6-2-0 [5]
5-0-0 (1)

1938
SEP. 24 H 15-0 WASHINGTON
OCT. 1 H 16-7 NEBRASKA
OCT. 8 H 7-0 PURDUE
OCT. 15 HC 7-6 MICHIGAN [6]
OCT. 29 A 3-6 NORTHWESTERN [17]
NOV. 5 H 28-0 IOWA
NOV. 12 H 0-19 NOTRE DAME [1]
NOV. 19 A 21-0 WISCONSIN
97-38 6-2-0 [7]
4-1-0 (1)

1939
SEP. 30 H 62-0 ARIZONA
OCT. 7 A 0-6 NEBRASKA [18]
OCT. 14 H 13-13 PURDUE
OCT. 21 HC 20-23 OHIO ST. ▼ [15]
NOV. 4 H 7-14 NORTHWESTERN
NOV. 11 A 20-7 MICHIGAN [7]
NOV. 18 A 9-13 IOWA [9]
NOV. 25 H 23-6 WISCONSIN
154-82 3-4-1 [U]
2-3-1 (7)

1940
SEP. 28 H 19-14 WASHINGTON [10]
OCT. 5 H 13-7 NEBRASKA [7]
OCT. 19 A 13-7 OHIO ST.
OCT. 26 HC 34-6 IOWA
NOV. 2 A 13-12 NORTHWESTERN [8]
NOV. 9 H 7-6 MICHIGAN [2]
NOV. 16 H 33-6 PURDUE
NOV. 23 A 22-13 WISCONSIN
154-71 8-0-0 [1]
6-0-0 (1)

1941
SEP. 27 A 14-6 WASHINGTON
OCT. 11 H 34-6 ILLINOIS
OCT. 18 H 39-0 PITTSBURGH
OCT. 25 A 7-0 MICHIGAN [5]
NOV. 1 HC 8-7 NORTHWESTERN [11]
NOV. 8 H 9-0 NEBRASKA
NOV. 15 A 34-13 IOWA
NOV. 22 H 41-6 WISCONSIN
186-38 8-0-0 [1]
5-0-0 (1)

COACH: DR. GEORGE HAUSER

1942
SEP. 26 H 50-7 PITTSBURGH
OCT. 3 H 6-7 IOWA SEAHAWKS [2]*
OCT. 10 A 13-20 ILLINOIS
OCT. 17 A 15-2 NEBRASKA
OCT. 24 HC 16-14 MICHIGAN [9]
OCT. 31 H 19-7 NORTHWESTERN
NOV. 7 H 0-7 INDIANA
NOV. 14 H 27-7 IOWA
NOV. 21 A 6-20 WISCONSIN [1]
152-91 5-4-0 [19]
3-3-0 (5)

1943
SEP. 25 H 26-13 MISSOURI
OCT. 2 H 54-0 NEBRASKA
OCT. 16 H 13-7 CAMP GRANT
OCT. 23 A 6-49 MICHIGAN ▼ [3]
OCT. 30 A 6-42 NORTHWESTERN [9]
NOV. 6 HC 7-14 PURDUE ▼ [5]
NOV. 13 A 33-14 IOWA
NOV. 20 H 25-13 WISCONSIN
NOV. 27 H 0-32 IOWA SEAHAWKS [2]**
170-184 5-4-0 [U]
2-3-0 (4)

1944
SEP. 23 H 13-19 IOWA SEAHAWKS [6]**
SEP. 30 H 39-0 NEBRASKA
OCT. 7 H 13-28 MICHIGAN [8]
OCT. 14 H 39-27 MISSOURI
OCT. 28 A 14-34 OHIO ST. ▼ [2]
NOV. 4 HC 14-14 NORTHWESTERN
NOV. 11 H 19-14 INDIANA
NOV. 18 A 46-0 IOWA
NOV. 25 A 28-26 WISCONSIN
225-162 5-3-1 [U]
3-2-1 (4)

*ARMED SERVICES RANKING IN 1942
**ARMED SERVICES RANKED WITH COLLEGE TEAMS IN 1943 & 1944

COACH: BERNIE BIERMAN

1945
SEP. 22 H 34-0 MISSOURI
OCT. 6 A 61-7 NEBRASKA
OCT. 13 H 14-0 FORT WARREN
OCT. 20 HC 30-7 NORTHWESTERN
OCT. 27 H 7-20 OHIO ST. [12]
NOV. 3 A 0-26 MICHIGAN [6]
NOV. 10 H 0-49 INDIANA ▼ [4]
NOV. 17 A 19-20 IOWA
NOV. 24 H 12-26 WISCONSIN
177-155 4-5-0 [U]
1-5-0 (8)

1946
SEP. 28 H 33-6 NEBRASKA
OCT. 5 H 0-21 INDIANA [20]
OCT. 12 H 7-14 NORTHWESTERN
OCT. 19 H 46-0 WYOMING
OCT. 26 H 9-39 OHIO ST.
NOV. 2 H 0-21 MICHIGAN [6]
NOV. 9 HC 13-7 PURDUE
NOV. 16 H 16-6 IOWA
NOV. 23 A 6-0 WISCONSIN
130-114 5-4-0 [U]
3-4-0 (5)

1947
SEP. 27 H 7-6 WASHINGTON
OCT. 4 H 28-13 NEBRASKA
OCT. 11 H 37-21 NORTHWESTERN
OCT. 18 A 13-40 ILLINOIS
OCT. 25 A 6-13 MICHIGAN ▼ [1]
NOV. 1 H 29-0 PITTSBURGH
NOV. 8 HC 26-21 PURDUE
NOV. 15 A 7-13 IOWA
NOV. 22 H 21-0 WISCONSIN
174-127 6-3-0 [U]
3-3-0 (3)

1948
SEP. 25 A 20-0 WASHINGTON
OCT. 2 H 39-13 NEBRASKA
OCT. 9 H 16-19 NORTHWESTERN [7]
OCT. 16 H 6-0 ILLINOIS
OCT. 23 H 14-27 MICHIGAN ▼ [1]
OCT. 30 HC 30-7 INDIANA
NOV. 6 H 34-7 PURDUE
NOV. 13 A 28-21 IOWA
NOV. 20 A 16-0 WISCONSIN
203-94 7-2-0 [16]
5-2-0 (3)

1949
SEP. 24	H	48 – 20	WASHINGTON	
OCT. 1	A	28 – 6	NEBRASKA	
OCT. 8	H	21 – 7	NORTHWESTERN	
OCT. 15	A	27 – 0	OHIO ST. ▼	[6]
OCT. 22	A	7 – 14	MICHIGAN ▼ ☆	[7]
OCT. 29	HC	7 – 13	PURDUE	
NOV. 5	H	55 – 7	IOWA	
NOV. 12	A	24 – 7	PITTSBURGH	
NOV. 19	H	14 – 6	WISCONSIN	

231 – 80   7-2-0 [7]
4-2-0 (3)

1950
SEP. 30	A	13 – 28	WASHINGTON	[11]
OCT. 7	H	26 – 32	NEBRASKA	[17]
OCT. 14	A	6 – 13	NORTHWESTERN	
OCT. 21	H	0 – 48	OHIO ST. ☆	[10]
OCT. 28	H	7 – 7	MICHIGAN ▼	[6]
NOV. 4	HC	0 – 13	IOWA	
NOV. 11	A	0 – 27	MICHIGAN ST.	[8] ❧
NOV. 18	H	27 – 14	PURDUE	
NOV. 25	A	0 – 14	WISCONSIN	[20]

79 – 196   1-7-1 [U]
1-4-1 (7)

❧ THE MICHIGAN ST. LOSS IS NOT COUNTED AGAINST MINNESOTA IN THE ABOVE CONFERENCE STANDINGS. MICHIGAN ST. WAS A NEW BIG TEN MEMBER BUT BECAUSE THEY DIDN'T YET PLAY A FULL BIG TEN SCHEDULE THEY WERE NOT COUNTED IN THE CONFERENCE STANDINGS FROM 1950-1952

COACH: WES FESLER

1951
SEP. 29	H	20 – 25	WASHINGTON	
OCT. 6	A	14 – 55	CALIFORNIA ☆	[12]
OCT. 13	H	7 – 21	NORTHWESTERN	
OCT. 20	HC	39 – 20	NEBRASKA	
OCT. 27	A	27 – 54	MICHIGAN	
NOV. 3	A	20 – 20	IOWA	
NOV. 10	H	16 – 14	INDIANA	
NOV. 17	A	13 – 19	PURDUE	[14]
NOV. 24	H	6 – 30	WISCONSIN	[8]

162 – 258   2-6-1 [U]
1-4-1 (7)

1952
SEP. 27	A	13 – 19	WASHINGTON	
OCT. 4	H	13 – 49	CALIFORNIA	
OCT. 11	H	27 – 26	NORTHWESTERN	
OCT. 18	H	13 – 7	ILLINOIS	
OCT. 25	A	0 – 21	MICHIGAN	
NOV. 1	HC	17 – 7	IOWA	
NOV. 8	H	14 – 14	PURDUE ▼	[12]
NOV. 15	H	13 – 7	NEBRASKA	
NOV. 22	A	21 – 21	WISCONSIN ▼ ☆	[10]

131 – 171   4-3-2 [U]
3-1-2 (4)

1953
SEP. 26	A	7 – 17	USC	
OCT. 3	A	0 – 21	MICHIGAN ST. ▼	[3]
OCT. 10	A	30 – 13	NORTHWESTERN	
OCT. 17	A	7 – 27	ILLINOIS ▼	[7]
OCT. 24	H	22 – 0	MICHIGAN	[19]
OCT. 31	H	35 – 14	PITTSBURGH	
NOV. 7	HC	28 – 20	INDIANA	
NOV. 14	A	0 – 27	IOWA	[9]
NOV. 21	H	21 – 21	WISCONSIN	[14]

150 – 160   4-4-1 [U]
3-3-1 (5)

COACH: MURRAY WARMATH

1954
SEP. 25	H	19 – 7	NEBRASKA	
OCT. 2	A	46 – 7	PITTSBURGH	
OCT. 9	H	26 – 7	NORTHWESTERN	
OCT. 16	H	19 – 6	ILLINOIS	
OCT. 23	A	0 – 34	MICHIGAN	[15]
OCT. 30	HC	19 – 13	MICHIGAN ST.	
NOV. 6	H	44 – 6	OREGON ST.	
NOV. 13	H	22 – 20	IOWA	
NOV. 20	A	0 – 27	WISCONSIN	[9]

195 – 127   7-2-0 [20]
4-2-0 (4)

1955
SEP. 24	H	0 – 30	WASHINGTON	
OCT. 1	H	6 – 7	PURDUE	
OCT. 8	A	18 – 7	NORTHWESTERN	
OCT. 15	A	13 – 21	ILLINOIS	
OCT. 22	H	13 – 14	MICHIGAN ★	[12]
OCT. 29	HC	25 – 19	USC	
NOV. 5	A	0 – 26	IOWA	[19]
NOV. 12	A	14 – 42	MICHIGAN ST.	[2]
NOV. 19	H	21 – 6	WISCONSIN	

110 – 172   3-6-0 [U]
2-5-0 (8)

1956
SEP. 29 A 34-14 WASHINGTON
OCT. 6 H 21-14 PURDUE
OCT. 13 H 0-0 NORTHWESTERN
OCT. 20 H 16-13 ILLINOIS
OCT. 27 A 20-7 MICHIGAN [7]
NOV. 3 HC 9-6 PITTSBURGH [13]
NOV. 10 H 0-7 IOWA▼[3]
NOV. 17 H 14-13 MICHIGAN ST.☆[9]
NOV. 24 A 13-13 WISCONSIN
127-87 6-1-2 [9]
4-1-2 (2)

1957
SEP. 28 H 46-7 WASHINGTON
OCT. 5 H 21-17 PURDUE
OCT. 12 A 41-6 NORTHWESTERN
OCT. 19 A 13-34 ILLINOIS
OCT. 26 H 7-24 MICHIGAN
NOV. 2 HC 34-0 INDIANA
NOV. 9 A 20-44 IOWA [5]
NOV. 16 A 13-42 MICHIGAN ST. [1]
NOV. 23 H 6-14 WISCONSIN [14]
201-188 4-5-0 [U]
3-5-0 (8)

1958
SEP. 27 A 21-24 WASHINGTON
OCT. 4 H 7-13 PITTSBURGH
OCT. 11 H 3-7 NORTHWESTERN [17]
OCT. 18 HC 8-20 ILLINOIS
OCT. 25 A 19-20 MICHIGAN
NOV. 1 A 0-6 INDIANA
NOV. 8 H 6-28 IOWA▼[1]
NOV. 15 H 39-12 MICHIGAN ST.
NOV. 22 A 12-27 WISCONSIN [6]
115-157 1-8-0 [U]
1-6-0 (9)

1959
SEP. 26 H 12-32 NEBRASKA
OCT. 3 H 24-14 INDIANA
OCT. 10 A 0-6 NORTHWESTERN [16]
OCT. 17 A 6-14 ILLINOIS [11]
OCT. 24 H 6-14 MICHIGAN
OCT. 31 HC 20-6 VANDERBILT
NOV. 7 A 0-33 IOWA
NOV. 14 A 23-29 PURDUE
NOV. 21 H 7-11 WISCONSIN▼[6]
98-159 2-7-0 [U]
1-6-0 (10)

1960
SEP. 24 A 26-14 NEBRASKA
OCT. 1 H 42-0 INDIANA
OCT. 8 H 7-0 NORTHWESTERN
OCT. 15 HC 21-10 ILLINOIS
OCT. 22 A 10-0 MICHIGAN
OCT. 29 H 48-7 KANSAS ST. *(1961 ROSE BOWL)*
NOV. 5 H 27-10 IOWA▼[1]
NOV. 12 H 14-23 PURDUE [15]
NOV. 19 A 26-7 WISCONSIN [5]
JAN. 2 A 7-17 WASHINGTON [1]
228-88 8-2-0 [1]
6-1-0 (1)

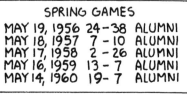

SPRING GAMES		
MAY 19, 1956	24-38	ALUMNI
MAY 18, 1957	7-10	ALUMNI
MAY 17, 1958	2-26	ALUMNI
MAY 16, 1959	13-7	ALUMNI
MAY 14, 1960	19-7	ALUMNI

MURRAY WARMATH

1961
SEP. 30 H 0-6 MISSOURI [11]
OCT. 7 H 14-7 OREGON
OCT. 14 A 10-3 NORTHWESTERN
OCT. 21 A 33-0 ILLINOIS
OCT. 28 HC 23-20 MICHIGAN
NOV. 4 H 13-0 MICHIGAN ST. ★[8]
NOV. 11 A 16-9 IOWA☆
NOV. 18 H 10-7 PURDUE [11]
NOV. 25 H 21-23 WISCONSIN [18]
JAN. 1 A 21-3 UCLA (1962 ROSE BOWL)
161-78 8-2-0 [6]
6-1-0 (2)

1962
SEP. 29 H 0-0 MISSOURI [12]
OCT. 6 H 21-0 NAVY
OCT. 13 H 22-34 NORTHWESTERN☆[16]
OCT. 20 HC 17-0 ILLINOIS [18]
OCT. 27 A 17-0 MICHIGAN
NOV. 3 A 28-7 MICHIGAN ST.
NOV. 10 H 10-0 IOWA
NOV. 17 H 7-6 PURDUE
NOV. 24 A 9-14 WISCONSIN▼[2]
131-61 6-2-1 [10]
5-2-0 (2)

1963
SEP. 28 H 7-14 NEBRASKA [5]
OCT. 5 H 24-8 ARMY
OCT. 12 A 8-15 NORTHWESTERN
OCT. 19 A 6-16 ILLINOIS▼[3]
OCT. 26 HC 6-0 MICHIGAN [10]
NOV. 2 H 6-24 INDIANA
NOV. 9 A 13-27 IOWA
NOV. 16 A 11-13 PURDUE
NOV. 28 H 14-0 WISCONSIN
95-117 3-6-0 [U]
2-5-0 (9)

1964
SEP. 26 H 21-26 NEBRASKA [6]
OCT. 3 A 26-20 CALIFORNIA
OCT. 10 H 21-18 NORTHWESTERN
OCT. 17 HC 0-14 ILLINOIS
OCT. 24 A 12-19 MICHIGAN▼[1]
OCT. 31 A 21-0 INDIANA
NOV. 7 H 14-13 IOWA
NOV. 14 H 14-7 PURDUE
NOV. 21 A 7-14 WISCONSIN
136-131 5-4-0 [U]
4-3-0 (4)

1965
SEP. 17 A 20-20 USC [9]
SEP. 25 H 13-14 WASHINGTON ST.
OCT. 2 H 6-17 MISSOURI [6]
OCT. 9 H 42-18 INDIANA
OCT. 16 A 14-3 IOWA
OCT. 23 HC 14-13 MICHIGAN
OCT. 30 A 10-11 OHIO ST. [11]
NOV. 6 H 27-22 NORTHWESTERN
NOV. 13 A 0-35 PURDUE [13]
NOV. 20 H 42-7 WISCONSIN
188-160 5-4-1 [U]
5-2-0 (3)

1966
SEP. 17 A 0-24 MISSOURI
SEP. 24 H 35-21 STANFORD
OCT. 1 H 14-16 KANSAS
OCT. 8 A 7-7 INDIANA
OCT. 15 HC 17-0 IOWA
OCT. 22 A 0-49 MICHIGAN
OCT. 29 H 17-7 OHIO ST.
NOV. 5 A 28-13 NORTHWESTERN
NOV. 12 H 0-16 PURDUE [6]
NOV. 19 A 6-7 WISCONSIN
124-160 4-5-1 [U]
3-3-1 (5)

1967
SEP. 23 H 13-12 UTAH
SEP. 30 A 0-7 NEBRASKA
OCT. 7 H 23-3 SOUTHERN METH.
OCT. 14 A 10-7 ILLINOIS
OCT. 21 HC 21-0 MICHIGAN ST.
OCT. 28 H 20-15 MICHIGAN
NOV. 4 A 10-0 IOWA
NOV. 11 A 12-41 PURDUE▼[9]
NOV. 18 H 33-7 INDIANA▼[4]
NOV. 25 H 21-14 WISCONSIN
163-106 8-2-0 [14]
6-1-0 (1)

1968
SEP. 21 H 20-29 U.S.C.★[2]
SEP. 28 H 14-17 NEBRASKA
OCT. 5 H 24-19 WAKE FOREST
OCT. 12 HC 17-10 ILLINOIS
OCT. 19 A 14-13 MICHIGAN ST.
OCT. 26 A 20-33 MICHIGAN [15]
NOV. 2 H 28-35 IOWA
NOV. 9 H 27-13 PURDUE☆[10]
NOV. 16 A 20-6 INDIANA
NOV. 23 A 23-15 WISCONSIN
207-190 6-4-0 [18]
5-2-0 (3)

1969
SEP. 20 A 26-48 ARIZONA ST.
SEP. 27 H 35-35 OHIO
OCT. 4 H 14-42 NEBRASKA [12]
OCT. 11 A 7-17 INDIANA
OCT. 18 HC 7-34 OHIO ST.★[4]
OCT. 25 H 9-35 MICHIGAN▼[8]
NOV. 1 A 35-7 IOWA
NOV. 8 H 28-21 NORTHWESTERN
NOV. 15 H 14-10 MICHIGAN ST.
NOV. 22 H 35-10 WISCONSIN
210-259 4-5-1 [U]
4-3-0 (4)

1970
SEP. 19	A	12-34	MISSOURI
SEP. 26	H	49-7	OHIO
OCT. 3	H	10-35	NEBRASKA[1]
OCT. 10	H	23-0	INDIANA
OCT. 17	A	8-28	OHIO ST. ▼[1]
OCT. 24	A	13-39	MICHIGAN[7]
OCT. 31	HC	14-14	IOWA
NOV. 7	A	14-28	NORTHWESTERN
NOV. 14	H	23-13	MICHIGAN ST.
NOV. 21	A	14-39	WISCONSIN

180-237 3-6-1 [U]
2-4-1 (7)

1971
SEP. 11	H	28-0	INDIANA
SEP. 18	A	7-35	N'EBRASKA[1]
SEP. 25	H	20-31	WASHINGTON ST.
OCT. 2	H	38-20	KANSAS
OCT. 9	A	13-27	PURDUE
OCT. 16	A	19-14	IOWA
OCT. 23	HC	7-35	MICHIGAN ▼[4]
OCT. 30	H	12-19	OHIO ST.
NOV. 6	A	20-41	NORTHWESTERN
NOV. 13	H	25-40	MICHIGAN ST.
NOV. 20	H	23-21	WISCONSIN

212-278 4-7-0 [U]
3-5-0 (6)

COACH: CAL STOLL

1972
SEP. 16	A	23-27	INDIANA
SEP. 23	H	6-38	COLORADO[14]
SEP. 30	A	0-49	NEBRASKA☆[4]
OCT. 7	H	28-34	KANSAS
OCT. 14	H	3-28	PURDUE
OCT. 21	HC	43-14	IOWA
OCT. 28	A	0-42	MICHIGAN ▼[6]
NOV. 4	A	19-27	OHIO ST. ▼[3]
NOV. 11	H	35-29	NORTHWESTERN
NOV. 18	H	14-10	MICHIGAN ST.
NOV. 25	A	14-6	WISCONSIN

185-304 4-7-0 [U]
4-4-0 (5)

1973
SEP. 15	A	7-56	OHIO ST. ▼☆[2]
SEP. 22	H	41-14	NO. DAKOTA
SEP. 29	A	19-34	KANSAS
OCT. 6	H	7-48	NEBRASKA[7]
OCT. 13	H	24-3	INDIANA
OCT. 20	A	31-23	IOWA
OCT. 27	HC	7-34	MICHIGAN ▼[6]
NOV. 3	A	52-43	NORTHWESTERN
NOV. 10	H	34-7	PURDUE
NOV. 17	A	19-16	ILLINOIS
NOV. 24	H	19-17	WISCONSIN

260-295 7-4-0 [U]
6-2-0 (3)

1974
SEP. 14	H	19-34	OHIO ST. ▼[3]
SEP. 21	H	42-30	NO. DAKOTA
SEP. 28	H	9-7	TEXAS CHRISTIAN
OCT. 5	A	0-54	NEBRASKA[8]
OCT. 12	A	3-34	INDIANA
OCT. 19	HC	23-17	IOWA
OCT. 26	A	0-49	MICHIGAN ▼[3]
NOV. 2	H	13-21	NORTHWESTERN
NOV. 9	A	24-20	PURDUE
NOV. 16	H	14-17	ILLINOIS
NOV. 23	A	14-49	WISCONSIN

161-332 4-7-0 [U]
2-6-0 (7)

1975
SEP. 13	A	14-20	INDIANA
SEP. 20	H	38-0	WESTERN MICH.
SEP. 27	H	10-7	OREGON
OCT. 4	H	21-0	OHIO
OCT. 11	A	23-42	ILLINOIS
OCT. 18	HC	15-38	MICHIGAN ST.
OCT. 25	A	31-7	IOWA
NOV. 1	H	21-28	MICHIGAN[8]
NOV. 8	H	33-9	NORTHWESTERN
NOV. 15	A	6-38	OHIO ST. ▼★[4]
NOV. 22	H	24-3	WISCONSIN

236-192 6-5-0 [U]
3-5-0 (7)

1976
SEP. 11	H	32-13	INDIANA
SEP. 18	H	28-14	WASHINGTON ST.
SEP. 25	H	21-10	WESTERN MICH.
OCT. 2	A	7-38	WASHINGTON
OCT. 9	HC	29-14	ILLINOIS
OCT. 16	A	14-10	MICHIGAN ST.
OCT. 23	H	12-22	IOWA
OCT. 30	A	0-45	MICHIGAN ▼★[3]
NOV. 6	A	38-10	NORTHWESTERN
NOV. 13	H	3-9	OHIO ST. ▼[5]
NOV. 20	A	17-26	WISCONSIN

201-211 6-5-0 [U]
4-4-0 (3)

1977
SEP. 10	H	10-7	WESTERN MICH.
SEP. 17	A	7-38	OHIO ST. ▼[12]
SEP. 24	H	17-13	UCLA
OCT. 1	H	19-17	WASHINGTON[9]
OCT. 8	A	6-18	IOWA
OCT. 15	HC	13-7	NORTHWESTERN
OCT. 22	H	16-0	MICHIGAN ▼★[8]
OCT. 29	A	22-34	INDIANA
NOV. 5	H	10-29	MICHIGAN ST.
NOV. 12	A	21-0	ILLINOIS
NOV. 19	H	13-7	WISCONSIN
DEC. 22	A	7-17	MARYLAND (HALL OF FAME BOWL)

171-187 7-5-0 [U]
4-4-0 (5)

1978
SEP. 16	H	38-12	TOLEDO
SEP. 23	H	10-27	OHIO ST.
SEP. 30	A	3-17	UCLA[12]
OCT. 7	H	14-17	OREGON ST.
OCT. 14	H	22-20	IOWA
OCT. 21	A	38-14	NORTHWESTERN
OCT. 28	A	10-42	MICHIGAN ▼[5]
NOV. 4	HC	32-31	INDIANA
NOV. 11	A	9-33	MICHIGAN ST. ▼
NOV. 18	H	24-6	ILLINOIS
NOV. 25	A	10-48	WISCONSIN

210-267 5-6-0 [U]
4-4-0 (5)

COACH: JOE SALEM

1979
SEP. 8	H	24-10	OHIO
SEP. 15	H	17-21	OHIO ST. ▼☆[4]
SEP. 22	A	14-48	USC★[2]
SEP. 29	A	38-8	NORTHWESTERN
OCT. 6	H	31-14	PURDUE[10]
OCT. 13	A	21-31	MICHIGAN[19]
OCT. 20	A	24-7	IOWA
OCT. 27	HC	17-17	ILLINOIS
NOV. 3	A	24-42	INDIANA[16]
NOV. 10	A	17-31	MICHIGAN ST.
NOV. 17	H	37-42	WISCONSIN

264-271 4-6-1 [U]
3-5-1 (6)

1980
SEP. 13	H	38-14	OHIO
SEP. 20	A	0-47	OHIO ST. ☆[15]
SEP. 27	H	7-24	USC[12]
OCT. 4	A	49-21	NORTHWESTERN
OCT. 11	A	7-21	PURDUE[16]
OCT. 18	HC	14-37	MICHIGAN ▼[4]
OCT. 25	H	24-6	IOWA
NOV. 1	A	21-18	ILLINOIS
NOV. 8	H	31-7	INDIANA
NOV. 15	H	12-30	MICHIGAN ST.
NOV. 22	A	7-25	WISCONSIN

210-250 5-6-0 [U]
4-5-0 (5)

1981
SEP. 12	H	19-17	OHIO
SEP. 19	H	16-13	PURDUE
SEP. 26		42-12	OREGON ST.
OCT. 3	A	29-38	ILLINOIS
OCT. 10	HC	35-23	NORTHWESTERN
OCT. 17	A	16-17	INDIANA
OCT. 24	A	12-10	IOWA ▼[15]
OCT. 31	H	13-34	MICHIGAN☆[10]
NOV. 7	H	35-31	OHIO ST. ▼[12]
NOV. 14	A	36-43	MICHIGAN ST.
NOV. 21	H	21-26	WISCONSIN

274-264 6-5-0 [U]
4-5-0 (6)

1982
SEP. 11	H	57-3	OHIO
SEP. 18	A	36-10	PURDUE
SEP. 25	H	41-11	WASHINGTON ST.
OCT. 2	H	24-42	ILLINOIS
OCT. 9	A	21-31	NORTHWESTERN
OCT. 16	HC	21-40	INDIANA
OCT. 23	H	16-21	IOWA
OCT. 30	A	14-52	MICHIGAN ▼[15]
NOV. 6	H	10-35	OHIO ST.[12]
NOV. 13	H	7-26	MICHIGAN ST.
NOV. 20	A	0-24	WISCONSIN

247-295 3-8-0 [U]
1-8-0 (10)

1983
SEP. 10 A   21 - 17 RICE
SEP. 17 H   13 - 84 NEBRASKA ★[2]
SEP. 24 H   20 - 32 PURDUE
OCT. 1   A   18 - 69 OHIO ST. [8]
OCT. 8   A   31 - 38 INDIANA
OCT. 15 HC 17 - 56 WISCONSIN
OCT. 22 A   8 - 19 NORTHWESTERN
OCT. 29 A   10 - 34 MICHIGAN ST.
NOV. 5   H   23 - 50 ILLINOIS ▼[10]
NOV. 12 H   10 - 58 MICHIGAN [8]
NOV. 19 A   10 - 61 IOWA [14]
             181 - 518 1-10-0 [U]
                        0-9-0 (10)

COACH: LOU HOLTZ

1984
SEP. 8   H   31 - 24 RICE
SEP. 15 A   7 - 38 NEBRASKA ★[3]
SEP. 22 A   10 - 34 PURDUE
SEP. 29 H   22 - 35 OHIO ST. ▼[12]
OCT. 6   H   33 - 24 INDIANA
OCT. 13 A   17 - 14 WISCONSIN
OCT. 20 HC 28 - 31 NORTHWESTERN
OCT. 27 H   13 - 20 MICHIGAN ST.
NOV. 3   P/   3 - 48 ILLINOIS
NOV. 10 A   7 - 31 MICHIGAN
NOV. 17 H   23 - 17 IOWA [15]
             194 - 316 4-7-0 [U]
                        3-6-0 (8)

1985
SEP. 14 H   28 - 14 WICHITA ST.
SEP. 21 H   62 - 17 MONTANA
SEP. 28 H   7 - 13 OKLAHOMA [1]
OCT. 5   H   45 - 15 PURDUE
OCT. 12 A   21 - 10 NORTHWESTERN
OCT. 19 H   22 - 7   INDIANA
OCT. 26 HC 19 - 23 OHIO ST. [11]
NOV. 2   A   26 - 31 MICHIGAN ST.
NOV. 9   H   27 - 18 WISCONSIN
NOV. 16 H   7 - 48 MICHIGAN [2]
NOV. 23 A   9 - 31 IOWA ▼[9]

COACH: JOHN GUTEKUNST

DEC. 21 A   20 - 13 CLEMSON (INDEP. BOWL)
             293 - 240 7-5-0 [U]
                        4-4-0 (6)

1986
SEP. 13 H   31 - 7   BOWLING GREEN
SEP. 20 H   0 - 63 OKLAHOMA [1]
SEP. 27 H   20 - 24 PACIFIC
OCT. 4   A   36 - 9   PURDUE
OCT. 11 HC 44 - 23 NORTHWESTERN
OCT. 18 H   19 - 17 INDIANA
OCT. 25 A   0 - 33 OHIO ST. ▼[6]
NOV. 1   H   23 - 52 MICHIGAN ST.
NOV. 8   A   27 - 20 WISCONSIN
NOV. 15 H   20 - 17 MICHIGAN ▼[7]
NOV. 22 H   27 - 30 IOWA [15]
DEC. 29 A   14 - 21 TENNESSEE (LIBERTY BOWL)
             261 - 316 6-6-0 [U]
                        5-3-0 (3)

1987
SEP. 12 H   24 - 7   NO. IOWA
SEP. 19 H   32 - 23 U. OF CALIFORNIA
SEP. 26 H   30 - 10 CENTRAL MICHIGAN U.
OCT. 3   H   21 - 19 PURDUE
OCT. 10 A   45 - 33 NORTHWESTERN
OCT. 16 HC 17 - 18 INDIANA [20]
OCT. 24 A   9 - 42 OHIO ST.
OCT. 31 A   17 - 27 ILLINOIS
NOV. 7   H   20 - 30 MICHIGAN [18]
NOV. 14 H   22 - 19 WISCONSIN
NOV. 21 A   20 - 34 IOWA [16]
             257 - 262 6-5-0 [U]
                        3-5-0 (6)

1988
SEP. 10 H   9 - 41 WASHINGTON ST. [16]
SEP. 17 H   35 - 3   MIAMI OF OHIO
SEP. 24 H   31 - 20 NO. ILLINOIS
OCT. 1   A   10 - 14 PURDUE
OCT. 8   HC 28 - 28 NORTHWESTERN
OCT. 15 H   13 - 33 INDIANA [20]
OCT. 22 H   6 - 13 OHIO ST.
OCT. 29 H   27 - 27 ILLINOIS
NOV. 5   A   7 - 22 MICHIGAN ▼[4]
NOV. 12 A   7 - 14 WISCONSIN
NOV. 19 H   22 - 31 IOWA
             195 - 246 2-7-2 [U]
                        0-6-2 (9)

1989
SEP. 16 A   30 - 20 IOWA ST.
SEP. 23 A   0 - 48 NEBRASKA [11]
SEP. 30 H   34 - 14 INDIANA ST.
OCT. 7   HC 35 - 15 PURDUE
OCT. 14 A   20 - 18 NORTHWESTERN
OCT. 21 A   18 - 28 INDIANA
OCT. 28 H   37 - 41 OHIO ST. [24]
NOV. 4   H   24 - 22 WISCONSIN
NOV. 11 A   7 - 21 MICHIGAN ST. [16]
NOV. 18 H   15 - 49 MICHIGAN ▼[7]
NOV. 25 A   43 - 7   IOWA
             263 - 283 6-5-0 [U]
                        4-4-0 (5)

1990
SEP. 8   H   29 - 35 UTAH
SEP. 20 H   20 - 16 IOWA ST.
SEP. 22 A   0 - 56 NEBRASKA [17]
OCT. 6   A   19 - 7   PURDUE
OCT. 13 HC 35 - 25 NORTHWESTERN
OCT. 20 H   12 - 0   INDIANA
OCT. 27 A   23 - 52 OHIO ST.
NOV. 3   A   21 - 3   WISCONSIN
NOV. 10 H   16 - 28 MICHIGAN ST. ▼[4]
NOV. 17 A   18 - 35 MICHIGAN ☆▼[7]
NOV. 24 H   31 - 24 IOWA ▼[16]
             224 - 281 6-5-0 [U]
                        5-3-0 (6)

1991
SEP. 14 H   26 - 20 SAN JOSE ST.
SEP. 21 A   0 - 58 COLORADO [15]
SEP. 28 H   13 - 14 PITTSBURGH
OCT. 5   A   3 - 24 ILLINOIS
OCT. 12 HC   6 - 3   PURDUE
OCT. 19 A   12 - 20 MICHIGAN ST.
OCT. 25 A   6 - 52 MICHIGAN ▼[4]
NOV. 2   H   8 - 34 INDIANA [23]
NOV. 9   H   6 - 35 OHIO ST.
NOV. 16 H   16 - 19 WISCONSIN
NOV. 23 A   8 - 23 IOWA [10]
             104 - 302 2-9-0 [U]
                        1-7-0 (10)

COACH: JIM WACKER

1992
SEP. 12 H   30 - 39 SAN JOSE ST.
SEP. 19 H   20 - 21 COLORADO [13]
SEP. 26 A   33 - 41 PITTSBURGH
OCT. 3   H   18 - 17 ILLINOIS
OCT. 10 A   20 - 24 PURDUE
OCT. 17 HC 15 - 20 MICHIGAN ST
OCT. 24 A   13 - 63 MICHIGAN ▼[5]
OCT. 31 H   17 - 24 INDIANA
NOV. 7   A   0 - 17 OHIO ST. [15]
NOV. 14 A   6 - 34 WISCONSIN
NOV. 21 H   28 - 13 IOWA
             200 - 313 2-9-0 [U]
                        2-6-0 (10)

1993
SEP. 4   A   20 - 38 PENN ST. [7]
SEP. 11 H   27 - 10 INDIANA ST.
SEP. 18 H   25 - 30 KANSAS ST.
SEP. 25 A   17 - 48 SAN DIEGO ST.
OCT. 2   H   19 - 23 INDIANA
OCT. 9   H   59 - 56 PURDUE
OCT. 16 A   28 - 26 NORTHWESTERN
OCT. 23 HC 28 - 21 WISCONSIN ▼[5]
NOV. 6   A   20 - 23 ILLINOIS
NOV. 13 H   7 - 58 MICHIGAN [19]
NOV. 20 A   3 - 21 IOWA
             253 - 354 4-7-0 [U]
                        3-5-0 (8)

1994
SEP. 3   H   3 - 56 PENN ST. ▼[2]
SEP. 10 H   33 - 7   PACIFIC
SEP. 17 H   40 - 17 SAN DIEGO ST.
SEP. 24 A   0 - 35 KANSAS ST.
OCT. 1   A   14 - 25 INDIANA
OCT. 8   A   37 - 49 PURDUE
OCT. 15 HC 31 - 37 NORTHWESTERN
OCT. 22 A   17 - 14 WISCONSIN
NOV. 5   H   17 - 21 ILLINOIS
NOV. 12 A   22 - 38 MICHIGAN [12]
NOV. 19 H   42 - 49 IOWA
             256 - 348 3-8-0 [U]
                        1-7-0 (11)

1995
SEP. 16 H 31 - 7   BALL ST.
SEP. 23 A 17 - 27 SYRACUSE
SEP. 30 H 55 - 7   ARKANSAS ST.
OCT. 7   H 39 - 38 PURDUE
OCT. 14 HC 17 - 27 NORTHWESTERN [7]
OCT. 21 A 31 - 34 MICHIGAN ST.
OCT. 28 H 17 - 52 MICHIGAN [17]
NOV. 4   H 21 - 49 OHIO ST. [2]
NOV. 11 H 27 - 34 WISCONSIN
NOV. 18 A 14 - 48 ILLINOIS
NOV. 25 A 3 - 45   IOWA [18]
         272 - 368 3 - 8 - 0 [U]
                    1 - 7 - 0 (10)

1996
SEP. 7   A 30 - 3   NORTHEASTERN LA.
SEP. 14 H 26 - 23 BALL ST.
SEP. 21 H 35 - 33 SYRACUSE [21]
OCT. 5   A 27 - 30 PURDUE
OCT. 12 A 24 - 26 NORTHWESTERN ▼ [15]
OCT. 19 HC 9 - 27   MICHIGAN ST.
OCT. 26 H 10 - 44 MICHIGAN [20]
NOV. 2   A 0 - 45   OHIO ST. ▼ [2]
NOV. 9   A 28 - 45 WISCONSIN
NOV. 16 H 23 - 21 ILLINOIS
NOV. 23 H 24 - 43 IOWA [18]
         236 - 340 4 - 7 - 0 [U]
                    1 - 7 - 0 (9)

COACH: GLEN MASON

1997
AUG. 30 A 3 - 17   HAWAII
SEP. 13 H 53 - 29 IOWA ST.
SEP. 20 A 20 - 17 MEMPHIS
SEP. 27 H 43 - 45 HOUSTON
OCT. 4   A 10 - 31 MICHIGAN ST.
OCT. 11 H 43 - 59 PURDUE [15]
OCT. 18 A 15 - 16 PENN ST. ★ [16]
OCT. 25 H 21 - 22 WISCONSIN
NOV. 1   A 3 - 24   MICHIGAN ▼ [1]
NOV. 8   HC 3 - 31   OHIO ST. [12]
NOV. 15 H 24 - 12 INDIANA
NOV. 22 A 0 - 31   IOWA
         238 - 334 3 - 9 - 0 [U]
                    1 - 7 - 0 (9)

1998
SEP. 5   H 17 - 14 ARKANSAS ST.
SEP. 12 A 14 - 7   HOUSTON
SEP. 19 H 41 - 14 MEMPHIS
OCT. 3   A 21 - 56 PURDUE [13]
OCT. 10 H 17 - 27 PENN ST. [11]
OCT. 17 A 15 - 45 OHIO ST. ★ ▼ [2]
OCT. 24 HC 19 - 18 MICHIGAN ST.
OCT. 31 H 10 - 15 MICHIGAN ▼ [12]
NOV. 7   A 7 - 26   WISCONSIN ▼ [5]
NOV. 14 A 19 - 20 INDIANA
NOV. 21 H 49 - 7   IOWA
         229 - 249 5 - 6 [U]
                    2 - 6 (7)

1999
SEP. 4   H 33 - 7   OHIO
SEP. 11 H 35 - 0   LA. MONROE
SEP. 18 H 55 - 7   ILLINOIS ST.
OCT. 2   A 33 - 14 NORTHWESTERN
OCT. 9   H 17 - 20 WISCONSIN ▼ O.T. [4]
OCT. 16 H 37 - 7   ILLINOIS [24]
OCT. 23 H 17 - 20 OHIO ST.
OCT. 30 HC 28 - 33 PURDUE [25]
NOV. 6   A 24 - 23 PENN ST. [11]
NOV. 13 A 44 - 20 INDIANA
NOV. 20 A 25 - 21 IOWA   (SUN BOWL)
DEC. 31 A 20 - 24 OREGON [18]
         368 - 196 8 - 4 [17]
                    5 - 3 (4)

2000
SEP. 2   H 47 - 10 N.E. LOUISIANA
SEP. 9   H 17 - 23 OHIO
SEP. 16 A 34 - 9   BAYLOR
SEP. 23 A 24 - 38 PURDUE ▼ [13]
SEP. 30 H 44 - 10 ILLINOIS
OCT. 7   H 25 - 16 PENN ST.
OCT. 14 A 29 - 17 OHIO ST.
OCT. 21 A 43 - 51 INDIANA
OCT. 28 HC 35 - 41 NORTHWESTERN ▼
NOV. 4   A 20 - 41 WISCONSIN [24]
NOV. 18 H 27 - 24 IOWA
DEC. 28 A 30 - 38 N. CAROLINA ST.
                     (MICRON.COMM BOWL)
         375 - 318
                    6 - 6 [U]
                    4 - 4 (5)

2001
AUG. 30 A 7 - 38   TOLEDO [22]
SEP. 8   H 44 - 14 LA. LAFAYETTE
SEP. 15 H -   BAYLOR (CANCELLED)
SEP. 29 H 28 - 35 PURDUE
OCT. 6   A 14 - 25 ILLINOIS ▼ [12]
OCT. 13 A 17 - 23 NORTHWESTERN
OCT. 20 HC 28 - 19 MICHIGAN ST.
OCT. 27 H 66 - 10 MURRAY ST.
NOV. 3   H 28 - 31 OHIO ST.
NOV. 10 A 10 - 31 MICHIGAN [20]
NOV. 17 A 24 - 42 IOWA
NOV. 24 H 42 - 31 WISCONSIN
         308 - 299 4 - 7 [U]
                    2 - 6 (10)

2002
AUG. 31 H 42 - 0   SW TEXAS ST.
SEP. 7   A 35 - 11 LA. LAFAYETTE
SEP. 14 H 31 - 21 TOLEDO
SEP. 21 H 41 - 17 BUFFALO
SEP. 28 A 15 - 28 PURDUE
OCT. 3   H 31 - 10 ILLINOIS
OCT. 10 HC 45 - 42 NORTHWESTERN
OCT. 19 A 28 - 7   MICHIGAN ST.
NOV. 2   A 3 - 34   OHIO ST. ▼ [1]
NOV. 9   H 24 - 41 MICHIGAN [12]
NOV. 16 H 21 - 45 IOWA ▼ [8]
NOV. 23 A 31 - 49 WISCONSIN
DEC. 30 A 29 - 14 ARKANSAS
                     (MUSIC CITY BOWL)
         376 - 319 8 - 5 [U]
                    3 - 5 (7)

2003
AUG. 30 H 40 - 10 TULSA
SEP. 6   H 48 - 7   TROY ST.
SEP. 13 A 42 - 20 OHIO
SEP. 20 H 48 - 14 LA. LAFAYETTE
SEP. 27 A 20 - 14 PENN ST.
OCT. 4   A 42 - 17 NORTHWESTERN
OCT. 10 H 35 - 38 MICHIGAN ▼ [6]
OCT. 18 H 38 - 44 MICHIGAN ST.
OCT. 25 A 36 - 10 ILLINOIS
NOV. 1   HC 55 - 7   INDIANA
NOV. 8   H 37 - 34 WISCONSIN
NOV. 15 A 22 - 40 IOWA [8]
DEC. 31 A 31 - 30 OREGON (SUN BOWL)
         494 - 285 10 - 3 [17]
                    5 - 3 (4)

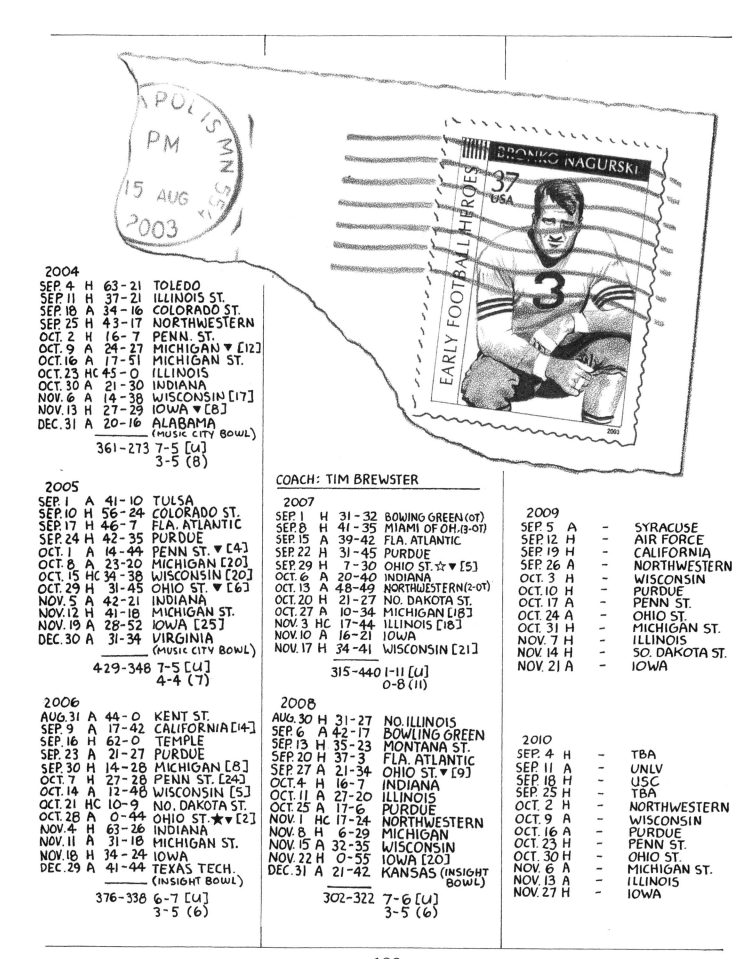

BRONKO NAGURSKI
37 USA
EARLY FOOTBALL HEROES
2003

2004
SEP. 4	H	63-21	TOLEDO
SEP. 11	H	37-21	ILLINOIS ST.
SEP. 18	A	34-16	COLORADO ST.
SEP. 25	H	43-17	NORTHWESTERN
OCT. 2	H	16-7	PENN. ST.
OCT. 9	A	24-27	MICHIGAN ▼ [12]
OCT. 16	A	17-51	MICHIGAN ST.
OCT. 23	HC	45-0	ILLINOIS
OCT. 30	A	21-30	INDIANA
NOV. 6	A	14-38	WISCONSIN [17]
NOV. 13	H	27-29	IOWA ▼ [8]
DEC. 31	A	20-16	ALABAMA (MUSIC CITY BOWL)

361-273 7-5 [U]
3-5 (8)

2005
SEP. 1	A	41-10	TULSA
SEP. 10	H	56-24	COLORADO ST.
SEP. 17	H	46-7	FLA. ATLANTIC
SEP. 24	H	42-35	PURDUE
OCT. 1	A	14-44	PENN ST. ▼ [4]
OCT. 8	A	23-20	MICHIGAN [20]
OCT. 15	HC	34-38	WISCONSIN [20]
OCT. 29	H	31-45	OHIO ST. ▼ [6]
NOV. 5	A	42-21	INDIANA
NOV. 12	H	41-18	MICHIGAN ST.
NOV. 19	A	28-52	IOWA [25]
DEC. 30	A	31-34	VIRGINIA (MUSIC CITY BOWL)

429-348 7-5 [U]
4-4 (7)

2006
AUG. 31	A	44-0	KENT ST.
SEP. 9	A	17-42	CALIFORNIA [14]
SEP. 16	H	62-0	TEMPLE
SEP. 23	A	21-27	PURDUE
SEP. 30	H	14-28	MICHIGAN [8]
OCT. 7	H	27-28	PENN. ST. [24]
OCT. 14	A	12-48	WISCONSIN [5]
OCT. 21	HC	10-9	NO. DAKOTA ST.
OCT. 28	A	0-44	OHIO ST. ★▼ [2]
NOV. 4	H	63-26	INDIANA
NOV. 11	H	31-18	MICHIGAN ST.
NOV. 18	H	34-24	IOWA
DEC. 29	A	41-44	TEXAS TECH. (INSIGHT BOWL)

376-338 6-7 [U]
3-5 (6)

COACH: TIM BREWSTER

2007
SEP. 1	H	31-32	BOWLING GREEN (OT)
SEP. 8	H	41-35	MIAMI OF OH. (3-OT)
SEP. 15	A	39-42	FLA. ATLANTIC
SEP. 22	H	31-45	PURDUE
SEP. 29	H	7-30	OHIO ST. ☆▼ [5]
OCT. 6	A	20-40	INDIANA
OCT. 13	A	48-49	NORTHWESTERN (2-OT)
OCT. 20	H	21-27	NO. DAKOTA ST.
OCT. 27	A	10-34	MICHIGAN [18]
NOV. 3	HC	17-44	ILLINOIS [18]
NOV. 10	A	16-21	IOWA
NOV. 17	H	34-41	WISCONSIN [21]

315-440 1-11 [U]
0-8 (11)

2008
AUG. 30	H	31-27	NO. ILLINOIS
SEP. 6	A	42-17	BOWLING GREEN
SEP. 13	H	35-23	MONTANA ST.
SEP. 20	H	37-3	FLA. ATLANTIC
SEP. 27	A	21-34	OHIO ST. ▼ [9]
OCT. 4	H	16-7	INDIANA
OCT. 11	A	27-20	ILLINOIS
OCT. 25	A	17-6	PURDUE
NOV. 1	HC	17-24	NORTHWESTERN
NOV. 8	H	6-29	MICHIGAN
NOV. 15	A	32-35	WISCONSIN
NOV. 22	H	0-55	IOWA [20]
DEC. 31	A	21-42	KANSAS (INSIGHT BOWL)

302-322 7-6 [U]
3-5 (6)

2009
SEP. 5	A	–	SYRACUSE
SEP. 12	H	–	AIR FORCE
SEP. 19	H	–	CALIFORNIA
SEP. 26	A	–	NORTHWESTERN
OCT. 3	H	–	WISCONSIN
OCT. 10	H	–	PURDUE
OCT. 17	H	–	PENN ST.
OCT. 24	A	–	OHIO ST.
OCT. 31	H	–	MICHIGAN ST.
NOV. 7	H	–	ILLINOIS
NOV. 14	H	–	SO. DAKOTA ST.
NOV. 21	A	–	IOWA

2010
SEP. 4	H	–	TBA
SEP. 11	A	–	UNLV
SEP. 18	H	–	USC
SEP. 25	H	–	TBA
OCT. 2	H	–	NORTHWESTERN
OCT. 9	A	–	WISCONSIN
OCT. 16	A	–	PURDUE
OCT. 23	H	–	PENN ST.
OCT. 30	H	–	OHIO ST.
NOV. 6	A	–	MICHIGAN ST.
NOV. 13	A	–	ILLINOIS
NOV. 27	H	–	IOWA

Big Ten

PRESIDENT JAMES H. SMART OF PURDUE CALLED A MEETING AT THE PALMER HOUSE IN CHICAGO ON JANUARY 11, 1895. THIS HISTORIC MEETING MARKED THE BIRTH OF THE BIG TEN, THE FIRST INTERCOLLEGIATE CONFERENCE. ITS ORIGINAL NAME WAS THE INTERCOLLEGIATE CONFERENCE OF FACULTY REPRESENTATIVES AND SERVED AS THE PATTERN FOR THE YET-TO-BE-CREATED N.C.A.A.— THE FOUNDING MEMBERS WERE PURDUE, MINNESOTA, MICHIGAN, WISCONSIN, NORTHWESTERN, ILLINOIS AND CHICAGO. LAKE FOREST COLLEGE WAS ALSO PRESENT BUT DIDN'T JOIN.

Standings

IN EARLY BIG TEN STANDINGS TIES WERE NOT COUNTED AGAINST A TEAM. IF IT HAD FOUR WINS, TWO TIES AND NO LOSSES IT HAD A 1000% RECORD JUST LIKE A TEAM WHO HAD WON ALL THEIR GAMES. TIES WERE COMPLETELY IGNORED.

THIS BUSINESS COULD CAUSE TROUBLE.

IN 1927 ILLINOIS HAD A PERFECT 5-0-0 RECORD AND MINNESOTA WAS 3-0-1. BOTH HAD A 1000% WIN RECORD AND A SHARE IN THE TITLE. UNIVERSITY OF MINNESOTA PRESIDENT LOTUS COFFMAN, HOWEVER, CONCEDED THE CHAMPIONSHIP TO ILLINOIS WITHOUT CONSULTATION WITH ANYONE ELSE. IT CAUSED A GREAT UPROAR AMONG GOPHER FOLLOWERS. A RECOGNITION RALLY WAS PUT ON AT THE MINNEAPOLIS AUDITORIUM FOR THE TEAM AND TO SHOW CONTEMPT FOR COFFMAN'S BOO-BOO. MINNESOTA LOST AN OFFICIAL FIRST PLACE IN THE STANDINGS, JUST THE SAME.

IN 1933 THE GOPHERS COMPILED A 2-0-4 RECORD TO SHARE A BIG TEN TITLE WITH 5-0-1 MICHIGAN. HEAD TO HEAD THESE TWO TEAMS TIED 0-0. ONCE AGAIN MINNESOTA DID NOT RECEIVE CREDIT.

BECAUSE OF THESE TWO SEASONS, OFFICIAL RECORDS TODAY SHOW MINNESOTA WITH TWO LESS CHAMPIONSHIPS THAN THEY, BY DEFINITION AND RIGHT, SHOULD HAVE. THIS RECORD SHOWS MINNESOTA AS IT OUGHT TO HAVE BEEN CREDITED. THE UNIVERSITY HAS DONE THE SAME.

IN 1946 THE SYSTEM WAS CHANGED TO WHERE A TIE WAS COUNTED AS A HALF-GAME WON AND HALF-GAME LOST. THE FOLLOWING CHART SHOWS HOW TEAMS ACTUALLY PLACED IN THE STANDINGS, TO THE LEFT OF THEIR NAME. TO THEIR RIGHT IS INDICATED THEIR FINISH IF TODAY'S SYSTEM HAD BEEN USED.

★ NATIONAL CHAMPIONS

1896
1 WI
2 NW
2 MI
4 CH
5 MN
6 IL
6 PU

1897
1 WI
2 CH
3 MI
4 IL
5 PU
6 NW
6 MN

1898
1 MI
2 CH
3 WI
4 IL
5 MN
6 NW
6 PU

1899
1 CH
2 WI
3 NW
3 MI
5 PU
6 MN
6 IL

1900
1 MN
1 IA 2
3 WI
3 NW 4
3 MI 4
6 CH

1901
1 MI ★
1 WI
3 MN
4 IL
5 NW
6 IN
7 CH
7 PU 8
7 IA 9

1902
1 MI ★
2 CH
3 MN
4 IL
5 PU
6 WI
7 IA
7 NW
7 IN

1903
1 MN
1 MI
1 NW 4
4 CH 3
5 IA
6 IN
7 IL
8 WI
8 PU 9

1904
1 MN
1 MI
3 CH
4 IL
5 NW
5 PU
7 IA
7 WI
7 IN

1905
1 CH ★
2 MI
2 MN
4 PU
5 WI
6 IN
6 IA 7
6 NW 7
6 IL 7

1906
1 WI
1 MN
1 MI
4 CH
5 IA
6 IN
6 PU

1907
1 CH
2 WI
3 IL
4 IA
5 MN
5 IN 6
5 PU 6

1908
1 CH
2 IL
3 WI
4 PU
4 IN
6 IA
6 MN
6 NW

1909
1 MN
2 CH
3 IL
4 WI
5 IN
5 NW
7 IA
7 PU

1910
1 IL
1 MN 2
3 IN
4 IA
5 WI
5 NW
5 CH 7
8 PU

1911
1 MN
2 CH
3 WI
4 IL
4 IA
6 PU
7 NW
8 IN

1912
1 WI
2 CH
3 PU
3 MN
5 NW
6 IL
6 IA 7
8 IN
- OS

1913
1 CH
2 MN
2 IA
2 PU 4
5 IL
6 WI
6 IN 7
6 OS 7
9 NW

1914
1 IL
2 MN
3 CH
4 WI
4 OS
4 PU
7 IA
8 IN
9 NW

1915
1 MN
1 IL 2
3 CH
3 OS 4
5 PU
6 WI
7 IA
8 IN
9 NW

1916
1 OS
2 NW
3 MN
4 IL
4 CH
6 WI
6 IA 7
8 IN
8 PU 9

1917
1 OS
2 MN
3 NW
3 WI
5 IL
5 CH
7 IN
8 MI
8 IA
8 PU

1918
1 IL
1 MI
1 PU
4 MN
4 IA
6 NW
7 WI
8 OS
8 CH
- IN

1919
1 IL
2 OS
3 CH
4 WI
4 MN
6 IA
7 MI
7 NW
9 IN
9 PU

1920
1 OS
2 WI
3 IN
4 IL
5 IA
6 MI
7 NW
8 CH
9 PU
9 MN

1921
1 IA
2 CH
2 OS
4 WI
5 MI
6 MN
6 IN
8 IL
9 PU
9 MN

1922
1 IA
1 MI
3 CH
4 WI
5 MN
6 IL
7 NW
8 OS
8 IN
9 PU 10

1923
1 IL ★
1 MI
3 CH
4 MN
5 IA
5 IN
7 WI
8 OS
8 PU
10 NW

1924
1 CH
2 IL
2 IA
4 MI
5 PU
6 MN
7 OS
7 NW 8
8 PU 8
10 WI 8

1925
1 MI
2 NW
2 WI
4 MN
5 IA
5 IN
7 WI
8 OS
9 IN
9 PU

1926
1 MI
1 NW
3 OS
4 PU
5 WI
6 IL
6 MN
8 IN
8 IA
8 CH

1927
1 IL ★
1 MN 2
3 MI
4 PU
6 OS
6 NW
8 IN
9 IA
9 WI

1928
1 IL
2 WI
3 MN
4 IA
4 OS
6 PU
7 NW
7 MI
9 IN
10 CH

1929
1 PU
2 IL
3 MN
3 NW
5 OS
5 IA
7 MI
7 IN
7 CH 9
10 WI

1930
1 MI
1 NW
3 PU
4 WI
5 OS
6 MN
6 IN
8 IL
9 IA
9 CH

1931
1 PU
1 MI
1 NW
4 OS
5 MN
6 WI
7 IN
7 CH 8
9 IA
9 IL 10

1932
1 MI ★
1 PU 2
3 WI
4 OS
5 NW
5 MN 6
7 IL
8 IN
8 CH 9
10 IA

1933
1 MI ★
2 MN 4
3 OS ★2
4 PU 3
5 IA
5 IL
7 NW
8 CH
8 IN
8 WI 9

1934
1 MN ★
2 OS
3 IL
4 PU
5 WI
5 NW
7 CH
8 IN
8 IA
10 MI

1935
1 MN ★
1 OS
3 IN
5 PU
5 NW
5 MI 6
5 CH 6
8 IA
9 IL
9 WI

1936
1 NW
2 MN ★
2 OS
4 IN
4 PU
6 IL
7 CH
8 IA
8 WI 9
8 MI 9

1937
1 MN
2 OS
3 IN
4 PU
4 WI
4 NW
4 MI
8 IL
9 CH
9 IA

1938
1 MN
2 MI
2 PU
4 NW
5 WI
5 OS 6
7 IL
8 IA
9 IN
10 CH

1939
1 OS
2 IA
3 PU
4 MI
4 NW 5
6 IL
7 MN
7 IN 8
9 WI
9 CH 10

1940
1 MN ★
2 MI
3 NW
4 WI
4 OS
6 IA
6 IN
8 PU
9 IL

1941
1 MN ★
2 MI
2 OS
4 NW
5 WI
6 IA
7 PU
7 IN
9 IL

1942
1 OS ★
2 WI ★
3 MI
3 IL
5 IN
5 IA
5 MN
8 PU
9 NW

1943
1 PU
1 MI
3 NW
4 IN
4 MN 5
6 IL
7 OS
8 WI
9 IA

1944
1 OS
2 MI
3 PU
4 MN
5 IN
6 IL
7 WI
8 NW
8 IA 9

1945
1 IN
2 MI
3 OS
4 PU
4 NW
6 WI
7 IL
8 MN
8 IA

1946
1 IL
2 MI
3 IN
4 IA
5 MN
6 OS
6 NW
8 WI
9 PU

1947
1 MI ★
2 WI
3 MN
3 IL
3 PU
6 IN
6 IA
8 NW
9 OS

1948
1 MI ★
2 NW
3 MN
4 OS
5 IA
5 PU
5 IN
8 IL
9 WI

1949
1 OS
1 MI
3 MN
4 WI
5 IL
5 IA
7 NW
8 PU
9 IN

1950
1 MI
2 OS
2 WI
4 IL
5 NW
6 IA
7 MN
8 IN
8 PU
- MS

1951
1 IL
2 PU
3 WI
4 MI
5 OS
6 NW
7 MN
8 IN
9 IA
- MS ★

1952
1 WI
1 PU
3 OS
4 MN
4 MI
6 IL
6 NW
6 IA
9 IN
- MS ★

1953
1 MS
1 IL
3 WI
4 OS
5 MI
5 IA
5 MN
8 PU
9 IN
10 NW

1954
1 OS ★
2 WI
3 MI
4 MN
5 IA
6 PU
7 IN
8 MS
8 NW
10 IL

1955
1 OS
2 MS
3 MI
4 PU
5 IL
6 WI
7 IA
8 MN
9 IN
10 NW

1956
1 IA
2 MN
2 MI
4 MS
4 OS
6 NW
7 PU
7 IL
9 WI
10 IN

1957
1 OS ★
2 MS ★
3 IA
4 WI
4 PU
6 MI
7 IL
8 MN
9 IN
9 NW

1958
1 IA ★
2 WI
3 OS
4 PU
5 IN
6 IL
7 NW
8 MI
9 MN
10 MS

1959
1 WI
2 MS
3 PU
3 IL
5 NW
6 IA
7 MI
8 IN
8 OS
10 MN

1960
1 MN ★
1 IA ★
3 OS
4 MS
5 IL
5 MI
5 NW
5 PU
9 WI
- IN

1961
1 OS ★
2 MN
3 MS
4 PU
5 WI
6 MI
7 IA
7 NW
9 IN
9 IL

1962
1 WI
2 MN
3 NW
3 OS
5 MS
5 PU
5 IA
8 IL
9 IN
10 MI

1963
1 IL
2 MS
2 OS
4 PU
5 NW
5 WI
5 MI
8 IA
9 MN
10 IN

1964
1 MI ★
2 OS
3 PU
4 IL
4 MN
5 MS
7 NW
8 IA
9 MN
9 IN

1965
1 MS ★
2 OS
3 PU
3 MN
5 IL
6 NW
7 MI
7 WI
9 IN
10 IA

1966
1 MS ★
2 PU
3 MI
3 IL
5 MN
6 OS
7 NW
7 WI
9 IN
10 IA

1967
1 IN
1 MN
1 PU
4 OS
5 IL
5 MI
5 MS
8 NW
9 WI

1968
1 OS ★
2 MI
3 PU
3 MN
5 IN
5 IA
7 MS
8 IL
8 NW
10 WI

1969
1 OS
2 MI
3 PU
4 MN
5 IA
5 IN
5 NW
5 WI
9 MS
10 IL

1970
1 OS ★
2 MI
2 NW
4 IA
5 WI
5 MS
7 MN
8 PU
9 IL
9 IN

1971
1 MI
2 NW
3 OS
3 MS
3 IL
6 WI
6 MN
6 PU
9 IN
10 IA

1972	1973	1974	1975	1976	1977	1978	1979	1980	1981	1982
1 MI	1 OS	1 MI	1 OS ★	1 MI	1 MI	1 MI	1 OS	1 MI	1 OS	1 MI
1 OS	1 MI	1 OS	2 MI	1 OS	1 OS	1 MS	2 PU	2 OS	1 IA	2 OS
3 PU	3 MN	3 MS	3 MS	3 MN	3 MS	3 PU	3 MI	2 PU	3 MI	3 IA
4 MS	4 IL	4 WI	3 IL	3 PU	4 IN	4 OS	4 IN	4 IA	3 IL	4 IL
5 MN	4 MS	5 IL	3 PU	3 IL	5 MN	5 MN	5 IA	5 MN	3 WI	5 WI
6 IN	4 PU	6 PU	6 WI	3 IN	6 PU	6 WI	6 MN	6 IN	6 MN	6 IN
6 IL	4 NW	7 MN	7 MN	7 IA	6 IA	7 IN	7 MS	6 WI	6 MS	7 PU
8 IA	8 WI	7 IA	7 IA	7 WI	7 WI	8 WI	7 WI	6 IL	8 PU	8 NW
9 WI	9 IN	7 NW	9 NW	7 MS	9 IL	9 IL	9 IL	9 MS	8 IN	8 MS
10 NW	9 IA	10 IN	10 IN	10 NW	10 NW	10 NW	10 NW	10 NW	10 NW	10 MN

1983	1984	1985	1986	1987	1988	1989	1990	1991	1992	1993
1 IL	1 OS	1 IA	1 MI	1 MS	1 MI	1 MI	1 IA	1 MI	1 MI	1 WI
2 MI	2 IL	2 MI	1 OS	2 IA	2 MS	2 IL	1 IL	2 IA	2 OS	1 OS
3 IA	2 PU	3 IL	3 IA	2 IN	3 IA	3 OS	1 MI	3 OS	3 MS	3 PS
4 OS	4 IA	4 OS	3 MN	4 MI	3 IL	3 MS	1 MS	3 IN	4 IL	4 IN
5 WI	4 WI	4 MS	5 MS	5 OS	5 IN	5 MN	5 OS	5 IL	5 IA	4 MI
6 PU	6 MI	6 MN	6 IL	6 MN	6 PU	6 IN	6 MN	6 PU	6 IN	4 IL
7 MS	6 MS	7 PU	8 NW	6 PU	7 OS	6 IA	7 IN	7 MS	6 WI	7 MS
8 IN	8 MN	8 WI	8 PU	8 IL	7 NW	8 PU	8 NW	8 WI	6 PU	8 IA
8 NW	9 NW	9 IN	8 WI	9 NW	9 MN	9 WI	8 PU	9 NW	6 NW	8 MN
10 MN	10 IN	9 NW		10 WI	9 WI	10 NW	10 WI	10 MN	10 MN	10 NW
										10 PU

1994	1995	1996	1997	1998	1999	2000	2001	2002	2003	2004
1 PS	1 NW	1 OS	1 MI ★	1 OS	1 WI	1 PU	1 IL	1 OS ★	1 MI	1 MI
2 OS	2 OS	1 NW	2 PS	1 WI	2 MI	1 MI	2 MI	1 IA	2 OS	1 IA
3 MI	3 MI	3 PS	3 OS	1 MI	2 MS	1 NW	3 OS	3 MI	2 PU	3 WI
4 MS	3 PS	3 IA	3 PU	4 PU	4 MN	4 OS	4 IA	4 PS	4 MN	4 NW
4 WI	5 MS	5 MI	5 WI	5 PS	4 PS	5 MN	4 PU	5 PU	4 IA	5 OS
6 IL	6 IA	5 MS	6 IA	6 MS	6 IL	5 WI	4 IN	5 IL	4 MS	5 PU
7 IA	7 WI	7 WI	7 MS	7 MN	6 PU	5 PS	4 PS	7 MN	7 WI	5 MS
8 IN	7 IL	8 PU	8 NW	7 IN	8 OS	8 IA	8 MS	8 WI	7 NW	8 MN
9 PU	9 PU	9 MN	9 MN	7 IL	8 IN	9 IL	8 WI	8 MS	9 PS	9 PS
10 NW	10 MN	9 IN	9 IN	7 IA	10 NW	10 NW	10 MN	10 IN	9 IN	10 IL
11 MN	11 IN	9 IL	11 IL	11 NW	11 IA	11 IN	10 NW	10 NW	10 IL	10 IN

2005	2006
1 PS	1 OS
1 OS	2 MI
3 WI	2 WI
3 IA	4 PS
3 MI	4 PU
3 NW	6 MN
7 MN	6 IN
8 PU	7 IA
9 MS	7 NW
10 IN	10 MS
11 IL	10 IL

2007	2008
1 OS	1 PS
2 IL	1 OS
2 MI	3 MS
4 WI	4 NW
5 PS	4 IA
5 IA	6 MN
7 IN	6 WI
7 MS	6 IL
7 PU	9 PU
7 NW	9 MI
11 MN	11 IN

Over-all Big Ten Standings

	AVERAGE STANDING	YEARS IN STANDING	NUMBER OF FINISHES PER STANDING											LAST * PLACE
			1	2	3	4	5	6	7	8	9	10	11	
MICHIGAN	2.87	103	42	19	12	7	8	4	5	3	1	2	0	4
OHIO STATE	3.04	96	33	16	13	14	6	4	3	6	1	0	0	2
PENN STATE	3.94	16	3	1	3	4	3	0	0	0	2	0	0	0
CHICAGO	4.56	45	6	7	6	6	3	1	5	5	3	2	0	9
MICHIGAN STATE	4.86	56	6	6	8	7	7	5	7	4	4	2	0	3
MINNESOTA	4.89	113	18	8	14	12	15	15	10	6	6	7	2	16
ILLINOIS	5.19	113	15	6	13	15	12	18	8	8	11	4	3	18
PURDUE	5.15	113	8	8	16	19	12	15	7	18	9	1	0	19
WISCONSIN	5.22	113	11	11	11	14	14	13	12	12	10	5	0	17
IOWA	5.54	109	11	5	7	13	16	16	14	13	9	4	1	26
NORTHWESTERN	6.22	111	8	6	8	8	13	12	18	10	10	17	1	29
INDIANA	6.93	107	2	1	7	7	10	16	14	17	23	8	2	33

* LAST PLACE HAS BEEN AS HIGH AS FIFTH IN THE STANDINGS. SINCE THE NUMBER OF TEAMS IN THE CONFERENCE HAS VARIED, LAST PLACES DO NOT SHOW UP IN THE STANDING NUMBER. SUCH EMBARRASSMENTS ARE POINTED OUT IN THIS COLUMN.

Win & Loss Trends at a Glance:

W-L-T

by Game:

1882 83 86 87 88 89 90 91 92 93 94 95 96
97 98 99 1900 01 02
03 04 05 06 07 08
09 10 11 12 13 14 15 16
17 18 19 20 21 22 23 24
25 26 27 28 29 30 31
32 33 34 35 36 37 38 39
40 41 42 43 44 45
46 47 48 49 50 51 52
53 54 55 56 57 58
59 60 61 62 63 64 65
66 67 68 69 70
71 72 73 74 75 76
77 78 79 80 81
82 83 84 85 86
87 88 89 90 91
92 93 94 95 96
97 98 99 2000 01
02 03 04 05 06
07 08

by Season:

1882 90 1900 10 20 30
40 50 60 70 80 90
2000

202

Winning Percentage Overall:

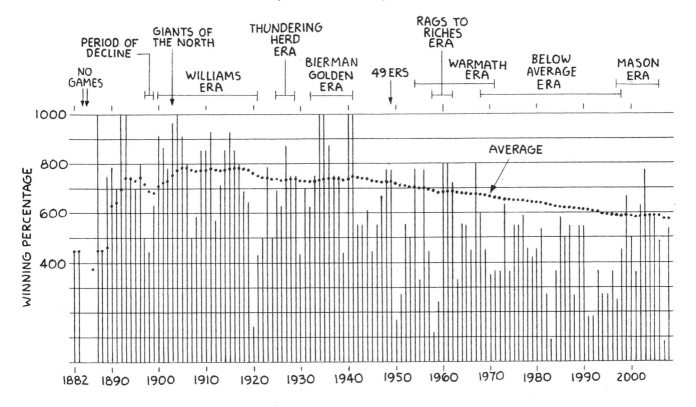

Winning Percentage in Big Ten:

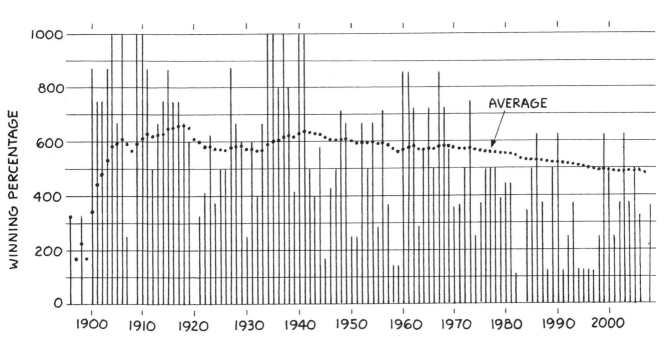

Scoring History

IT MAY BE INTERESTING TO LOOK AT THESE CHARTS TO SEE THE TRENDS OF SCORING PROFICIENCY, BUT AS MURRAY WARMATH INDICATED, ALL THAT IS NEEDED TO WIN IS "PLUS ONE" IN ANY GAME.

TEN TIMES THE GOPHERS HAD WINNING SEASONS WHILE SCORING LESS POINTS THAN THEIR OPPONENTS. SIX TIMES THEY SCORED MORE POINTS WHILE ENDING UP WITH A LOSING SEASON.

MINNESOTA SCORED 154 POINTS IN BOTH 1939 AND 1940. THEIR 1939 RECORD WAS 4-4-1 WHILE PLACING 7TH IN THE BIG TEN. 1940 SAW THEM WIN THE NATIONAL CHAMPIONSHIP WITH AN 8-0-0 RECORD... ALL WITH IDENTICAL SCORING.

Scoring Differential by Season

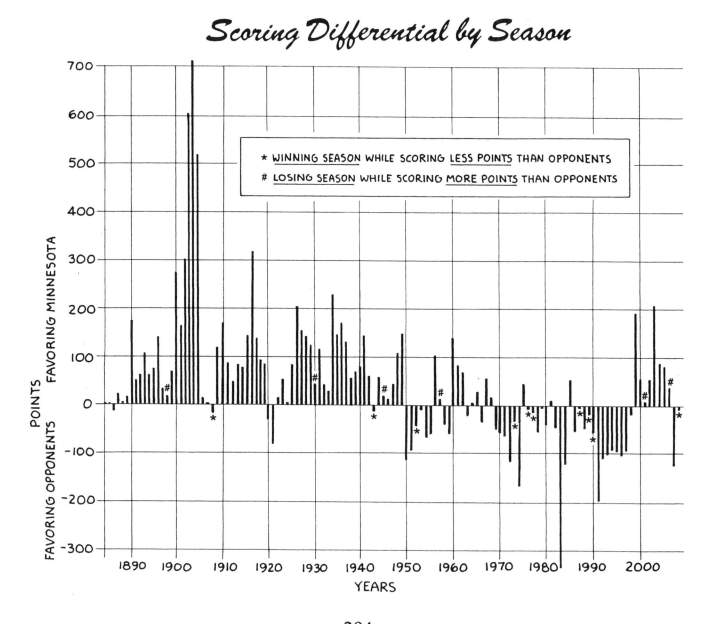

* WINNING SEASON WHILE SCORING LESS POINTS THAN OPPONENTS

\# LOSING SEASON WHILE SCORING MORE POINTS THAN OPPONENTS

Minnesota Scoring by Season

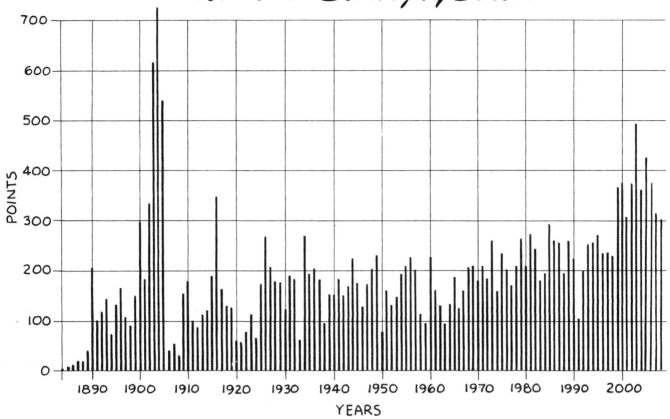

POINTS

YEARS

Opponent Scoring by Season

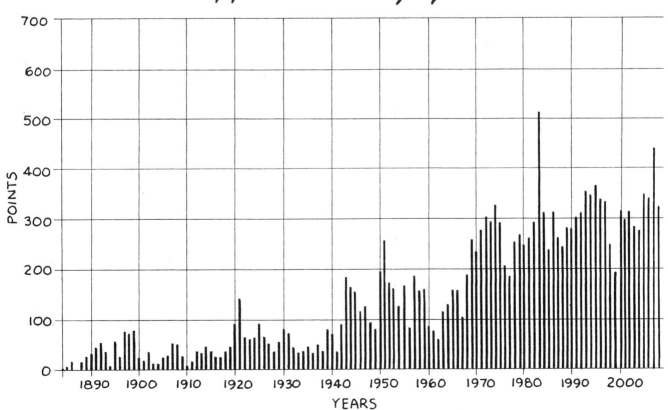

POINTS

YEARS

Coach Comparisons

COACH	YEARS COACHED	TOTAL SEASONS	TOTAL GAMES	CAREER GAME RECORD (W-L-T)	WIN/LOSS SEASONS (W-L-T)	WIN PERCENTAGE	BEST SINGLE SEASON (W-L-T)	WORST SINGLE SEASON (W-L-T)	SHUT-OUTS GIVEN	SHUT-OUTS TAKEN
(NO COACH)	1882	1	2	1-1-0	0-0-1	500	1-1-0	1-1-0	1	1
T. PEEBLES	1883	1	4	2-2-0	0-0-1	500	2-2-0	2-2-0	1	0
F. JONES	1886-88	3	6	3-3-0	1-1-1	500	2-0-0	0-2-0	3	0
D. McCORD A. McCORD F. HEFFELFINGER B. MORSE	1889	1	4	3-1-0	1-0-0	750	3-1-0	3-1-0	3	0
T. ECK	1890	1	7	5-1-1	1-0-0	786	5-1-1	5-1-1	4	1
E. MOULTON	1891	1	5	3-1-1	1-0-0	700	3-1-1	3-1-1	0	1
(NO COACH)	1892	1	5	5-0-0	1-0-0	1000	5-0-0	5-0-0	0	0
W. WINTER ☆	1893	1	6	6-0-0	1-0-0	1000	6-0-0	6-0-0	2	0
T. COCHRANE	1894	1	4	3-1-0	1-0-0	750	3-1-0	3-1-0	2	1
W. HEFFELFINGER ☆◇	1895	1	10	7-3-0	1-0-0	700	7-3-0	7-3-0	5	1
A. JERREMS	1896-97	2	18	12-6-0	1-0-1	667	8-2-0	4-4-0	9	4
J. MINDS ☆◇	1898	1	9	4-5-0	0-1-0	444	4-5-0	4-5-0	3	3
W. LEARY J. HARRISON	1899	1	11	6-3-2	1-0-0	636	6-3-2	6-3-2	4	2
H. WILLIAMS ★	1900-21	22	180	136-33-11	19-2-1	786	13-0-0	1-6-0	104	22
W. SPAULDING	1922-24	3	22	11-7-4	1-0-2	591	5-1-1	3-3-1	7	6
C. SPEARS ☆◇	1925-29	5	40	28-9-3	5-0-0	738	6-0-2	5-3-0	12	2
F. CRISLER ★	1930-31	2	18	10-7-1	1-1-0	583	7-3-0	3-4-1	8	5
B. BIERMAN ☆▽★ ₿	1932-41 1945-50	16	134	93-35-6	13-3-0	716	8-0-0	1-7-1	36	15
G. HAUSER ☆₿	1942-44	3	27	15-11-1	3-0-0	574	5-3-1	5-4-0	3	2
W. FESLER ☆◇	1951-53	3	27	10-13-4	1-1-1	444	4-3-2	2-6-1	1	3
M. WARMATH ▼	1954-71	18	172	87-78-7	9-9-0	526	8-2-0	1-8-0	20	17
C. STOLL	1972-78	7	78	39-39-0	4-3-0	500	7-4-0	4-7-0	4	5
J. SALEM	1979-83	5	55	19-35-1	1-4-0	355	6-5-0	1-10-0	0	2
L. HOLTZ ★	1984-85	2	22	10-12-0	1-1-0	455	6-5-0	4-7-0	0	0
J. GUTEKUNST	1985-91	6+	68	29-37-2	3-2-1	441	6-5-0	2-9-0	1	5
J. WACKER	1992-96	5	55	16-39-0	0-5-0	291	4-7-0	2-9-0	0	3
G. MASON ▲	1997-06	10	121	64-57	5-4-1	529	10-3	3-9	5	2
T. BREWSTER ₿	2007-	2	25	8-17	1-1	320	7-6	1-11	0	1
TOTALS:	1882-2008	125	1135	635-456-44	76-38-11	579	13-0-0	1-11-0	241	105

▽ COACH OF THE YEAR: 1935, 1941   ☆ COACHES WHO WERE ALL-AMERICANS IN THEIR PLAYING DAYS
▼ COACH OF THE YEAR: 1960   ◇ COACHES WHO MADE THE HALL OF FAME AS PLAYERS
▲ COACH OF THE YEAR: 1999   ₿ COACHES WHO MADE ALL-BIG TEN IN THEIR PLAYING DAYS
★ COACHES HALL OF FAME

AVERAGE GAME SCORE MN.-OPP.	CAREER POINTS	LONGEST UNDEFEATED STRING	LONGEST WIN STRING	LONGEST LOSS STRING	POST SEASON GAMES W-L-T	CHAMPIONS OF NW/MIDWEST	CONFERENCE RECORD W-L-T	CONFERENCE WIN PERCENTAGE	CONFERENCE TITLES	AVERAGE STANDING IN CONFERENCE	ALL-CONFERENCE PLAYERS	ALL-AMERICAN PLAYERS	NATIONAL TITLES
-1	4 - 2	1	1	1	—	—	—	—	—	—	—	—	0
-2	9 - 8	2	2	1	—	—	—	—	—	—	—	—	0
0-7	57 - 43	2	2	2	—	—	—	—	—	—	—	—	0
-7	46 - 28	2	2	1	—	—	—	—	—	—	—	0	0
0-0	208 - 3	5	2	1	—	1	—	—	—	—	—	0	0
0-9	102 - 46	4	2	1	—	1	—	—	—	—	—	0	0
4-11	122 - 56	5	5	0	—	1	—	—	—	—	—	0	0
5-6	148 - 38	6	6	0	—	1	—	—	—	—	—	0	0
0-2	74 - 8	3	3	1	—	0	—	—	—	—	—	0	0
-6	136 - 58	3	3	1	—	0	—	—	—	—	—	0	0
2-6	280 - 101	7	7	4	—	0	1-5-0	167	0	5.50	3	0	0
0-8	92 - 72	2	2	3	—	0	1-2-0	333	0	5.00	0	0	0
-7	151 - 79	6	5	2	—	0	0-3-0	000	0	6.00	0	0	0
6-5	4727 - 819	34	24	6	0	3	50-25-5	656	8	2.86	51	12	0
-9	261 - 188	6	3	3	0	—	5-6-3	464	0	5.33	4	2	0
5-7	1015 - 297	11	8	2	0	—	13-7-2	636	1	3.40	13	6	0
-9	317 - 153	3	3	2	1-0-0	—	4-5-0	444	0	5.50	2	1	0
-9	2586 - 1235	28	21	5	0	—	57-28-6	659	7	3.13	32	24	5
0-16	547 - 437	4	3	3	0	—	8-8-1	500	0	4.33	1	0	0
-22	443 - 589	4	3	4	0	—	7-8-4	474	0	5.33	3	1	0
-16	2881 - 2755	7	7	10	1-1-0	—	66-57-4	535	2	4.89	24	12	1
-23	1424 - 1788	4	4	5	0-1-0	—	27-29-0	482	0	5.43	11	0	0
-29	1176 - 1598	3	3	10	0	—	12-32-1	278	0	7.40	5	0	0
-25	467 - 543	3	3	4	0	—	7-10-0	412	0	7.00	0	0	0
-25	1324 - 1703	5	5	6	1-1-0	—	18-28-2	395	0	6.50	8	0	0
-31	1217 - 1723	3	3	7	0	—	8-32-0	200	0	9.60	2	0	0
-22	3179 - 2641	7	7	7	3-4	—	32-48	400	0	6.70	16	6	0
-30	315 - 440	4	4	10	0-1	—	3-13	188	0	8.50	2	0	0
-17	26,504 - 19,518	34	24	10	6-8-0	7	319 - 346 - 28	486	18	4.88	177*	64*	6

* PLAYERS WHO REPEATED THEIR ACCOMPLISHMENTS ARE COUNTED ONCE AND ONLY UNDER THE FIRST COACH THEY RECEIVED THEIR DISTINCTION. GOPHERS RECEIVING THEIR DISTINCTIONS WHILE AWAY FROM MINNESOTA ARE NOT COUNTED.

Postgame Credits

The following sources were helpful to my research for this book.

PERIODICALS

Ariel (University of Minnesota newspaper), 1882–98.

Gopher (University of Minnesota yearbooks), 1888–1962, 1964–66.

Minneapolis Directory, 1883, 1884, 1886.

The Minneapolis Journal, 1903–36.

The Minneapolis Star, 1901–82.

The Minneapolis Times, 1941.

The Minneapolis Tribune, 1903–42.

Minnesota Daily (University of Minnesota newspaper)

St. Paul Directory, 1895.

St. Paul Pioneer Press

Star and Tribune (Minneapolis–St. Paul), 1982–87.

Star Tribune (Minneapolis–St. Paul), 1987–2007.

University of Minnesota Football Press Guide, 1954–83, 1987–89, 1997, 1998, 2003.

University of Minnesota Game Program, 1903–90.

University of Minnesota General Alumni Catalogue, 1916.

SPORTS PUBLICATIONS

1936 Minnesota Huddle, published by Stan Carlson, Minneapolis, Minnesota.

1937 Minnesota Huddle, published by Stan Carlson, Minneapolis, Minnesota.

1987 Big Ten Football Yearbook. Schaumburg, Illinois, 1987.

1987 N.C.A.A. Football. Michael V. Earle, ed. N.C.A.A., 1987.

1988 N.C.A.A. Football. Michael V. Earle, ed. (with Steve Boda Jr. and James M. Van Valkenburg). N.C.A.A., 1988.

1989 N.C.A.A. Football. Michael V. Earle, ed. (with Steve Boda Jr. and James M. Van Valkenburg). N.C.A.A., 1989.

Barns Football Record Book, 1942.

College Football. Nashville: Athlon Sports Communications, Inc., 2007.

Deitch, Scott, ed. *Official 2003 N.C.A.A. Football Records.* Indianapolis, 2003.

Dickinson, Frank G. *Dickinson's Football Ratings from Grange to Harmon.* Omaha: What's What Publishing Company, 1941.

Greunke, Lowell R., ed. *Football Rankings.* Jefferson, N.C.: McFarland Publishing, 1984.

Menke, Frank G. *The New Encyclopedia of Sports.* New York: A. S. Barns and Company, 1947.

Spaulding Football Record Books, 1913, 1920, 1921.

Spaulding Official Football Guide, 1940.

Sports News (St. Paul, Minnesota), 1989–98.

Summers, J. Gregory, ed. *N.C.A.A. Football: The Official 1996 College Football Record Book.* Overland Park, Kansas, 1996.

Waldorf, John. *N.C.A.A. Football Rules Committee Chronology of 100 Years, 1876–1976.* N.C.A.A., 1975.

Who's Who in Minnesota Athletics. Richard Charles Fisher, ed. Who's Who in Minnesota Athletics, 1941.

BOOKS AND ARTICLES

Akers, Tom, and Sam Akers. *The Game Breaker.* Wayzata, Minn.: Ralph Turtinen Publishing Company, 1977.

Brown, Lyle. *Sports Quiz.* New York: Pocket Books, Inc., 1954.

Carlson, Stan W. *Dr. Henry L. Williams, a Football Biography.* Minneapolis, 1938.

"Football at Minnesota." *The Minnesota Alumni Weekly* 14, no. 9 (November 9, 1914).

Furlong, William Barry. "How the War in France Changed Football Forever." *Smithsonian* (February 1986).

Loken, Newt, and Otis Dypwick. *Cheerleading.* New York: A. S. Barns and Company, Inc., 1945.

Newell, Martin, ed. *History of Minnesota Football.* Minneapolis: General Alumni Association of the University of Minnesota, 1928.

O'Neil, John. "Gold Country Revival," *Minnesota Daily* 75, no. 22 (September 1973).

Powers, Francis J. *A. A. Stagg, Grand Old Man of Football.* St. Louis: C. C. Spink and Son, 1946.

Quirk, James P. *Minnesota Football: The Golden Years, 1932–1941.* 1985.

Rainbolt, Richard. *Gold Glory.* Wayzata, Minn.: Ralph Turtinen Publishing Company, 1972.

Roppel, Joel. *Memorable Moments in Minnesota Sports.* St. Paul: Minnesota Historical Society Press, 2003.

South St. Paul Centennial, 1887–1987: The History of South St. Paul, Minnesota. South St. Paul Area Chapter of the Dakota County Historical Society, 1987.

Thornley, Stew. *On to Nicollet.* Minneapolis: Nodin Press, 1988.

Turtinen, Ralph, ed. *One Hundred Years of Golden Gopher Football.* Minneapolis: Men's Intercollegiate Athletic Department of the University of Minnesota, 1981.

White, Mervin, and Gordon S. White Jr. *Big Ten Football.* New York: Macmillan Publishing Company, 1977.

Wilkinson, Mike. *The Autumn Warrior.* Edina, Minn.: Burgess International Group, Inc., 1992.

HISTORICAL RECORDS

Atlas of the City of Minneapolis, Minnesota. Minneapolis: C. M. Foote Publishing Company, 1882.

Davidson, C. Wright. *The Davidson Map of Minneapolis.* 1881.

Davidson's Atlas Map of Minneapolis, Hennepin County, Minnesota. 1888.

George B. Wright's Map of Minneapolis. Lithographed and published by Rice and Company, St. Paul, Minnesota. 1873?

Honorable Mention

The following individuals helped make this book possible. They loaned knowledge, time, books, photographs, stories, and advice. With their assistance, the long task of creating this book was a pleasant experience. I am grateful to:

Mertle Allen	Robyn Kannas	Jeff Papas
Marie Angle	Penny Krosch	Jon W. Papas
Bob Beebe	Jane Lee	Bob Patrin
Sarah Berhow	Mary Lacroix	K. C. Poehler
Phillip Brain Jr.	Francis "Pug" Lund	David Samuelson
Jack William Brown	Millie Marple	Millie Smith
Marilyn Brown	Donald Marshall	George Svendsen
Bill Crumley	Cynthia Martinson	Lt. Col. Roger Syverud
John Dunnigan	Muriel McEachern	Chris Thornby
Otis Dypwick	Gary McVey	James Walker
Bill Garnaas	Winifred Midler	Jeff Ward
K. C. Gillman	Martha Muxlow	Dick Westby
Louis Gross	Bronko Nagurski	Dr. John Williams
Rosemary Hannah	Ellen Oliver	Karen Zwach
Louis Hendrickson	Donita Papas	
Marcus Johnson	Jack Papas	

I also appreciate the contributions of the following organizations: Big Ten Offices, Clemson University Sports Information Department, Dakota County Historical Society, Hamline University News Bureau, Hennepin County Historical Society, Independence Bowl, Matthews Community Center, Minneapolis Public Library, Minnesota Historical Society, National Football Foundation Hall of Fame, St. Paul Public Library, Shattuck High School, Stanford University Sports Information Department, University of Illinois Sports Information Department, University of Minnesota Archives and Libraries, University of Minnesota Athletic Communications Department, University of Pennsylvania Sports Information Department, University of Wisconsin Band, and Yale University Sports Information Department.

Al Papas Jr. is a freelance artist and lifelong Gopher football fan. He worked as a sports cartoonist and newsroom artist for the *Minneapolis Star–Tribune* and has created artwork for the U.S. Hockey Hall of Fame and for teams in the NBA, ABA, and NHL.